BRITISH ROMANTICISM AND THE JEWS

British Romanticism and the Jews

History, Culture, Literature

Edited by
Sheila A. Spector

palgrave
macmillan

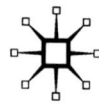

BRITISH ROMANTICISM AND THE JEWS
Copyright © Sheila A. Spector, 2002, 2008.

All rights reserved.

First published in hardcover in 2002 by
PALGRAVE MACMILLAN®
in the US—a division of St. Martin's Press LLC,
175 Fifth Avenue, New York, NY 10010.

Where this book is distributed in the UK, Europe and the rest of the world, this is by Palgrave Macmillan, a division of Macmillan Publishers Limited, registered in England, company number 785998, of Houndmills, Basingstoke, Hampshire RG21 6XS.

Palgrave Macmillan is the global academic imprint of the above companies and has companies and representatives throughout the world.

Palgrave® and Macmillan® are registered trademarks in the United States, the United Kingdom, Europe and other countries.

ISBN-13: 978-0-230-60251-9
ISBN-10: 0-230-60251-7

Library of Congress Cataloging-in-Publication Data is available from the Library of Congress.

A catalogue record of the book is available from the British Library.

Design by Newgen Imaging Systems (P) Ltd., Chennai, India.

First PALGRAVE MACMILLAN paperback edition: July 2008

10 9 8 7 6 5 4 3 2 1

Printed in the United States of America.

Transferred to digital printing in 2008.

Contents

Acknowledgments   vii
Contributors   ix
Introduction   1
Sheila A. Spector

Part I   Cultural Contexts   17

1. Great Britain or Judea Nova? National Identity, Property, and the Jewish Naturalization Controversy of 1753   19
Alan H. Singer

2. Abraham Goldsmid: Money Magician in the Popular Press   37
Mark L. Schoenfield

3. Halakhic Romanticism: Wordsworth, the Rabbis, and Torah   61
Lloyd Davies

4. "What Are Those Golden Builders Doing?": Mendelssohn, Blake, and the (Un)Building of *Jerusalem*   79
Leslie Tannenbaum

Part II   British Romantics and the *Haskalah*   91

5. "For Luz is a Good Joke": Thomas Lovell Beddoes and Jewish Eschatology   93
Christopher Moylan

6. Scott's Hebraic Historicism   105
Esther Schor

7. Maria Edgeworth's *Harrington:* The Price of
   Sympathetic Representation   121
   Neville Hoad

8. Imagining "the jew": Dickens' Romantic Heritage   139
   Efraim Sicher

   Part III   Jewish Writers and British Romanticism   157

9. British–Jewish Writing of the Romantic Era and the
   Problem of Modernity: The Example of David Levi   159
   Michael Scrivener

10. Not for "Antiquaries," but for "Philosophers":
    Isaac D'Israeli's Talmudic Critique and His
    Talmudical Way with Literature   179
    Stuart Peterfreund

11. Hyman Hurwitz's *Hebrew Tales* (1826): Redeeming the
    Talmudic Garden   197
    Judith W. Page

12. Grace Aguilar: Rewriting Scott Rewriting History   215
    Elizabeth Fay

13. *Alroy* as Disraeli's "Ideal Ambition"   235
    Sheila A. Spector

14. Harold's Complaint, or Assimilation in Full Bloom   249
    David Kaufmann

Glossary   265
Works Cited   269
Index   287

Acknowledgments

At the 1999 meeting of the American Conference on Romanticism, I found myself wandering around like the Ancient Mariner stopping one in three to ask: "Where are the Jews?" Having spent the better part of the previous two decades exploring the relationship between Blake and Kabbalism, I had come up for air and was astonished to find that in a major conference on Romanticism, attended by a group of international scholars whose interdisciplinary focus transcended virtually all boundaries of time and space, there was absolutely no presentation devoted to the Jews, not even by the Israeli scholars who were there. Yet, as my own research amply demonstrated, there were, indeed, strong historical, cultural, and literary connections between British Romanticism and the Jews, ranging from the legal problems of English Jews, to Christian interests in Judaica and Anglo-Jewish literature, through the post-Holocaust Jewish American critics who opened up the field of Romanticism for the rest of us.

My first thought was to organize a special session on British Romanticism and the Jews for the next ACR Conference, but the deadline had already passed, so I did the next best thing. I advertised for a special session at the next MLA convention. Considering NASSR-L, the list-serv for the North American Society for the Study of Romanticism, as the most efficient means of contacting the largest group of Romanticists, I sent out a call for papers, and as an afterthought, indicated that if there was enough interest, I would be happy to compile an anthology of original essays on any aspect of the intersection between British Romanticism and the Jews. As the rich variety of this volume testifies, there was, indeed, a great deal of interest in the topic, just no appropriate mode of publication. So it is with great pride that I have edited what I hope will be but the first of many different forms of scholarship that help illuminate the wealth of as-yet unexplored material dealing with the interaction between Romanticism and Judaica.

Since January 2000, when I first announced my interest in compiling this volume, I have made many new friends who have been extremely generous with their time and knowledge, in order to bring this project to fruition. Lilach Lachman, of Tel-Aviv University, whom I met at that first ACR Conference, has provided invaluable advice and guidance from the beginning; and Jeanne Moskal of the University of North Carolina, although not contributing an essay herself, became an e-mail pal, passing on to me any information she thought might be useful, and providing good advice when I had problems. Similarly, I wish to extend a special thanks for the moral and intellectual support provided by Clifford Marks of the University of Wyoming, whose ill health prevented his being a more active partner in the project. Judith W. Page, of the University of Florida, and Esther Schor, of Princeton University, both of whom did write essays for this volume, have served as de facto co-editors, generously helping me with all of the problems that befall a first-time editor, from basic information about the content of papers to advice about the best way to get this kind of anthology published. I also wish to thank all of the other contributors to the project, whose personal attention has helped make this volume more than simply another collection of essays. Marilyn Gaull, of Temple and New York Universities—who considered this book her Christmas present—has been an enthusiastic and informed advocate, generating Palgrave's interest in the concept of the project and providing her own editorial skill for its execution. Without Marilyn's unstinting assistance, this anthology would not have made nearly the contribution that it does. Finally, I would like to thank Kristi Long, Senior Editor at Palgrave, Roee Raz, her Editorial Assistant, and Donna Cherry, Palgrave's Production Manager, for turning this project into a reality. Its strengths are due to all those who believed in the project; its weaknesses, unfortunately, are my own.

CONTRIBUTORS

LLOYD DAVIES received his Ph.D. in Literature from Duke University's Graduate Program in Literature. He is an associate professor of English Literature at Western Kentucky University with research interests in Romanticism, literary theory, and Jewish studies. He recently concluded a dialogue with several other literary critics, published in the journal *Christianity and Literature,* on the possibilities of traditional Judaic textual studies as a theoretical model for contemporary literary criticism. He is currently working on a book-length project, inspired by the work of Harold Fisch, entitled *Romantic Hebraism: The Covenantal Turn in English Romanticism.*

ELIZABETH FAY, Associate Professor of English at the University of Massachusetts at Boston, specializes in Romanticism and Gender Studies. In addition to two books—*Becoming Wordsworthian, A Performative Aesthetics* (University of Massachusetts Press, 1995), and *A Feminist Introduction to Romanticism* (Blackwell, 1998)—she has a book forthcoming on British Medievalism (Palgrave), and she has written "Romanticism and Feminism," for *The Blackwell Companion to Romanticism,* edited by Duncan Wu (Blackwell, 1998); co-edited with Alan Richardson "British Romanticism: Global Crossings," a special issue of the *European Romantic Review* (Spring 1997); and is the editor of a special issue on Grace Aguilar, in *Romantic Circles* (Spring 1999).

NEVILLE HOAD received a B.A. and M.A. from the University of the Witwatersrand, Johannesburg, South Africa; and the Ph.D. from Columbia University, New York. He was a William Rainey Harper postdoctoral fellow in the Humanities Division at the University of Chicago, and is currently an Assistant Professor in the Department of English at the University of Texas at Austin. He has published articles in *Postcolonial Studies, GLQ: A Journal of Lesbian and Gay Studies, Development Update, Jewish Affairs,* and *Repercussions;* and he has written reviews for *Current Anthropology, Windy City Times,* and the *Voice Literary Supplement.*

DAVID KAUFMANN, Chair of the Philosophy and Religious Studies Department at George Mason University, has written extensively about contemporary theory. In addition to a full-length study, *The Business of Common Life: Novels and Classical Economics between Revolution and Reform* (The Johns Hopkins University Press, 1995), he has published numerous essays in *New German Critique, The Burlington Magazine, Modern Judaism, Modern Philology, Yale Journal of Criticism, ELH,* and *PMLA,* among others.

CHRISTOPHER MOYLAN, Associate Professor of English at the New York Institute of Technology, is primarily interested in the influence of Jewish eschatology on Romanticism, especially as it relates to T. L. Beddoes. In preparation for a book-length study, he has published "T. L. Beddoes and the Hermetic Tradition" (*The Beddoes Society,* 1999); "T. L. Beddoes and the Advent of Therapeutic Theater" (*Studia Neophilologica,* 1991); and "The Idea of Therapeutic Theater in English and German Romanticism" (*Text and Presentation,* 1993).

JUDITH W. PAGE is Professor of English at the University of Florida and is also an affiliate faculty of the Center for Jewish Studies. She is the author, most recently, of *Imperfect Sympathies: Jews and Judaism in British Romantic Literature and Culture* (Palgrave Macmillan, 2004).

STUART PETERFREUND, Professor of English at Northeastern University in Boston, directs the graduate program there, having formerly served as chair of the department from 1991 to 1999. His most recent books are *William Blake in a Newtonian World: Argument as Art and Science* (1998), and *Shelley among Others: The Play of the Intertext and the Idea of Language* (2002). Long interested in the role played in British culture by religious issues and religious controversy, Peterfreund is currently at work on a book dealing with British natural history writing from Bacon to Darwin. A chapter dealing with Bacon recently appeared in the journal *The Eighteenth Century: Theory and Interpretation,* and another on Gilbert White is forthcoming in a collection by several hands.

MARK L. SCHOENFIELD, Associate Professor of English at Vanderbilt University, is the author of *The Professional Wordsworth: Law, Labor, and the Poet's Contract* (University of Georgia Press, 1996). His work includes essays in *Studies in Romanticism, The Wordsworth Circle,* and *Prose Studies,* and he is currently working on a book tentatively titled *British Periodicals and Romantic Identity.*

ESTHER SCHOR, Associate Professor and former Acting Director of Jewish Studies at Princeton University, is the author of *Bearing the Dead: The British Culture of Mourning from the Enlightenment to Victoria* (Princeton University Press, 1994). In addition, she is the co-editor of *The Other Mary Shelley: Beyond Frankenstein* (Oxford University Press, 1993), and *Women's Voices: Visions and Perspectives* (Random House, 1990). Currently, she is editing the *Cambridge Companion to Mary Shelley* (in progress).

MICHAEL SCRIVENER, Professor of English at Wayne State University, converted to Judaism as an adult, and is the author of three books: *Radical Shelley* (Princeton University Press, 1982); *Poetry and Reform* (Wayne State University Press, 1992); and *Seditious Allegories: John Thelwall and Jacobin Writing* (Penn State University Press, 2001). He is at present working on Jewish representations in Romantic literature.

EFRAIM SICHER is Associate Professor of English and Comparative Literature at Ben-Gurion University of the Negev, Beer-Sheva, where he teaches the nineteenth-century British novel, as well as contemporary drama and fiction. His publications cover a wide range of topics from Charles Dickens and George Eliot to modern dystopia and post-war memory. His several books include *Beyond Marginality: Anglo-Jewish Literature After the Holocaust* (SUNY Press, 1985), and a collection of essays on the literary aftermath of the Holocaust, *Breaking Crystal: Writing and Memory after Auschwitz* (University of Illinois Press, 1998). His recent study of representation in Dickens' novels, *Rereading the City/Rereading Dickens: Representation, the Novel and Urban Realism,* is forthcoming from AMS Press, New York.

ALAN H. SINGER, who received his Ph.D. in Modern British History at the University of Missouri-Columbia in 1999, is currently a Visiting Assistant Professor of the History of the Western Civilization at Marquette University in Milwaukee. He has taught courses on British, Jewish, and European history at Stephens College and the University of

Missouri, and is in the process of completing a monograph, *Aliens and Citizens: Jewish and Protestant Naturalization in the Making of the Modern British Nation, 1689–1753.*

SHEILA A. SPECTOR is an independent scholar who has devoted her career to exploring the intersection between the British and Jewish cultures, primarily in the Romantic Period. She has published *Jewish Mysticism: An Annotated Bibliography on the Kabbalah in English* (Garland, 1984), and her two-volume study of Blake as a Kabbalist— *"Glorious incomprehensible": The Development of Blake's Kabbalistic Language,* and *"Wonders Divine": The Development of Blake's Kabbalistic Myth*—was published by Bucknell University Press in 2001.

LESLIE TANNENBAUM, Associate Professor of English at The Ohio State University, is author of *Biblical Tradition in William Blake's Early Prophecies: The Great Code of Art* and of articles on Blake, Mary Shelley, and Byron.

INTRODUCTION
Sheila A. Spector

Judging from the most comprehensive works produced by the most respected scholars and published by the most prestigious presses of our time, one could hardly escape the conclusion that there was minimal contact between the British and Jewish cultures in the interim between the Enlightenment and the Victorian era. In the most extensive coverage, Iain McCalman's outstanding compilation, *An Oxford Companion to The Romantic Age: British Culture 1776–1832,* includes a scant four references to the Jews in the discursive essays of Part One, while in the encyclopedic Part Two, McCalman's one-page entry, "Jews," refers only briefly to earlier misconceptions, citing a few of the more notable British Jews of the period.[1] This is not to suggest that McCalman, or others— like Duncan Wu, whose *Companion to Romanticism* indexes but a single reference to "Jewish history"—are deliberately misrepresenting or minimizing a relationship that, in fact, did exist between the two cultures.[2] Rather, the distortions found in these texts arise from the dearth of information available. While during the past few decades, scholars have unearthed masses of heretofore ignored materials regarding various issues of race, class, and gender, for the most part they have overlooked the significance of the Jews to the overall development of what might loosely be defined as British Romanticism.[3] Yet, as the essays contained in this volume demonstrate, not only were both cultures shaped in significant ways by the presence of the *other,* but it is difficult to overestimate the importance of their interaction for the formation of what would eventually become the modern British Empire.

In order to gain a full perspective on the complex relationship between the British and Jewish cultures between the 1750s and the 1850s, it is necessary first to establish the broader intellectual context. Traditionally, the histories of the British-Christian and the British-Jewish communities in the interim between the mid-eighteenth and mid-nineteenth centuries have been studied separately.[4] From the perspective of the dominant culture, this is the Romantic Period,[5] the period between the end of the Enlightenment and the consolidation of Victorianism, during which time England evolved into Great Britain, replacing its narrow sectarian self-image as a white, Anglo-Saxon Protestant country into a pluralistic empire, unified around the values of freedom and liberty. For the minority, this is the *Haskalah,* the Jewish Enlightenment, the period between the repeal of the Jewish Naturalization Bill in 1753 and Emancipation in 1858, during which time the Jews, who resided primarily in London, became acculturated, learning how to dress, speak, and work like subjects of the Crown.[6] This artificial separation, however, obscures the interactions between the two cultures. While it is true that each had its own legal, social, political, and religious challenges, in fact, both communities were engaged in comparable evolutionary processes. Although coming from diametrically opposite histories, it was during this century of transformation that both the British Christians and the British Jews developed a viable means of integrating with the world at large while still retaining their own cultural and ethnic identities. The result was the so-called Judeo-Christian tradition, a merger of the two cultures that has provided the basis for post-Romantic Great Britain to today.

Not simply a function of Enlightenment attitudes, this cultural blending can best be understood in terms of the historical factors that separated the Jewish and Christian traditions in the first place.[7] Although they originated from the same religion, Judaism and Christianity developed fundamentally different linguistic and exegetical traditions that yielded contradictory attitudes toward eschatology. Historically, Jewish messianism has revolved around a communal restoration to the geographical Jerusalem, while Christian millenarianism has focused on a prophesied Second Coming of Christ, His return signifying the individual's salvation and restoration to a spiritual city of God.[8] Both religions claim that their doctrines are validated by the "Bible," but while normative Judaism relies on the rabbis' exegesis of the Hebrew Scriptures, Christianity turned from the beginning to the Church Fathers' interpretation of the combined Old and New Testaments, as eventually translated into Latin.[9] Thus, despite the fact that Christianity is predicated on the assertion that the "Jewish" Bible prophesies the coming of Christ, actually, Christians used a translation of a text that had already undergone numerous modifications before Jerome codified the Catholic version in the fourth century. Consequently, despite their respective contentions that their religions can be justified with comparable claims of Scriptural authority, actually, both religions rely on derivative sources, each of which had been transformed before being separately canonized by the two religions.

By the Middle Ages, linguistic and textual anomalies began to force both traditions to reexamine their attitudes toward their particular versions of Holy Writ. In the ninth century, Jewish scholars started questioning the integrity of their text. It had always been assumed that the received Bible comprised in its totality the Divine Word. However, by the twelfth century, Abraham Ibn Ezra explicitly claimed, and then in the sixteenth century, Elias Levita expanded, the theory that the diacritical marks used to punctuate the biblical text were later additions.[10] From then on, Jewish scholars had to determine which—if any—portions of the Bible could be considered of Divine origin, and what relationship the later additions had to the original text. Responses would range from a total rejection of the Ibn Ezra/Levita position that the diacritical marks were not coeval with the text, to an insistence that though later additions, they, too, represented God's Word, to a rejection of the Divinity of the text in its entirety.

Though originating as an internal matter, the validity of the Hebrew text became an essential factor in the Reformation. When Protestants repudiated the Roman Church, they rejected, as well, the Catholic Bible, that is, the Latin translation and its accompanying exegesis. In order to return to the original text, however, they had to deal with Jewish grammarians and exegetes, there having been no significant Christian hebraic tradition before the Renaissance. Consequently, not only were Christians forced to rationalize for themselves the question of diacritics, but, even more significantly, they had to justify turning to Jews—whose exegetical tradition patently did not find Christian prophecy in the Hebrew Bible—for instructions on deciphering that same text so that it would do just the opposite, validate Christian eschatology. By the Enlightenment, the Jews and Christians would find themselves in comparable positions: in both cases, their linguistic and exegetical traditions had been undermined by questions that eventually would coalesce into the High Criticism of the Bible, leaving Christians and Jews alike with two extreme alternatives—blind faith or skeptical rationalism.

These problems were magnified in England.[11] When establishing the Anglican Church, the Tudors had relied on a negative theology, dissociating themselves from Rome, though without positing an alternate doctrine to replace the discredited Catholic beliefs. Rather, theologians developed a religious methodology comprised of three primary elements: the authority of Scripture; the use of reason; and the appeal to antiquity.[12] By the mid-eighteenth century, however, English nationalistic myth would combine with distortions of these three elements to undermine faith in the constitutionally established Church of England.

Historically, the myth of Joseph of Arimathea had enabled the English to fabricate a direct connection with Christian history, to the point, as Blake would speculate in the Preface to *Milton*, that Jesus had been in England, and that London was the true Jerusalem:

> And did those feet in ancient time,
> Walk upon Englands mountains green:
> And was the holy Lamb of God,
> On Englands pleasant pastures seen!

Amplifying this belief, by the seventeenth century the English began generating the myth of the Anglo-Israelites, the theory that the English were the true descendants of Noah, via Japhet, and consequently, the truly chosen people, as opposed to the ancient Hebrews, who were cast in the role of usurpers. To justify this belief, Anglo-Israelites created a wholly specious linguistic association between the English and Hebrew languages. Assuming that Japhet brought with him the remnant of the ur-language spoken by Adam, and thus the language of God Himself, Christian Hebraists began a process of dissociating biblical Hebrew from the Jews, asserting that regardless of motivation (that is, whether out of ignorance or malice), the rabbis had distorted the ancient tongue, with the result that the true prophecy of Christ had been occluded. Rather, as the most extreme Anglo-Israelites asserted, the means of discerning the truth of Scripture was to bypass rabbinic Hebrew entirely, and trace the route backwards from English to the true Hebrew, and from thence, to God Himself.[13]

Thanks to these theories, as well as the Reformation's return to the Hebrew text, the study of Hebrew became popular in seventeenth-century England, though the published resources could range from normative grammars to free-wheeling fantasies that interpreted the language through ahistorical, anti-linguistic methodologies.[14] If the purpose was to liberate Scriptures from the Jews, the effect was to sever the Hebrew Bible from any reliable linguistic or exegetical standard, enabling sectarians to produce "Bibles" that would justify their own particular viewpoints. While King James did, in 1611, authorize what he anticipated would be the most reliable translation of the Bible to date, as time progressed, those who wished to separate themselves from the Anglican Church could easily find versions more amenable to their theologies. With the proliferation of radical sects and dissenting churches, the authority of the Bible became a sectarian matter, dependent upon which translation one used.[15]

If the authority of Scripture was undermined, so, too, were the other methods advocated by the established Church. Believing that God made man rational, Anglicans thought that reason could be used as a means of understanding passages that were unclear or ambiguous. However, by the Enlightenment, that same rational faculty had led advocates of natural religion to reject the authority of the Bible entirely, as they questioned its textual accuracy and Divine origins. Thus, by the Romantic Period, the centuries-old relationship between throne and altar was in jeopardy. The established religion had no doctrinal justification for privileging itself over the onslaught of non-Anglicans, including the Scottish Presbyterians and the Irish Catholics, both formally incorporated into the Empire, and all sorts of sectarians, notably Dissenters, Evangelicals, Unitarians, and Free-Thinkers, who were not. Yet, paradoxically, during this same period, when Anglicanism was being undermined, the British attributed their economic progress and military prowess in no small measure to their constitutionally established religion. Consequently, the interim between 1750 and 1850 turned into a period of reconciliation, as the British mediated between the contradictory impulses of millenarians and skeptics, on the one hand, and of reform-minded Oxford Tractarians, who advocated a return of Anglicanism to its high-church origins, and of utilitarian disestablishmentarians, who wished to sever completely the ties between church and state, on the other. In addition, as a colonizing empire, Great Britain required a method by which to incorporate non-Christians into its fold. Thus, the British experienced what has been called a "Romantic reformation," as the theological basis of Anglicanism was reconfigured to accommodate a Protestant identity with the core values of liberty and freedom.[16] Overlooked, however, has been the fact that a significant aspect of that cultural renovation can be attributed to the internal changes occurring within the British-Jewish community at the same time.

Although the Jewish version of Enlightenment occurred chronologically later than its Christian counterpart, the *Haskalah* contributed an intellectual base that would be exploited by the British as they effected their Romantic reformation.[17] Most frequently described in terms of the German experience of the 1770s, the *Haskalah* is usually associated with the theories of Moses Mendelssohn (1729–86), the German-Jewish philosopher who attempted to combine strict adherence to faith with the Enlightenment values of tolerance and rationalism, in order to enable the Jews to assimilate into the dominant community while still retaining their ethnic identity. To that end, *maskilim*, as followers of the *Haskalah* were called, advocated an expansion of traditional education beyond the religious subjects so that the Jews would be able to earn a livelihood in the outside world, while completing the religious training needed for reinvigorating the Jewish community. A major component of Mendelssohn's philosophy involved the translation of Hebrew texts, especially the Bible. Believing that the vernacular might be used as a conduit to bring Jews back to Hebrew studies, Mendelssohn published a Jewish translation of the Bible into German, in 1783.

Despite Mendelssohn's original intentions, the *Haskalah* eventually led to large-scale assimilation, as vocational education provided many Jews with the means of leaving their origins behind. Others, seeking a smoother integration between their secular and religious lives, fostered the theological changes that would in the nineteenth century consolidate into the Reform Movement of Judaism, including the use of the vernacular in worship, and a relaxation of the laws regarding Sabbath observance, marriage, and divorce.[18] Most significantly, reformers advocated a secularized interpretation of Zionism. While historically, the hope for a return to a Jewish homeland had held the community together, by the post-Enlightenment period, traditional Zionism was seen by many as an impediment to the possibility of citizenship, as modern Europeans questioned the dual loyalties of the Jews. Some *maskilim* even considered traditional Zionism to be unpatriotic, indicating that the Jews were not committed to their lives in the West. Therefore, as the movement evolved, Reformed Jews universalized the concept of Jewish messianism, associating a now-metaphorical Zion with the enlightened values of reason and liberty.

Given the unique development of British-Jewish history, the manifestation of the *Haskalah* in Great Britain was somewhat different from the German model.[19] Historically, the earliest Jewish settlers came with the Normans, though within a scant two centuries, in 1290, they were expelled, not to be granted formal reentry until the seventeenth century.[20] Some few Jews did, however, remain, to be joined in time by others escaping from persecution on the Continent, most notably by crypto-Jews fleeing the Inquisition at the end of the fifteenth century. In the sixteenth, when the English required the assistance of Hebraists to consolidate the new Anglican religion, authorities loosened the ban against the Jews, not formally readmitting them though permitting their unofficial settlement. Hoping for a change in their legal status under the Protectorate, the Jews argued, in part, that their exclusion from England was an impediment to Christian eschatology, which required the dispersal of the Jews to the four corners of the earth as a prerequisite to the Second Coming. Still, despite their theological argument, not to mention Cromwell's attempt to associate the Puritan Revolution with the liberation from slavery in Egypt, popular anti-Semitism precluded anything more than an unofficial grant of reentry. So, too, with Charles II who, at the Restoration, let matters stand where they had been. It would be another century before the Jews would again try to improve their legal status, but though the Jewish Naturalization Bill was passed in May 1753, anti-Semitism led to its eventual repeal the following December.

Between 1753 and 1858, during the period when the British Christians were engaged in their Romantic reformation, British Jews experienced their version of the *Haskalah*. In contrast to the larger, more firmly established Jewish communities on the Continent, London's was fairly small and undeveloped; yet, at the same time, overall conditions in England were relatively stable—the protesters had demanded the repeal of the "Jew Bill," not the deportation of the Jews.[21] Consequently, community leaders concentrated more on social reforms than religious, introducing the educational changes that would acculturate the Jews for their lives in Great Britain, but not attempting to modify attitudes toward Jewish law or Zionism.

The most important effect of the *Haskalah* in Britain involved the publication of accurate Hebrew grammars and dictionaries, translations of the Bible, and studies of Jewish antiquities.[22] Before the *Haskalah*, most materials, even those by the most respected scholars of their time, had been ideologically skewed to demonstrate the author's belief in the superiority of Christianity. Whether blatantly anti-Semitic, intended to demonstrate the absurdity of Judaism, or more subtly philo-Semitic, designed to convert the Jews, these texts contained distortions that at best avoided anything that might present a negative view of Christianity. In the 1780s and 90s, native-born David Levi (1742–1801) published a series of works eventually to include: *A Succinct Account, of the Rites, and Ceremonies of the Jews* (1782); *Lingua Sacra* (3 vols.; 1785–87), the first comprehensive Hebrew grammar and dictionary; and an annotated edition of the Pentateuch (1787).[23] In addition, Levi wrote pamphlets defending the Jews against Unitarians (1789), millenarians (1795), and Deists (1797). Levi was joined later by Hyman Hurwitz (1775/6–1844), a friend of Coleridge's who would eventually be appointed the first Jewish professor of Hebrew at the University of London. Hurwitz published studies of Hebrew language (1807; 1831), and of Jewish antiquities, including the *Hebrew Tales, Selected and Translated from the Writings of the Ancient Hebrew Sages; to which is Prefixed, An Essay, on the Uninspired Literature of the Hebrews* (1826).[24]

Missing from the British *Haskalah* were the kinds of religious innovations that would culminate in Reform Judaism on the Continent and in America by the middle of the nineteenth century. Whether it was because the British-Jewish community of the time could not support its own seminary, or just that the Jews were too insecure to risk any radical changes, the internal governance remained essentially Orthodox, leaving individual Jews with no alternatives other than conformity with the communal leaders or de facto excommunication. Consequently, when he quarreled with religious authorities, Isaac D'Israeli (1766–1848), a strong admirer of Mendelssohnianism, felt he had no alternative but to withdraw from the community and, further, that he should have his children baptized, so that they could enjoy the full rights of citizenship.[25]

Thus would Isaac's son Benjamin (1804–81) become the living embodiment of the combined Judeo-Christian tradition as it consolidated in the British Romantic reformation.[26] Frequently identifying himself as the blank page between the two Testaments, Disraeli remained throughout his life both a practicing Anglican and an ethnic Jew, developing in the 1840s a peculiar racial theory that combined the two religions through a secularized messianism not very different from that advocated by the Reformed Jews. In his novel *Tancred, or The New Crusade* (1847), the hero travels to Jerusalem in order to affirm his faith as an Anglican, explaining that "Christianity is Judaism for the multitude, but still it is Judaism" (427). As if to actualize that belief, in 1875 Disraeli arranged, with the financial assistance of the Rothschilds, Britain's purchase of the Suez Canal, thus paving the way simultaneously for the British to achieve their imperialistic ambitions and for the Jews to realize their Zionistic aspirations.

The purpose of *British Romanticism and the Jews: History, Culture, Literature* is to explore the mutual influences exerted by the British-Christian and British-Jewish communities during the period between the Enlightenment and Victorianism, demonstrating how the texts produced by the *Haskalah* provided a significant resource for Romantic intellectual revisionism, in much the same way that British Romanticism provided the cultural basis through which the British-Jewish community was able to negotiate between the competing obligations to ethnicity and nationalism. The collection is divided into three sections: the first, *Cultural Contexts,* establishing the historical and philosophical bases from which the mutual interactions can be explored in the second, *British Romantics and the Haskalah,* and in the third, *Jewish Writers and British Romanticism.*

Cultural Contexts

In establishing the broader cultural context, the first group of chapters effectively undermines the commonly held belief that the British Christians and British Jews existed separately, with little cultural interaction between the two. Historically, in the interim between December 20, 1753, when the "Jew Bill" was repealed, and July 26, 1858, when Baron Lionel de Rothschild was permitted to assume his seat in the House without first having to swear an oath as a Christian, British attitudes toward the Jews shifted radically. It is conventional to view the change in terms of internal acculturation, as the Jews learned how to speak and dress like Englishmen, and became adept in the trades and professions that would liberate them from the pushcart. Absent the visibility of the peddler, whose peculiar dialect and disheveled appearance drew unwarranted attention to the Jews as a group, it is asserted, the British became less offended by and more willing to integrate these aliens into their culture. While the importance of these social changes should not be minimized, this approach tends to ignore the extent to which the two communities shared cultural interests. Although the leaders of both religions preferred that they remain separate from each other, there is evidence that throughout history, not only did the two traditions exert significant influence on each other, but, more important, there existed an underground ecumenical movement composed of non-sectarians who combined into what has been called a "brotherhood of letters," an informal group of like-minded people who minimized the differences between Christianity and Judaism, in order to explore the core of beliefs they held in common. Eventually, the underground movement began to surface, as the Western Enlightenment created the rational basis, and the *Haskalah* provided the heretofore inaccessible texts, for the two traditions to explore their common ground in the open.

The first two chapters of this section establish the historical context. Opening the volume, Alan H. Singer's "Great Britain or Judea Nova? National Identity, Property, and the Jewish Naturalization Controversy of 1753" argues that the popular reaction against the "Jew Bill" was connected to the way in which, by the mid-eighteenth century, the British had replaced religious anti-Semitism with a secular form, one in which developing notions of national identity and property rights were used to project the Jew as being anti-British, rather than strictly anti-Christian. Illustrating Singer's thesis, Mark L. Schoenfield explores the role of the media in constructing the popular representation of Jews, demonstrating in "Abraham Goldsmid: Money Magician in the Popular Press" that though native born, the financier's ethnicity greatly affected the way he was depicted in the press.

The following two chapters focus on the shared intellectual concerns of the British Christians and Jews. Lloyd Davies, in "Halakhic Romanticism: Wordsworth, the Rabbis, and Torah," explores the affinity between Wordsworth and his older Jewish contemporaries, the Gaon of Vilna and Shneyur Zalman of Liady, as revealed through their common adherence to a life of *halakhah*—that is, a life lived in covenantal response to the Law conceived of as Torah, or Divine Instruction. In contrast, Leslie Tannenbaum's "'What Are Those Golden Builders Doing?': Mendelssohn, Blake, and the (Un)Building of *Jerusalem*" reads William Blake's *Jerusalem* as an intellectual response to the kind of arguments raised in Moses Mendelssohn's *Jerusalem,* especially its vision of religion predicated on principles of Enlightenment rationalism, in opposition to the kind of Jewish and Christian pietism invoked by Blake's epic.

British Romantics and the *Haskalah*

The anti-Semitic protests that followed the passage of the "Jew Bill" in 1753 resulted from a complex of attitudes, ranging from religious bigotry and economic fear to a perceived threat against political hegemony. By 1858, when the Jews were no longer excluded from public life, many of these issues had been resolved. Thanks to both Jewish and British educational reforms, the Jews had become acculturated into the British world; with the development of capitalism, the British were no longer as dependent on Jewish financiers; and through the process of colonial expansion, Anglo-Saxon xenophobia was being supplanted by British imperialism. As a result, during this period, much of the historical anti-Semitism was transformed into its mirror image, philo-Semitism, the belief that if reasoned with calmly, the Jews would of their own accord convert to Christianity. In the midst of these cultural changes, Christian writers used both religious and secular manifestations of Judaica as the means by which to articulate their own relationship with British culture. While historically, the conventional Jewish stereotypes had provided the British with ready-made symbols of the *other,* by the nineteenth century many British Romantics, who themselves felt alienated from their own culture, turned to the Jews as the vehicle through which to analyze their attitudes toward Great Britain.

The four chapters in this section consider the dimensions of religious, political, and sociological change that occurred during the period. In the first, "'For Luz is a Good Joke': Thomas Lovell Beddoes and Jewish Eschatology," Christopher Moylan analyzes Thomas Lovell Beddoes's adaptation of Talmudic references to "*luz* of the spine," as the central symbol of the illusory nature of the social and religious constructions of identity. Next, Esther Schor argues, in "Scott's Hebraic Historicism," that Scott appropriated Jewish attitudes toward kingship and Zionism to portray the conflict between the Scottish Covenanters and the English Crown. Taking a sociological approach, in "Maria Edgeworth's *Harrington:* The Price of Sympathetic Representation," Neville Hoad considers how the historical reaction to the Naturalization Bill of 1753 is replicated in the novel's structure, exposing the difficulty of attempting to naturalize the Jews into the Protestant country. Yet, by the mid-1840s, according to Efraim Sicher's "Imagining 'the jew': Dickens' Romantic Heritage," the narrative of the *other* had changed so radically that Dickens was publicly vilified for his anti-Semitic portrayal of Fagin in *Oliver Twist*.

Jewish Writers and British Romanticism

It was also during this period that British-Jewish writers began to explore the relationship between their ethnic identity and their place in the secular community. Before the Enlightenment, the Jews, with a few notable exceptions, had two basic choices: they could remain within their own ghettoes, or they could apostatize, leaving their heritage behind as they assimilated into the Christian world. However, as the reforms of the *Haskalah* expanded educational possibilities, and as the liberalism of Romanticism expanded economic opportunities, the Jews were confronted with the more complex challenge of establishing a balance between their ethnicity and their nationality. As they became acculturated, learning the language and literature of Great Britain, they explored different ways by which they might best serve their co-religionists, though without betraying their countrymen who, often despite personal animosity, did eventually emancipate the Jews in their midst. The final six chapters of the collection explore these concerns, the first three concentrating on Jewish writers who attempted to incorporate Judaica into British culture, the last three on those who tried to make space for their Jewish ethnicity within the larger Christian world.

Opening this section, Michael Scrivener's "British-Jewish Writing of the Romantic Era and the Problem of Modernity: The Example of David Levi" introduces David Levi, the Anglo-Jewish theological controversialist who used the public sphere to "English" Judaism, to defend the Jewish community, and to assimilate British and Jewish cultures with each other. Next, in "Not for 'Antiquaries,' but for 'Philosophers': Isaac D'Israeli's Talmudic Critique and His Talmudical Way with Literature,"

Stuart Peterfreund identifies the essentially Jewish intellectual and conceptual base that comprises the foundation of Isaac D'Israeli's secular literary output. Finally, in "Hyman Hurwitz's *Hebrew Tales* (1826): Redeeming the Talmudic Garden," Judith W. Page argues that Hurwitz's *Hebrew Tales*, analogous to the *Lyrical Ballads*, was designed to redeem and reconcile traditional Judaic learning with contemporary English culture.

The final three chapters of the collection explore the ways Jewish writers negotiated between their ethnicity and the larger community. In "Grace Aguilar: Rewriting Scott Rewriting History," Elizabeth Fay explains how Aguilar uses her Jewish identity to construct a literary and authorial identity. In contrast, Sheila A. Spector, in *"Alroy* as Disraeli's 'Ideal Ambition,'" interprets Benjamin Disraeli's only "Jewish" novel as a Christian apologetic, a fictionalized defense of Disraeli's own apostasy. Finally, bringing the theme to the present, David Kaufmann considers the significance of the modern Jewish critic to British Romantic studies, in "Harold's Complaint, or Assimilation in Full Bloom," analyzing in particular Harold Bloom's theory of influence as a method for allegorizing the place of Jews in the literary academy.

As the chapters in this collection indicate, during the period between 1753 and 1858, the British-Christian and British-Jewish communities were both able to develop a viable relationship between their respective ethnic heritages and their place in the British Empire. In the interim between the Enlightenment and the consolidation of the British Empire under Victoria, the British expanded their self-definition to embrace a large proportion of the minorities within their domain; and though it would take another century for the process to mature, it was during this period that they began to recognize the contributions of these *others* to the nation as a whole. For this reason, too, as American universities in the twentieth century eased the quotas against Jewish students and increased the hiring of Jewish faculty, it was inevitable that so many Jewish scholars would be attracted to British Romanticism, for by studying how the British of the Romantic Period were able to incorporate minorities into the larger community, these post-Holocaust American Jews could through their Romantic literary criticism help adapt the process to the twentieth century.

As a unique anthology, *British Romanticism and the Jews: History, Culture, Literature* establishes the foundation for further study of the intersection between British Romanticism and Judaica, an aspect of both disciplines that has remained essentially buried. Expanding our understanding of the so-called Judeo-Christian tradition (not to mention the more current "Abrahamic tradition," that includes Islam as well), a label now used to project a harmoniously integrated pluralistic ethos, this volume explores some of the ways in which post-Enlightenment Great Britain began to formulate this cultural amalgamation, as the Christians and Jews both independently and together came to terms with their own attitudes toward the relationship between ethnicity and nationalism. Ultimately, the purpose of this collection is to illuminate some of the ways in which the process evolved specifically during the interim between the "Jew Bill" of 1753 and Emancipation in 1858.

Notes

1. Iain McCalman, *An Oxford Companion to the Romantic Age: British Culture 1776–1832* (Oxford: Oxford University Press, 1999), 563–4. Specifically, the index refers to: the existence of a Jewish community dating from readmission in the mid-seventeenth century, in R. K. Webb's essay, "Religion" (94); the exclusion of the Jews from the universities, in Ian Britain's "Education" (164); the significance of a Jewish national history, in Marilyn Butler's "Antiquarianism (Popular)" (336); and William Jones's attitude toward Jewish mythology, in Nigel Leask's "Mythology" (341). Among those Jews given their own entries are Isaac D'Israeli, Jonathan King and David Ricardo.
2. Duncan Wu, *Companion to Romanticism* (Oxford: Blackwell, 1998). The reference to the Jews occurs in relation to a discussion of Freud in Douglas B. Wilson's essay on "Psychological Approaches" (424).
3. There are some significant exceptions, notably David B. Ruderman's *Jewish Enlightenment in an English Key: Anglo-Jewry's Construction of Modern Jewish Thought* (Princeton: Princeton University Press, 2000); Michael Ragussis's *Figures of Conversion: "The Jewish Question" and English National Identity* (Durham: Duke University Press, 1995); Frank Felsenstein's *Anti-Semitic Stereotypes: A Paradigm of Otherness in English Popular Culture, 1660–1830* (Baltimore: The Johns Hopkins University Press, 1995); and Brian Cheyette's *Constructions of "the Jew" in English Literature and Society: Racial Representations, 1875–1945* (Cambridge: Cambridge University Press, 1993). While all of these books explore particular aspects of the intersection between Romanticism and Judaica, none considers its full impact on the development of each culture as a distinct entity or on the direction taken by the more encompassing British Empire as it developed later in the nineteenth century, and on into the twentieth.
4. Of the most significant recent histories, Linda Colley's *Britons: Forging the Nation 1707–1837* (New Haven: Yale University Press, 1992), has little to say about the British-Jewish community, while conversely, Todd Endeleman's work, notably *The Jews of Georgian England: Tradition and Change in a Liberal Society* (Philadelphia: Jewish Publication Society of America, 1979; reprint, with a new preface, Ann Arbor: University of Michigan Press, 1999), and *Radical Assimilation in English Jewish History, 1656–1945* (Bloomington: University of Illinois Press, 1990), focus more on internally Jewish matters. David S. Katz does explore the intersection between the two cultures, though he concentrates

primarily on the seventeenth century. A major exception is his book *The Jews in the History of England, 1485–1850* (Oxford: Clarendon Press, 1994).
5. "The Romantic Century" is a term coined by Susan J. Wolfson to encompass the period between 1750 and 1850 (see "50–50? Phone a Friend? Ask the Audience?: Speculating on a Romantic Century, 1750–1850," *European Romantic Review* 11, 1 [Winter 2000]: 1–11).
6. The Jewish Naturalization Bill was an attempt to remove disabilities against Jews' owning land and ships, and conducting trade. When first introduced into the House of Lords on April 3, 1753, and into the House of Commons on April 17, the bill generated little discussion; however, by May 7, opposition began to develop, and although the bill was passed on May 22, public outcry against the "Jew Bill" was so strong that it was repealed the same year, on December 20. For a detailed discussion of the Jew Bill, see Alan H. Singer's essay in this volume, "Great Britain or Judea Nova? National Identity, Property, and the Jewish Naturalization Controversy of 1753."
7. See the three-volume collection of essays, *Jewish and Christian Self-Definition*: Volume 1: *The Shaping of Christianity in the Second and Third Centuries*, ed. E. P. Sanders; Volume 2: *Aspects of Judaism in the Greco-Roman Period*, ed. E. P. Sanders, with A. I. Baumgarten and Alan Mendelson; Volume 3: *Self-Definition in the Greco-Roman World*, ed. Ben F. Meyer and E. P. Sanders (Philadelphia: Fortress Press, 1980–2).
8. Gershom G. Scholem provides a cogent differentiation between Jewish and Christian eschatology in "Toward an Understanding of the Messianic Idea in Judaism," in *The Messianic Idea in Judaism and Other Essays on Jewish Spirituality* (New York: Schocken, 1971), 1–36. Also, see the essays in Marc Saperstein's anthology, *Essential Papers on Messianic Movements and Personalities in Jewish History*, Essential Papers on Jewish Studies, gen. ed. Robert M. Seltzer (New York: New York University Press, 1992). Of special interest are the two overviews: R. J. Zwi Werblowsky, "Messianism in Jewish History" (35–52); and Eliezer Schweid, "Jewish Messianism: Metamorphoses of an Idea" (53–70). Providing a corrective to the tendency to overestimate the differences between Jewish and Christian eschatology, Richard H. Popkin explores the overlapping areas between the two in "Jewish Messianism and Christian Millenarianism," in *Culture and Politics from Puritanism to the Enlightenment*, ed. Perez Zagorin (Berkeley: University of California Press, 1980), 67–90.
9. A good survey of biblical history can be found in the three-volume *Cambridge History of the Bible*: Volume 1: *From the Beginnings to Jerome*, ed. P. R. Ackroyd and C. F. Evans; Volume 2: *The West from the Fathers to the Reformation*, ed. G. W. H. Lampe; Volume 3: *The West from the Reformation to the Present Day*, ed. S. L. Greenslade (Cambridge: Cambridge University Press, 1963–70).
10. Ibn Ezra and Levita can be said to have introduced what would develop into the school of biblical "high criticism," the secular study of the Bible, an approach that was extended in the seventeenth century by René Descartes and Hugo Grotius among Christians, and Benedict Spinoza in the Jewish community. In the following century, Christians Gotthold Ephraim Lessing and Immanuel Kant were joined by the Jewish Moses Mendelssohn. See W. Neil's essay, "The Criticism and Theological Use of the Bible, 1700–1950," in *The Cambridge History of the Bible* (3:238–93).

INTRODUCTION / 15

11. There is a long history of Christian Hebraism in England. On the Renaissance, see G. Lloyd Jones, *The Discovery of Hebrew in Tudor England: A Third Language* (Manchester: Manchester University Press, 1983); on the seventeenth century, see David S. Katz's "Babel Revers'd: The Search for a Universal Language and the Glorification of Hebrew," the second chapter of *Philo-Semitism and the Readmission of the Jews to England, 1603–1655* (Oxford: Clarendon Press, 1982), 43–88; and on the eighteenth century, my essay, "Blake as an Eighteenth-Century Hebraist," in *Blake and His Bibles,* ed. David V. Erdman, Locust Hill Literary Studies No. 1 (West Cornwall, CT: Locust Hill Press, 1990), 179–229. On the importance of sectarianism in the eighteenth century, see Katz's "The Hutchinsonians and Hebraic Fundamentalism in Eighteenth-Century England," in *Sceptics, Millenarians and Jews,* ed. Katz and Jonathan I. Israel, Brill's Studies in Intellectual History, vol. 17 (Leiden: E. J. Brill, 1990), 237–55. Finally, the first two chapters of Ruderman's *Jewish Enlightenment in an English Key*—"'The Scripture Correcting Maniae': Benjamin Kennicott and His Hutchinsonian and Anglo-Jewish Detractors" (23–56), and "The New and 'Metrical' English Bible: Robert Lowth and His Jewish Critic, David Levi" (57–88)—explore the relationship between Christian Hebraism and the English *Haskalah.*

12. See Ian Green, "Anglicanism in Stuart and Hanoverian England," in *A History of Religion in Britain: Practice and Belief from Pre-Roman Times to the Present,* ed. Sheridan Gilley and W. J. Sheils (Oxford: Blackwell, 1994), 168–87. On various uses of the Bible, see Christopher Hill, *The English Bible and the Seventeenth-Century Revolution* (1993; New York: Penguin, 1994).

13. For a detailed discussion of the impact Anglo-Israelism had on Christian Hebraism in the eighteenth century, see "Contexts: The Languages of Eighteenth-Century England," the first chapter of my monograph, *"Glorious incomprehensible": The Development of Blake's Kabbalistic Language* (Lewisburg, PA: Bucknell University Press, 2001), 35–56.

14. For a bibliography of Hebrew grammars and dictionaries, see Cecil Roth's *Magna Bibliotheca Anglo-Judaica: A Bibliographical Guide to Anglo-Jewish History,* new ed. (London: Jewish Historical Society of England, 1937), 361–71.

15. For a general overview, see Michael Mullett, "Radical Sects and Dissenting Churches, 1600–1750," in *A History of Religion in Britain: Practice and Belief from Pre-Roman Times to the Present,* ed. Sheridan Gilley and W. J. Sheils (Oxford: Blackwell, 1994), 189–210.

16. See Robert M. Ryan, *The Romantic Reformation: Religious Politics in English Literature 1789–1824,* Cambridge Studies in Romanticism 24, gen. ed. Marilyn Butler and James Chandler (Cambridge: Cambridge University Press, 1997).

17. The most recent comprehensive history of European Jewry during this period is David Vital, *A People Apart: The Jews in Europe 1789–1939,* Oxford History of Modern Europe, gen. ed. Lord Bullock and Sir William Deakin (Oxford: Oxford University Press, 1999).

18. On the history of Reform Judaism, see Michael A. Meyer, *Response to Modernity: A History of the Reform Movement in Judaism* (New York and Oxford: Oxford University Press, 1988), especially the first two chapters,

"Adapting Judaism to the Modern World" (10–60), and "Ideological Ferment" (62–99).
19. In the past, it has been argued—especially by Endelman—that English Jewry experienced no real *Haskalah*. Opposing Endelman, Ruderman wrote *Jewish Enlightenment in an English Key* to argue that while the English did not follow the German model, they generated their own kind of *Haskalah*, one that responded to their own political and social conditions in Great Britain. I follow Ruderman's lead in this introduction, and the essays in this collection effectively support his thesis that the British *Haskalah*, like its Continental counterparts, reflects the attempt of a post-Enlightenment Jewish community to negotiate between conflicting ethnic and national identities.
20. Todd M. Endelman is currently working on a British-Jewish history to supercede Cecil Roth's older *A History of the Jews in England*, 3rd ed. (Oxford: Clarendon Press, 1964). Also useful is David S. Katz's *The Jews in the History of England, 1485–1850;* and on the Romantic Period in particular, see Endelman's *The Jews of Georgian England: Tradition and Change in a Liberal Society.* The earliest British-Jewish history is D'Blossiers Tovey's *Anglia Judaica or A History of the Jews in England* (Oxford, 1738).
21. Unlike Jews on the Continent, those in Great Britain did not press for their own emancipation when Napoleon liberated the French Jews. While Vital attributes Jewish acquiescence to the small size and relative stability of the Jewish community within the Empire (37–42), equally as significant, during this same period, non-Anglicans, especially Catholics, were seeking their own emancipation, and the English would find it far easier to assimilate other Christians into their fold, than the Jews. Finally, it must be remembered that many British attributed their victory over the secular French state to their constitutionally established Church. Thus, during the war years, it would have been highly imprudent for the Jews to call too much attention to their presence in Great Britain.
22. In *Jewish Enlightenment in an English Key*, Ruderman includes chapters on Jewish contributions to English controversies over the biblical text, the Hebrew language, Deism, political radicalism, science, and, finally, Jewish assimilation.
23. A detailed discussion of David Levi can be found in Michael Scrivener's contribution to this collection, "British-Jewish Writing of the Romantic Era and the Problem of Modernity: The Example of David Levi."
24. On Hurwitz's *Hebrew Tales*, see Judith W. Page's "Hyman Hurwitz's *Hebrew Tales* (1826): Redeeming the Talmudic Garden."
25. On Isaac Disraeli, see Stuart Peterfreund's "Not for 'Antiquaries,' but for 'Philosophers': Isaac D'Israeli's Talmudic Critique and His Talmudical Way with Literature."
26. By placing Disraeli within his Romantic and Jewish contexts, the essays contained in Charles Richmond and Paul Smith's collection, *The Self-Fashioning of Disraeli, 1818–1851* (Cambridge: Cambridge University Press, 1998), correct the older view of Disraeli as an out-of-place Victorian. See also my essay in this collection, "*Alroy* as Disraeli's 'Ideal Ambition.'"

Part I
Cultural Contexts

Chapter 1

Great Britain or Judea Nova? National Identity, Property, and the Jewish Naturalization Controversy of 1753

Alan H. Singer

In the September 1, 1753, issue of *Jackson's Oxford Journal*, a song entitled *Advice to the Freeholders* appeared. The chorus, repeated four times, warned that for their sins, Britons were going to lose their "Liberties, Properties, and their Fore-Skins."[1] According to the lyricist, it was apparent that a national, Divine retribution was about to be unleashed, rendering the British people propertyless and circumcised slaves. The verses recounted the national transgressions that would bring such a stiff sentence. The primary sin was the ratification of the Jewish Naturalization Act the previous May. *Advice to the Freeholders* was one of the many pieces of propaganda designed to incite public opinion to effect the repeal or preservation of the legislation. Polemicists published dozens of pamphlets, broadsides, and newspaper articles in the spring and summer of 1753 attacking and defending the legislation.

The Jewish Naturalization Act was, in actuality, extremely narrow in scope and should not have attracted such virulent opposition. Its authors simply created the law to clarify the legal position of foreign-born Jews residing in England. These foreigners suffered significant legal and economic disabilities. Most of the legislators in 1753 recognized that Jewish disabilities were in place largely by accident. Jews were inadvertent victims of the anti-Catholic and anti-Dissenting measures taken after the Glorious Revolution of 1688. To prevent Catholics and Dissenters from obtaining property and positions of power, the state required oaths of loyalty to the Anglican Church, "upon the true faith of a Christian." Because practicing Jews could not possibly pass this test, the law restricted them from rights, including prohibitions on attending universities or holding any municipal or Parliamentary office. Foreign-born Jewish merchants were forced to pay exorbitant alien duties. These impositions included special port fees and customs rates that were often twice as much as those for native merchants.[2] Finally, the law also prohibited the Jews from owning real property or land. This ultimately discouraged relatives of native-born Jews from settling in England.[3]

The so-called Jew Bill allowed individuals professing Judaism to apply for a private act of naturalization without having to take the Christian oaths. The text of the legislation made clear that this was not a general naturalization and Jews were still prohibited from holding many forms of property and public offices. After some moderate debate, Parliament ratified the Jewish Naturalization Act. The initial success of the Whigs only persuaded the opposition to increase their propaganda to achieve a repeal of the legislation. Monopolistic merchants and Tories opposed the law for reasons of economic self-interest and politics. Established trading companies saw Jews as a competitive threat. By the middle of the eighteenth century, political economists and much of the political and economic elite were moving more in favor of free trade policies. As a result, monopolists felt threatened. The Tories and some dissenting Whigs also had reason to inflame the public over the Jewish Naturalization Act. With a highly contested general election coming in 1754, the opposition created the clamor with the intent of manufacturing popular indignation against the Pelhamite Whigs.

For the opposition, a massive public incitement against the naturalization legislation was necessary to break the Whig's controlling grip on patronage and influence. In the press and on the pulpit, the supporting politicians and church leaders were branded as "Jews" and traitors. Tory newspapers such as the *London Evening Post, London Magazine,* and *The Craftsman* published items attacking the law almost daily. The opposition's appeal to the public also set off a virulent pamphlet war. Through the late spring and summer of 1753, the combatants published approximately eighty pamphlets arguing either side of the issue. Both professional and hack writers were eager to submit their contributions to the debate.

The opposition succeeded in effecting the withdrawal of the Jewish Naturalization Act. By the end of July, the Pelham government was considering how to rescind the legislation, and simultaneously dissociate themselves from supporting Members of Parliament who were sure to lose their seats in the upcoming elections. Pelham devised a plan in which the Ministry itself would introduce a bill to repeal, thereby creating a comfortable distance from those who had originally voted for it in Parliament. By the end of November, both Houses ratified the repeal.[4]

One of the most fascinating aspects of the Jewish naturalization episode was how the opposition could pass the Jews off as such a serious threat, especially since they were so few in number and the scope of the legislation was so limited. The recent work of historians of British nationalism, such as Gerald Newman and Linda Colley, may be able to help explain why such a strong anti-Jewish public opinion developed in a short period of time.[5] Colley demonstrated that the creation of a Catholic *other* helped solidify a Protestant, British national identity. She wrote, "Self-evidently, the Protestant construction of British identity involved the unprivileging of minorities who would not conform: the Catholic community, most Highland Scots before 1745, and the supporters of the exiled Stuart dynasty, those men and women who were not allowed to be British so that others could be."[6] Colley did not include Jews on her list of British *others*. Perhaps she does not discuss Jews because of their small numbers. With a population of only around eight thousand persons in 1753, the Jews did not compare with the omnipresence of Catholics in and around Britain. The controversy over Jewish naturalization should, however, be considered an important episode in the development of national identity in the eighteenth century. Despite the lack of a large Jewish physical presence, the clamor displayed an extremely telling British perception of Jews in 1753, ultimately offering the careful observer an opportunity to see how cultural nationalism influenced social and political conflict.

Although there were few Jews in Great Britain, the idea of a Jewish *other* was remarkably strong. Unlike the very real Catholic threat, the Jewish one was wholly imaginary. Very few Jews had any property in England and a number of laws, including the Jewish Naturalization Act itself, prohibited them from holding positions of power. Furthermore, the scope of the new legislation was extremely limited. A better informed public would have known that there would be no massive Jewish immigration in 1753. For the opposition, it was absolutely necessary to exaggerate and distort the scope and contents of the Jew Bill.

The anti-Jew Bill propagandists were able to add Jews to the *other* list by attaching them to already existing fears of exploitation. It is not difficult to understand that it would be effective to cast the Jews as threats to property, wealth, and livelihood. The enemies of the Pelhamite Whigs portrayed the Jews as the quintessential type of economic victimizers that many lesser merchants, artisans, small landholders, and tenants feared in the eighteenth century. In his classic discussion of the rebellious traditions of the lower classes during this period, E. P. Thompson wrote, "The conservative culture of the plebs as often as not resists, in the name of custom, those economic rationalizations and innovations (such as enclosure, work-discipline, unregulated 'free' markets in grain) which rulers, dealers, or employers seek to impose."[7] As will be seen, according to the opposition, the Jews were already the dealers and would soon become the rulers and employers Thompson mentioned. According to the Government's adversaries, the free market designs of the Whigs put the nation in peril by unleashing historically exploitative Jews into their community.

The opposition was ultimately victorious because it could cast a very wide net over the public by appealing to issues, whether real or imagined, that concerned practically all. The intended audience of their literature was not a specific group of politicians or social class. As many of their pamphlets read, the opposition appealed to the British nation. This was done by presenting the Jews as *both* capitalistic exploiters and the thieves of what all Britons supposedly shared despite class differences— a common national identity. Property and class interest may have meant different things for different groups in British society in the eighteenth century, but the opposition was able to perpetuate a form of nationalism that cast the Jews as a common enemy for all.

Jonas Hanway, the renowned merchant, traveler, philanthropist, and founder of the Marine Society, made some of the most persuasive arguments against Jewish naturalization within a nationalistic context.[8] In two pamphlets, Hanway unleashed a barrage of attacks on the legislation. Both writings represented the Jews as the antithesis to the British establishment.

Hanway started with the supposition that the British nation and polity were founded upon Protestant Christianity.[9] The Glorious Revolution and its settlement protected the British nation from the "ecclesiastical tyranny" of Catholicism. Hanway believed that the primary goal of the state was to ensure the Protestant Succession and spread the Anglican gospel. He asserted that the state's main concern should be the conversion of the Irish to Protestantism, rather than the naturalization of Jews.[10]

For Hanway, at a time when the British were conflicting with fellow Christians, the idea of naturalizing Jews was absurd. The inclusion of those who rejected Christ into a system that was based on the absolute connection of Church and State was unacceptable. Hanway was willing, however, to include Protestant Dissenters in his nation. He pointed out that Dissenters both were natural-born subjects and did not differ "with us, with regards to the fundamental principles of Christianity." Jewish naturalization, in contrast, "appears to me to constitute as unnatural a mixture in the body politic, as bread and arsenic in the human body; and therefore such a mixture could produce no happiness, but on the contrary, dishonor and reproach.[11] Hanway concluded, then, that the Jews could only poison the British establishment.

In his writings, Hanway strengthened his argument by stating that the Jews were not only outsiders, but also were a nation of their own. At a time when the idea of a modern British nation-state was developing, the notion of an antithetical Jewish nation was a powerful tool. Hanway referred to the crucifixion story as follows:

> Our business now is to enquire, if it is our honor, and our politics, to naturalize Jews. For this purpose we may consider the subject in an enlarged view, with regard to the prophecies previous to their great national crime of crucifying the Lord of life; and their national punishment in consequence of that unparalleled act of iniquity. From hence we may possibly be led to believe, that as they are not suffered to establish any Government of their own, nor permitted to incorporate with any other nation therefore they ought not to be naturalized.[12]

Hanway did not speak of the Jews only as a separate religion that rejected Christ. He also attempted to characterize them as a dangerous nation. The Jews' great "national" crime of crucifixion and their Divinely mandated "national" punishment further separated them from the British.

Jonas Hanway's pamphlets were likely the most important pieces written for the opposition.[13] William Romaine, a Methodist minister also in London, however, was probably the most important oppositional voice. Himself the son of Huguenot immigrants, Romaine became a very popular preacher among the London crowd. He was an ardent follower of George Whitefield and gave fiery sermons to very large gatherings. Romaine's attraction of the multitudes reportedly upset the "fashionable people" at his church in Hanover Square. He was eventually removed by the courts to a more plebeian parish.[14]

Romaine published at least one pamphlet arguing against Jewish naturalization.[15] In *An Answer to a Pamphlet, entitled, Considerations on the Bill to permit Persons professing the Jewish Religion to be naturalized; Wherein, the False reasoning, Gross Misrepresentation of Facts, and Perversion of Scripture, Are fully laid open and detected* (London, 1753), he stressed the fact that the British Constitution was founded upon Christian principles. He also argued that because the Jews openly rejected Christianity, they could never be incorporated. Romaine asserted that the Crown had never treated the Jews as free-born subjects in England. For him, considering the Jews as such would destroy what he believed to be the cornerstone of the British establishment. The British nation was based on the idea that "The Christian Religion is true, and therefore it ought to be maintained."[16]

After establishing that the British state and nation were fundamentally Christian, Romaine concentrated on the idea of the natural-born subject. According to him, because the Jews collectively murdered Christ, they could never be natural-born subjects of Great Britain. Jewish immigration was prohibited because, as a nation, the Jews were collectively guilty of the Deicide. Romaine wrote: "Nothing can be more absurd, than to think of uniting them with us in the Bonds of Society, whose Enmity to us is implacable: For who ever heard of making such Foreigners our natural-born Fellow Subjects, who had a natural-born Enmity to us. This is worse than tying a living Man to a dead Carcasse."[17]

Like Jonas Hanway, Romaine believed that religion and state were absolutely inseparable. The Jews were cast as the foreign enemy because they were not Protestant. Indeed, the Protestant, British nation was a "living man" and the nation of Jews, "a dead Carcasse." Romaine continued:

> The Jews Murdered Christ, and would murder us if they had Power: They blaspheme Christ and his Religion; so that they are Murderers and Blasphemers Convict; and who ever heard of a natural-born Murderer, or a natural-born Blasphemer? For murdering and blaspheming Christ, God drave them out of the Holy Land, and made them Vagrants all over the Earth, and who ever heard of a natural-born Vagrant? Of a natural-born English Foreign Jew? i.e., a free Slave-born in the Liberty of Bondage.[18]

Romaine's use of the terms "natural-born Murderer," "Blasphemer" and "natural-born English Foreign Jew" clearly demonstrates his abhorrence of the concept of a naturalized Jew. Jews could not be British because they were the very nation that always threatened Christianity.

By explaining that Jews were dangerous to Protestant Christianity, both Hanway and Romaine also reveal a newly constructed concept of nation and national identity. The *otherness* of the Jews, as with Catholics, was used to demonstrate what Britons were supposedly not. For both of these polemicists, the British nation was likened to a masculine human being. Romaine's evocations of Great Britain as "a living man" and the Jews as a "carcasse," and Hanway's representation of Jews as "arsenic" in the British body were clearly designed to frighten and bolster nativistic feeling.

Other opposition writers followed Hanway and Romaine in asserting that the Jews represented an anti-nation. They found it very effective to characterize Jews as rebels. By again reviving the Deicide story, the pamphleteers translated Jewish theological infidelity into civil treason. The fear of political rebellion was still very real in many people's minds in the 1750s. The memory of the last serious attempt at a Jacobite rebellion in 1745–46 was still prominent in Protestant national consciousness. An anonymous pamphlet entitled *A Modest Apology for the Citizens and Merchants of London, Who petitioned the House of Commons against Naturalizing the Jews* (London, 1753), played on such fears. In the introduction, the author wrote, "We look upon the Jews, who lived in the Time of Christ as Traitors, Rebels against God. The Act of Rebellion was rejecting Jesus for the promised Messiah, and crucifying him for a Malefactor."[19] He wrote that present-day Jews were also guilty of this treason because they continued to defend their ancestors' rebellion.

An author pseudonymously known as "Britannia" continued the theme of a separate nation. This writer posed the following question: "If an Artful Rabbi should spirit his Nation up with the Expectation of a future Restoration of the Jewish Kingdom, as History informs us has been often done, who would be able to defend the Crown itself from a people, that have at all times and Places, where the least Success has bouy'd em up, left Examples of their imperious and rebellious Spirit?"[20] Again, the author plays upon the idea that the Jews themselves are a nation and could not possibly have loyalty toward the Crown.

The condemnation of the Jews based on their supposed role in the demise of Christ was an old and familiar practice. All of Christendom effectively used this accusation to force the Jews into *otherness* status during the Middle Ages and early modern era. By the eighteenth century, Britons had adopted this ancient accusation into contemporary political and national language. We can see evidence of this change in how the opposition referred to Christ. When they traditionally characterized Christ as the Son of God, the Jews' crime was Deicide. In the middle eighteenth century, Christ was frequently referred to as "King." This allowed the opposition to condemn the Jews of regicide.

The crime of regicide played upon real, contemporary national fears. In the eighteenth century, the memory of the execution of Charles I was strong and negative.[21] Cromwell was repeatedly called "the usurper." In 1753, the idea of a Jacobite threat was still alive.[22] The author of the *Modest Apology* advised his readers to consider that the Jews "took away the life of the King" and are the "Aider[s] and Abettor[s] of the Regicide," and Christians could only "pray for the Conversion of all of them, who rebel against Jehovah, and against his Christ."[23] The author's choice of political terms was clearly meant to emphasize the Jews as a serious threat to the political and national establishment.

"Britannia" went to great lengths to show that the Jews had no part in the British nation. The author ultimately characterized the Jews as a rebellious, disobedient, covenant-breaking nation.[24] Again, it is important to recognize "Britannia"'s emphasis on the supposedly rebellious character of the Jewish people. In 1753, attacking the Jews as being merely heretical was not sufficient. Although their different religion placed them in *otherness* status, it was their disobedience in general that made them dangerous to the nation.

Along with warning of Jewish national infidelity, the opposition also predicted the condition of the British nation if the Jews were naturalized. Many of these prophecies were both fantastic and absurd, but they are important in showing that they could play upon fear of national peril. All the predictions of life after Jewish naturalization have a similar conclusion: the British nation would disappear.

The opposition published some of the most interesting predictions in the *London Evening Post* and the *London Gazetteer*. Many of them are written as if the Jews had already taken over Great Britain. One such entry was a commentary on the state of Great Britain one hundred years after naturalization. The nation was now called "Judea Nova." This piece, in the form of an obituary, reads: "On Wednesday last died at his grace, the duke of Hebron's in Barkshire, Sir Nadah Issachar, attorney general. He was esteemed a sound lawyer, an able politician, and a friend to the Sandherim [sic] he is to be succeeded in his office by Moses Da Costa, Esq.; of Lincoln's Inn." Another read, "On Monday last a dispensation passed the great seal to enable Abraham Levy, to hold a living in the synagogue of Paul's together with the rectory of the Rabbi in the diocese of Litchfield."[25] Both pieces intend to inflame the reader by asserting that the Jews would take over the most important legal and political positions in Britain. The opposition also emphasized that the Jews would seize the most sacred symbols of Protestant Great Britain. Parliament was to be renamed the Sanhedrin, and even St. Paul's Cathedral was to become a synagogue.

According to the prophecies, the Jews who would assume positions of power were usually men who had distinguished themselves in wars against Christians. These stories were written with the contemporary European diplomatic situation in mind. The realities of wars between Catholics and Protestants became conflicts between Protestant Christians and Jews. Another contrived obituary described the career of a noble during Jewish rule:

> At two o'clock this morning died at his house in Grosvenor square, the right honourable the earl of Balaam, baron of Zimri, the knight of the most noble order of Melchizidec. He succeeded his father in estate and title in the year 1821; went twice lord lieutenant to Ireland; was plenipotentiary at the states of Holland during the late war against the christian league, called the Jewisade, and has since served principle secretary of state.[26]

Under Protestant, British rule, this Secretary of State would have been the ideal patriot. He was a member of the nobility, Lord Lieutenant for Ireland, and diplomat in Holland. The career of the above deceased could have been that of the Duke of Newcastle or Marlborough. This, however, was not the era of Jewish rule that began with their naturalization in 1753. The man in the obituary is named Earl of Balaam of the noble order of Melchizidec. An unfamiliar, un-Christian world turned upside down was now the destiny of the British nation.

Another theme that pervades these futuristic tales is the persecution of Christians under Jewish rule. The announcement sections of the *London Evening* and the *Gazeteer* included imaginative accounts of how Jews were persecuting Christians. Some of these items read:

> John Heartwell, shoemaker, was whipped around Duke's Place for speaking in disrespectful terms of the coming of the Messiah.
>
> Last week was brought up to Newgate, under a strong guard George Briton, the outlawed smuggler, who was taken on the coast of Sussex in very fact of running pork into this kingdom, in defiance of the many penal laws enacted to prohibit the same.
>
> This day was republished *christianity not founded upon argument,* and we hear, that a statue is to be erected in Westminster-Abbey to the memory of its author.
>
> Last night the bill for naturalizing christians was thrown out of the Sanhedrim [*sic*] by a very great majority.[27]

These announcements, although fictional and ridiculous, contain many indications of how the British saw themselves and how they perceived the Jews as an antithetical nation. The writers chose the names of the supposed newsmakers carefully. A man named "Heartwell" was whipped for questioning the imminent first coming. A man named George Briton was arrested for smuggling pork into the kingdom. Lastly, it is significant that the writer suggested that in Judea Nova, the *Sanhedrin* would soundly defeat a Christian naturalization bill.

A British national identity that was based on Anglican Protestantism was a powerful tool against Jewish naturalization. The idea of mass Jewish immigration provided an excellent opportunity for the opposition to defeat the Whigs by using nationalistic rhetoric as a weapon. Inciting anti-Semitism was easy for the opposition. Ancient and medieval notions of Jewish heresy and treachery made it possible for the anti-Whig propagandists to cast the Jews up against modern notions of what it meant to be British. It was not merely for religious and political treason, however, that the Jews were cast as a people to fear. Older established suspicions of Jewish financial treachery, combined with eighteenth-century ideals of property, wealth, and power, solidified the anti-Jew Bill argument and perhaps gave it its sharpest teeth.

On May 17, 1753, the *London Evening* ran a letter to the editor from "Old England." The main argument in the letter was summed up in the following lines: "...this supposed Bill is nothing less than giving ourselves, our Liberty, Property, and Religion, into the Hands of the Jews. For it is an open, full invitation of the whole scatter'd Race to come and take Possession of all our Estates."[28] "Liberty, property, and religion" was indeed a maxim for the eighteenth-century British patriot. It is necessary here to examine why wealth and property issues were also so prevalent in the Jewish naturalization controversy. I would like to suggest that the debate reveals much evidence both that property issues were a major concern for members of all classes in Britain, and more importantly, that the supposed right to own property was considered as essentially a national birthright. Private ownership was an important component of Britishness.

A thorough examination of the anti-Jew Bill literature often reveals themes that tie the Jews negatively to both the market and property ownership. The opposition revived one of the most persistent subjects in Anglo-Jewish relations since the Middle Ages. The characterization of the avaricious and usurious Jew was easy to propagate in 1753 because it had been a recurring myth for centuries. The theater frequently revived Shakespeare's Shylock, greatly contributing to traditional, English popular lore. By the middle of the eighteenth century, it was easy to build upon and exaggerate further. The late seventeenth and early eighteenth centuries are noted for having gone through a financial revolution when, after the Glorious Revolution, new institutions, such as the Bank of England, the National Debt, and the Stock Exchange, were created. Great Britain's imperial successes and relative political and domestic stability were tied to its publicly funded debt and efficient financial system.[29] The Jews, who were traditionally associated with money lending, were now connected to the modern economic reality of capitalism. Medieval and early modern Christian society previously castigated the Jews for supposed individual acts of financial treachery. After 1689, elements in modern British culture and society berated the Jews as the representatives of the uglier side of capitalism.

Although the Jewish Naturalization Act would have permitted only a few wealthy Jews access, the opposition insisted that actually hordes of Jews would enter and buy up all of the landed estates. Land was the most highly coveted form of property in Britain. The strategy was an attempt to influence the smaller landed gentry against the legislation. The Tory opposition argued that the Whig elite had already sold themselves out to the Jews. The smaller landlords, however, were represented as most in danger when the Jews infiltrated the land market. The supposed Jewish threat to landed property alarmed not only its owners, but also the tenants. Without Christian mercy, the Jews were certain to raise rents and even evict good British Christians.

William Romaine and Jonas Hanway were among the more serious anti-Jew Bill writers who were concerned with Jewish property ownership. Both attempted to apply logic and the law to argue that the Jews could not own property. In a reply to a recently published pro-Jew Bill pamphlet that argued that Jews could own landed property, Romaine resorted to Lord Coke. Romaine quoted the seventeenth-century legal scholar as having written, "That Jews born here are in every Respect to be deemed natural-born Subjects, and may consequently purchase and hold what Land Estates they please, is to me a Doctrine that seems quite inconsistent with the whole Tenor of our Laws, and with the very Essence of our Constitution."[30] Although English-born Jews already safely held land in England, Romaine argued that this was illegal. Not only did Romaine claim that the Jewish possession of landed estates was unconstitutional, but he also warned of Jewish power. He commented that the Jews were "brought in" to get "Power and Influence." Ultimately, this power was "inseparable from holding...Estates." Romaine further commented that the new rich and powerful Jews, "may have Influence enough over the Poor to get some false Messiah set up and make our Country a Scene of Blood and Desolation."[31] He concluded, then, that Jewish naturalization would lead to revolution.

Jonas Hanway also emphasized the Jewish seizure of land. There was an attempt by the supporters of the legislation to argue that naturalization did not mean the British were obligated to sell land to the Jews. Hanway wrote that many landlords managed their property poorly, often being forced to sell. After naturalization, the Jews would be in a position to take advantage of property owners' misfortunes. Hanway argued that the Jews should remain merchants in Britain but it would be disastrous if they became landlords. He commented, "If it should be the case with half the island to change hands; and the estates were purchased by our own moneyed people, though it left the Jews the only merchants in the land, it would certainly be much better, than that a Jewish landed interest should predominate."[32]

Hanway directly tied landownership with power. In perhaps a more sober tone than his allies', he concluded, "The Jews, like fire and water, I am willing to think, are good servants in a commercial state; but they are very improper masters for a free people."[33] For Hanway, the Jewish acquisition of landed property automatically implied Jewish power.

Opposition pamphlets and newspapers chose a number of ways to argue the Jews would obtain landed estates. They also insisted, even more forcefully than Romaine and Hanway, that Jewish property and power were synonymous. The author of *A Letter from a Gentleman to his Friend Concerning the Naturalization of the Jews* (London, 1753), warned that in every great city in Europe, the Jews were kept separate from the rest of the population. This was done so the Jews could not "make any great impressions on the minds of the common people."[34] Jewish naturalization, according to this author, gave the Jews unlimited power to purchase lands. In a few years, the common people would be left without the "*example, influence,* or *protection* of any man above their own level ex[c]ept a Jew" (author's italics). The legislation was, then, an invitation for the Jews to become masters of the countryside through their landownership.

Whereas the author of the above *Letter from a Gentleman* argued that every important city in Europe took prudent steps to keep the Jews separate from the rest of their populations, especially by not allowing them to own land, "Britannia," the author of *An Appeal to the Throne,* chose to offer a different story. He argued that the Jews were significant landowners in France. This was undoubtedly false, Jews being permitted to own lands in only a few rare instances. Nevertheless, according to "Britannia," in Paris, the Jews had "almost half of the City into their Possession, which gave 'em an uncontroulable Power, and Boldness to insult all that opposed 'em."[35] By using the supposed French example, Britannia posed the following questions: "Would not such Possessions entitle them to Privileges of Freeholders? Would not they both by their Money and Sway among their Tenants be able to carry many Elections[s] for Parliament-men, if not to get into the House themselves? Would not a Christian be overawed frequently by a Jew Justice of the Peace. And might it not be feared that, in future Ages, some of these Israelites might buy themselves a Place too near the Throne?"[36]

Fear of Jewish power was a most important weapon in the opposition's arsenal. The *London Evening Post* often warned of Jewish domination as the main reason for contesting the Jewish Naturalization Act. An item dated June 23, 1753, queried:

> Doth not this give rise to a new interest in Great Britain, which never was known or heard of before? A Jewish landed interest? ... will not dominion follow property? Or are our present managers in possession of a secret of frustrating the operation of this hitherto uncontested principle? Can they allow the Jews to purchase the half, or three parts, of the lands of the kingdom, and still withhold from them that weight and influence which is the consequence of property?[37]

Unless the Government had some secret plan to overturn the "hitherto uncontested principle" that dominion followed property, the Jews were sure to seize power. Another item in the *London Evening Post*, this one on May 17, 1753, carried this warning further. It commented that the "Vices and Extravagancies" of this "corrupt age" were continually bringing estates to the market. The piece further claimed that "it is more probable, that in Ten Years our Tenants may have jewish Landlords. Two thirds of our Free holders be oblig'd to be circumcised, or vote as they are order'd, ... God preserve us from Jewish Power!"

Conclusion

The most intriguing aspect of the Jewish naturalization controversy was most certainly how, for a brief period, Jews were elevated to the pariah status of Catholics in the British establishment. This was all the more fascinating because while the Catholics were a real threat with very real armies and navies, the Jewish peril was wholly imaginary. It should be noted that much of Professor Colley's conception of the British nation was theoretically informed by the work of Benedict Anderson, who defined nations loosely as "imagined political communities."[38] A nation was imagined because its inhabitants, who never met the vast proportion of their fellow citizens, felt that they belonged to the same community. Furthermore, a nation was imagined because, as Anderson wrote, "regardless of the actual inequality and exploitation that may prevail in each, the nation is always conceived as a deep, horizontal comradeship."[39] In this case, the British imagined themselves as a coherent nation while they imagined the Jews as an anti-nation.

The Jewish naturalization episode provides a vivid demonstration of Anderson's hypothesis. By proclaiming the Jewish Naturalization Act as an affront to the ideals of *all* Britons, the opposition found the necessary ammunition to defeat the oligarchical Whigs. At a time when class differentiation and conflict were becoming more acute, the political opposition found in the Jews another point around which the entire nation could rally. The patriotic feelings that were allowed to surface were strong enough to cause the Government to retreat.

In this chapter, I have explained how nationalist rhetoric pervaded the oppositional literature. I should also add here that it was not only the legislation's detractors who resorted to patriotism to support their argument. The proponents of Jewish naturalization, perhaps reacting to the success achieved by the opposition's use of nationalism, responded in kind. At least one important pamphlet emphasized that allowing Jews to be naturalized was a patriotic, all-British measure. The pamphlet, *The Crisis, or an Alarm to Britannia's True Protestant Sons,* was pseudonymously written by "a disinterested, independent, and Truly Protestant BRITON."[40] The author first explained the benefits of Jewish naturalization:

> ... it only empowers rich Foreigners to purchase Lands, and to carry on a free and extensive Commerce by importing all sorts of Merchandise and Raw Materials, allow'd by Law to be imported, for the Employment of our own People, and then exporting the Surplus of the Produce, Labour, and Manufactures of our own Country, upon cheaper and better Terms than is done at present. This is all the Hurt that such a Bill can do.[41]

This is perhaps the most concise argument made for Jewish naturalization. It is an exclusively economic argument. The author conceded that Jews (or "rich foreigners") would purchase land and become more involved in trade, but this could only benefit the entire country. His British nation included a "free and extensive commerce," full employment, and cheaper labor.

The author of *The Crisis* switched easily between giving a specifically economic argument on the merits of free trade and liberal policies toward Jews, and extolling post-Revolutionary, Whiggish tolerance as distinctly British virtues. The pamphlet ends with the following statement:

> Let not the Panick of our Anti-Christian Jacobite Enemies, whether feigned or real, seize upon Britannia's true Protestant Sons. There were they in great Fear, where no Fear was, in the Character of none of the best of Men. Let a Tucker (our British Hero), the Merchant's Letter, or Considerations, the Jews Advocate, the Serious Address to our Electors,

and several other Pieces wrote with a true Protestant Spirit and patriot Zeal, be attentively read, and impartially considered; and then believe, if you can, that either the Christian Religion, the protestant Succession, our happy Constitution, the English Hierarchy, the British Peerage, the landed or trading Interest of our Nation, are the least indangered [sic] by the Act before us.[42]

The author of *The Crisis* attempted to discredit *all* of the opposition's arguments with one blunt hit. The Christian religion, Protestant Succession, Constitution, English hierarchy, peerage, land, and trade—the British nation itself—was not to be harmed by the Jewish Naturalization Act.

It is very significant that *both* sides used nationalism when constructing their respective arguments. The proponents did use this strategy on a much smaller scale and only after their adversaries already proved that this tactic was effective. The supporters of Jewish naturalization initially believed that the economic benefits alone would be sufficient to convince their countrymen. The importance, however, lies in the fact that British national identity and its correlating issues of property and power were regular components in the social and cultural ideals and language of the eighteenth century. All sides, factions, parties, and classes adopted this language for their own use. The debate of 1753 affords us an excellent example of how a mundane legislative event erupted into a vitriolic public debate when the right chords were struck. In this case, the ill-fated attempt to naturalize Jews individually uncovered a valuable glimpse into the social and cultural tenor of eighteenth-century Britain.

Notes

1. *Jackson's Oxford Journal*, September 1, 1753.
2. Thomas W. Perry, *Public Opinion, Propaganda, and Politics in Eighteenth-Century England: A Study of the Jew Bill of 1753* (Cambridge: Harvard University Press, 1962), 13.
3. Perry, *Public Opinion,* 14. The Sephardic community initiated the process that would ultimately lead to the Jewish Naturalization Act. On January 14, 1753, Joseph Salvador, a wealthy merchant and *parnas* of Bevis Marks synagogue formally requested that Parliament naturalize any Jewish person in the future without his having to take the Oaths of Supremacy. The Government and the Pelhamite Whigs in Parliament welcomed Salvador's and the Sephardic community's position. In the Government, the so-called Triumvirs—Henry Pelham; his brother, the Duke of Newcastle; and Philip Yorke, the Lord Chancellor Hardwicke—firmly supported the Jew Bill. In the House of Commons, Robert Nugent advocated Jewish naturalization

after initiating several failed general naturalization bills. Lord Halifax, the president of the Board of Trade, introduced the Bill into the upper House, where it passed easily. After a couple of petitions were presented to the Commons, some debate ensued. The proponents succeeded. The Jewish Naturalization Act passed by a vote of ninety-six to fifty-five.

4. Few historians have attempted to examine the Jewish naturalization episode for causes or consequences other than those that were purely political. In 1962, T. W. Perry characterized the entire event as a serious ministerial and party conflict in a period when, according to Sir Lewis Namier and his followers, the political seas were supposedly calm. In a more recent book that has become an essential contribution to the current renaissance in Anglo-Jewish history, David S. Katz described the Jew Bill as insignificant (*The Jews in the History of England, 1485–1850* [Oxford: Clarendon Press, 1994], 27). Todd M. Endelman was the first scholar to break from a purely political examination. In *The Jews of Georgian England, 1714–1830: Tradition and Change in a Liberal Society* (Philadelphia: The Jewish Publication Society of America, 1979; reprint, Ann Arbor: University of Michigan Press, 1999), Endelman demonstrates that among the arguments made on both sides, the limited scope of the Jew Bill was largely ignored (59). This suggests that the participants had other points to make rather than concentrating on the truly mundane character of the legislation. More recently, two literary scholars, James Shapiro, in *Shakespeare and the Jews* (New York: Columbia University Press, 1996), and Frank Felsenstein, in *Anti-Semitic Stereotypes: A Paradigm of Otherness in English Popular Culture, 1660–1830* (Baltimore: The Johns Hopkins University Press, 1995), examined the Jew Bill controversy solely through its literature and have demonstrated what they both believe is a large amount of anti-Semitism in British society. It can be argued that they exaggerated the level of hostility toward Jews. Indeed, Endelman questioned whether Felsenstein's examination of anti-Semitic literature really "illuminate[s] how English men and women interacted with Jews—in the market place, the drawing room, and the public house, in associational life and public forums" (xx).

5. Gerald Newman, in *The Rise of English Nationalism: A Cultural History, 1740–1830* (New York: St. Martin's Press, 1987), and Linda Colley, in *Britons: Forging the Nation 1707–1837* (New Haven: Yale University Press, 1992), have informed us that during the eighteenth century, the English, Welsh, and Scottish peoples invented an overarching national, or British, identity. Colley argues that Protestantism became the most important unifying force in the development of British nationalism. Protestants ultimately developed a national identity by creating *others*. Colley correctly believes that the main *other* group was the Catholics. The French and their co-religionist allies were a *real* threat, persistently challenging the British at home and abroad.

6. Colley, 53.

7. E. P. Thompson, *Customs in Common: Studies in Traditional Popular Culture* (New York: The New Press, 1993), 9.

8. Hanway produced at least two important pamphlets against Jewish naturalization in 1753: *A Review of the Proposed Naturalization of the Jews: Being an*

Attempt at a dispassionate Enquiry in to the present State of the Case, with some Reflections on General Naturalization; and *Letters Admonitory and Argumentative from J. H———y, Merchant to J. S———r, Merchant. In Reply to Particular Passages and the General Argument, of a Pamphlet, entitled Further Considerations on the Bill, &.* There is only one fairly recent biography of Hanway. James Stephen Taylor's *Jonas Hanway, Founder of the Marine Society: Charity and Policy in Eighteenth-Century Britain* (London: Scolar, 1985), concentrates on Hanway as the most important philanthropist of the period. Taylor briefly mentions Hanway's role in the controversy, correctly attributing Hanway's opposition to a belief that the legislation threatened the necessity of the union between Church and State. These were indeed the crucial elements in the construction of the British nation.

9. In *Britons*, Professor Colley discusses Hanway as a merchant who joined and formed patriotic associations in an effort to extol the virtues of economic and cultural nationalism (91). Curiously, she does not mention his pamphlets on Jewish naturalization, which are among his strongest pronouncements on the very subject she is writing about. Hanway's emphasis on Protestantism being at the core of Britishness would have greatly supported her own thesis.
10. Hanway, *A Review*, 5.
11. Hanway, *Letters Admonitory*, 22.
12. Hanway, *A Review*, 7.
13. James Stephen Taylor rightly believes that Hanway had an influential role in the debate, perhaps not because of any particular argument he may have made, but because his ideas reflected those of "a significant number" of international merchants in London. See Taylor's *Jonas Hanway*, 50.
14. *Dictionary of National Biography*, s.v., "William Romaine."
15. William Romaine, *An Answer to a Pamphlet, entitled, Considerations on the Bill to permit Persons professing the Jewish Religion to be naturalized; Wherein, the False Reasoning, Gross Misrepresentation of Facts, and Perversion of Scripture, Are fully laid open and detected* (London, 1753). A number of pseudonymously written pamphlets can probably be attributed to Romaine.
16. Romaine, *An Answer*, 8.
17. Romaine, *An Answer*, 21–2.
18. Romaine, *An Answer*, 21–2.
19. Anonymous, *A Modest Apology of the Citizens and Merchants of London, who petitioned the House of Commons against Naturalizing the Jews* (London, 1753), vi–vii.
20. Britannia, *An Appeal to the Throne against the Naturalization of the Jewish Nation: In which we are Exposed to Those practices for which the Jews were expelled out of England: and the fatal Consequences that may follow, should the Act of their Naturalization take Place* (London, 1753), 22.
21. Linda Colley has noted that every January 30 until 1859, Protestants throughout England and Wales fasted and prayed in the memory of Charles I's execution in 1649. She added that every May 29, the anniversary of the Restoration, was celebrated with bonfires and bells (19).

22. Colley also points out that there were Jacobite invasion scares as late as 1759 (24).
23. *Modest Apology,* viii.
24. *Britannia,* 12–13.
25. Anonymous, *A Collection of the Best Pieces in Prose and Verse, Against the Naturalization of the Jews* (London, 1753), 66.
26. Anonymous, *A Collection,* 68.
27. Anonymous, *A Collection,* 66–8.
28. Old England, *London Evening Post,* May 17, 1753.
29. The best works that argue this point are P. G. M. Dickson's classic, *The Financial Revolution in England: A Study in the Development of Public Credit, 1688–1756* (New York: St. Martin's Press, 1967), D. W. Jones' *War and Economy in the Age of William III and Marlborough* (Oxford: Blackwell Ltd., 1988), and John Brewer's, *The Sinews of Power: War, Money, and the English State, 1688–1783* (Cambridge: Harvard University Press, 1990).
30. Romaine, 11.
31. Romaine, 51.
32. *A Review,* 75.
33. *A Review,* 75.
34. Anonymous, *A Letter from a Gentleman to his Friend Concerning the Naturalization of the Jews* (London, 1753).
35. *Britannia,* 21.
36. *Britannia,* 21–2.
37. *London Evening Post,* June 23, 1753.
38. Benedict Anderson, *Imagined Communities: Reflections on the Origin and Spread of Nationalism* (London: Verso, 1983), 6.
39. Anderson, 7.
40. The full title is *The Crisis, or an Alarm to Britannia's True Protestant Sons. In Two Parts, With an Appendix in each of them. Among a Variety of Things, An Address to King George* (London, 1754).
41. *The Crisis,* 9.
42. *The Crisis,* 22. The titles mentioned in this quotation were the best pro-Jew Bill pamphlets produced in 1753. Josiah Tucker, Dean of Gloucester Cathedral, wrote at least five pamphlets emphasizing free trade and liberal naturalization policies. For a more detailed description of Tucker's role in the Jewish naturalization controversy, see my thesis, "Aliens and Citizens: Jewish and Protestant Naturalization in the Making of the Modern British Nation, 1689–1753" (Ph.D. diss., University of Missouri-Columbia, 1999).

Chapter 2
Abraham Goldsmid: Money Magician in the Popular Press

Mark L. Schoenfield

If I can, I shall keep my death from saying anything that my life has not already said
—Michel de Montaigne, circa 1574.[1]

When the financier Abraham Goldsmid died of a self-inflicted gunshot wound on September 25, 1810, just two years after his brother and business partner Benjamin Goldsmid had killed himself, polite magazines and newspapers throughout Great Britain reported the event. The disastrous effect of his death on the public stocks was immediate, and political economists speculated on—and sought to mitigate—the extended ramifications. *The European Magazine and London Review* ran four different pieces in its October 1810 edition. Its second article (longer than its first on the King's Jubilee and accompanied by a frontispiece portrait of Goldsmid) began by announcing: "There has, in the *commercial* and *moral* world, scarcely ever occurred an event that has excited a more general sensation of sorrow, or in a greater degree stimulated the emotions of sensibility."[2] A poem by "J. M." immediately followed on the next page, declaring that:

> Blessed with those qualities which men hold dear
> Wealth, honour, fame, attended his career,
> His death a grateful nation seem'd to feel.
> So Florence mourn'd—so drooped commercial pride,
> When Cosmo perish'd, and Lorenzo died.[3]

The chiasmus—"Florence mourn'd—so drooped commercial pride"—coordinates the social and commercial responses to these deaths through sentimentalizing personifications. A later poem, Mr. [Samuel?] Pratt's "Lines, Occasioned by the Death of Benjamin Goldsmid, *Esq.*" elides the distinction between the brothers. By collapsing the interval between their deaths, Pratt's poem implies that the death of the first not only occasions, but amounts to, the death of the second. As with J. M.'s fictive reconstruction of the Medici into a modern commercial enterprise, here, the collapse of the public firm is tantamount to the destruction of the private individual. "Lines" continues in a sentimental vein by declaring that, despite his dying a suicide, "The *rich* who lov'd, the *poor* who bless'd thy worth, / Whate'er the cause, shall consecrate thy earth."[4] This poem is followed by a report of the inquest and burial of Abraham Goldsmid; the inquest marshaled evidence for a verdict of "*insanity*" that included his "occasional depressions of spirits, in the highest degree alarming to his family" and an "accident" in which an ox and cart struck him and "contributed to the derangement of his nervous system, and rendered him more susceptible to the mortifications and embarrassments to which the late depreciation of omnium exposed him." Despite this legal mitigation, however, the article reports that "in conformity to the Mosaic laws, they ['high priest and elders'] withheld from him the customary funeral rites."[5]

If more extensive than the notices in other periodicals, the *European Magazine*'s presentation of Goldsmid is typical in several respects. It marks a tension between British and Jewish identity, here evident in the difference between the British and Jewish legal determinations regarding Goldsmid's suicide. Goldsmid's philanthropy, however, becomes a sign of the universal in which Jewish and British identities can converge. The continual association of "wealth, honour, and fame" mark the public nature of the banker's career as it negotiates contradictory impulses and representations. Goldsmid's suicide is usually delineated as an aberration in his career, one produced by a confluence of external circumstances distinct from his public character. I would like to suggest, however, that the ability to disassociate his death from his life is both characteristic of and made possible by the public nature of his identity as it is reiterated within a print culture for which the continuity of selfhood inheres not in individual identity but in the public location of the self. In the first part of this chapter, "Creating Credit," I sketch out Goldsmid's own production of his public self within the matrix of emerging British financial markets; in the second part, "Competing Parties," I explore William Cobbett's exploitation of that public character in the aftermath of Goldsmid's suicide. If *The European Magazine and London Review* seeks to mediate tensions of British economic policy (and an anxiety about its reliance on immigrant Jews) through panegyric, Cobbett attempts to replicate those tensions as threats to British economic well-being.

Creating Credit

The public association of Jews with the English financial markets is an eighteenth-century truism generated throughout popular print and theatrical cultures. Describing his chameleon nature, Addison's *Spectator* notes that "I have been taken for a Merchant upon the *Exchange* for above these ten Years, and sometimes pass for a *Jew* in the assembly of Stock-jobbers at *Jonathan's*."[6] Susanna Centlivre's *A Bold Stroke for a Wife* (first printed in London, 1735), similarly locates a key financial scene among the stockjobbers at Jonathan's; there, the hero Colonel Fainwell, disguised as a Dutch merchant, dupes Changelove as part of the elaborate marriage plot. Stockjobbers provide the ambience of confusion that culminates in the Second Stockjobber's exclamation: "Zounds, where are all the Jews this afternoon? Are you a bull or a bear today, Abraham?" The Third Stockjobber replies that he is a bull today and will be a bear next week.[7] In both Addison's and Centlivre's representations, the Jewish presence at the nascent stock exchange registers the uncertainty of its trading procedures and its dependence upon a stabilizing discourse. Such cultural representations ranged from pro-Semitic commentary that credited Jewish stockjobbers with providing crucial stability, to vicious anti-Semitism that identified the financial uncertainties of the market as the creation of the Jewish brokers. These caricatures overstated a genuine but limited phenomenon, the influx of Jewish immigrants with mercantile and financial skills, from Amsterdam and other places on the Continent, who, in concert with others, transformed the English monetary markets. Although Jews were declared to characterize the financial merchant industry, the law limited the number of licensed Jewish financial merchants to a dozen, and although many other Jews worked as unlicensed merchants (a status that denied them either the right to sue for their fees or to testify in court, but allowed certain other benefits, including the ability to act simultaneously as principle brokers in a transaction), at no time did they constitute more than a substantial minority of the financial market.[8]

Edmund Burke, defending his construction of English constitutionalism, recognized that political, and even military, success in modern Europe depended upon the viability of financial markets, which, in turn, relied on the stability of money as a representation of public credit. He proposes a series of analogies that link the economy of ideas to that of monetary exchange. Distinguishing the English revolutionaries under Cromwell from the contemporary French revolutionaries, Burke insists on the "long view" of the former: "They were not like Jew brokers, contending with each other who could best remedy with fraudulent circulation and depreciated paper the wretchedness and ruin brought on their country by their degenerate councils."[9] In associating in 1791 the French National government with Jews, Burke works to erode French financial credit in part by associating it with Jewish anti-Christianity: church-wardens should not "so much as to trust the chalice in their sacrilegious hands, so long as Jews have assignats on ecclesiastical plunder, to exchange for the silver stolen from churches."[10] His own attack on the French Assignats served as rhetorical supplements to British attacks on French currency waged through counterfeiting, monetary manipulation, and restrictions on the availability of gold. Such tactics not only corrupted French economic stability—and contributed to both Robespierre's defeat of the more moderate Girondins and Napoleon's later rise—but distressed England's own financial markets as the national debt soared and markets responded to rumors about the flow of gold out of the country.

Huge draws on the Bank of England made by the government to wage war and to support foreign allies meant that gold was leaving the country and the Bank had to repurchase its own gold at considerable loss. The resulting economic situation spawned an industry of financial pamphlets that attempted to assure an uneasy public of British economic stability. Financiers recognized that the faith of the nation in economic stability was partly a self-fulfilling prophecy. For example, the ability of banks to circulate gold-backed notes depended on a sufficiently high confidence in the ability to redeem the notes that few holders would elect to do so, since it was economically infeasible to maintain sufficiently high reserves of gold. Such delicate balances were exacerbated when, on February 20, 1797, country banks in Newcastle had failed, and the subsequent run on banks resulted in a collapse of the monetary market. The directors of the Bank of England, in concert with prime minister William Pitt and King George III, suspended cash payments. This meant that where before one could redeem paper notes for the gold that they signified, now, although they technically continued to signify their value with respect to gold, they could not be converted into it. So what had money become? Metaphors proliferated as anxious answers were proposed. Lord Lansdowne, in a passionate speech before the House of Lords, compared public credit to the soul of England. He continued in this metaphorical vein, insisting that a "fever is as much a fever in London as in Paris or Amsterdam";[11] paper money was, for Lansdowne, the sign of a sick, and contagious, body-politic. The government's analysis of the situation, by contrast, was designed to calm fears rather than distribute accurate information—although in theory, the calming of fears would validate the government's confidence in recovery.

The practice of accepting Bank of England notes without gold backing was institutionalized on February 27 by agreement of the principle merchants to "take the Bank of England notes and to promote the circulation of them." In order to compel adherence as a patriotic duty, newspaper reports emphasized the similarity of this measure to those taken in 1745 to counter the Jacobite rebellion. The measure was "in consequence of the unusual demand that had been made upon the metropolis, arising from ill-founded or exaggerated alarms in different parts of the country." This rationale blamed the information system, rather than the material drain on gold caused by government policies and to which the alarm was rationally responding.[12] The public display by the merchants of support for the suspension of species, despite—and partly because of—their private reservations about the effect, required the mobilization of the press; and periodicals such as the *Gentleman's Magazine* applauded the honorable conduct of the merchants. With great rapidity, the basis of the Bank of England's stability shifted from the gold in its coffers to the confidence of the merchant class. By March 3, 1797, the *Times* reported that "not a guinea was to be had in exchange for Bank-notes on any of the public roads," and the cohesion of the banking industry had minimized damage. More than three thousand firms and individuals were named over several days in the *Times* as resolving to accept and to pay using Bank of England notes. This was both a crisis of economy and a crisis of representation, or, more precisely, this crisis revealed that economic solidity was grounded only in its own persuasive representation.

Among the chief agents of this stabilizing effort was the Jewish firm of Abraham and Benjamin Goldsmid, two brothers, the children of an immigrant Dutch merchant. From the perspective of their career, which from the early 1790s relied increasingly on the public representation of their own stability as intermediaries within various financial markets, the events of 1797 were less a crisis (although they did lose considerable money) than a developmental stage in the financial markets that required merchants to represent persuasively their financial stability. In 1792, a "landmark [year] in the firm's history," they had moved "from a house on the close and cramped Jewish quarter to more spacious premises in Capel Court, within a stone's throw of the Bank of England and the Royal Exchange, and the move was the outward sign of the growing prestige and importance of the firm."[13] There, they were positioned to befriend

Abraham Newland, the "famous, popular" and "very speculative" chief cashier of the Bank of England; Paul Emden speculates that "this very close acquaintanceship" might be better described as "a very silent partnership" from which "both sides benefited."[14] Like Newland, as they extended their professional relationships, the Goldsmids also developed their public personæ as philanthropists and patriots.

Benjamin Goldsmid's biographer maintains that the brothers took up "the business of a *Bill Broker*," that is, "the middle man between the Merchant and the Monied Interest; a concern wholly unknown on the Royal Exchange till that time," that is, about 1771.[15] Their ancestor, Rabbi Uri Halevi, was reputed to have been an alchemist capable of transforming base metals into gold,[16] and although the myth was, I presume, not widely believed, it still contributed to the popularization of the notion of Abraham Goldsmid as financial magician. Summarizing their career as it had been captured in the periodical press, John Francis compares their "entertainments" to "the glories of the Arabian nights" and characterizes their success in lotteries as "little inferior to romance"; he grants them a particularly relevant form of clairvoyance: "they knew as if by instinct a bill of exchange with a bad name to it."[17] Even their father's death was surrounded with an aura of the mystical, as Levy Alexander relates "a mysterious circumstance" that "occasioned much talk among our people," i.e., English Jews; Aaron Goldsmid had been left a "packet of papers carefully sealed" by a "Cabalistical Doctor," accompanied by the "severest injunction" not to break the seal. Obedience to this command would make Aaron's family "highly prosperous in all their undertakings," and breaking it would have "fatal consequences." Succumbing to curiosity, Aaron Goldsmid eventually opened the scroll and was found dead "the same day" next to a scroll "covered with Cabalistic figures and Hieroglyphics."[18] In part, this narrative is meant to account symbolically for the complex careers of the Goldsmids, financially highly successful but culminating in Benjamin's suicide. But its emphasis on the power of representational figures themselves corresponds to the market transformations in which the Goldsmids participated, in which, as Karl Polanyi has argued, money (and other representors of value) emerged as commodities in their own right, that is, as objects capable of being produced for sale and deployed for gain;[19] the cabbalistic manipulation of figures presaged the economic legerdemain of Abraham Goldsmid.

The government in 1797 had moved quickly to link its financial troubles to its war effort, and consequently to correlate financial loyalty to the government with patriotism. Having already been instrumental in

Pitt's 1795 Loyalty Loan, the Goldsmids undertook brokering numerous loans for the Navy and lent the Prince of Wales considerable funds. In this environment, they were able to transform both their own fortunes and the financial markets. S. R. Cope notes that the Goldsmids "were referred to at various times as bill brokers, money dealers, loan contractors, dealers in the funds, monied men, merchants, and so on. They were in fact all of these... [although] they usually called themselves simply merchants."[20] By 1803, the annual *Public Characters* noted they had an international reputation "as merchants particularly in the line of exchange, in which lucrative line of merchandise the Goldsmids are unrivalled";[21] that same year, Robert Dighton painted a portrait of Abraham Goldsmid that was reproduced in print form.[22] As England became more mired in the expenses of hostilities with France, the Goldsmids' position as bill brokers and as close friends of Abraham Newland, the signatory for the Bank of England, allowed them to act as the intermediary between the Exchequer and the Bank of England; Cope estimates that on a single day in 1802, B. & A. Goldsmid sold 85,000 pounds to the Bank, and that between 1797 and 1810, they sold some 300 million pounds of Exchequer notes to private firms. For the English financial market, the legacy of public anti-Semitism, exploited by Burke in his attack on the French National Assembly, became a liability. If before, shadowy Jewish figures were acknowledged as a necessary evil, now, the public presentation of both the Jewish community and of specific Jewish financiers was part of the project of English economic recovery, and for the Goldsmids, the new alchemy consisted of the transformation of loans into wealth, Jewish monetary magic into English patriotism.[23] This presentation availed itself of rapidly emerging newspaper and periodical industries, through which it negotiated the double-bind of the public performance of hybrid nationality—to be Jewish and to be British.

    The process by which this fame was achieved was a combination of financial innovations, public presentation, and social maneuvering that included situating the Goldsmid firm visibly within the financial community and developing important friendships. Just as their much-advertised personal friendship with the Prince of Wales aided their business (and his), Abraham's "commercial transactions have, in a manner, identified him with the Government of the country," as a newspaper reported in 1806.[24] This account also notes that while "Bounaparte is assembling the Jews at Paris," Britain should exult that "a British merchant should hold so distinguished and eminent a rank in society, that the first characters in the kingdom are anxious to pay respects to his invitation, to become the guests at his hospitable and munificent table." Such rhetoric is replicated in the *Anti-Jacobin Review,* which notes that while the French have their Goldsmidt (a spy), the British have theirs as well—the financier. This difference between the two Goldsmi(ths) serves as a metonymy for the difference between French and British society and finance.[25] The brothers deployed their money in highly visible charity projects, carefully balanced between specifically Jewish and British causes. Further, they were able to represent the visible markers of their own success as indicators of British success as well. The Goldsmids recognized that the physical appearance of their property was part of their public persona. Benjamin had his estate at Roehampton designed by James Spiller, who had designed the Great Synagogue of London, while J. T. Groves, the "official Clerk of Works for Whitehall and Westminster," designed Morden for Abraham Goldsmid.[26] In addition to the *Times,* several periodicals reported on the feast Abraham Goldsmid held to celebrate the completion of his estate at Morden, to which accounts Cobbett alludes five years later.[27] The *Courier* (August 26, 1806) reported "Mr Goldsmid's Superb Fete," at which "Yesterday evening Mr GOLDSMID was honoured at his newly erected villa at Morden, with the presence of His Royal Highness the Prince of WALES, his Royal Brothers, the LORD CHANCELLOR of England, and a select assembly of the first persons of distinction." Elaborate descriptions of the grounds, interwoven with that of the event, begin the next paragraph: "A more picturesque and romantic place in point of rural scenery cannot be imagined. Before the house is a beautiful lawn, diversified with orange and lemon trees, aloes, and the various exotics of the most luxuriant climes." As with their earlier business move to Cadel Court, adjacent to the Bank of England, Abraham's personal establishment at Morden reflects financial stability, though here that stability is linked explicitly to a sense of culture and acculturation. Included in the festivities were songs by John Braham, including one with this refrain:

> Fill then the bowl with myrtle bound
> Let Morden's roof with mirth resound
> And every tongue this strain declare
> "Long live Britannia's Joy and Heir."[28]

This imagery of permanence is similarly reflected both in Abraham Goldsmid's image as a "Pillar of the community" and in the conspicuous presence of pillars at both Morden and Roehampton, Benjamin's estate where "Every thing" is presented "on a scale of magnificence and beauty equal to any Nobleman's country seat."[29] The breakfast room at Roehampton was adorned with "genealogical pictures," some of which were "executed by the most eminent Masters viz. WEST, SIR JOSHUA REYNOLDS AND BEECHY," and this room was "introduced [to] its visitors" by "A vestibule of the most beautiful and expensive marble pavement supported by Corinthian pillars"[30] (the association of pillars and financial stability continued, as seen in an 1829 print of Nathan Rothschild beside a pillar, ambiguously entitled "A *PILLAR* of the Exchange").[31] David Hughson includes in his extensive guide to the neighborhoods of London an illustration of Morden, with the pillars emphasized; the text identifies it as "the elegant mansion of Abraham Goldsmid, Esq. The structure is formed upon a lively and beautiful model ... part of the roof is supported by twelve porphyry pillars."[32]

Goldsmid's public reputation, once established, was available for cooption in a variety of ways. Philo-Judaeis, in his *Letter to Abraham Goldsmid*, responding to a proposal for taxation to ameliorate the condition of the Jewish poor, addresses his pamphlet as a letter to Abraham Goldsmid.[33] After a brief Preface detailing the argument he intends to refute and pointing out that taxation is likely to have no positive effect because Jewish philanthropists "cheerfully" donate, and "in every instance, their bounty has been *more* than *apportioned* to their means," the author addresses Goldsmid: "Sir, Persuaded that you merit every eulogium, and confirmed in that opinion, by the testimony of those, who have had opportunity of experiencing how justly they are bestowed, I am induced, although a stranger, to address you." In particular, Philo-Judaeis cautions Goldsmid about lending his name, which is accompanied by such immense public recognition, in a scheme that "appears" to be "pregnant with the most mischievous consequences to your nation [i.e., Judaism]." Despite never having met Goldsmid, the author seeks to assure Goldsmid he is actuated by concern for Goldsmid's own character. In such a move, the author uses the name "Goldsmid" and its public associations metonymically for Jewish philanthropy, and even this is expanded by the subsequent claim that should Van Oven's scheme be enacted, "responsibility" for its practical flaws would devolve on "*you*, as the *ostensible head of the Jews* in this country." Such praise seeks to advance a disciplinary agenda regarding British Jews, as Philo-Judaeis simultaneously uses Goldsmid's own success within British culture— especially "your [Goldsmid's] noble example" of "lavish" "benefactions to the Christian poor" (30)—to produce an assimilation argument, in which any specifically Jewish culture emerges from anti-Semitic persecution that is best combated by avoiding any legislative or rabbinic measures to consolidate Jewish society beyond gestures of personal acts of charity. The appeal to Goldsmid, then, functions to position his "genuine charity" as part of a "pure, and unostentatious humanity" (13) and not a sense of Jewish identity, even as this humanity manifests those "long habituated" rights, the "franchises and privileges of Englishmen" that Goldsmid's fellow Jews "conceive themselves entitled [to] by inherent right" (31–2).

A less ideologically trenchant, but still illustrative example of the public force of Goldsmid's name appears in the *Newgate Calendar*. Levi Mortgen and Joseph Luppa were convicted of conspiring to swindle a Piccadilly innkeeper. Posing as agents of Russian princes, they "borrowed" eight pounds in order to obtain appropriate passports for the Russian aristocrats, and they concocted the story that Mortgen "had got an order to draw on Abraham Goldsmid, esq., to the amount of five hundred pounds, and that on his return in the evening he would deposit one hundred pounds in order to ensure the keeping of the rooms."[34]

A letter of recommendation for a Mr. Phineas vouches for him on the word of "Mr Abm Goldsmid," and continues that "Lord Nelson will feel much obliged to any Captain who may be pleased to show attention to the recommendation of Lord Nelson's friend and neighbor Mr. Goldsmid."[35] The Goldsmids' friendship with Lord Nelson, as with the Prince of Wales, was integrated into their public credit. After the Battle of Trafalgar, "The Discourse of the Three Sisters" (London, 1805), N. I. Valletine's poem issued in Hebrew and English, memorialized Nelson through the speaking voices of England, Scotland, and Ireland; it was dedicated to Benjamin Goldsmid as Nelson's closest friend and one of his public champions. Both brothers were mourners at Nelson's funeral, and the story that Nelson had chosen to stay at Benjamin Goldsmid's house on his final night before embarking to Trafalgar was widely repeated and corroborated by the later diary reminiscence of Benjamin's son, Lionel, who, eight years old in 1805, longed to go to sea with Nelson.[36]

Competing Parties

In his 1812 Preface to *Paper against Gold,* William Cobbett explains that the "greater part of this work" was "written in, and dated from the '*State Prison, Newgate*'" where Cobbett was incarcerated for sedition. As an indication of the esteem in which the public held him, he describes the celebration occasioned by his release: "A great dinner was given in London for the purpose of receiving me, at which dinner upwards of

600 persons were present."[37] Within the narrative of the Preface, additional public ceremonies, bell-ringings, and fetes secure Cobbett's reputation and position him to relaunch his perennial attack on government fiscal policy, here organized as a series of republished letters. *Paper against Gold* begins with a consideration of the Bullion Report, a document produced by Parliament that favored extending the suspension of gold payments for a limited period of time. Demonstrating his contempt for the government's motives for the suspension of cash payments, Cobbett notes that the government committee that authored the Bullion Report opened its investigation by "sen[ding] for several persons, whom they examined as *witnesses,* touching the matter in question. There was SIR FRANCIS BARING, for instance, the great loan-maker, and GOLDSMIDT, the rich Jew, whose name you so often see in the newspapers, where he is stated to give grand dinners to princes and great men." In italicizing "witnesses," Cobbett is reminding his audience of the interested positions of these witnesses, who were not economists but financiers. Where the parties in Cobbett's own honor—depicted as spontaneous overflows of admiration—validate his character and integrity, Abraham Goldsmid's celebrations, like his testimony, are presented as calculated public-relations tactics consistent with Goldsmid's strategic and highly public charity and that serve as an integral part of his financial operations, operations that Cobbett represents as a sophisticated form of theft. His misspelling of Goldsmid's name, even within quotations otherwise accurate, insists upon the banker's unassimilatable foreignness and insinuates that the Anglicization constitutes a breach of public trust, in a system increasingly reliant on accurate signatures and the ability to recognize fiscal origins of bills and notes.

In his first letter, Cobbett substitutes Goldsmid's public representation, as the producer of grand parties and ubiquitous newspaper articles, for an analysis of Goldsmid's particular evidence before the Committee. He intends Goldsmid's tainted presence itself to compromise the Bullion Committee. Cobbett's attack is ad hominem, focusing not on the content of the testimony, which is insignificant relative to that of other witnesses, but on his public character. In his two brief appearances before the Committee, Goldsmid primarily reported on fluctuations in the price of gold in Amsterdam and Hamburg.[38] When asked pointedly about the key issue, the effect of "the circulating medium, as entirely confined to paper in this country," Goldsmid demurred, replying that he was not "competent to give [his] opinion on that" (121). By contrast, his nephew, the lesser known Aaron Asher Goldsmid, who testified on four separate occasions, had indicated that, as a bullion merchant, he "did not make any distinction between Bank paper and coin" (41); although Aaron Goldsmid articulates precisely the position attacked in *Paper against Gold,* Cobbett completely ignores both his testimony and similar accounts by many witnesses, including other Jews. In contrast, David Ricardo, in his "Notes on the Bullion Report," recognized both the import of Aaron Asher's evidence and the insignificance of Abraham's.[39] Cobbett's decision, then, to target the less relevant Abraham Goldsmid indicates that his animosity stems from sources other than the information the banker had provided for the *Bullion Report.*

Cobbett excoriates Goldsmid's means of establishing personal public credit, which he interprets as a deceit analogous with one he sees inscribed on the bills from the Bank of England, namely, that although on their face, they read "payable on demand," such payment in specie had been suspended and the Bullion Commission had recommended extending the suspension for at least an additional two years. Abraham Goldsmid negotiated his public figure as both immigrant Jew and loyal Briton during the financial upheavals that spanned his professional career, and Cobbett's response accurately registers Goldsmid's use of the public press, not least because Goldsmid's methods resembled Cobbett's development of his own public character. The viciousness of Cobbett's anti-Semitism focuses on Goldsmid at this moment because of the success of that public performance—whether it was deliberately orchestrated by Goldsmid through payments, as Cobbett maintains, or was a predictable consequence of his actions in a society increasingly attuned to fame—and because Cobbett recognized that, in a paper-money economy, such public performances were crucial to the development of a discourse about the enactment of public credit. Rhetorically, by misrepresenting Goldsmid's centrality to the Bullion Committee, Cobbett insinuates that its hearings were designed for public consumption and not a genuine investigation of the issue. Ricardo similarly acknowledges the social utility of Goldsmid's presence as a witness, when he notes that John Sinclair implies Goldsmid's sanction in attributing a particular opinion to "the authority of persons of practical detail."[40]

I am not concerned here with the merit of Cobbett's claim about the purposes of the Committee but, rather, with his appropriation of Goldsmid's public persona to make the claim. His ability to do so depended upon the rise of a periodical industry that corresponded to, and complemented, the economic expansions in which both Goldsmid and Cobbett participated. The risk of deploying the press in public self-representation, exacerbated for Goldsmid by the dependence of his business on credit as both commodity and metaphor, is baldly illustrated by a brief excerpt from an obituary in the *Morning Post*, of October 1, 1810, just days after his suicide: "His benevolence was *so enlarged*—his public and private character was so *princely,* embracing *men of all persuasions*— he was so *unostentatious* in his habits." Cobbett quotes this passage as evidence of its own untruth; he argues that its very appearance—as a remnant of Goldsmid's own public relations machine designed to "keep the public from *grudging*"—demonstrates that "[n]ever was anything more *ostentatious* than the acts of *benevolence*" that have been "carefully *printed* and *published.*"[41] Cobbett was not alone in making such assertions. As Endelman points out, the anonymous author of *The Commercial Habits of the Jews* (1808) announces that Goldsmid "has been exhibited in the windows of the printshops, with scrolls of paper dangling out of his pocket, enumerating the whole of his splendid gifts... our contempt and disgust are excited when we learn, that it was not the result of gratuitous adulation, but a wretched design and plot upon the admiration of the public."[42] By contrast, contemporary apologists for the Goldsmids, such as Benjamin's biographer Levy Alexander, characterized their charity as "too conspicuous to be hidden."[43]

The theory of credit—in which bills depend on both the solvency of their signatory and the fluidity of the paths in which they circulate— made it both possible and requisite for a banker like Goldsmid to produce his public image as credit. To do so, Goldsmid negotiated a growing periodical industry and used that industry not only to balance his allegiances to both Judaism and Britain, but to represent them as coextensive, rather than contradictory. His public ability to pass in a circle of friendships that included the Prince of Wales and Prime Ministers, while he provided special wheat for the *mazah* of the Chief Rabbi of London, expressed these allegiances by signaling the depth of his personal credit. Cobbett is attempting to vilify Goldsmid for having a public character, although, as I have already argued, such a character was required and produced by the historical context in which Abraham Goldsmid operated.

Roughly a month after Cobbett began publishing the serialized letters *Paper against Gold* from Newgate prison, the newspapers reported the suicide of Abraham Goldsmid by gunshot wound. In the two years since Benjamin's death, he suffered recurrent despondency, and in 1810, as his firm suffered significant financial losses from having overextended its credit, he appeared increasingly agitated. Chaim Bermant, in *The Cousinhood,* reports that on the last day of his life, Goldsmid "felt that everything and everybody was ranged against him. 'I will have my revenge,' he kept roaring, shaking a fist at an unseen adversary."[44]

Cobbett's Letter IX,[45] nearly the longest of the collection, is dated October 2, 1810; therefore, he must have written it immediately and quickly, recognizing both the import of the event and the need to participate in the public shaping of its meaning, by challenging other public representations that he considered beholden to Goldsmid's own self-presentations and the government's investment in them. As Cobbett puts it, "the circumstances connected" with the suicide "afford, perhaps, a more striking and satisfactory illustration" of the "*loan-making transaction.*"

Cobbett begins by relaying the consternation reported in the *Courier* and *Times* when the news of Goldsmid's death reached "the city of London" from "his house, or rather palace." The *Times* reports that "the FUNDS felt the effect... stock fell from 661/2 to 631/2"; the *Courier* announces that a special messenger was dispatched to alert the King and Prince of Wales. The hyperbole included the *Courier*'s assertion that "Words would be inadequate to express the surprise, the *alarm* and the *dismay* that were visible" (Cobbett's italics). Cobbett then marshals a series of rhetorical questions that restate these claims in a sarcastic register, culminating in: "Is there truth in the shameful fact, that a Jew Merchant's shooting himself produced *alarm* and *dismay* in the capital of England, which is also called... the emporium of the world." Similarly, he ridicules the *Times* for labeling Goldsmid and Baring, who had also died recently, "PILLARS OF THE CITY"; compared with the whole body of public servants, such as the Mayor and Aldermen to whom the "kingdom have been indebted for the preservation of their liberty," and private individuals such as "ingenious Tradesmen" who constitute what Cobbett regards as the city's genuine wealth, Goldsmid and Baring are merely "the names of a couple of dealers in funds and paper money." In contrast to the *Times*' construction of the Stock Exchange as a synecdoche for the British response to Goldsmid's death, Cobbett attempts to isolate Baring and Goldsmid—reducing them to their names as objects of commercial and periodical circulation. He contrasts them to the producers of material wealth—laborers, apprentices, artisans—and those protectors of liberty (with whom he associates himself and his publication, in opposition to the government's organs, such as the *Times*). He ridicules the association of Goldsmid with architectural materiality by shifting the metaphor, accusing the government of establishing "CAPITAL, CREDIT, and CONFIDENCE" as "pillars of national strength," when they are in reality "three words instead of one, merely for the sake of the sound." The repetition of sound, like that of public appearance, leads to an illusion of materiality, but also to linguistic absurdity, so that these synonyms are "the *pillars* of the nation" and

Baring and Goldsmid are "the *pillars* of our CREDIT." This illogical imagery is sustained, Cobbett maintains, through circulation; he traces a series of articles about stock values and notes that "these paragraphs were *circular*" in two related senses—first, they circulate "through all the daily news-papers" (and likely "the weekly newspapers too"); and second, they perform in self-fulfilling ways, as public representations of credit designed to bolster public credit.

Cobbett insists that the newspapers' claim that the monetary markets depend on individuals—which had been meant to bolster it by constructing those merchants as modern economic heroes—will itself "destroy all confidence in the FUNDS and STOCKS: for what man in his senses can possibly confide in that which leans for support upon the life of individuals...who, from the perils of their very calling, are liable to be driven to commit acts of suicide." Where Goldsmid had associated his monetary magic with an ethical and vital public self, Cobbett now attempts to resituate it—calling the financier's work "tricks of the money-Jobbers" bolstered by the "*erroneous* opinions" of the "political writers." Cobbett makes the suicide the culmination and logical consequence of Goldsmid's empty representations; his "outward show" cannot finally conceal "his essential practices, still a money-loving, a money-amassing Jew." Typically anti-Semitic, Cobbett locates Goldsmid's greed in the fetishization of money itself as a collectable object of desire, rather than in its ability to represent and purchase. It is, for Cobbett, precisely a fetishized object because it is no object at all, but becomes one through its systematic treatment by collusive organizations, such as the Bank of England, which was legally obliged to conceal the amount of its gold reserves, the Exchequer, and Goldsmid's firm. The inexorable mark of Cobbett's anti-Semitism is his construction of even those moments of lavish spending as part of Goldsmid's miserliness; Cobbett is forced to this construction, I suggest, because of his own resemblances to Goldsmid, as a character inventing himself before a public and relying on its accreditation.

To undermine Goldsmid's charity, Cobbett chooses a particular example that invokes the governmental institutions; he asserts, incorrectly, that the sum of Goldsmid's charitable contributions were less than half of his profits from the single day in which, by using his connections, he was able to get inside the Bank to discount 350,000 pounds of Exchequer bills while other merchants waited outside for their opportunity.[46] This event, Cobbett insists, rather than those produced in the periodical press, demonstrates Goldsmid's "real character," which can be adduced "from these facts alone, facts which cannot be denied." Like Goldsmid, Cobbett is committed to the production of "facts," which necessarily embody interpretations, but by associating Goldsmid's facts with paper money and its system of manipulation, Cobbett presents his own as genuine: produced through his unalienated labor as writer/editor/publisher within the objective space of the "prison," in opposition to the "palace" that Goldsmid occupies. Neither Goldsmid nor Cobbett operates outside the system of public representations, but both rely on systems of differentiation by which to construct their identities. Both recognized that even genuine emotion needed to be performed and would serve rhetorical purposes, and both sought to graft their public character onto public institutions. For Cobbett, to oppose paper money was to oppose Goldsmid, precisely because of Goldsmid's successes within not only the financial marketplace but the periodical marketplace.

Cobbett's stridency was not the only public response to the assertion that the death of Goldsmid was a catastrophe for the market. "Erinaceus" published *Remarks on the Present State of Public Credit and the Consequences Likely To Result from the Decease of Mr. A. Goldsmid & Sir F. Baring: In A Letter To William Manning, Esq. M. P. Deputy-Governor Of The Bank* within weeks of Goldsmid's death. He notes that the "public funds have not been inaptly termed the political barometer of the state," and that the recent "very material depression of the stocks" was "particularly calculated to depress Mr. Goldsmid." As with the suicide of his brother Benjamin, the public mood, reflected in the stock depressions, is incorporated into the private person of the banker. Erinaceus describes Goldsmid's situation through a series of metaphors, such as "standing alone in the midst of a labyrinth," and seeing "a storm gathering over him"; similarly, the "general confusions" caused by news of his death meant that "the richest commercial man scarcely felt the ground secure beneath his feet." This series of matching metaphors is meant to convey a temporary state of affairs, and when "consternation and amazement had relaxed their grip on the public mind, the funds revived." He asserts that, ultimately, Goldsmid's death "may be placed amongst those private evils which contribute to the public good."[47] His vision is of a hypnotic trance that broke: "the monopoly [on the Loan industry established by Goldsmid and Barings] which paralyzed the inferior merchants, like a spell, has been suddenly dissolved; the giants of the Stock-exchange, who stalked majestically to and fro, holding every stock-holder and merchant in awe, have fallen... the streams of opulence, no longer arrested in their regular course, will revert to their accustomed channels." Through his mixed metaphors, Erinaceus replaces the correspondence of credit between Goldsmid and the public funds with a natural image of English wealth, which the monopoly of Baring and Goldsmid diverted, as a kind of magic.

Although Erinaceus is sympathetic to Goldsmid as a suffering human being, his purpose is to disrupt the continuity between the personalities of the leading financial figures and the behaviors of the financial markets. He insists that the presence of Goldsmid and Baring constitutes a kind of exceptional aberration, and their absence will restore a personality-less normality, characterized by the circulation of money through "accustomed channels." This rhetorical position is consistent with his representation of public credit not as the aggregate of the creditability of individual and corporate financiers, but as a reflection of the British "spirit of enterprise" and a steady domesticity of the English worker, "possessed of a humble cottage, sufficiently capacious for his wants and wishes; … he has a spot of ground where he raises his vegetables" (20). He continues this description of rural felicity, which includes "a pig in his stye" for a full page, noting that the peasant would dispute representations of "his unhappiness." Linking commerce to agriculture—"the same cause which fetters commerce will also fetter agriculture"—Erinaceus locates the economic barometer in someone who has no name, but is himself an aggregate, the idealized farmer (21). This figure, immune from melancholia, is meant to replace Goldsmid in the public imagination as the emblem of British credit.

Afterimage

Economic and Jewish history has located Abraham Goldsmid and his family on the periphery of the Rothschilds and Montefiores, in part because of the Goldsmid's suicides, which set them outside the Jewish burial ground, and in part because the structure of metonymic credit, which the Goldsmids developed, was more enduringly employed by the Rothschilds. Nonetheless, as late as 1850, the myth of the Goldsmid's public figure continued to reverberate. In his history of the stock exchange, John Francis wrote that the newspapers "bore an almost daily testimony to their [the Goldsmids'] munificence. On one day the grandeur of an entertainment to royalty was recorded, and on the next a few words related a visit of mercy to a condemned cell."[48] Just as in the eighteenth century, when the presence of Jewish merchants became metonymic for the financial market itself and thus sheltered other British merchants from potential public animosity, here the periodical, but hardly even monthly, appearance of the Goldsmids in the public press is exaggerated into "daily testimony" in keeping with the figure of the Jew as a trope of exaggeration and over-extended credit.

I wish to conclude by glancing at an American novel, which, in its comic bluntness, schematizes the historical construction of Goldsmid that emerges from his public persona. James Kirke Paulding, writing in 1830, exploits the interchange of cultural and financial economics in a scene presumably placed in 1810. Early in his *Chronicles of the City of Gotham*, an argument about the literary merits of a novel devolves into a struggle of authority, in which citation completely replaces reasoning:

> "Dr. Johnson affirms"—
> "The Edinburgh Review says"—
> "The London Quarterly lays it down"—
> "The London Literary Gazette"—screamed Lucia—
> "Blackwood's Bombazine"—cried Mrs. Coates, yet louder.

This appeal to periodical authority begins with the reasonableness implied by the verbs associated with the magazines, as the sequence moves chronologically through major reviews. Johnson, as honored precursor, "affirms"; the *Edinburgh Review* assertively "says," while its rival *Quarterly* "lays it down," as a kind of challenge. The verbs shift, however, from the journals speaking for themselves to their only being summoned in hyperbolic, competitive tones—Lucia "screamed," and Mrs. Coates "cried...yet louder" the names of their respective champions. This comic moment depends upon the cultural credit that has accrued to the periodical press, but simultaneously notes the ease of its manipulation. Unresolved, this argument takes another turn with the arrival of Highfield, a worldly but indifferent student:

> "What do you think of Goldsmith?" asked Miss Appleby, after the compliments.
> "Goldsmid?" said he [Highfield], "why really I think he was a great fool to shoot himself."
> "Shoot himself?" screamed Mrs. Coates, "what, is he dead?"
> "Yes, madam—his affairs fell into confusion, and he shot himself; I thought you had seen it in the papers, by your asking my opinion."
> "Lord!" said Miss Appleby, "I don't mean Goldsmid, the broker, but Goldsmith, the poet and novelist; what is your opinion of him?"[49]

These juxtaposed conversations signal Goldsmid's currency within the popular discourse dominated by the periodical press. The confusion between Goldsmid and Goldsmith plays on the permeability of literary and economic figures, but also points to the historical confusions from which the discursive distinctions themselves emerged. Highfield assumes that Miss Appleby draws her interests from the current newspapers, but her own shock at Goldsmith's mistaken death is comic precisely because he has been dead for nearly forty years. His literary self, impressed through print culture, obscures his own death and allows him to compete, as the discussion develops, against Byron, the modern poet who is "all passion"; by contrast, Goldsmith appears to Highfield as "one of the most agreeable, tender, and sprightly writers in the language," and as insipid to the Byron-inspired Puddingham and Goshawk, who insist he lacks "power" and "force." The Byronic force to which these characters refer is the corporate production of Byronism that, as Jerome Christensen has demonstrated, skillfully merged and evaded economic and aesthetic imperatives.[50] Within the structure of this conversation, in which Goldsmith's lack of suicidal impulses marks his insipidness, Goldsmid occupies the position of Byron. His sensitivity to his "affairs falling into confusion" marks his passionate impulses. This discursive slippage is underscored by the historical impossibility of the events, Goldsmid having died long before the formation of some of the reviews mentioned and before the establishment of Byronism as the gold standard of poetic passion. Thus, his currency in the newspaper is as implausible as the *recent* news of Goldsmith's death in 1810.[51] Written in 1830, James Kirk Paulding's *Chronicles of the City of Gotham* registers the currency of Goldsmid's fame and locates it within specific modes of literary productions, precisely those that Goldsmid himself exploited by enacting press-worthy performances of charity, celebration, and civic duties, as part of his system of securing the public credit necessary for his firm to operate.

Notes

1. "That intention is judge of our Actions," in *The Complete Essays of Montaigne*, trans. Donald Frame (Stanford: Stanford University Press, 1957), 20.
2. 58 (October 1810): 243.
3. J. M., "Poem," *The European Magazine and London Review* 58 (October 1810): 244.
4. *The European Magazine and London Review* 58 (October 1810): 244.
5. *The European Magazine and London Review* 58 (October 1810): 313–14.
6. Joseph Addison and Richard Steele, *The Spectator,* ed. Donald Bond (Oxford: Clarendon Press, 1965), 1:4.
7. Susanna Centlivre, *A Bold Stroke For a Wife,* ed. Nancy Copeland (New York: Broadview Press, 1995), IV. i.19–22.

8. See Harold Pollins, *Economic History of the Jews in England* (Rutherford: Fairleigh Dickinson University Press, 1982), especially chapter 2, "Merchants and Brokers: The Commercial and Financial Revolutions."
9. *Reflections on the Revolution in France*, ed. J. C. D. Clark (Stanford: Stanford University Press, 2001), 204.
10. *A Letter From Mr. Burke To A Member Of The National Assembly In Answer To Some Objections To His Book On French Affairs* (1791) (Smartboard Website: http://www.ourcivilisation.com/smartboard/shop/burkee/tonatass, 2000). Burke follows up with a blistering paragraph: "I am told, that the very sons of such Jew-jobbers have been made bishops; persons not to be suspected of any sort of Christian superstition, fit colleagues to the holy prelate of Autun, and bred at the feet of that Gamaliel. We know who it was that drove the money-changers out of the temple. We see, too, who it is that brings them in again. We have in London very respectable persons of the Jewish nation, whom we will keep; but we have of the same tribe others of a very different description, house-breakers, and receivers of stolen goods, and forgers of paper currency, more than we can conveniently hang. These we can spare to France, to fill the new episcopal thrones: men well versed in swearing; and who will scruple no oath which the fertile genius of any of your reformers can devise."
11. Quoted in Andreas Michael Andreades, *History of the Bank of England, 1640 to 1903*, trans. Christabel Meredith, preface by H. S. Foxwell, 4th ed., Reprints of Economics Classics (New York: A. M. Kelley, 1966), 199.
12. The government's position is reflected in the thinking of the teenaged Francis Horner, five years from becoming the *Edinburgh Review*'s chief economic writer for its early issues and eventual chair of the Bullion Committee; emphasizing his belief that, despite "violent attacks made on the rights of the subject," the "propriety of supporting the government" was at once a moral imperative and economic necessity, he wrote to his father: "I am happy that you think the late apprehensions with respect to pubic affairs, exceed what the occasion could justify; indeed, the panic is now in a great measure worn off, I hope from no other cause than its being discovered to have been unfounded, Paper money still circulates without depreciation, and must be found, in the mean time, a great relief to the market; for many reasons, especially the enlargement of the Bank discounts. All political reasonings point out the increase of paper currency as a most pernicious evil; but it is to be hoped that matters may yet go well, provided it be used only as a temporary expedient" (Leonard Horner, *Memoir and Correspondence of Francis Horner* [London: John Murray, 1853], 34–5).
13. S. R. Cope, "The Goldsmids and the Development of the London Money Market during the Napoleonic Wars," *Economica* 9 (1942): 184–5.
14. Paul Emden, "The Brothers Goldsmid and the Financing of the Napoleonic Wars," *Transactions of the Jewish Historical Society of England* 14 (1935–9): 233. Emden notes that, on his death, Newland left each brother £500, with the proviso "to buy mourning rings" (234).
15. Levy Alexander, *Memoirs of the Life and Commercial Connections, Public and Private, of the Late Benj. Goldsmid, Esq. Of Roehampton, Containing A*

ABRAHAM GOLDSMID: MONEY MAGICIAN / 57

Cursory View of the Jewish Society and Manners, Interspersed with Interesting Anecdotes of Several Remarkable Characters (London, 1808), 16, 100.
16. Marcus Arkin, *Aspects of Jewish Economic History* (Philadelphia: Jewish Publication Society, 1975), 159.
17. *Chronicles and Characters of the Stock Exchange* (London: Willoughby and Co., 1849), 162–3.
18. Alexander, 45–7.
19. *The Great Transformation*, forward by Robert M. MacIver (New York: Rinehart, 1944; reprint, Boston: Beacon Press, 1985), chapter 1.
20. Cope, 181.
21. [Alexander Stephens et al.], "The Goldsmids," in *Public Character of 1802–03,* from the ten-volume *Public Characters of…* (London: R. Phillips, 1798–1810), 4:50–1. The author announces that the "principle inducement" for this particular article is "to remove the film of prejudice" which has been so exacerbated by both "mystery" and "misrepresentations" that "it is by no means surprising to meet with persons actually doubting, whether the millions of wealth which pass through the hands of the Goldsmids be conjured up by some art as black as magic, or extorted by some means as despicable as the '*gamester's tools'*" (4:50). *Public Characters of 1803–4* includes a sketch of John Braham (who would sing at the commemoration of Abraham Goldsmid's estate), that details the interactions between his talents as a singer and his success as a public figure; the author, Mr. Busby, notes that "the publicity of his late powers had not only produced him numerous admirers, but many *friends,* among whom the most conspicuous were the Goldsmids, a family as well known to the public as respected by their private connections" (376).
22. See Alfred Rubens, *Anglo-Jewish Portraits: A Biographical Catalogue of Engraved Anglo-Jewish and Colonial Portraits from the Earliest Times to the Accession of Queen Victoria* (London: The Jewish Museum, 1935), especially 40–3. Rubens' study demonstrates the visibility, in both representation and caricature, of English Jews, including the Goldsmid family and estates.
23. I am not implying that their patriotism was not sincere but, rather, I wish to insist that patriotism, however genuine, needed to be publicly enacted and could be used to align national imperatives and self-interest.
24. "Mr. Goldsmid's Fete," FC 47 "*Aug 22nd 1806"* [date penciled]; from the Archive at Morden Lodge. Katie Fretwell, whom I thank for generously sharing her research with me, has supplied the transcripts, as transcribed by Judith Goodman, of the various newspaper accounts from the Archive at Morden Lodge referred to in this paragraph. In some cases, because the archive contained only newspaper and periodical clippings, it has not been possible to provide a complete citation.
25. It appears, ironically, that the "French" Goldsmith was actually a paid British propagandist, and when in England, he was released from a charge of high treason through the intercession of Abraham Goldsmid, "who introduced him to Spencer Percecval, the Prime Minister" (Alfred Rubens, "Portrait of Anglo-Jewry, 1656–1836," *Transactions of the Jewish Historical Society* 19 [1960]: 41).

26. Edward Jamilly, "Anglo-Jewish Architects, and Architecture in the 18th and 19th Centuries," *Transactions of the Jewish Historical Society of England* 18 (1953–5): 140.
27. See Katie Fretwell and Judith Goodman, "The Fete of Abraham Goldsmid: A Regency Garden Tragedy" (London: The National Trust, 2000), www.ntenvironment.com/environment/html/gardens/_fspapers/fs_gold1.htm.
28. Printed in *The Englishman*, no. 167 (August, 1806). FC 46 in Archive at Morden Lodge.
29. Alexander, 95.
30. Alexander, 90.
31. Described in Rubens, *Anglo-Jewish Portraits*, 98. Rubens includes a narrative from an 1833 *Observer*, in which Rothschild is "prevented from taking his usual station, with his back leaning against one of the pillars," by a Mr. Rose, who gets there first.
32. David Hughson, *London; being an accurate History and Description of the British Metropolis and its Neighborhood, to Thirty Miles Extent*, 6 vols. (London: J. Stratford, 1805–9), 5:293–4. In his 1806 2-volume edition, Hughson indicated that "the generous and opulent proprietor" had "spared no expense" in making the villa "perhaps one of the most complete and elegant in this kingdom"; besides noting six particular pillars, he mentions "a curious well, two hundred feet deep, with an inscription alluding to Abraham's finding water" (quoted in Fretwell).
33. Philo-Judaeis, *A Letter to Abraham Goldsmid, Esq. Containing Strictures on Mr. Joshua Van Oven's Letters on the Present State of the Jewish Poor. Pointing out the Impracticability of ameliorating their condition through the medium of Taxation and Coercion, with a Plan for Erecting a Jewish College, or Seminary, &c.* (London: Blacks and Parry, 1802). Subsequent references to Philo-Judaeis's *Letter* will be cited parenthetically in the text. For a discussion of Van Oven's plans and Goldsmid's interests in them, see Todd M. Endelman, *The Jews of Georgian England, 1714–1830: Tradition and Change in a Liberal Society* (Philadelphia: The Jewish Publication Society of America, 1979; reprint, Ann Arbor: University of Michigan Press, 1999), 231–6. The scheme that Van Oven had proposed to combat Jewish "poverty and criminality" was "the creation of a communally financed, government-supported agency for the relief and the control of the Jewish poor"; this entailed the creation of a "Jewish poor relief board to be invested by Parliament with quasi-governmental powers," including that of taxation of wealthier Jews (Endelman, 231–2).
34. *The Complete Newgate Calendar*, reprint, Tarlton Law Library, Law in Popular Culture Collection, Web Site Reproduction of *The Complete Newgate Calendar* (London: Navarre Society Ltd., 1926), http://tarlton.law.utexas.edu/lpop/etext/completenewgate.htm, 5:82–3.
35. Quoted in Bernard Susser, *The Jews of South-West England: The Rise and Decline of their Medieval and Modern Communities* (Exeter: Exeter Press, 1993), 101.
36. Cecil Roth, "Nelson and Some Jews," in his *Essays and Portraits in Anglo-Jewish History* (Philadelphia: The Jewish Publication Society of America,

1962), 232–6. In the *European Magazine*, J. M.'s elegiac poem to Abraham Goldsmid is followed immediately by a brief article, "An anagram on the Name of Horatio Nelson"; both items emphasize the personal honor and public virtues of their respective subjects in language suggesting the deliberate placement of them in the same column (58 [October, 1810]: 245).

37. William Cobbett, *Cobbett's Paper against Gold: containing the history and mystery of the Bank of England, the funds, the debt, the sinking fund, the bank stoppage, the lowering and the raising of the value of paper-money,* 2nd ed. (London, 1817), iv, viii. For the details of Cobbett's prosecution and imprisonment for sedition, based on his articles in the *Political Register* protesting the flogging of British troops, see G. D. H. Cole, *The Life of William Cobbett* (New York: Harcourt, Brace, and Co., 1924), chapters 9 and 10. Cole suggests that *Paper against Gold*, "a full examination of the paper-money system," was "the main literary labour of his imprisonment" (169).

38. Francis Horner et al., *Report, Together with the Minutes of Evidence and Accounts from The Select Committee on the High Price of Gold Bullion* (London: J. Johnson, 1810), 114–15. Future references to Horner's *Report* will be cited parenthetically in the text.

39. In *The Works and Correspondence of David Ricardo*, ed. Piero Sraffa and M. H. Dobb, vol. III: *Pamphlets and Papers 1809–10* (Cambridge: Royal Economic Society, 1951), 350, 358.

40. Ricardo, 359.
41. Cobbett, 104–5.
42. Endelman, 252.
43. Alexander, 100.
44. Chaim Bermant, *The Cousinhood: The Anglo-Jewish Gentry* (New York: Macmillan, 1971), 21. The *European Magazine* reported the description of the incident as given at the inquest in gentler terms: "On Thursday, while on change, he betrayed more than usual impatience and irritability, and spoke very incoherently as to the revenge he proposed to himself, in the punishment of the two parties opposed to him in the money market" (58 [October 1810]: 314).
45. Cobbett, 99–120.
46. This scandal had prompted a Parliamentary investigation, and though it was clear that Goldsmid acted improperly, it appears that he was not discounting his own bills, so that his profits would have been small, though clearly he saw an advantage in the transactions, as he "made a gift of at least £5000 stock to the clerks of the Exchequer Bill Office" (Cope, 189).
47. Erinaceus, *Remarks on the Present State of Public Credit and the Consequences Likely To Result from the Decease of Mr. A. Goldsmid & Sir F. Baring: In A Letter To William Manning, Esq. M. P. Deputy-Governor Of The Bank* (London: J. Johnston, 1810), 38, 39, 41. Future references to Erinaceus' *Remarks* will be cited parenthetically in the text.
48. Francis, 162.
49. James Kirke Paulding, *Chronicles of the City of Gotham* (New York: Carvill Press, 1830), 29–30.

50. See Jerome Christensen, *Lord Byron's Strength: Romantic Writing and Commercial Society* (Baltimore: Johns Hopkins University Press, 1993).
51. In addition, the reference to the "Great Unknown" appears despite the historical detail that Walter Scott was as yet not "Unknown" since the anonymous *Waverly* had not been published and he was already famous for his poetry.

Chapter 3
Halakhic Romanticism:
Wordsworth, the Rabbis, and Torah

Lloyd Davies

The year 1796 marks the beginning of William Wordsworth's enormously productive friendship with Samuel T. Coleridge in Dorset, England. That same year, in Vilna, Lithuania, the leading representative of Lithuanian *mitnagged* Rabbinic Judaism, R. Elijah, the Vilna Gaon, issued a *ḥerem* or letter of excommunication, condemning *Ḥasidism* as a pantheistic heresy. Also in that year the *Ḥasidic* Rebbe Shneyur Zalman of Liady published his *Tanya*, a work whose objective was to secure *Ḥasidism*'s legitimacy within traditional Rabbinic Judaism.[1] Only four years earlier, in Königsberg, Prussia, just two hundred miles from Vilna, Immanuel Kant, the premier philosopher of the Enlightenment, had published *Religion within the Boundary of Pure Reason*. Kant's friend and fellow native of Königsberg, J. G. Hamann, the radical Christian polemicist, had died just eight years earlier. Moses Mendelssohn, the leading German–Jewish exponent of the *Haskalah*, the Jewish Enlightenment, had also died recently (1786) in Berlin, a mere three hundred miles from Königsberg.[2]

These names and places are not easily brought into relationship with each other, for, despite their contiguity in time and space, they occupy distinct universes of discourse, alien to each other and increasingly distant to us. Yet the simultaneity of events, of lives lived in conjunction with each other, of trajectories falling within the often eccentric orbits of these other worlds—this phenomenon calls for commentary and understanding, for a faithful tracing of the shifting constellations in the night sky of our common history. When we penetrate the obscurities cast up by the cumulative clouds of post-Enlightenment life and thought and consider Wordsworthian Romanticism in conjunction with eighteenth-century Rabbinic Judaism, a surprising core of common practices and affirmations is revealed. That is to say, a distinct affinity exists between

Wordsworth, the preeminent poet of English Romanticism, and such distinguished representatives of eighteenth-century Eastern European Judaism as his older contemporaries, the Gaon of Vilna and Shneyur Zalman of Liady. That affinity reveals itself as a common adherence to a life of *halakhah*—that is, a life lived in covenantal response to the Law conceived of as Torah, or Divine Instruction.

The question of law was a major philosophical, religious, and political issue for eighteenth-century Europe. Where is the law located? In an age of science and rationality, nature is understood to be determined by mathematical and physical laws, but what laws, ethical and moral, govern human behavior? Is the law exterior to ourselves, necessitating submission to an external authority, or is it something we freely produce out of our own beings, either individually or as part of a social collective? A major thrust of Enlightenment thought, including its Jewish manifestation in the *Haskalah,* was toward a radical division of law into two distinct categories: the physical laws of the natural world and the freely chosen laws of the autonomous human subject. However, in understanding Torah as Law, *ḥasidic* Judaism, *mitnagged* Judaism, and Wordsworth alike perceive the world as a realm unified by a Divine Summons that calls all of creation, both man and nature, to an active response. In this sense, "Torah" comprehends all the ways in which law is manifested—not only the Mosaic Law, but also, in Judaism, the Oral Law and its tradition. The *halakhic* life that develops out of a lived relationship with the Law, while rooted in obedience to a transcendent commandment, is nevertheless worked out in the ordinary, empirical realities of everyday human existence. For Wordsworthian Romanticism, this opens up the possibility of *Halakhah* as response not only to Torah understood as Scripture, but also to Torah as read in the face of the natural world.

This chapter, then, intends to develop a connection between the Wordsworth of such poems as "Tintern Abbey," "Home at Grasmere," "Ode to Duty," and "Nuns fret not at their convent's narrow room," and an eighteenth-century Judaic sensibility rooted in classical *halakhic* Judaism.[3] It should be understood from the outset that I am not postulating any direct influence or communication between Wordsworth and the Jews of his time. There is little evidence that Wordsworth had any particular interest in Jewish practices or doctrines. We do know from letters and journals written by Wordsworth and his sister Dorothy from Germany in 1798 that they observed sympathetically the ill treatment of Jews in Hamburg and commented on the exemplary honesty of a Jewish woman in comparison to other German shopkeepers.[4] Perhaps these experiences led to the poem published in the 1800 edition of the *Lyrical Ballads,* the "Song for the Wandering Jew," as Kenneth R. Johnston suggests in *The Hidden Wordsworth.*[5] But despite such occasional references, there is certainly no sustained engagement on Wordsworth's part with Judaism. And, from the other side of the equation, there was also no contact; though the Gaon of Vilna was noted for taking an interest in contemporary intellectual developments, and supported such projects as Moses Mendelssohn's translation of the Torah into German, there is no reason to suppose that he knew of the cultural and intellectual stirrings in either Germany or England that would soon burst forth into what we now call Romanticism. Yet, just as it is claimed that Wordsworth's thinking "frequently parallels that of his philosophical German contemporaries," though he "never read a word of German metaphysics,"[6] so too it is possible to establish a parallel between Wordsworth and his Jewish contemporaries, though he never read a word of Talmudic commentary.

Fifty years ago, in his essay "Wordsworth and the Rabbis," Lionel Trilling pondered "why Wordsworth is no longer the loved poet he once was, why, indeed, he is often thought to be rather absurd and even a little despicable."[7] Taking note of "the hostile uneasiness that Wordsworth can arouse in us," he sought to understand the gulf of sensibility separating us from the poet.[8] Trilling proposed that what made Wordsworth unattractive to the modern world, and no longer an "intellectual possibility" for us, is a certain "Judaic quality" to his writings.[9] While confessing that his knowledge of the Jewish tradition was not sufficient to allow him to develop his hypothesis, Trilling nevertheless argues provocatively that "between the Rabbis and Wordsworth an affinity existed"; further, "between the Law as the Rabbis understood it and Nature as Wordsworth understood that, there is a pregnant similarity."[10] According to Trilling, Wordsworth viewed Nature with the same attention that the rabbis showed to the Torah; Nature was a "great object, which is from God and might be said to represent Him as a sort of surrogate, a divine object to which one can be in an intimate passionate relationship, an active relationship ... which one can, as it were, handle, and in a sense create, drawing from it inexhaustible meaning by desire, intuition, and attention."[11] Trilling also notes "the plain living," the "desire for the humble life and the discharge of duty" that marks both the rabbis and Wordsworth.[12] And, finally, he notes a similar lack of "militancy of spirit" between the rabbis and Wordsworth—Wordsworth's Happy Warrior "derives his courage not from his militancy of spirit but from his calm submission to the law of things." This involves a kind of quietism, one "which is not in the least a negation of life."[13] Wordsworth "loved to affirm the dizzy raptures of sentience," but he also "loved to move down the scale of being," where he found that even passive, unconscious, and insentient beings had a blessed existence. Trilling comments, "Nothing could be further from the tendency of our Western culture, which is committed to an idea of consciousness and activity, of motion and force."[14] The tendency of modern Western culture to judge Wordsworth as unattractive, absurd, even despicable—as no longer an intellectual possibility—also applies to traditional Judaism in precisely the same way. David Hartman, in *A Living Covenant: The Innovative Spirit in Traditional Judaism*, locates the core of modernity's condemnation of Judaism in its "alleged excessive concern with the law"—that is, its legalism.[15] Modern critics of religion object to "a religious anthropology which offends against a Zeitgeist that celebrates the unfolding of human powers and creative potential." This critique of Judaism follows Benedict Spinoza (1632–77), who claimed in the *Tractatus theologico-politicus* (Amsterdam, 1670), that the purpose of Judaic law was so that "men should do nothing of their own free will but should always act under external authority, and should continually confess by their actions the thought that they were not their own masters, but were entirely under the control of others."[16] With that view of classical Judaism and its practices, Spinoza withdrew from the Jewish community, becoming one of the first philosophers of the Enlightenment. In his intellectual wake came the *Haskalah*, the Jewish Enlightenment, led by such figures as Moses Mendelssohn (1729–86), who, though remaining devoutly observant of traditional Judaism, also embraced modern secular learning. Then, following Mendelssohn's delicate and unstable balancing act between the authority of the Talmudic tradition and the free thought of the secular intellect, German Reform Judaism quickly leaned toward rejecting *halakhah* altogether. By the late 1700s the Talmud had become what *The Encyclopædia Britannica* calls a "medieval anachronism,... legalistic, casuistic, devitalized, and unspiritual."[17] The *Britannica*, participating in the very attitude of enlightened modernist thought it describes, assumes that classical Judaism suffers from a fundamental deficiency, noting at one point the periodic need in Jewish history for "esoteric doctrines to transcend the legalistic formalism and confining dogmas of normative Judaism."[18] The *Britannica*'s negative portrayal of classical Judaism's view of the Law follows a long Greco-Christian tradition, exemplified, for instance, by Matthew Arnold, who, in his essay "Hellenism and Hebraism," sneers at the Jew who will not rest "till, as is well known, he ha[s] at last got out of the law a network of prescriptions to enwrap his whole life, to govern every moment of it, every impulse, every action."[19]

Against this critical view of its detractors Judaism must defend itself. This, too, is where Wordsworth's defense against a hostile modernity must be made, for it is precisely here, in the matter of *halakhah*, of life covenantly constituted as an obligatory response to a Divine call, that the affinity between Wordsworth and the rabbis is most clear, and most at odds with the zeitgeist of modernity. This affinity connects Wordsworth not only with the rabbis of *Pirke Aboth*, as Trilling demonstrates in his essay, but also with eighteenth-century Judaism and its modern inheritors, such as the philosopher Emmanuel Levinas and Rabbi Joseph Soloveitchik.[20]

Through the last years of the eighteenth century, while Wordsworth was developing his revolutionary poetics, Eastern European Jewry was deeply divided over two contending forces: *Ḥasidism*, the joyous and spontaneous spirituality of the Jewish masses, and *Mitnaggedism*, its scholarly and intellectual opponent. Since then this conflict has been exploited by polemicists for a variety of reasons; *Ḥasidism* especially has been made to appear as a kind of forerunner of a romantic and natural religion of modernity, while *mitnagged* Judaism has been portrayed as elitist and scholastic. Given this opposition, it would seem that the Romantic Wordsworth should be aligned with *ḥasidic* spirituality, not with *mitnagged* scholarship. Yet, in historical perspective, it is clear that the differences between the two movements were relatively insignificant in comparison to their crucial unity on the question of faithful observance of Torah and the Oral Law of Talmudic tradition. It is on that point of agreement that their common opposition to the *Haskalah* is rooted. Romanticism, of course, was also in large measure a reaction to the Enlightenment and its values. We may more accurately align Wordsworth with traditional Judaism if we see that he represents a strand of Romanticist thought that takes its stand in opposition to the "freedom from the Law" affirmed by Enlightenment thinkers. Wordsworth is truly connected with both *Ḥasid* and *Mitnagged* precisely by his sense of obligation toward fulfilling the requirements of the Law.

The similarities between *Ḥasidism* and Wordsworth are certainly notable. *Ḥasidism* originated with the life and teachings of the Ba'al Shem Tov, who, as a young man, would often wander in the woods, where, "amidst the beauties of nature, he felt more in the presence of God than in the schoolroom."[21] The Ba'al Shem Tov proclaimed that God's presence could be known by the common man without access to rabbinic learning, and that this immediacy should be the cause for a joyous attitude toward life: "Now, therefore, leave sorrow and sadness; man must live in joy and contentment, always rejoicing in his lot."[22] The first principle of Ḥasidism is, according to Charles Chavel,

> the absolute nearness of the Divine Presence to the material world, especially to man.... The universe in its various manifestations is but the outward embodiment of the Infinite Glory of the Divine Majesty, and does not exist independent of His Province.... The nearness of God to the world surrounding man entails the principle of *Simhah* (Joy): Man must banish all melancholiness and be ever joyful in the presence of the Almighty.[23]

Wordsworth, the Romantic lover of nature, expresses similar thoughts in "Expostulation and Reply," turning away from the study of books to embrace a natural world "Of things for ever speaking" (26). In "Ode: Intimations of Immortality" he says, "Oh evil day! if I were sullen/While Earth herself is adorning, ... I hear, I hear, with joy I hear!" (42–3, 50). And, in "Tintern Abbey," Wordsworth writes, "And I have felt/A presence that disturbs me with the joy/Of elevated thoughts; ... A motion and a spirit, that impels/All thinking things, all objects of all thought,/And rolls through all things" (93–5, 100–2). Wordsworth's natural world can clearly be charged with a revelatory, Divine character; in this respect Wordsworth, like the *Ḥasidim*, flirts with Pantheism: both read Divinity in the face of nature.

This linkage of Wordsworth with *Ḥasidism* reflects the typical attitudes of a Romanticist modernity—particularly its desire to turn away from the external authority of the Law, of Torah, in order to claim the interior subjective freedom of the spirit. From this perspective, *Ḥasidism's* joyful embrace of the natural world as a manifestation of God's presence frees the individual from the tedious and interminable mediations of the traditional *halakhic* system of *miẓvot* –a Judaism seen as inimical to the new spirit of *Haskalah*. In his essay "Rationalism, Romanticism, Rabbis and Rebbes," Allan Nadler notes that in the late 1800s there was "a sympathetic reappraisal of Ḥasidism inspired by the influence of European romanticism, in particular the writings of Schopenhauer and Nietzche [sic]."[24] For these Jewish Romantics, *Ḥasidism* represented

> a re-birth of the natural, subconscious spirit of the Jews. The primal nature of Hasidism's religious enthusiasm, and its rejection of the sophisticated, scholarly religion of the Talmudists, heralded an almost miraculous reincarnation of the spirit of ancient Israel, a return from the shackles of exile symbolized by the restrictions of Halakha, to Jewish authenticity, and the beginning of the difficult trek back to *Eretz Yisrael*.[25]

This essentially modernist interpretation of *Ḥasidism* was advanced by such figures as Shmuel Abba Horodetsky (1871–1957), a Russian

Zionist, who rejected the Talmud as alien to authentic Judaism, merely part of the "exilic religion of reason and law." For Horodetsky, *Hasidism* represented the rebirth for contemporary Jews of the "primal, natural faith of their ancient homeland."[26] In this interpretation of Judaism we see a deliberate rejection of centuries of traditional Jewish law. *Halakhah* is no longer the way to incarnate the spirit of ancient Israel; instead, religious authenticity grounds itself upon a subjective feeling of spiritual enthusiasm. In this revisionary re-alignment, *Hasidism*, with its emphasis on the "inner life," appears much closer to certain eighteenth-century forms of Protestant Pietism—and both of these to a Romantic sensibility based upon feelings—than to classical Judaism.

However, modernist efforts to drive a wedge between *mitnagged* Judaism—rationalistic, legalistic, and artificial—and *Hasidism*—spiritual, liberating, and authentic—stumble upon *Hasidism*'s ultimate fidelity to Torah, *mizvot*, and *halakhah*. Despite the *Hasidic* affirmation "that the mystical experience can be attained through the spiritualization of the here and now,"[27] *Hasidism* never broke with the Torah as Law, nor did it reject Rabbinic *halakhah* as the proper working out of Jewish observance of the law. In any case, as Nadler makes clear, from the viewpoint of the Enlightenment, "hasidim and misnagdim were equally backward and medieval, and their doctrines equally offensive."[28] What most offended *Haskalah* sensibilities in both *hasidic* and *mitnagged* Judaism was precisely the sense of obligation to the Law as a transcendent authority, an obligation obviously foundational for traditional *halakhah*, and yet also able to assimilate *hasidic* experience: in Judaism the experience of God's immanence is not only conformable to Torah and Talmud, it inheres within the *halakhic* life itself. It would seem then that Romantic Jewish modernists, in their attempted appropriation of *hasidic* spirituality, fundamentally misread the spiritual character of normative Judaism.

Since Spinoza and Kant, critics of normative Judaism have charged that *Halakhah* encourages a slave mentality; they have claimed that a life devoted to the observance of *mizvot* is devoid of personal moral responsibility. According to Hartman's analysis, modern critics believe that "an all-encompassing external coercive dimension is present in a disciplined normative life governed by the Orthodox *halakhah*."[29] Against these charges Hartman characterizes Judaism "in terms of a covenantal anthropology that encourages human initiative and freedom," and argues that a "covenantal vision of life, with *mitzvah* (Divine commandment) as the central organizing principle in the relationship between Jews and God, liberates both the intellect and the moral will."[30]

Hartman turns to *Halakhic Man*, the classic text of his teacher Rabbi Joseph Soloveitchik, for support in his argument. Soloveitchik's powerful tripartite typology of personalities—*homo religiosus*, cognitive man, and halakhic man—was meant to establish the viability of classical Judaism as a kind of third way in the modern world's opposition between transcendental and other-worldly religion on one hand and rational, scientific materialism on the other. While Soloveitchik's profile of halakhic man is generally considered to derive from the *mitnagged* Judaism of his ancestors, Allan Nadler contests that assumption, claiming in his article "Soloveitchik's Halakhic Man: Not a *Mithnagged*" that "Soloveitchik's ideal halakhic personality has nothing at all in common with the earlier mithnagdic philosophy of man."[31] Nadler cites fundamental points where *mitnagged* Judaism differs from Soloveitchik's ideal type, particularly in what he calls its philosophical dualism, spiritual transcendentalism, and general pessimism and asceticism.[32] While Nadler does acknowledge a shared "central religious value, . . . the attachment of supreme sanctity to the act of Torah study and the glorification of the Rabbinic scholar,"[33] he neglects the other obvious common element: the rabbinic scholar's *halakhic* life, which he derives from that very Torah study. Whatever pessimistic and dualistic elements were present in the theoretical and philosophical writings of the *mitnaggedim*, their observance of *halakhah* forced them, as it forced the Ḥasidim, to remain within the orbit of the principles of what Soloveitchik calls "Halakhic Man."

In response to those modernist accusations that Judaism merely imposes an external authority, Hartman argues that *halakhic* man does not accept the requirements of Torah as an externally imposed law. Instead, as Soloveitchik puts it, it is "as though he discovered the norm in his innermost self, as though it was not just a commandment that had been imposed upon him but an existential law of his very being."[34] The law is at once an expression of transcendence as well as inwardness. Comparable here are the thoughts of Emmanuel Levinas, who, in *Of God Who Comes to Mind*, says that the Infinite becomes known to us in our responsibility for the other, "speaking to me through my own mouth . . . . One might give the name 'inspiration' to this intrigue of infinity in which I make myself the author of what I hear."[35] According to Levinas, to hear the Law as emanating from within one's own being is to participate covenantally in the giving of the Law—it is to take on an ultimate ethical responsibility that becomes the very ground for consciousness of the self; I find my interior self only through an external pressure, or inspiration, that I make my own and accept as binding upon me.

Halakhic man's subjectivity is constituted only insofar as it is called into being, or interpellated, by a transcendent voice that it makes its own. Wordsworth's sense of self emerges from similar pressures or inspirations. For what Wordsworth reads in Nature, and embraces with joy, is not liberation from all authority, but rather the freedom to join with forces equally present in the external world and in his own interior life of feeling and thinking. As he affirms in "Tintern Abbey,"

> And I have felt
> A presence that disturbs me with the joy
> Of elevated thoughts; a sense sublime
> Of something far more deeply interfused,
> Whose dwelling is the light of setting suns,
> And the round ocean and the living air,
> And the blue sky, and in the mind of man:
> A motion and a spirit, that impels
> All thinking things, all objects of all thought,
> And rolls through all things. (93–102)

These lines certainly refer to an inspiring inner presence—something that disturbs Wordsworth with thoughts and sensations, and is "in the mind of man,"—but this presence is also externally manifest as a universal law, a governing, empowering force "that impels/All thinking things, all objects of all thought,/And rolls through all things." Thus, Wordsworth says, he is

> well pleased to recognize
> In nature and the language of the sense,
> The anchor of my purest thoughts, the nurse,
> The guide, the guardian of my heart, and soul
> Of all my moral being. (107–11)

These lines, advocating a constraint upon the free autonomy of the individual, echo Psalm 119's celebration of Torah in their praise of the Divine Presence as anchor, nurse, guide, and guardian— as constituting, through a law-bound relationship, Wordsworth's identity as a person. Wordsworth speaks as well in *The Prelude* (1805) of a Nature that "early tutor'd me/To look with feelings of fraternal love/Upon those unassuming things, that hold/A silent station in this beauteous world" (XII. 49–52). Here Nature takes on the personified role of a tutor or instructor, who, while external to Wordsworth, nevertheless teaches him to connect his inner life of thoughts and feelings with the world. Wordsworth's acceptance of that instruction is experienced as a personal deepening, an inwardness that can accommodate the silent and "unassuming things" of the world.

In Wordsworth's sonnet, "Nuns fret not at their convent's narrow room," the sonnet form becomes a symbol of the paradoxical freedom manifest within the constraints of law. The poem itself demonstrates the way in which the exterior limitations of form, inherent in the laws of the sonnet, become interiorized in the creative response of the poet bound by its requirements:

> Nuns fret not at their convent's narrow room;
> And hermits are contented with their cells;
> And students with their pensive citadels;
> Maids at the wheel, the weaver at his loom,
> Sit blithe and happy; bees that soar for bloom,
> High as the highest Peak of Furness-fells,
> Will murmur by the hour in foxglove bells:
> In truth the prison, unto which we doom
> Ourselves, no prison is: and hence for me,
> In sundry moods, 'twas pastime to be bound
> Within the Sonnet's scanty plot of ground;
> Pleased if some Souls (for such there needs must be)
> Who have felt the weight of too much liberty,
> Should find brief solace there, as I have found.

One of the restrictions for any poet entering the "narrow room" of the sonnet is working within the normal division between the octave and sestet, which includes a turn of meaning or thought at the ninth line. Yet Wordsworth begins the turn early, at the eighth line, with an enjambment connecting the eighth and ninth lines so that there can be no doubt of his intentions: "In truth the prison, into which we doom/Ourselves, no prison is." Wordsworth demonstrates his freedom, within the requirements of form, through this creative response to the rules for the sonnet: the prison of the sonnet is, in truth, no prison, if its affirmation becomes an instance of that truth.

In Wordsworth's hands the sonnet becomes the symbol for a kind of relationship between the individual and law that is best described by the hebraic term *covenant*. In a covenantal relationship the covenanting parties bind themselves to mutual obligations and responsibilities. But while the covenant involves limitations, it also calls for creative enactment of the positive requirements of the Law. In classical Rabbinic Judaism that meant that the Oral Law took on the status of Torah along with the Books of Moses, precisely because those bound by the commandments of the Law had a responsibility to actualize the Law in the everyday world. The Law—transcendent, Divine, holy—needed to be brought down into the empirical world, to be realized in a specific historical and social setting. In the same way, the requirements of the sonnet can only be manifest through a poet accepting the limitations of its form, agreeing to be "bound/Within the Sonnet's scanty plot of ground," and then responding as though the traditional form were in fact an expression of the poet's individual freedom. Wordsworth makes the form his own; just so *halakhic* man makes the Torah his own.

In "Ode to Duty," one of Wordsworth's most powerful poems on the theme of submission to the Law, he pledges himself as Bondman to Duty, personified here as the "Stern Daughter of the Voice of God" (1).[36] Acknowledging that he has for too long followed only his own thoughts, Wordsworth confesses that he is tired of "unchartered freedom"—that is, a freedom without contractual obligations, without covenant, a freedom without Law. Longing for a "repose that ever is the same" (40), and having been made "lowly wise" (61), Wordsworth's sentiments here are what Trilling had in mind when he noted that Wordsworth's poetry displays a calm submission to the "law of things" and a "desire for the humble life and the discharge of duty"—thoughts that are clearly counter to modern Western culture's commitment to "an idea of consciousness and activity, of motion and force."

If "Duty" can be understood as the obligation that one party to the covenant has to the other, the metonymic sign for the covenantal relationship, then Wordsworth is clearly affirming the Law in "Ode to Duty," as he does in "Tintern Abbey," as a universal covenant between God, mankind, and Nature. Duty is not only the "Stern Lawgiver," and "A light to guide, a rod/To check the erring, and reprove" (49, 3–4); Duty's guidance to mankind also extends to the natural world, which is the "smile upon th[e] face" of Duty:

> Flowers laugh before thee on their beds
> And fragrance in thy footing treads;
> Thou dost preserve the stars from wrong;
> And the most ancient heavens, through Thee, are fresh and strong. (53–6)

These affirmations concerning Duty, the "Daughter of the voice of God," echo the biblical words in Proverbs, spoken by a personified Wisdom, who, in Judaism, has traditionally been identified with Torah:

> When he prepared the heavens, I was there:
> When he set a compass upon the face of the depth:
> When he established the clouds above:

> When he strengthened the fountains of the deep:
> When he gave to the sea his decree, that the waters should
>   not pass his commandment:
> When he appointed the foundations of the earth:
> Then I was by him, as one brought up with him:
> And I was daily his delight, rejoicing always before him;
> Rejoicing in the habitable part of his earth;
> And my delights were with the sons of men.
> Now therefore hearken unto me, O ye children:
> For blessed are they that keep my ways. (8:27–32)

Torah Wisdom, present with God from the beginning, oversees the work of creation, setting the stars in motion and commanding the seas; Wisdom then exhorts mankind, "Now therefore hearken unto me." For the hebraic mind there is a seamless continuity between the laws governing nature and those calling mankind to obedience: they are all Torah. In a strikingly similar way Wordsworth calls upon Duty, who gives the law to flowers, stars, and all of nature, to also guide *him:* "To humbler functions, awful Power!/I call thee: I myself commend/Unto thy guidance from this hour" (57–9). Wordsworth invokes for himself and others the same power that preserves the stars from erring, asking that those who "Live in the spirit of this creed" may hold to "a blissful course" (21, 23).

"Ode to Duty," in its sense of harmony with the cosmic order and the possibility of aligning the course of earthly human life with the course of the stars in the heavens, moves beyond the fearful ambiguities of an earlier Wordsworth poem, "A slumber did my spirit seal." In that poem, a mysterious "she," who has no motion or force, who "neither hears nor sees," is "Rolled round in earth's diurnal course,/With rocks, and stones, and trees" (6–8). Here humanity seems to have been negated and swallowed up in the indiscriminate processes of an impersonal nature, but in "Ode to Duty" the course that mankind takes in conformity to nature is a positive affirmation of the human—a "blissful course" (21), taken up in the "quietness of thought" (36) and offering serenity, calm, and joy.

The path chosen by Wordsworth in "Ode to Duty," the decision to follow a Torah-like course of wisdom rather than stray in "smoother walks" (31), had already led Wordsworth, in 1799, to the vale of Grasmere in the Lake District, where he and his sister Dorothy would establish their home far from the social and cultural centers of England. Here, as he says in "Ode to Duty," he would "serve more strictly" (32) that Stern Lawgiver whose presence he recognizes in the smiling face of Nature. "Home at Grasmere," Wordsworth's poem justifying this decision to retreat into apparent obscurity, provides clear evidence of his sense of Divine Law as both an exterior reality and an interior experience. In the early version of the poem (MS B), for instance, Wordsworth claims that "The Lord of this enjoyment is on Earth/And in my breast" (87–8).[37] Later in the poem, Wordsworth apostrophizes that Divine Presence in nature, invoking it as a guide to his own inner life:

> Hail to the visible Presence, hail to thee,
> Delightful Valley, habitation fair!
> And to whatever else of outward form
> Can give us inward help, can purify,
> And elevate, and harmonize, and soothe ... (388–92)

Kenneth Johnston calls this enthusiasm for the "human embracing of the divine" an "unnerving sight," and a "dizzying, surreal absurdism." He pictures the poem as attempting to transcend the world and yet failing: "At the very height of his '*O altitudo!*' Wordsworth looks down, sees poverty, death, and evil, and plunges to the ground."[38] Johnston claims,

> Contrary to sentimental views of Wordsworth's happy return to the Lake District—views which often make much of the phrase "home at Grasmere"—the poem of that title challenges and indeed destroys the sentimental view, showing Wordsworth's clear awareness that his greatness as a poet could never be built on Grasmere, the Lake District, or even all of Nature.

Johnston summarizes his argument: "No empire, no earthly place, was big enough for his godlike conception of imagination"; Wordsworth learns instead "the inadequacy of a literal faith in natural transcendence." For Johnston there is something incongruous in Wordsworth's desire to fulfill his calling as a poet in the narrow and limiting vale of Grasmere; life in Grasmere is inadequate for the bold, transcendent poetic ambition Wordsworth clearly displayed. Yet his conception of transcendence assumes movement away from the world toward some "godlike" realm of the imagination—that is, he holds a typically "Romanticist" conception—while Wordsworth's affirmations and practices instead suggest a much more hebraic understanding of transcendence that is brought down and made real in the mundane details of the everyday world. Wordsworth experiences transcendence precisely as a Divine commandment calling him to a life of strict service, through which the transcendent becomes immanent. After all, Wordsworth did in fact choose to live and work in Grasmere, and, as Johnston admits, "While this terrific creative struggle was working in Wordsworth's mind... he was living a very ordinary and happy life."[39] It is this ordinary and happy life—but one that is taken up in obedience to a Divine summons—that is so parallel to the Rabbinic sense of *halakhah* voiced by Rabbi Soloveitchik. For Soloveitchik it is precisely the life of *halakhah* that "brings the Divine Presence into the midst of empirical reality"; the "true sanctuary," he says, "is the sphere of our daily, mundane activities,... it is there that the realization of the Halakhah takes place."[40]

The transcendence that Wordsworth reads in the face of Nature does not remove him from the demands of the world; rather, it penetrates his inner being as inspiration, as a Torah-like imperative to action and duty:

> But 'tis not to enjoy, for this alone
> That we exist; no, something must be done.
> I must not walk in unreproved delight
> These narrow bounds, and think of nothing more,
> No duty that looks further, and no care. (875–9)

The narrow bounds of the vale of Grasmere, like the convent's narrow room or the sonnet's "scanty plot of land," become the scene for an active, personal response to "the law supreme/Of that Intelligence which governs all" (774–5). Wordsworth's personal response is to accept the calling of a poet as a covenantal vocation. He thus affirms that he has been "divinely taught" and "privileged to speak as I have felt/Of what in man is human or divine" (907–9). Wordsworth also makes a daring allusion to Moses and the Israelites in the wilderness, who followed a cloud covering the Tabernacle, so that "in the place where the cloud abode, there the children of Israel pitched their tents" (Numbers 9:17): "—Beauty—a living Presence of the earth,... waits upon my steps;/Pitches her tents before me as I move,/An hourly neighbor" (795–800). Here Wordsworth places himself among the people of the covenant, claiming for himself the same Divine election and guidance as Israel.

In the English poetic tradition following Wordsworth, belief in the poetic vocation as a Divine calling to which the poet responds in imaginative obedience, the sense of God's Law discernable in the beauty of the created world or in the face of one's neighbor, and the commitment to everyday, ordinary life as the legitimate realm of the transcendent—all would be eclipsed by the modern world, its conflicting ideologies and its terrible wars. So, too, eighteenth century *halakhic* Judaism in Eastern Europe and its internal struggles between *Ḥasidim* and *mitnaggedim* would be overshadowed, first by the powerful onslaught of modernity upon traditional Jewish life, and then by the obliterating black clouds of the Holocaust. Yet, now, a half century after commenting on the perceived unattractiveness of both Wordsworth and Judaism in our culture, Trilling would probably be surprised to discover that Judaism continues to thrive in a proliferation of Orthodoxies, and that Wordsworth still inspires and consoles new generations of grateful readers. Though these groups—Orthodox Jews and Wordsworth readers—rarely overlap, their mutual presence in the modern world testifies to the enduring power of an essentially Judaic sense of covenantal obligations toward Torah. That sense, which sustains observant Jews in a life of *mizvot* and *halakhah,* may also be felt by the modern reader through Wordsworth, who has given us not only some of the most memorable and beloved poetry in the English language, but also an intimation of the profound obligations and surprising joys of such a life.

Notes

1. The Gaon of Vilna, Elijah ben Solomon Zalman (1720–97), a famed Talmudic scholar, led the *mitnagged* (literally, one who is against) opposition to the Ḥasidic movement. His most noted disciple is Rabbi Hayyim of Volozhin (1749–1821), who founded the Yeshiva of Volozhin, the most influential center for Talmudic studies of its time. On the Gaon of Vilna, see Bernard Martin, *A History of Judaism,* Vol. II: *Europe and the New World* (New York: Basic Books, 1974), 137–40, and Solomon Schechter, "Rabbi Elijah Wilna, Gaon," in his *Studies in Judaism,* first series (Philadelphia: Jewish Publication Society, 1896), 73–98. On R. Hayyim of Volozhin, see Norman Lamm, *Torah Lishmah: Torah for Torah's Sake in the Works of Rabbi Hayyim of Volozhin and his Contemporaries* (Hoboken, NJ: KTAV Publishing House, 1989). Ḥasidism originated with R. Israel ben Eliezer (1700–60), the Ba'al Shem Tov ("Master of the Good Name"). Rabbi Shneyur Zalman of Liady (1748–1813) developed a more intellectual version of Ḥasidism known as Ḥabad Ḥasidism in his *Likkutei Amarim,* popularly known as the *Tanya.* On Ḥasidism, see Martin, 168–88; on R. Shneyur Zalman, see Charles B. Chavel, "Shneyur Zalman of Liady," in *Understanding Rabbinic Judaism: From Talmudic to Modern Times,* ed. Jacob Neusner (New York: Ktav Publishing House, 1974), 317–35.
2. On Mendelssohn, see Leslie Tannenbaum's essay in this volume, "'What Are Those Golden Builders Doing?': Mendelssohn, Blake, and the (Un)Building of *Jerusalem*" (ed.).
3. Unless otherwise noted, quotations from William Wordsworth's poetry are taken from the standard *Poetical Works of William Wordsworth,* ed. Ernest de Selincourt and Helen Darbishire, 5 vols. (Oxford: Clarendon, 1940–49). Dates and references to specific poems mentioned in the text are as follows: "Expostulation and Reply" (1798), 4:56; "Ode: Intimations of Immortality" (1802–4), 4:279–85; "Tintern Abbey" (1798), 2:259–63; "Nuns fret not at their convent's narrow room" (1802), 3:1–2; "Ode to Duty" (1804), 4:83–6; and "A slumber did my spirit seal" (1799), 2:216. *The Prelude, or, Growth*

of a Poet's Mind (1805/1850), is edited separately by de Selincourt and Darbishire (2nd ed. [Oxford: Clarendon, 1959]). The text of "Home at Grasmere" presents special difficulties. Begun in 1800 and completed in 1806, it exists in two primary versions: the earlier MS B and the final version, MS D. Beth Darlington's edition, *Home at Grasmere,* The Cornell Wordsworth (Ithaca, NY: Cornell University Press, 1977), provides parallel texts of both MS B and MS D. For the present essay, unless otherwise indicated, I have used the text edited by William W. Heath, which closely follows MS D (in his *Major British Poets of the Romantic Period* [New York: MacMillan, 1973], 239–47).

4. See, for instance, Dorothy Wordsworth's "Journal of Visit to Hamburgh and of Journey from Hamburgh to Goslar (1798)," in *Journals of Dorothy Wordsworth,* ed. Ernest de Selincourt (London: Macmillan, 1952), 1:19–34.
5. *The Hidden Wordsworth: Poet, Lover, Rebel, Spy* (New York: Norton, 1998), 735.
6. M. H. Abrams, *Natural Supernaturalism: Tradition and Revolution in Romantic Literature* (New York: Norton, 1971), 278.
7. Lionel Trilling, "Wordsworth and the Rabbis," in *The Opposing Self: Nine Essays in Criticism* (New York: Viking, 1955), 119.
8. Trilling, 132.
9. Trilling, 123.
10. Trilling, 125.
11. Trilling, 127.
12. Trilling, 128.
13. Trilling, 131.
14. Trilling, 131.
15. David Hartman, *A Living Covenant: The Innovative Spirit in Traditional Judaism* (New York: The Free Press, 1985), 1.
16. Quoted in Hartman, 2.
17. "Judaism," *The Encyclopaedia Britannica,* 15th ed. (Chicago, 1992), 22:429.
18. "Judaism," 22:421.
19. Mathew Arnold, "Hebraism and Hellenism," in *Culture and Anarchy,* ed. J. Dover Wilson (Cambridge: Cambridge University Press, 1961), 131.
20. *Pirke Aboth: The Ethics of the Talmud, Sayings of the Fathers* (trans. and ed. R. Travers Herford [New York: Schocken, 1962]), a tractate of the *Mishnah,* is a collection of the sayings of the ancient rabbis, sometimes translated as "Ethics of the Fathers." Emmanuel Levinas (1906–95) was born into the Jewish community of Kovno, Lithuania. Following studies in France and Germany, he became a French citizen, introducing the thought of Edmund Husserl and Martin Heidegger to the French intellectual world. He continued to maintain an active engagement with the rabbinic tradition, including the Lithuanian Judaism of the Gaon of Vilna and R. Hayyim of Volozhin. See *Nine Talmudic Readings,* trans. Annette Aronowicz (Bloomington: Indiana University Press, 1994), 197, and *Difficult Freedom: Essays on Judaism,* trans. Seán Hand (Baltimore: The Johns Hopkins

University Press, 1990), in which he says, in the intellectual tradition of the Vilna Gaon, that the only viable path in a Jewish "return to Judaism ... brings us back to the source, the forgotten, ancient, difficult books, and plunges us into strict and laborious study" (52). Rabbi Joseph Soloveitchik (1903–92), a leading twentieth-century Orthodox theologian and talmudic scholar, comes from a distinguished Lithuanian rabbinic family. He is most noted for his *Halakhic Man* (Philadelphia: Jewish Publication Society, 1983).
21. Martin, 172.
22. Quoted in Martin, 174.
23. Chavel, 319.
24. Allan Nadler, *Rationalism, Romanticism, Rabbis and Rebbes* (New York: YIVO Institute for Jewish Research, 1992), 10.
25. Nadler, *Rationalism,* 11.
26. Nadler, *Rationalism,* 12.
27. Allan Nadler, "Soloveitchik's Halakhic Man: Not a *Mithnagged*," *Modern Judaism* 13 (1993): 134.
28. Nadler, *Rationalism,* 20.
29. Hartman, 68.
30. Hartman, 3.
31. Nadler, "Soloveitchik's Halakhic Man," 119.
32. Nadler, "Soloveitchik's Halakhic Man," 128.
33. Nadler, "Soloveitchik's Halakhic Man," 127.
34. Joseph B. Soloveitchik, *Halakhic Man,* trans. Lawrence Kaplan (Philadelphia: Jewish Publication Society, 1983), 64–5.
35. Emmanuel Levinas, *Of God Who Comes to Mind,* trans. Bettina Bergo (Stanford: Stanford University Press, 1998), 75–6.
36. Wordsworth's Duty, the "Stern Daughter of the Voice of God," has its antecedent in the Jewish idea of the *bat kol,* "The Daughter of the Voice," who in rabbinic literature was a source of direct communication with God following the era of prophecy.
37. Darlington, 42. See my "'Home at Grasmere,' or Romantic Contentment," in *Prism(s): Essays in Romanticism* 9 (2001), 109–20, for an extended discussion of "Home at Grasmere," especially in relationship to the thought of Levinas and Soloveitchik.
38. Johnston, 704.
39. Johnston, 711–12.
40. Soloveitchik, 94–5.

Chapter 4
"What Are Those Golden Builders Doing?": Mendelssohn, Blake, and the (Un)Building of *Jerusalem*

Leslie Tannenbaum

If William Blake had heard that Moses Mendelssohn was called the "Socrates of Berlin,"[1] Blake would have responded, "That's just his problem." And Mendelssohn would have said the same thing if he had heard that Blake regarded himself as an incarnation of "the ever-apparent Elias," "the Spirit of Prophecy" (*Milton* 24:71).[2] For both writers, at least nominally, squared off on opposite sides of the Enlightenment, and the site of this contestation is a discursive space called Jerusalem, which is the title of the major work of each writer. Both Moses Mendelssohn's and William Blake's *Jerusalem*, besides sharing the same title and the same position in the canon of each writer, also share an intriguing and informative congruence, even in their very differences. Yet, when we closely examine the net effect of both writers' works, we will find that their most important common factor is their tendency to undo the very project that they attempt to establish.

Both the Jewish philosopher and the Christian poet invoke Jerusalem as a historical and theoretical construct in order to envision an ideal society in which liberty—particularly religious liberty—could flourish. Mendelssohn's *Jerusalem*, a philosophical treatise published in 1783, was written in response to an anonymous pamphlet, written by a Christian, which challenged him to reconcile his philosophical ideas with his Jewish faith.[3] As a German Jew living in Berlin whose political situation was always precarious, Mendelssohn was aware that the stakes in his project—for himself and for the Jewish community—were more than theoretical. His subtitle, "On Religious Power and Judaism," reflects that awareness. Mendelssohn's *Jerusalem*, so named because it was his "vision of the ideal,"[4] attempts to achieve nothing less than the "social and intellectual emancipation of Jews in Central Europe"[5] by envisioning his Jerusalem as a ground upon which Jews and Christians can meet, a discursive space created by rationalism and a potentially shared belief in historic revelation. Equally liberatory was the project of Blake's *Jerusalem,* an illustrated prophetic poem of epic proportions that he wrote between 1804 and 1827,[6] in response to what he saw as the philosophical and political threats to the liberty of the British people, especially British Christians. Blake's image of Jerusalem, based on traditional biblical images and their interpretative traditions, is both historical and mythic, rather than rational. Blake's Jerusalem is both a city and a woman, as envisioned by the prophet Ezekiel (Ez. 16) and by St. John in the book of Revelation (21:2).[7] She explicitly represents Liberty in Blake's poem, as he stated in the repeated phrase, "Jerusalem is called Liberty among the Children of Albion" (53:5); and she is the true bride of Albion, a male figure who represents all of Great Britain. In the poem's complicated narrative of the separation and reunion of Albion and Jerusalem, Blake is attempting to create a congruence between England and Jerusalem as geographical and symbolic entities, so that, like Mendelssohn, he can create a space in which liberty can flourish. Jews play an important part in that space, but the ground upon which they and Christians meet is mythic rather than rational, according to Blake's vision of Judaism.

Given the shared titles and the diametrically opposed grounds and methodologies of Mendelssohn's and Blake's *Jerusalems,* it is tantalizing to see Blake's work as a direct reaction to Mendelssohn's, especially since Blake was a close friend of the Swiss painter Henry Fuseli, who was in turn a friend of Johann Kaspar Lavater, the man who had earlier challenged Mendelssohn into writing his first public defense of Judaism.[8] Blake himself was strongly connected to Lavater through Lavater's written work, having engraved the frontispiece for Fuseli's translation of Lavater's *Aphorisms on Man* (1789), which Blake also heavily annotated, and also having provided engravings for a translation of Lavater's *Physiognomy* (1789–98).[9] Also, it was Fuseli who was largely responsible for disseminating a lot of information about German literature and philosophy in England,[10] since he wrote many reviews of German material for the *Analytical Review,* which was published by Joseph Johnson, whose circle both Blake and Fuseli belonged to. Thus, although Blake did not read or speak German, and although Mendelssohn's *Jerusalem* was not translated into English during Blake's lifetime, there is a good chance that he had heard about the work. Yet even if Blake had not, we see in his version of *Jerusalem* a direct engagement with the kind of arguments that Mendelssohn was raising.

While Mendelssohn's *Jerusalem* grounds its vision of religion on principles of Enlightenment rationalism, in opposition to Jewish and Christian pietism, Blake's work invokes that very pietism. As several scholars have noted, Mendelssohn's religious thought was influenced by the English Deists and by Leibniz and his disciple, Christian Wolff.[11] Like Wolff and his followers, who were inspired by Newton and the scientific revolution,[12] Mendelssohn tried to reconcile Divine revelation with human reason, attempting to do for Judaism what those philosophers were doing for Christianity. In this project of aligning Jewish thought with contemporary Enlightenment ideas, Mendelssohn did not completely abandon the rabbinic traditions that strongly influenced Jewish thought, but he rejected those aspects of rabbinic tradition that did not support his own thinking.[13] This was particularly the case in terms of kabbalistic tradition and the allegorical interpretation of Scripture.[14] He expresses his mistrust of symbols and symbolic readings in a long digression in Chapter 2 of *Jerusalem,* which is an attack on such symbols as an appropriate means of communicating religious truths (76–89).

This attack was based on Mendelssohn's understanding of the Church and State's appropriation and manipulation of such symbols as a means of coercion. In a remarkable—if not distorted—statement about the Jewish written tradition, Mendelssohn writes, " Judaism has no symbolic books" (72). He believes that idolatry arises from such heavy reliance on symbols, including written symbols and print culture in general. Privileging the Jewish oral tradition over written symbols as a means of communicating abstract concepts, Mendelssohn claims that ignorance and the ravages of time cause people to mistake the sign for the thing signified, a confusion that results in idolatry (*Jerusalem* 84–8):

> It was well known that idolatry was actually the dominant religion nearly everywhere for several centuries. Images lost their value as symbols. The spirit of truth which they were meant to preserve evaporated, and the empty container that remained behind was transformed into a dangerously poisonous substance. The notions of the deity, lingering on in folk religions, were so distorted by superstition, so corroded by hypocrisy and priestcraft, that one had every reason to doubt whether atheism would not actually have been less harmful to human happiness, whether godlessness, so to speak, would not have been less godless than such a religion. (*Jerusalem* 87)

His own project is to deprive these signs of their power by de-mystifying them through rational analysis.

Blake, unlike Mendelssohn, depends entirely on the less rational aspects of Jewish and Christian tradition. As a poet who relies heavily on symbols as a means of communicating religious truth, he deliberately offers allegory (including the Kabbalism that Mendelssohn rejected), myth, and pseudo-history in opposition to Mendelssohn's rationalist-historical position. Blake called his own writings—based on his reading of the Bible and biblical tradition—a "sublime allegory" or "Allegory addressed to the Intellectual Powers while it is altogether hidden from the Corporeal Understanding" (Letter to Thomas Butts of July 6, 1803, E 730); and it is clear that in private and public practice, Blake advocated a spiritual/allegorical interpretation of Divine revelation. In his famous letter to Reverend Trusler of August 23, 1799, Blake cites symbolic or allegorical works—such as those of Aesop, Plato, Homer, Moses, and Solomon—as being the best way of communicating Divine truths (E 702). Following traditions of Jewish and Christian biblical exegesis and scholarship, Blake—unlike Mendelssohn—constantly pointed to the Bible's use of symbols as a model for the use of images taken from the material world as the best means of communicating spiritual truths.[15] Also, Blake's use of Kabbalism has been acknowledged and studied ever since Yeats and Ellis published their edition of Blake's works in 1893.[16] As Sheila A. Spector has most recently and most thoroughly pointed out, Kabbalism informs a great deal of Blake's thought and art, from his idea of a fourfold world or four levels of consciousness, to his whole orientation toward myth.[17] *Jerusalem*, according to Spector, derives its narrative structure, its central concepts and its myth from kabbalistic tradition.[18] The kabbalistic figure of *Adam Rishon* the pre-lapsarian man who originally contained all things within himself, informs Blake's concept of Albion, and the kabbalistic *Adam Kadmon*, primordial man, informs the character of Los[19]; and here Blake explicitly acknowledges his awareness of his sources in his prologue to Chapter 2 of *Jerusalem*, addressed to the Jews: "You have a tradition, that Man anciently contained in his mighty limbs all things in Heaven & Earth" (*Jerusalem* 27, E 171). Similarly, the figures of Jerusalem, Albion's emanation or female counterpart, and Vala, the false shadow of Jerusalem, are derived from the kabbalistic figures of the *Shekhinah*, "the Divine Presence" or "feminine concept of the Divinity,"[20] and the *pargod*, the curtain or veil.[21] In this appropriation of what Mendelssohn rejected, Blake is clearly articulating a method of thought at odds with Mendelssohn's Enlightenment project. Although Blake agrees with Mendelssohn about the dangers of taking the sign for the thing signified, Blake saw the act of imaginative appropriation or re-appropriation,[22] rather than rational de-mystification, as the means of combating this tendency. In many ways, Blake's pietism was close to that of Lavater, Mendelssohn's early Christian opponent.[23]

Since both works partake of these opposing approaches to religion, Blake's and Mendelssohn's *Jerusalem*s offer opposing theories of the interrelationship of revelation, reason, and law. While Mendelssohn believes in Divine revelation, he circumscribes it by locating it in the historical past (the revelation to Moses on Sinai), by limiting this revelation to a body of laws, and by maintaining that these laws related only to human actions rather than beliefs:

> I believe that Judaism knows nothing of a *revealed religion* in the sense in which Christians have defined this term. The Israelites possess a *divine legislation*—laws, commandments, statutes, rules of conduct, instruction in God's will and in what they are to do to attain temporal and eternal salvation. Moses, in a miraculous and supernatural way, revealed to them these laws and commandments, but not dogmas, propositions concerning salvation or self-evident principles of reason. (61)

Mendelssohn's whole argument for the civil rights of Jews is based on his attempt to align Judaism with natural religion, to show that Judaism is concerned with actions rather than a body of doctrines. For people who do not properly understand Judaism, Mendelssohn argues, "[s]upernatural *legislation* has been mistaken for a supernatural *revelation* of religion" (61). Having set up this important distinction, Mendelssohn asserts that in matters of belief Judaism does not teach anything that is not in accord with the principles of reason, or what he calls "the universal religion of mankind" (69), that this kind of revelation is available to everyone: "... I do not believe that human reason is incapable of perceiving those eternal truths which are indispensable to man's happiness or that God, therefore, had to reveal these truths in a supernatural way" (65). The Jewish Scriptures, according to Mendelssohn, are essentially a body of laws binding only on the Jewish people, as well as a collection of universal precepts that can also be validated by unaided reason (70–1). And those laws that bind the Jews to their God, although revealed by God, are aligned with reason in that they make no attempt to enforce belief and therefore leave the mind free for untrammeled intellectual inquiry (101–5).

In Mendelssohn's *Jerusalem*, then, reason becomes the ground upon which Judaism, Christianity, and other religions can meet in a diverse world of mutual tolerance; and neither law nor revelation impinges upon matters of belief that might harmfully separate these groups. To further seal this connection between Jews and other believers, Mendelssohn adds one more perspective on the law, which is aimed primarily at the traditional Christian critique of Jewish legalism. For one of the few times in *Jerusalem,* he resorts to poetry and myth to evoke an appreciation of what Mendelssohn obviously holds out as his own love of the law. Looking back with nostalgia at the time of the Mosaic constitution, a time when civil and religious life were united, Mendelssohn relates that nostalgia for a historico-mythic past to similar nostalgic gestures in pagan and Christian culture:

> Just as Plato spoke of an earthly and a heavenly love, one might also speak of earthly and heavenly politics. Take a fickle adventurer, currying favor, the kind of man found on the streets of every metropolis. Talk to him of the Song of Songs, or of the love of primeval innocence in Paradise, as Milton described it. He will think you indulge in dreams or want to demonstrate to him how well you have learned to besiege the heart of a demure damsel with the help of Platonic endearments. A politician will understand you just as little when you speak to him of the simplicity and moral grandeur of our original constitution. (102–3)

And Mendelssohn clinches his argument about the dignity and validity of Jewish attachment to the law by arguing that Jesus himself observed the law and did not release Jews from their obligation to follow that law (105–6).

Blake, as a radical antinomian, immediately parts company with this vision of the law and of Jesus' adherence to it. In his earlier *The Marriage of Heaven and Hell,* Blake has one of his satirical devils demonstrate how Jesus broke all of the Ten Commandments (pl. 22–3, E 43–4), and in *Jerusalem,* Jesus is envisioned as a figure who liberates the human race from the "bondage" of the law. As opposed to Mendelssohn's nostalgic image of a lost ideal theocracy, Blake posits an anarchistic pre-lapsarian past that was simultaneously located in Britain and Israel. In the Preface to Chapter 2 of his *Jerusalem,* Blake's address "To the Jews," this myth of a pre-lapsarian past that was free from the law, is articulated in the poem that begins "The fields from Islington to Marybone," where Blake asserts that "Jerusalems pillars" stood in England and that Jesus and Jerusalem, his bride, walked through England's green fields, "Forgiving trespasses and sins/Lest Babylon with cruel Og,/With Moral & Self-righteous Law/Should Crucify in Satan's Synagogue" (27:4, 21–4, E 171–2). Amalgamating the Jewish law with the pagan idolatry that it was intended to combat, Blake's vision asserts that the coming of the law, which he posits in opposition to a true Christian vision, marks the fall of Britain. Blake calls Christ the "Divine Vision" and associates Him with imagination; he follows Mendelssohn in associating reason with the law, but with an obviously different valuation. Given this reversed alignment of reason, law, and revelation, it goes without saying that Blake regarded Divine revelation as an active ongoing process and believed that eternal truths come to us not through reason but through imagination. In the very opening of *Jerusalem,* Blake invokes the revelation on Sinai in a move that opens up the past event, rather than closes it off, as Mendelssohn had done:

> Reader! [lover] of books! [lover] of heaven,
> And of that God from whom [all books are given,]
> Who in mysterious Sinais awful cave
> To Man the wond'rous art of writing gave,
> Again he speaks in thunder and in fire!
> Thunder of Thought, & flames of fierce desire: (3:1–5, E 145)

Furthermore, it is clear from these lines that Blake did believe, contrary to Mendelssohn, that the God of Sinai teaches doctrine rather than law. And in the face of Mendelssohn's mistrust of written symbols and print culture in general, Blake is asserting the efficacy of that culture.

In his emphasis on the power and the form—rather than the content—of God's revelation on Sinai, Blake underscores the power that is inherent in the God-given gift of writing, in the imagination's ability to create symbols and invest them with Divine truths. God speaks again and again through "Thunder of Thought, & flames of fierce desire," which have the power to destroy error and convincingly posit truths that have a more immediate impact on human thought than abstract principles revealed by reason. And Blake claims authority for these visions by grounding them in traditional myths and symbols, especially those that unite different groups, places, or religions. Blake's myth of the fall of universal man from a state of wholeness is an amalgam of kabbalistic symbolism,[24] Arthurian legend,[25] and the Pauline notion of the mystical body of Christ.[26] Blake appropriates the kabbalistic myth of the universal man in his concept of Albion, or Britain, who originally contains the whole world in his limbs but loses his pre-lapsarian wholeness by rejecting the Divine Vision or Imagination and by embracing reason and the law. Blake also appropriates Jewish history in his use of Anglo-Israelite typology[27] for his own version of Britain's history. According to Blake, the Hebrew patriarchs and the British Druids were one and the same, and they lived in a state of wholeness or harmony until the coming of the law, which Blake describes as "compulsory cruel Sacrifices" (27, E 174). In both the myth of Albion and the historical myth of Britain's patriarchal roots, Judaism exists in harmony with Christianity insofar as it is divested of the law and of its associations with reason—in other words, insofar as it ceases to be Judaism as Blake and Mendelssohn understand it.

Thus, while Mendelssohn's *Jerusalem* is written in part as response to the continual attempts by such non-Jewish admirers as Johann Kaspar Lavater to convert him to Christianity, Blake (who was familiar with Lavater's works) re-invokes the same conversionist attitudes that Mendelssohn had tried so hard to combat. Perhaps the darkest aspect of Blake's supposedly liberatory poem is his participation in the very kinds of conversionist discourse that Mendelssohn spent all his life—and much of his energy—fighting. The entire address to the Jews in the prologue to Chapter 2 of Blake's *Jerusalem* is both an appropriation and denial of the culture that Mendelssohn belonged to, and it exposes the limits of Blake's liberalism. As Michael Meyer has observed, it is the usual tendency among Christian writers that as soon as they admire something about Jews, their next impulse is to convert them to Christianity;[28] and in this regard, Blake is no exception. Blake's rhetoric contains the highest praise for Jews, as he purports to ground his own mythology in Jewish kabbalistic tradition and as he proclaims, "If Humility is Christianity; you O Jews are the true Christians" (27, E 174).[29] But, as the double-edged nature of this compliment indicates, Blake is interested only in appropriating what he understands—or misunderstands—about Jewish culture in order to subsume it within his Christian program, as Blake ends up proclaiming, "Take up the Cross O Israel & follow Jesus" (27, E 174). Blake's idea of liberty, then, apparently does not include one group of people or at least offers that liberty at the expense of erasing the culture that it seeks to liberate.

Yet before we are too harsh on Blake, it is important to note that Mendelssohn's own project offers a similar erasure of Judaism, albeit on different grounds, and that Blake's vision of Christianity effects a similar erasure of his own religion. Mendelssohn, in his attempt to establish Judaism as a natural religion that was congruent with Enlightenment values, created a version of Judaism that was not recognizable or acceptable to most other Jews of his time.[30] As David Sorkin has pointed out, while some contemporaries, like Heine, saw Mendelssohn as a liberator "who overturned the Talmud as Luther had the Papacy," other Jews saw him as a renegade or as a heathen;[31] and both contemporary Jews and their successors had trouble with seeing the God of Israel as merely a God of law and reason.[32] Similarly, Blake's universalized, anthropomorphic, and ultimately humanistic Christianity was a far cry from what most of his contemporaries would be willing to recognize as Christianity at all. Blake's attempts in *Jerusalem* to negate the moral law, to say that the only thing that Jesus taught was the forgiveness of sin, and to negate any separation between the human and the Divine presented a brand of Christianity that most Christians during his own time—and since— could not accept as being Christianity at all. While Frederick Tatham, who became Blake's executor after Catherine Blake's death, claimed that Blake was an orthodox Christian, there was a larger chorus of attempts to pin other labels on him, such as a Spinozist, Platonist, Swedenborgian, Marcionist Gnostic, or a Joachite—to name just a few.[33] If the vision of *Jerusalem* is mythic, the real-life Christians to whom it is ultimately addressed are apparently equally mythic. Thus, while both Blake and Mendelssohn sought to establish a universal religion that would promote greater freedom for all, such gains were made at the expense of the unique doctrines and the people attached to those religions. Paradoxically, each writer, while effecting this virtual erasure of his own religion, also strongly asserts the superiority of his religion, despite each writer's gestures toward humility and religious pluralism.

Mendelssohn ends his *Jerusalem* with an eloquent plea for religious diversity in a world in which all religions are equally valuable; yet, in his earlier emphasis on the Jewish oral tradition as being superior to the written codes of other religions (91), in his celebration of the Mosaic dispensation as an ideal utopian world, in his insistence that Judaism is more free of dogma and mystery than Christianity,[34] and in his proclaiming that the Jews were chosen as a nation of priests to instruct the rest of mankind (89),[35] Mendelssohn is also setting up Judaism as the superior religion. Blake also ends up vaunting the very religion that he claims to be one of humility, at the expense of other religious points of view. Besides negating the validity of the Jewish point of view, in his prologue to Chapter 2 of *Jerusalem* and throughout the poem, Blake also attacks the Deists and natural religion in general, since Natural Religion is represented in Blake's myth as Rahab and Tirzah, two manifestations of the Great Whore of Babylon who must be identified and cast out before Jerusalem can return to Albion. Despite his attempts to create a universal vision of Christianity and his claim in an early tractate that *All Religions are One* (E 1), Blake is clearly promoting Christianity at the expense of all other religions, as he states in his preface to Chapter 3 of *Jerusalem*, which is addressed to the Deists: "Man must & will have Some Religion; if he has not the religion of Jesus, he will have the Religion of Satan" (52, E 201). While nominally sharing Mendelssohn's fear of a society that threatens to absorb everything into an oppressive unity, Blake's either/or position is promoting his own kind of forced unity.

These seemingly odd contradictions within the work of Mendelssohn and Blake were the result, in part, of both writers' needs to negotiate among a number of different audiences and among different aspects of their own complicated lives and thought. As David Sorkin and others have noted, Mendelssohn was always dealing with a dual community: the Jewish community that he belonged to and often defended or represented, and the larger European culture that he sought to have a place in—and to relocate Judaism within.[36] His Judaism kept him from completely embracing Enlightenment thought[37] and kept him at odds with enlightened non-Jews who wondered how someone with such a great mind could continue to be a practicing Jew; and his commitment to Enlightenment thought and secular learning kept him from completely embracing—or being embraced by—the Jewish community.[38] Also, he had the rhetorical problem of having to address this dual audience, attempting to live up to the responsibility of justly representing the oppressed group that he belonged to and attempting at the same time to avoid any offense to Christian society that could result in a threat to the already limited rights of Jews in Germany.[39] Blake, who allied himself with Deists like Tom Paine, and Unitarians such as Joseph Priestley,[40] at least in terms of their questioning of orthodoxy and in terms of their political allegiances, also had to continuously distinguish his religious beliefs from theirs. For instance, his annotations to Bishop Watson's *Defense of the Bible,* an orthodox Christian response to Paine's *The Age of Reason,* provide an instructive example of the kind of tightrope walking between Deism and Christian orthodoxy that Blake had to perform. While he attacks Deism in *Jerusalem,* especially in his preface to Chapter 3, addressed directly to the Deists: "You O Deists profess yourselves the Enemies of Christianity: and you are so: you are also the Enemies of the Human Race & Universal Nature" (pl. 52); Blake also defends Paine's deistic critique of Christianity, as we see in the conclusion to Blake's annotations to Bishop Watson's apology: "It appears to me Now that Tom Paine is a better Christian than the Bishop. I have read this Book with attention & find that the Bishop has only hurt Paines heel while Paine has broken his head the Bishop has not answered one of Paines grand objections" (E 620).

Here Blake, whose spiritual approach to Christianity cannot abide the rationalist approach of Deism, takes sides with the Deists in the face of the greater threat of established orthodoxy. Thus Blake, like Mendelssohn, often had to temper his beliefs with practical politics. Another source of contradiction in Blake's art and thought resided in the very structure of Christian thought. Blake's attempts to overcome traditional dualisms in

Christian thinking were constantly being undermined by the very structure of the symbols that he was appropriating. As long as Judaism was associated with the Law and with a God of Judgment—as opposed to a God of Mercy[41]—Judaism would always be located on the opposite side of grace, in Blake's Christian scheme. Given these external and internal conflicts that Mendelssohn and Blake had to confront, it is not surprising that each writer's *Jerusalem*, like all such attempts to transcend the limitations of their own times, have greater meaning for us as extremely accurate barometers of the very pressures they so brilliantly tried to resist.

Notes

1. David Sorkin, *Moses Mendelssohn and the Religious Enlightenment* (Berkeley and Los Angeles: University of California Press, 1996), xx.
2. All references to Blake's works are from *The Complete Poetry and Prose of William Blake*, ed. David V. Erdman, with commentary by Harold Bloom, newly rev. ed. (New York: Doubleday, 1988), and will be noted parenthetically within the text. References to Blake's poetry will have plate and line numbers, and references to his prose works will be indicated by an E, followed by the page number. All references to Moses Mendelssohn's *Jerusalem* are from *"Jerusalem" and Other Jewish Writings*, trans. and ed. Alfred Jospe (New York: Schocken, 1969), and will be noted parenthetically within the text.
3. Mendelssohn wrote *Jerusalem* in response to an anonymous pamphlet entitled *The Search for Light and Right* (1782), supposedly written by an Austrian convert named Joseph von Sonnenfels (Mendelssohn, 159 n2), but actually written by one August Cranz, with a postscript written by an army chaplain named David Ernst Mörschel (Sorkin, 118–19).
4. Michael A. Meyer, *The Origins of the Modern Jew: Jewish Identity and European Culture in Germany, 1749–1828* (Detroit: Wayne State University Press, 1967), 48.
5. Alfred Jospe, "Introduction" to *Jerusalem, or On Religious Power and Judaism*, in *"Jerusalem" and Other Jewish Writings*, trans. and ed. Alfred Jospe (New York: Schocken, 1969), 1.
6. Joseph Viscomi, *Blake and the Idea of the Book* (Princeton: Princeton University Press, 1993), 338–57.
7. All citations of the Bible are from the Authorized (King James) Version.
8. Lavater, in his preface to his translation of Charles Bonnet's *Inquiry into the Evidences of Christianity* (1769), publicly challenged Mendelssohn to defend his Jewish faith. Mendelssohn replied in an *Open Letter* to Lavater that was published the same year (Meyer, *The Origins of the Modern Jew*, 30–1; Sorkin, 25–9; Maurice Samuels, *Memoirs of Moses Mendelssohn, the Jewish Philosopher*, 2nd ed. [London: Longman, 1827], 43–8).
9. Leonard M. Trawick, "William Blake's German Connection," *Colby Library Quarterly* 13, 4 (1977): 231–3.
10. Trawick, 31.

11. Meyer, *The Origins of the Modern Jew*, 1–22; Sorkin, xxi, 6–8, 38; Julius Guttmann, *Philosophies of Judaism: The History of Jewish Philosophy from Biblical Times to Franz Rosenzweig* (New York: Holt, Rinehart and Winston, 1964), 293–6.
12. Sorkin, 6.
13. Sorkin, 6.
14. Meyer, *The Origins of the Modern Jew*, 21–2; Sorkin, 47.
15. Leslie Tannenbaum, *Biblical Tradition in Blake's Early Prophecies: The Great Code of Art* (Princeton: Princeton University Press, 1982), 55–85.
16. Sheila A. Spector, *"Wonders Divine": The Development of Blake's Kabbalistic Myth* (Lewisburg: Bucknell University Press, 2001), 11.
17. Spector, 19–24.
18. Spector, 140–68.
19. Spector 109–10, 142–3.
20. Spector, 110.
21. Spector, 140.
22. Tannenbaum, 60–4.
23. Trawick, 230.
24. Spector, 147–52.
25. Jason Whittaker, *William Blake and the Myths of Britain* (London: Macmillan, 1999), 47–8.
26. See Jean H. Hagstrum, "Christ's Body," in *William Blake: Essays in Honour of Sir Geoffrey Keynes*, ed. Morton D. Paley and Michael Philips (Oxford: Clarendon Press, 1973), 129–56.
27. For a discussion of this typology, see Tannenbaum 22, 88, 95, 300–1 n84.
28. *The Origins of the Modern Jew*, 34.
29. Actually, Blake derives his myth from the Christian kabbalistic tradition— see Spector, 29–32.
30. Michael A. Meyer, "Judaism as a Vehicle of the Enlightenment: The Contribution of Moses Mendelssohn," *Studies on Voltaire and the Eighteenth Century* 263 (1989): 574.
31. Sorkin, xviii.
32. Jospe, 7.
33. J. G. Davies, *The Theology of William Blake* (Oxford: Clarendon Press, 1948), 1–3.
34. Meyer, *The Origins of the Modern Jew*, 38, 49.
35. See Sorkin, 60.
36. Sorkin, 8.
37. Sorkin, xxii–xxiii.
38. Meyer, *The Origins of the Modern Jew*, 38–42.
39. Sorkin, 29.
40. G. E. Bentley, Jr., *Blake Records* (Oxford: Clarendon Press, 1969), 40–1.
41. See Tannenbaum, 206–10, for an account of how Blake articulates this tradition in his earlier prophetic book, *The Book of Urizen*.

Part II
British Romantics and the *Haskalah*

Chapter 5

"For Luz is a Good Joke": Thomas Lovell Beddoes and Jewish Eschatology

Christopher Moylan

"What is the lobster's tune when he is boiling?" asks the would-be overman Isbrand in *Death's Jest-Book*, the Gothic drama Thomas Lovell Beddoes wrote and revised from 1825, when he was a medical student at the University of Göttingen, until his suicide in 1849. Answers to this question come in the songs scattered throughout the *Jest-Book*: in the scatological ballads of the oviparous tailor and flatulent new Cecilia, the eerie complaint of a mis-evolved new dodo crying with frog voice in the gloom, and the siren lisp of "the little snakes of silver throat/ever singing 'die, oh die.'"[1] The strangeness and emotional extremes of Beddoes' poetry have long attracted a small but devoted following. Only in the last thirty years or so, however, have critics integrated what were once considered Beddoes' eccentricities—social and political estrangement, homosexuality, and emotional difficulties—into a reading of questions of identity in the grotesque world of his play.

It is perhaps fitting, within the bleak ironies of Beddoes' writing, that a trope of central importance in the *Jest-Book*, and arguably the subject of one of the most peculiar episodes in his life, has been largely ignored in studies of his work. In the spring of 1827, Beddoes gave his late evenings to dissecting corpses in the hope of finding the bone of *luz*, associated in various Talmudic sources with the resurrection of the dead. He came to this legend through his encounters with Benjamin Bernhard Reich, a fellow medical student at Göttingen and, like Beddoes, a poet and republican radical. Reich, a Russian Jew, impressed Beddoes as "a man who has a quantity of brain but no breeches, and for Hebrew incomparable, for I presume there are few Jews or Christmas-pious folks who can or have translated Schiller, written songs &c. in that desolated and abandoned language."[2] The friendship began at a time when Beddoes was reading hermetic and mystical texts, often in the original languages, as background research for the *Jest-Book*. Reich set him on a new direction, tutoring Beddoes in that "desolated and abandoned language," Hebrew, and serving as a guide to the Kabbalah and its magical variants, the so-called practical Kabbalah. The two men roomed together, off and on, for two years, and one can assume from Beddoes' later history that they were lovers.

Beddoes' appropriation of the *luz* story arises from a personal and scholarly immersion in Judaism and Hebrew rare among the English Romantics. Rarer still, he employs Jewish symbolism, and, indirectly, the figure of the Jew, in terms respectful of their origins. That is, although *luz* and related references appear in a satirical iconography of social estrangement and marginalization, Judaism and the Jew are not satirized or subjected, as far I can discern, to anti-Semitic distortion. Yet, it is important to stress that Beddoes appropriates the legend for his own purposes. The failure of his anatomical search for the bone of *luz* appears to have dispelled his eschatological hopes, if he ever in fact had any. The resurrection scene in which *luz* figures is about the body as site of metaphysical, spiritual, and sexual disillusionment. Death is an issue in the *luz* scene— it is always an issue with Beddoes—but the body, the libidinous, confused body, is primary. In exploring these issues of identity and sexuality, my work is informed by the writing of Slavoj Zizek in particular, and by Lacanian and psychoanalytic approaches generally. Any writer on Beddoes, however, is familiar with the need to acquaint readers with his work and writings. Within the limitations that this necessity imposes, the emphasis on the discussion that follows will be on establishing the iconographic and textual contexts in which the *luz* legend plays a role. I will begin, then, with the sexual connotations of the *luz* legend, and turn to Beddoes' thinking about death and the afterlife just before he wrote this scene.

The bone of *luz* is hardly common knowledge, receiving brief mention even in specialized texts on Jewish eschatology. "Old anatomists, as Bartholinus, Vesalius, &c. mention it," Beddoes writes in a note to the 1829 text of *Death's Jest-Book*, "but are not certain what bone was so designated."[3] Rabbinical sources, he continues, make clear that *luz* must be under the eighteenth vertebra. In other words, it is associated with the coccyx. A curious passage on the subject occurs in *Genesis Rabbah* (28:3): "Even the nut [*luz*] of the spinal column, from which the Holy One, blessed be he, will make a man sprout [in his resurrection in] the age to come was blotted out."[4] Legends about the bone had to do with its resistance to damage from fire, water, hammer blows, and the like, and it is quite possible that Beddoes' research involved similar kinds of tests. Reich's interest, it appears, was more scholarly; the note mentions a study on resurrection in Judaism, since lost. Reich's influence can be seen directly where Beddoes offers an etymological analysis, partly in Hebrew, of *luz*, concluding that the word refers to the almond shape of the coccyx. The note acknowledges a scholarly relationship between Reich and Beddoes, noteworthy in itself, given Reich's religious background. Beddoes ends by thanking Reich, who is

> to publish soon an academical disquisition on the subject which, enriched as it will be, with many very ingenious suppositions and curious discussions on the philosophy and language of the Jews and other orientals, will form a very acceptable Essay towards the history of the remarkable doctrine [of the] resurrection, and many other points of Judaical physiology & [religion].[5]

The depth of their personal relationship is left unstated, not surprisingly. Yet, if one is inclined to look, or if one were tipped off to begin with, the *luz* could easily be seen as a semiotic key to a homoerotic subtext in *Death's Jest-Book*. Beddoes' sexual identity is well established. The fact that writers on his work have not commented on this subtext implies what is in effect a kind of sexual and religious invisibility in his work. Invisibility, as I will demonstrate below, is an important trope in the *Jest-Book*. Before doing so, I would like to take a look, as it were, at the symbolism of seeds and semen associated with *luz*.

In the play, the bone is referred to as a seed or nut, as it is in rabbinical sources. As a seed or germ, *luz* places itself in an eschatological iconography established in Judaism and taken up in early Christian sources. In the Torah and the Talmud, comparisons between the resurrection and blossoms or sprouting seeds are common, as in Ecclesiastes 12.5: "The almond tree shall blossom," and Psalms 72:16: "Let men sprout up in towns like country grass." In the Babylonian Talmud, *Ketuboth* IIIb: "If a grain of wheat that is buried naked sprouts up with many coverings, how much more so the just who are buried in their shrouds."[6] Isaiah refers to the bones of the dead flowering like herbs at the resurrection. The importance of the Holy Land as a chthonic center or even vessel of Divine benevolence encouraged a belief that the bones of the righteous will roll through cavities underground to Jerusalem.[7] The bodies thus prepared for resurrection are again compared to sprouting wheat.[8] The sexual, or generative, symbolism of these images of seeds and tunnels is more direct in other Talmudic references. In several rabbinical sources from the sixth and seventh centuries, the resurrection is compared to the growth of semen or an egg in the womb, and the buried body to a fetus in the womb.[9] In short, the tradition suggests a continuity in the cycles of sexual generation and the grand cycle of life, death, and resurrection. Sex and death are, if not one, then part of the same process. As Michael Bradshaw points out, images of the dead as risen seed occurred in Beddoes' work well before he met Reich.[10] Such images are common in the New Testament, where Beddoes is likely to have encountered them first. Reich, however, returned this symbolism to the body, first as the locus of an eschatological promise, and second as the locus of desire. The two become enmeshed in the *Jest-Book*, as no doubt they did in Beddoes' life.

The action of the *Jest-Book* revolves, in an endless circle, between a pit, where at the start of the play three of the principal characters—Duke Melveric, Sibylla, and the knight Wolfram—take turns in a death-in-life imprisonment, and a tomb near the Duke's court at Grussau, where Wolfram, Sibylla, and Melveric, among others, are interred more or less impermanently. But if these symbols owe more to alchemical symbolism, as I have argued elsewhere,[11] than to Jewish practices and beliefs, the many references to the dead as grass and seeds do show the influence of Beddoes' studies with Reich. These are concentrated in Act III, scene iii, the *luz* scene, specifically when the magician Ziba describes the disposition of the dead. "Flesh, thou grass, mown wert thou long ago/Now comes the brown dry after-crop,"[12] he says of the dead. Conversely, the dead are "seed that now is dust." A tale of a flower rising from a lover's grave, harkening to Beddoes' early writing, serves as a prelude to the legend of *luz*. "This was a cheat," says Duke Melveric, who has been promised the resurrection of his dead wife:

> The herb was born out of a seed,
> Not raised out of a bony skeleton.
> What tree is man made of?
> Ziba.   Of a ghost;
> Of his night-coming, tempest-waved phantom:
> And even as there is a round dry grain
> In a plant's skeleton, which being buried
> Can raise the herb's green body up again;
> So there is in man, a seed-shaped bone,
> Aldabaron, called by the Hebrews Luz,
> Which, being laid into the ground, will bear
> After three thousand years the grass of flesh,
> The bloody, soul-possessed weed called man.[13]

"Luz is an excellent joke," writes Beddoes in a letter,[14] and part of the joke—trick might be a better word—is the hermetic layering of references. The seed is also a term in alchemy for a stage in the purification of metal. The magician Ziba, insistently described as black, represents nigredo, or the blackening and putrefaction of the metal, allegorically represented as a body, before burning. The man he will raise, Wolfram, is named for a white metal, consistent with the dualism operative throughout the play.[15] Yet Luz is renamed Aldabaron, and distanced from its origins in Judaism. One might hunt out Arab references to *luz,* or trace the many stories of the "little jew bone," as it was called, in medieval Germany,[16] were it not for the suspicion that the joke is that all this erudite layering is rather beside the point.

On the surface the *luz* scene reads as a bitter exercise in Tieckian Romantic irony. When Ziba invokes the power of *luz* in an attempt to resurrect the wife of Melveric, he raises not one but two bodies, neither of them belonging to his wife. First, Homunculus Mandrake emerges from the tomb, the stirring bones within having disturbed his prosaic slumber. Next, the Duke's murder victim, Wolfram, steps forth, his corpse having been switched earlier for that of the wife. As the scene ends, Mandrake sets off for the "mummy country" of Egypt in search of magic potions, and the Duke and the resurrected Wolfram leave together, to watch the bleak continuation of the internecine struggles at court. Friend murders friend, brother destroys brother, and the women over whom they battle drift listlessly to their graves. Eventually, Melveric follows Wolfram alive into the tomb.

In short, the murderer resurrects his victim, the magus resurrects his clownish alter ego, and resurrection perpetuates rather than resolves the dreary problems of life. Even this irony, however, is a feint. Magic aside, the salient feature of the scene is not the Prufrock-like moment of unimpressive raising from the dead, but the repeated annunciation of men rather than a woman to the waiting Duke. The scene is about men uniting and reuniting with men. Here it is important to point out that the Duke and Wolfram had sworn, when they were friends, that the first of them to die would come back from the grave to visit the other. Even when the Duke dismisses this pact as void, his words are laden with the eroticism of the Romantic sub-genre of late night hauntings by the beloved:

> Yet never has his bond or his revenge
> Raised him to my bed-side, haunting his murderer
> Or keeping blood-scaled promise to his friend.[17]

Duke Melveric brings to life the homoerotic desire he cut off with the murder of his friend. Thus the irony of the scene is not that Ziba resurrects the wrong bodies, but that he resurrects the right ones—bodies right each other. Once Wolfram returns to his side there is no thought of resurrecting the wife to join them. Thus homoeroticism subsumes the hermetic references. The tomb as vessel or container of the seed, the seed as spirit or identity undergoing transformation, the identity of the male figured initially as friend, or rival in love—each is re-inscribed in terms of homoerotic desire. Even inscription is re-inscribed. In an in-joke, Mandrake alludes to the reference to Reich's book on resurrection, mentioned in Beddoes' note to the play. "For my part, I was always dead against my will," he says, "and shall write an Essay on it to be dedicated to my black friend here."[18]

This would make Homunculus Mandrake a stand-in for Beddoes. The choice of name is significant. In the theory of preformation, the homunculus is the little person in the germ cell, fully formed and so tiny as to be invisible to the naked eye. Mandrake as root, homunculus as seed or germ: he is *luz* embodied, and he is also nothing. At the start of the play, Mandrake is accidentally doused with a potion that renders him invisible, leading him to conclude that he has died. Later, a blow to the head knocks him out and restores his visibility, leading others to take him for dead. Waking in the tomb, Mandrake speaks of a loss of self: "I could weep, or rather I could think that I wept, for it appears to be too true that I have given up the body. Well, what is, is, and what is not, is not; and I am now what I was—for I am what I was not; I am no more I for I am no more: I am no matter, being out of all trouble, and nobody at all, but poor Mandrake's pure essence."[19] The dead self is no self, an empty category; "I am no more I for I am no more." Yet this very absurdity, this void, re-inscribes the dead self in the problematics of identity as such. "Death cannot be presented," writes Michael Bradshaw, "it can only be represented, and in this respect of being tantalizingly vacuous, blank and ripe for inscription, it becomes a figure of all non-signifiable others."[20] But the self can only be represented, rather than presented. Since "poor Mandrake's pure essence" is so easily detached from the signified (he believed that he was dead when he was not, that he was risen when he was not, and so forth), he has, in effect, no essence.

Mandrake is "A living somebody or nobody," says Isbrand earlier, "a false coin of flesh that may pass at Court as a tolerable counterfeit of humanity, so indeed that all who see but skin-deep might take it for scurvy human creature."[21] In the tomb and out of the tomb, in sight and out of sight, identity is contingent and unreliable.

Mandrake, one of many fools distributed throughout the play, satirizes the spiritual craving that led Beddoes to the search for the bone of *luz*, and the quasi-scientific determination with which he pursued this search. As a homunculus and mandrake, two non-existent or mythical creatures trapped for a time in an invisible (so he thought) visible body, he embodies the impossibility of this research, or, to borrow a phrase from Slavoj Zizek, he "positives the lack and inconsistency of our scientific explanation,"[22] in this case for any theory of an after-life or resurrection. Thus, the hostility he receives on his false resurrection has less to do with his foolishness than with the fragility of the eschatological hopes he tramples accidentally. From the beginning of the play on, he is an unintentional trouble-maker, misunderstood and unfairly [if harmlessly] persecuted. As such, he is a parody of the Jew of anti-Semitic discourse. "The (anti-Semitic figure of the) 'Jew' is not the positive cause of social imbalance and antagonisms," writes Zizek; "social antagonism comes first, and the 'Jew' merely gives body to this obstacle."[23]

Mandrake, the false Lazarus, is also a false or foolish scapegoat. To return to a comparison made earlier, he is Beddoes associating himself with the Jew. Ziba, closer to the real thing, or Reich, is a necromancer and a revolutionary, plotting first with Isbrand to overthrow the Duke, then against Isbrand. Ziba's race, so often thrown back at him as a taunt, corresponds to what we now term *otherness* or marginal status in Reich and Beddoes, and Mandrake's invisibility to a closeted if irrepressibly vital "eccentricity."

Thus the raising of the two men by way of seed, and Jewish seed at that, is a codified form of sexual and social self-declaration, complicated by Beddoes' close identification with his lover. But much as the Jew is a figure of attraction and power for Beddoes, in the *Jest-Book* he is also a figure of vulnerability, uncertainty, and secretiveness. Reich's identity is nested in that of Ziba, and his Jewishness concealed in Ziba's exotic blackness. Beddoes' identity is nested in that of Mandrake, and Mandrake's identity, in turn, is displaced by his invisibility, and earlier by his fool's cap and bells.

The trope of invisibility suggests a corresponding ambivalence; Beddoes would be seen, and not seen as author of the *Jest-Book*. This is reflected in his remarks on the reception of the play. The *Jest-Book*, Beddoes wrote in the preface, "is written for those who can find entertainment in it."[24] As for the critics, he had nothing but contempt: "To annoy and puzzle the fools and amuse oneself with their critical blunders, is the only admissible plea for printing, for anyone who has been a few years from school."[25] Unfortunately, when he sent the play to his friends for comment, they had many misgivings, the most serious being the strangeness of the grotesques and Homunculus Mandrake. His friends suggested cutting all of them. In a sense, they were asking Beddoes to cut himself, and Reich, from the play. He responded by attempting to commit suicide.

So, Beddoes nearly gives the critics what they want—his silencing and disappearance, or his death. Then, failing to die, he returns to revise the play and plan for its publication. Beddoes approaches death and backs away, and he will repeat the process later in life, finally poisoning himself at age forty-six—though not before writing a note leaving a sum for his nephew to buy a case of Moet Chandon to drink his health with, and money for his doctor to buy Reade's best stomach pump. This ambivalence is written in the title of the play. The *Jest-Book* belongs to death as much as to Beddoes. The jokes are on death, but they are also on him. In a letter he wrote a couple of months before he met Reich, Beddoes revealed perhaps more than he intended of the erotics of this attraction and repulsion. Concerning his frustrated attempts to find a spiritual or material escape from death, he writes:

> I am now already so thoroughly penetrated with the conviction of the absurdity & unsatisfactory nature of human life that I search with avidity for every shadow of a proof or probability of an after-existence, both in the material & immaterial nature of man. Those people, perhaps they are few, are greatly to be envied who believe, honestly and from conviction, in the Xtian doctrines: but really in the New T. it is difficult to scrape together hints for a doctrine of immortality. Man appears to have found this secret for himself, & it is certainly the best part of all religion and philosophy, the only truth worth demonstrating: an anxious question full of hope & fear & promise, for which Nature appears to have appointed one solution—Death.[26]

Here, as often with Beddoes, one finds the language of desire chasing its subject through a circuit of evasions and displacements. Searching with avidity amid the notional shadows of an evasive proof, he follows the erotics of his search back to the point that penetrated him. That is, given that Beddoes is convinced that this life is absurd and unsatisfactory, what would impel him to search for another? Is he not, in fact, simply searching for a way out—of life, and of the restlessness that impels the search? To turn to religion: how can it be that Beddoes fails to discover in the New Testament the resurrection stories, some basis for a Christian doctrine of resurrection, unless that is not what he is looking for in the first place? The answer, the only truth worth demonstrating, as he puts it, is somewhere else, and something else. He discovers it in the *other*. Man—and the privileging of gender here is worth preserving against the backdrop of Beddoes' sexuality—is invested with a resilient and yet unformed apprehension or "secret." The secret is not a sense or intuition of a life beyond ours. The "best part" or the "only truth" is not an after-life, but a non-life, a solution that is not a solution. The "best part" is death. Death, the secret to be approached with "hope & fear & promise," opens a sudden gap in the construction of the passage. Resurrection and the afterlife vanish, and in their place we find the Lacanian "Das Ding," the Thing as lack or absence that paradoxically generates the erotics of Beddoes' search. The "only truth worth demonstrating," then, is paradoxically that which cannot be demonstrated, or experienced. It is, to quote Slavoj Zizek, "a cause which in itself does not exist—which is present only in a series of effects, but always in a distorted, displaced way."[27] In *luz,* Beddoes found or thought he found the kernel or seed of this constantly withdrawing, evasive object-cause of desire. It is appropriate that the coccyx, the bone associated with *luz,* is vestigial, an evolutionary leftover, a nub of an identity lost and yet not entirely annihilated over time. Dissecting corpses late at night, Beddoes searched for this trace or kernel, the *objet petit a,* of a lost, not entirely annihilated desire. In this research, however, Beddoes simply ritualized his own isolation—the "void of his desire" to use another Lacanian phrase. So many bodies would be alive to him if they were not already—out of whatever unhappy combination of his social displacement and personal idiosyncrasy—dead to him. He might retrieve and revive the original kernel of desire, if it were not already lost. Death, for Beddoes, is where the achievement or resolution of desire locates itself as absence or lack.

Hebrew, "that desolate and abandoned language," thus appeals inasmuch as it is dead and present, abandoned and omnipresent, if in the wider culture only through translation and Christian exegesis. It speaks the Diaspora—Reich translating Schiller into Hebrew—reclaiming, like Wolfram leading Melveric alive into the tomb, the living for the dead. Reich, as a scholar of Hebrew and Judaism, embodies this dual existence and, as a homosexual, adds another layer of presence (as Beddoes' lover) and absence (inasmuch as he was forced to deny his sexual identity outside the relationship with Beddoes). Thomas Lovell Beddoes' preference is for this ambiguity—in later years, one of his lovers was described on a visit to England as an "inamorata in disguise."

The eschatological context is part of this as well. In Judaism, it appears that Beddoes saw the disbursal of the kernel or seed to all bodies, or to the body as other, in contrast to the Christian mediation of a risen messiah. The resurrection, after all, is the resurrection of all. The risen bodies will, as he writes in his unfinished poem "Doomsday," "overwhelm the sands/With an eruption of the naked millions." The end of humanity, the annihilation of the *other,* brings a release, a generalized *jouissance:*

> The buried navies
> Shall hear the call, and shoot up from the sea

Whose wrecks shall knock against the hollow mountains
And wake the swallowed cities in their hearts ... [28]

The sexual symbolism of the passage, no less than the overt invocation of the buried dead, is clearly pathetic rather than triumphant or prophetic. The poem is anti-apocalyptic, in the sense that it is about what will not happen, what will not be experienced by the speaker or the recipient of these words. The doomsday vision is necessarily fragmented, and impossible, for the subject could apprehend or realize it fully only through death, or the extinction of the subject. So life, this life, requires a complete exile from that which completes it. Each breaks off in silence.

For a time Beddoes found the paradox of companionship in existential estrangement by living with Bernard Reich, a Diaspora Jew removed at Göttingen from his place of exile. In fact, Reich was to be uprooted again, following Beddoes to Zürich and a year later wandering off like Mandrake or dying, it is not clear which. In any case, he disappears from the records. Beddoes led a wandering life as well—moving on to Berlin, Geneva, and Zürich again, rarely visiting friends and family in England. He was a physician disinclined to practice, a writer averse to publishing. His radical politics brought him into conflict with the authorities, and barred him from an academic career. He went bankrupt at one point, and was forced to sell most of his possessions. But certain books and medical instruments remained with him. One of the items that was found in his room after his suicide was a Hebrew dictionary.

Notes

1. Thomas Lovell Beddoes, *Selected Poems*, ed. Judith Higgens (Manchester: Carcanet Press, 1976), 48.
2. Thomas Lovell Beddoes, *The Works of Thomas Lovell Beddoes,* ed. with intro. H. W. Donner (London: Oxford University Press, 1935; reprint, New York: AMS Press, 1978), 634.
3. Beddoes, *Works,* 488.
4. *Genesis Rabbah: The Judaic Commentary to the Book of Genesis, A New Translation,* trans. Jacob Neusner (Atlanta: Scholars Press, 1985), 1:295. *Genesis Rabbah,* also called *Bereshith Rabbah,* is an *aggadic midrash* on the Book of Genesis. For other *midrashic* references to *luz* of the spine, see George Foote Moore, *Judaism in the First Centuries of the Christian Era, the Age of the Tannaim,* 3 vols. (1927–30; Cambridge: Harvard University Press, 1996), 2:385.
5. Beddoes, *Works,* 488.
6. Quoted in Neil Gilman, *The Death of Death: Resurrection and Immortality in Jewish Thought* (Wooodstock: Jewish Lights, 1997), 132.

7. Moore, 2:379–80.
8. Caroline Walker Bynum. *The Resurrection of the Body in Western Christianity, 200–1336* (New York: Columbia University Press, 1995), 54.
9. Bynum, 25.
10. Michael Bradshaw, *Resurrection Songs: The Poetry of Thomas Lovell Beddoes* (Burlington: Ashgate, 2001), 102–3.
11. Christopher Moylan, *T. L. Beddoes and the Hermetic Tradition* (Belper: Thomas Lovell Beddoes Society, 1999).
12. Beddoes, *Works,* 439.
13. Beddoes, *Works,* 436.
14. Beddoes, *Works,* 640.
15. Moylan, 3.
16. Julius Preuss, *Biblical and Talmudic Medicine*, trans. and ed. Fred Rosner (New York: Sanhedrin Press, 1978; reprint, Northvale, NJ: J. Aronson, 1993), 65.
17. Beddoes, *Works,* 336–7.
18. Beddoes, *Works,* 441.
19. Beddoes, *Works,* 400.
20. Bradshaw, 11.
21. Beddoes, *Works,* 333.
22. Slavoj Zizek, *The Plague of Fantasies* (London: Verso, 1997), 76.
23. Zizek, 76.
24. Beddoes, *Works,* 534.
25. Beddoes, *Works,* 635.
26. Beddoes, *Works,* 629–30.
27. Zizek, 163.
28. Beddoes, *Selected Poems,* 44.

Chapter 6
Scott's Hebraic Historicism
Esther Schor

David B. Ruderman's *Jewish Enlightenment in an English Key* and Tom Segev's revisionary study of the Mandate period, *One Palestine, Complete* (in Hebrew, *Yamei Kalaniot*), both have enriched our understanding of relations between English Jews and the Britons among whom they lived, worked, studied, and worshiped.[1] Ruderman, in particular, suggests that Jews played a variety of roles in religious debates among Anglicans and dissenters, both actively and passively.[2] While it may seem untoward to suggest that a historical novel about seventeenth-century Presbyterians has implications for the later development of Zionism, I want to argue that Sir Walter Scott's *Old Mortality* (1816) richly imagines a Hebrew State, if not a Jewish one. Moreover, the reception of Scott's novel by Scottish Presbyterian readers suggests how complex, even contradictory, are the uses of "the Jews" in debates about Presbyterian dissent. As we shall see, anti-dissenting rhetoric during the Covenanting wars often identifies dissenters with both Jews and biblical Hebrews; as we shall see presently, this gesture is made on both sides of the issue, for historically, Presbyterian apologists have also invoked Jews and Hebrews in arguing for the purity of their Presbyterian faith against the corruptions of Anglicanism.

My point of departure is an impassioned, polemical critique of Scott's novel by his contemporary Thomas M'Crie, a Scottish minister. In a fiery three-part review published in 1817 in *The Edinburgh Christian Instructor* and reprinted in 1824 as a pamphlet, M'Crie eschews contemporary notions of Scott's historicism as civilized and urbane, claiming that the novel constitutes a violation of Presbyterian civil rights. When M'Crie explores Scott's use of anti-Presbyterian sources, he explores how such sources malign the Covenanters by pointing to their affinities with another "covenanting" group, the Jews. Jews are also implicated in M'Crie's contention that Scott travesties the

Covenanters by putting a farrago of biblical language in their mouths. In fact, M'Crie's objection centers on the fact that the Covenanters refer rarely—in many cases, not at all—to Christian revelation. In other words, Scott is charged with drawing on various anti-Semitic traditions to represent the Covenanters as a violent party, willfully blind to the charitable morals of Christian revelation.

Before turning to M'Crie's *Vindication of the Scottish Covenanters,* as the pamphlet version of the review was called, let me summarize the issues that brought the Covenanters into being.[3] The 1638 "National Covenant" signed in Edinburgh had a double purpose. For the Scottish nobility, it served to warn Charles I against infringing on their economic power; for the lower ranks, it opposed the institution of "Prelacy," or the Anglican Church and its observances, on the membership of the Scottish Reformed Church, known as "Presbyterians" after their representative scheme of church government. The stakes of the Covenant escalated in the Revolutionary climate of 1642, when the English Parliament proposed an alliance with the Scottish Presbyterians; in 1643, a "Solemn League and Covenant" was transacted between the English republicans and the Scottish rulers. Its somewhat quixotic terms exchanged Scottish support for Parliament for a promise that the Scottish Reformed Church would become established not only in Scotland, but in England and Ireland as well. By the end of the decade, the Scottish nobility had defected to the Crown, and a radical faction from the southwest, known as "Whigs" (after the so-called Whiggamore Raid), began a prolonged period of insurgency. Though the alarmed Charles II attempted a rapprochement with the Covenanters after his father's execution, he renounced the Covenant shortly after the Restoration; ejecting and fining the radical preachers, who took to preaching in outdoor conventicles, Charles II eventually offered royal "indulgences" to the more moderate preachers. The exact ratio of "indulged" moderates to radicals at various points in the conflict is still debated. In *Old Mortality,* Scott is generally thought to have superimposed on events of the relatively calm 1670s, the violent mood and rhetoric of the following decade, known as the "killing time": during the 1680s, an extreme wing of Covenanters, known as "Cameronians," met their match in the ruthless John Graham of Claverhouse, who became famous for ordering summary executions of entire families.[4] The conflict was by and large resolved when William of Orange established the Presbyterian Church in Scotland in 1690, though pockets of Cameronian resistance remained for several decades.

"chargeable offences"

Thomas M'Crie, a Presbyterian minister alive to the contemporary resonance of Scott's novel, writes from critical premises strikingly different from those of Scott's English reviewers.[5] Instead of viewing the novel's historicism as a civilized withdrawal from political discourse, M'Crie argues that the author's mixing of fiction and history infringes on civil liberties, rendering him culpable of two "chargeable offences": "*first*, of partiality to the persecutors; and, *secondly*, of injustice to the persecuted Presbyterians. And as we do not mean to blink the charge, we wish to be understood as accusing the work of *gross* partiality and injustice."[6] These offences, it develops, are an "attempt" both on the "spirit of [the] fathers" of "the good people of Scotland" (49) and also an attack on "the established religion of Scotland" (63).

M'Crie's critique of Scott's novel dwells at length on the Covenanters' egregious use of the language of Scripture. M'Crie refutes this representation by associating the ubiquity of Scripture in Scottish culture with literacy and enlightenment. He deems the Scots' intimate acquaintance with the Bible to have "raise[d] [the Scots'] character, in point of intelligence, above that of the lower orders in any other country" (71); "the Bible is to the common people what the writings of Homer are to the learned," serving as their "Greek or Roman classics" (72). He cites the Anglican Bishop Burnet's account of attempts to subdue—and proselytize to—the Presbyterians: "We were indeed, amazed to see a poor commonality so capable to argue upon points of government, or on the bounds to be set to the power of princes in matters of religion: upon all these topics they had texts of Scripture at hand" (108). Here the Anglican bishop plays directly into M'Crie's hand: The Bible is not merely cited by all ranks of society; it has also made possible an enlightened discourse of government. Moreover, an evident "thirst for knowledge" (107), even among the aged, is attributed to the presence of a Bible in every family. In an impassioned defense of field preaching, M'Crie assails "[p]uling complaints that their sermons did not display good taste, and were devoid of elegant frippery" (80): "It was not elegant diction, apt s[i]miles, well-turned periods, or elaborate reasonings, that the people ... needed. They needed to be taught the word of God ... to have their minds prepared for that death with which they were daily threatened" (81). But it is not simply that Scott has misrepresented the meanings of Scripture. M'Crie's attack specifically indicts the "ludicrous perversions of Scripture" (73) committed by Scott's Covenanters. Why "perversion"? Surely Scott's offense is more than putting into Presbyterian mouths "gross and ludicrous misapplications" (71) of Scripture; more also, than his casual practice of "cull[ing] a few phrases from Scripture, and scraps from this sermon and that dying speech" (77). Why does M'Crie charge Scott with a "wanton abuse" of the Bible, "designed to give pleasure to an infidel reader... because they gratify this disposition to laugh at the Bible" (79)?

On closer inspection, Scott's "perversion" of Scripture appears to be a suppression of the New Testament in favor of references to the Hebrew Bible. While M'Crie does not make his intuition explicit, it guides his entire analysis of scriptural allusion. Let me give a few examples. He takes exception to a dialogue between Mause, an old garrulous Covenanter, and the preacher Kettledrumle in which "the words are part of a description expressly and repeatedly applied in the New Testament to the sufferings of the Saviour of Men" (79). M'Crie drives the point home by citing at length the historical documents on which Scott, according to Calder, drew for the characters of Mause and Kettledrumle. The document drawn on for Mause is a compendium of "dying testimonies" of Presbyterian martyrs called *A Cloud of Witnesses*.[7] M'Crie quotes a portion of the "dying speech" of Isabel Alison in which the only scriptural allusion is to the words of Pontius Pilate: "Then they [her 'inquisitors'] said, your blood be on your own head; we shall be free of it. I answered, so said Pilate... but ye have nothing to say against me but for owning of Christ's truths, and his persecuted members: to which they answered nothing" (75). For the words of Kettledrumle, Scott drew on another such collection, *Naphtali*, which contains the "dying speech" of John King, a minister taken prisoner at Drumclog. King denies that "the Gospel preached [as he preached it] was a rendevousing in rebellion, (as it is termed)"; he goes on to assert that "I walked according to the light and rule of the word of God, and as it did become... a minister of the Gospel" (76). Strikingly, both Alison and King cite the Gospels rather than any Old Testament source, and by so doing distinguish themselves from *virtually every one* of Scott's Bible-soaked Covenanters. The only Covenanter chiefly associated with Christian revelation, as M'Crie himself notes, is Bessie Maclure, a blind and elderly widow who serves as a type of Christian Charity. Having given two sons to the Covenanting cause, she makes an early appearance in the novel to warn the Covenanting assassin Burley to safety, and a late appearance to nurse and protect the wounded Royalist Evandale after Bothwell Bridge. Told by fellow Presbyterians that she *should* have played Jael to Evandale's Sisera, Bessie negates the reference to Judges by claiming that to save the wounded enemy "was baith like a woman and a Christian" (452).

But Bessie Maclure's case is singular and, given its presence in the denouement, quite possibly palinodic. The preponderance of biblical allusions in the novel cite the Deuteronomic history of the Hebrew Bible—the historical sweep following the death of Moses through Joshua, Judges, First and Second Samuel, and First and Second Kings—with a secondary source in the major prophets Isaiah and Jeremiah. Parenthetically, the few New Testament allusions pertain not to the Gospels, Acts, or Epistles, but to the florid imagery of Revelation, images barely distinguished from their quoted counterparts in Isaiah, Jeremiah, and the minor prophets of the Hebrew Bible. I use the term "Hebrew Bible" in lieu of "Old Testament" to make a point: For Scott's Covenanters, the Bible is not primarily legible as a prefiguration of the New Testament of Christian revelation. Nor, signally, does it prefigure a stern, Calvinist theology of election. Instead, it evokes a hebraic understanding of history, in which Scripture makes contemporary history intelligible.[8] And the particular phase of hebraic history invoked is one in which the primary cause of historical crisis was understood to be a dissonance between the will of God and the theocratic monarchy of Israel. In other words, at the heart of hebraic historicism lies a conflict between the agency of its rulers and the will of God propounded through law and later elaborated through prophecy. Scott, who wrote a biography of Dryden in 1808, was thoroughly familiar with the use of biblical allegory for contemporary events. Of *Absalom and Achitophel,* Dryden's biblical allegory of the Monmouth rebellion of 1685, Scott wrote: "The poem is written in the style of a scriptural allusion; the names and situations of personages in the holy text being applied to those contemporaries to whom the author assigned a place in his piece."[9] Dryden's Whig imitators, writes Scott, also "[gave] Jewish titles to their heroes."[10] If Dryden's "scriptural allusion" makes meaning of contemporary events by alluding to a scriptural pretext, Scott's Covenanters take this method to an extreme degree by interpreting contemporary events *exclusively* as fulfillments of biblical prefigurations.

Let us consider three kinds of evidence for Scott's hebraizing of the Covenanters. First, I will treat two passages in which Scott abrades a distinction between the "uncivil" biblical language of the Covenanters and the ostensibly civil language of the Royalists. In these passages, Scott's Covenanters are cast as monotheistic Hebrews against the idolatrous Royalists, who worship manners, tokens, and signs. Next, I'll consider biblical allusions in sermons by a trio of Covenanting preachers in *Old Mortality;* and finally, I'll examine a striking gesture of hebraism in the novel's climactic "Drumshinnel episode."

"uncivil" Language

Not surprisingly, passages where biblical allusions are most concentrated are also passages thick with the incivilities of Scots dialect.[11] Such a passage occurs early in the novel, when Scott introduces the Covenanting Mause Headrigg in tandem with the Royalist Lady Margaret Bellenden of Tillietudlem Castle. Though the loquacious self-importance of both Mause and Lady Margaret ordinarily provides Scott with a good deal of comedy (anti-feminist in flavor, if not in purport), their conversation in Chapter 7 proves to be the first of the novel's many scenes of inquisition. The "high-born dame" (118), carrying an "ivory headed cane," enters "the cottage of the delinquents" to challenge Mause for violating "the faith you owe to God and the king and to me, your natural lady and mistress" (117). Mause rises "like an accused party on his first appearance in presence of his judge, before whom he is, nevertheless, determined to assert his innocence" (116). In self-defense, Mause cites a higher authority, reminding Lady Margaret that "prelacy is like the great golden image in the plain of Dura, and that as Shadrach, Meshach, and Abednego, were borne out in refusing to bow down and worship, so neither shall Cuddie Headrigg [Mause's son]...make murgeons or Jenny-flections, as they ca' them, in the house of the prelates and curates" (119). Mause's wish that Lady Margaret "may be brought to see the error of your ways," elicits a contemptuous response: "The error of *my* ways, ye uncivil woman?" (120). Lady Margaret summarily ejects Mause and her son Cuddie from the estate of Tillietudlem, fearing "the next thing wad be to set up a conventicle in my very withdrawing room" (120). This fear is less hyperbole than an admission that not only Lady Margaret's civility, but her political allegiance to the Crown, are staked on a singular act of drawing-room hospitality; as anyone who sets foot in Tillietudlem is told, Lady Margaret once presided over a breakfast taken by Charles II and "seldom afterwards partook of that meal...without detailing the whole circumstances of the royal visit, not forgetting the salutation which his majesty conferred on each side of her face, though she sometimes omitted to notice that he bestowed the same favour on two buxom serving-wenches" (76). Though the King went directly from breakfast to receive a sound thrashing by Cromwell at Worcester, Lady Margaret united herself "exclusively to the fortunes of the Stewarts" (76). Clearly Mause's citation of "the great golden image in the plain of Dura" (119), is meant to indict Lady Margaret's daily burnishing of the golden image of her King. Mause, far from being laughable, achieves a moment of quiet dignity when her son Cuddie upbraids her for parading her "non-enormity": "'Non-conformity, hinnie,' sighed Mause, 'is the name that thae warldly men gie us'" (122). But Cuddie is partly right, for the plot catches fire from the friction between Mause's social "Non-enormity" and her enormous assertion of opinion. This scene of inquisition is soon echoed when a troop of Royalist dragoons storms the household at Milnwood, where Cuddie and Mause have taken refuge. Mause cannot hold her tongue, aligning the red-coated dragoons with both "the Red Dragon" of Revelation and the "Edomites" associated in Genesis with the line of Esau and the color red. Bothwell reminds Mause that "every bull of Bashan and Red Dragon will not be so civil as I am, or be contented to leave you to the charge of the constable and ducking-stool" (137), but his civility is primarily enacted by the extraction of "civility-money"—a bribe for leniency. Both constable and ducking-stool are soon ruled out by Mause's incendiary diatribe; as Bothwell puts it, she is soon "primed and loaded again since her first discharge" (138). Mause's second volley cites, by chapter and verse, the abuses of Kings Ahab and Hezekiah, who jeopardized the northern kingdom of Israel by the paying of tributes to neighboring empires; Calder notes that Ahab is an error for Ahaz, but whether this is Mause's error or Scott's is unclear.[12] Mause painstakingly interprets her text to Bothwell as an allegory of fines exacted by the Crown from the Presbyterians of her own northern kingdom. When the housekeeper of Milnwood vows that Mause will never cross their threshold again, she, Mause, makes a rare allusion to Exodus: "there's nae mark on [this] threshold for a signal that the destroying angel should pass by" (140). Ironically, this allusion to the Passover liberation inaugurates the exiled Mause's captivity at the hands of the dragoons.

In both of these scenes, civility becomes unmasked as a form of idolatry. The point is sent home in Chapter 21 in a debate between the moderate hero Morton and the Covenanting guerilla, John Balfour of Burley. Morton provides a civil foil for what Daniel Whitmore has called Presbyterian "bibliolatry."[13] Having learned that a council of Covenanters has just elected him captain, Morton declares:

> I will own frankly ... much of this sort of language which, I observe, is so powerful with others, is entirely lost on me .... I revere the Scriptures as deeply as you or any Christian can do. I look into them with humble hope of extracting a rule of conduct and a law of salvation. But I expect to find this by an examination of their general tenor, and of the spirit which they uniformly breathe, and not by wresting particular passages from their context, or by the application of Scriptural phrases to circumstances and events with which they have often very slender relation. (259)

Earlier, Morton had been "impressed" by Burley's reading from the Bible: Morton had heard it as a "strong and emphatic" language, rendered more impressive by the "Orientalism of Scripture" (108). At this juncture, however, Morton turns away from such "Orientalism" to proclaim his "reverence" for the scriptural provision of "rule" and "law." The requisite "examination" of Scripture is to ignore particular "phrases" and attend instead to its general "tenor" or "spirit." Burley rightly understands Morton to declare a Pauline preference for living spirit over killing letter, but he counters by associating carnality with Morton's reason, "which is, for the present, thy blind and imperfect guide" (259). And when the zealous preacher Macbrier interrupts to call the interests of Charles II "carnal," Morton's reasoned approach to Scripture is severely undercut; his reading of Scripture exposes his desire to find in it a reflection—not a source—of his principles. As the chapter closes, Morton announces that "I join a cause supported by men engaged in open war, which it is proposed to carry on according to the rules of civilized nations" (266). Ironically, both Morton and the radicals find that Scripture yields the "rules" by which war is to be waged.

In Chapter 18, following their success in the skirmish at Drumclog, the Presbyterians gather "on the ground which they had won" (236). The phrase is resonant, and it is followed by the impromptu sermons of three ejected field-preachers who celebrate reclaiming the literal grounds of their ministry. Inspired largely by passages from the Hebrew Bible, these sermons soon reveal exactly what sort of "spirit" these biblical passages "uniformly breathe." The two-hour preaching of Kettledrumle centers on a vengeful text from Isaiah 49, which reads in part: "And I will feed them that oppress thee with their own flesh; and they shall be drunken with their own blood as with sweet wine" (238). A mixture of sublimity and burlesque, as Scott puts it, the sermon makes no reference to Christ, identifying the Savior and Redeemer as "the Mighty One of Jacob" (238). Kettledrumle is "uncourtly" not only in style but in substance; he closes with an attack on the Crown, likening Charles II to Jeroboam, Omri, and Ahab, "and every other evil monarch recorded in the Chronicles" (239). These are the "hard names" (239), of course, of the despised kings of the Northern Kingdom of Israel, which fell to the Assyrians in 722 BCE.

The oratory of Macbrier, an Anglican-born proselyte, comes in for more praise from the narrator than Kettledrumle's; in "the most affecting colours" (240), he feminizes the Church by likening it to Hebrew heroines such as Hagar, Deborah, and Rachel. But rising into a "rough sublimity" (240), he compares the present victory favorably to the sacrifice in

Solomon's temple; "with the rocks for your altars, and the sky for your vaulted sanctuary, and your own good swords for the instruments of sacrifice" (241). In one breath, he invokes the desolation of Jeremiah, the heroism of "the valiant Maccabeus," the mighty Sampson, and "Gideon, which turned not back from slaughter" (241). Not surprisingly, among his major themes is the conflation of the Covenanters with biblical "children of the Covenant" (241).

A third preacher enters the novel in Chapter 22, the grizzled, unkempt, eagle-clawed Habakkuk Mucklewrath, said to have lost his reason during a long captivity by the Crown. But what Morton regards with disgust as "utter abomination and daring impiety... the mingled ravings of madness and atrocity" (273), are regarded by the most radical faction of Covenanters as prophesy itself: "Our violent brethren will have it," reports the moderate Poundtext, 'that he speaketh of the spirit, and that they fructify by his pouring forth" (272). Like Kettledrumle, Mucklewrath cites Scripture against the inclination toward mercy, invoking God's merciless treatment of the Northern Kingdom—here Jezebel, rather than Ahab—as his example. Like Ezekiel, whom he quotes, Mucklewrath is a prophet of fasting and silence: "Six days he hath not spoken nor broken bread, and now his tongue is unloosed" (274). After Mucklewrath's rant, Burley tells an appalled Morton that "it is not men of sober and self-seeking minds, who arise in these days of wrath to execute judgment and to accomplish deliverance" (274), and against such assertions, M'Crie portrays the Covenanters as "sober and pious men, desirous of living peaceably" (70). When Morton, much chastened, insists that such violence was not known by his father's generation, those Roundheads who showed "wisdom and moderation with which they conducted their civil and military affairs" (275), he matches the Covenanters' bibliolatry with patriolatry. But Burley, who fought side by side with Morton's father in the Civil Wars, knows better. While Burley quotes the first book of Kings—"I will bring a sword upon you that shall avenge the quarrel of my Covenant"—the enthusiast of civil patriarchy dreams of "softening the horrors of civil war" (275).

The horrific episode at Drumshinnel in Chapter 33 has been controversial not simply because here the portrait of the Covenanters reaches its violent verge, but because, as one critic puts it, the tale "has no basis in Covenanting history."[14] Indeed, in a note to the Magnum edition of 1830, Scott writes that he based the story on an anecdote by a deceased "Excise man" who was taken captive by a band of Sabbath-observing smugglers: "A regard for the sanctity of the Sabbath evening, which still oddly subsisted among these ferocious men, amidst their habitual violation of divine and social law, prevented their commencing their intended cruelty until the Sabbath should be terminated" (575). At Drumshinnel, a similar delicacy about the Sabbath obtains; Morton anxiously watches as a clock—an anachronism lambasted by M'Crie[15]—ticks the remaining Sabbath-hours away," on the brink between this and the future world" (373). But the "future world" he anticipates must wait until a most ancient world is recuperated: the world of ritual sacrifice. Mucklewrath declares Morton "a ram caught in the thicket, whose blood shall be a drink-offering to redeem vengeance from the church, and the place shall from henceforth be called Jehovah-Jireh, for the sacrifice is provided. Up then, and bind the victim with cords to the horns of the altar!" (369). Ironically, this horrific allusion to the binding of Isaac points to the instant of Divine reprieve, the ram provided "for a burnt offering in the stead of [Abraham's] son" (Gen. 22:13). In Genesis, the provision of the ram closes the convulsive episode of Abraham's test; the same deity who had threatened to bring Abraham's line to a bloody end, now showers him and his descendants with blessings. But when Mucklewrath identifies Morton as the innocent "ram," Scott evokes Augustine's association of the ram with Christ's sacrifice. Morton's Drumshinnel is his Gethsemane; meditating on his faith while reciting from the *Book of Common Prayer,* he passes the night "with less agitation than he himself could have expected, had the situation been prophesied to him" (372). But Scott's grotesque emphasis lands firmly on the horrific wrath of the Cameronians who humiliate, surround, and threaten Morton—that is, on an anti-Semitic tradition of Jews as the killers of Christ. The allusion has a second, strange resonance, for it invokes not only the Jews' guilt as Christ's ostensible murderers, but also the blood libels of the thirteenth century that resulted in the expulsion of Jews from England in 1290.

Scott, Jews, and Hebrews

The evidence I have discussed here points to one conclusion: that Scott's "perversion" of Scripture is hardly the mimesis of incoherence and madness it has been taken to be by critics from his day to ours, but rather a pervasive emphasis on affinities between the "uncivil" Covenanters and the biblical Hebrews. That M'Crie regarded such a representation of the Covenanters with alarm raises the important question of what is at stake—politically, culturally, aesthetically—in Scott's hebraizing gesture. First, it is clear that Scott draws on various anti-Semitic traditions, and not only in conveying the brutalities at Drumshinnel. The novel evokes images of Jews as contentious, self-defeated infidels; as scriptural literalists; as slavish observers of ritual; as benighted, as crafty, as clannish, and as un-English. We are reminded that M'Crie begins the *Vindication* by bristling at Scott's assertion that the Presbyterians practiced a "judaical observance" (15) of the Sabbath. In fact, parties hostile to nonconformists often invoked anti-Semitic diatribes against "judaizing" practices dating back to the vituperations of St. John Chrysostom. But the preponderance of such anti-Semitic material originates in the anti-Presbyterian writings on which Scott drew heavily, which conflated the 1643 Covenant with that of the Jews, and asserted roundly that both Covenants rendered their "sectaries" unfit for full civil liberties. This conflation of Jews and nonconformists in the seventeenth century was hardly casual; bear in mind that during that century, and until the passage of the short-lived Jew Bill of 1753, the civil rights of both Jews and nonconformists were subject to identical restrictions. Moreover, both M'Crie and the seventeenth-century anti-Presbyterians were probably aware of traditions (some based on medieval Scottish chronicles) tracing the Scots back to various branches of the Hebrew patriarchs: to the line of Zerah, the son of Judah; to the line of Noah's grandson, Gomer, and so forth. Taking a slightly different tack, John Toland's 1714 *Reasons for Naturalizing the Jews in Great Britain and Ireland* (based in part on Simone Luzzatto's *Discorso circa il stato de gl'Hebrei*, published in Venice in 1638), attributes "a remarkable Aversion to pork and black-puddings to this day," to intermarriage between Scots and Jews fleeing the expulsion of 1290.[16] Finally, in the factional politics of the seventeenth century, Jews played a precarious and ambiguous role, ingratiating themselves with Oliver, then Richard Cromwell; seeking indulgences and protections from the restored monarchy; and later financing, from Amsterdam, the glorious expedition of William of Orange.[17] It is worth noting also that the first openly Jewish community in England since the expulsion in 1290 was ratified during the Protectorate in 1656, shortly after the Whitehall conference found no legal basis on which to expel the appellant Jews. The ambiguity of the Jews' allegiances within the English scene was compounded by a greater ambiguity of identity: While not liable to expulsion, Jews maintained until the mid-nineteenth century an ambiguous status as "endenized" subjects—something like resident aliens. The paranoia and suspicions within the ranks of Scott's Covenanters—suspicions often allegorized in *Old Mortality* and in contemporary sources by base and mercenary Jewish kings—may have had a historical basis in pervasive suspicions of Jewish allegiances.

In Scott's own day, as I have already suggested, the ideology of conversion succeeded in portraying Jews in a passive, often feminized role; Jews needed the custodial care of the tolerant state Church as much as they needed conversion. Four decades later, George Eliot lavished praise on both Stowe's novels and Scott's *Old Mortality,* for exhibiting "what we may call Hebraic Christianity."[18] What exactly George Eliot intends by this term is not clear, but if she was reading Scott's stance on Jews through the philo-Semitic *Ivanhoe,* she would not have been alone. (If only to counterbalance this received wisdom about Scott's philo-Semitism, one notes that Scott was also the author of the 1827 *Surgeon's Daughter,* whose half-Jewish protagonist is an unstable, erratic, and violent figure who traffics in women.)

But does this bring us any closer to resolving the matter of Scott's stance on the Jews? As Michael Ragussis has shown in *Figures of Conversion,* the decade in which the Waverley novels appeared closed upon contrasting developments in Britain and Germany vis-à-vis the "Jewish question."[19] While Germany saw an outbreak of anti-Semitic actions that specifically invoked the medieval Crusades, Britain's long tradition of tolerance for Jews became subsumed by a millenarian urgency to convert the Jews. As Ragussis notes, one plank of English nationalism, since before the Glorious Revolution, was the notion that English tolerance for Jews distinguished England from many Continental nation-states, a notion immeasurably complicated by Napoleon's emancipation of French Jews in 1808.[20] Ragussis, taking *Ivanhoe* to question severely the notion that tolerance and conversion can be mutually reinforcing, credits Scott with motivating a liberal, philo-Semitic strain running through *Daniel Deronda* on to Joyce's *Ulysses.* And a crucial feature of this strain, according to Ragussis, is "disengaging the representation of Jewish identity from the sphere of biblical discourse—that is, from the narrow notion of 'God's ancient people.'"[21]

But the example of *Old Mortality* presents several obvious difficulties with Ragussis' argument, at least as it pertains to Scott. First, as M'Crie shrewdly observes, Scott's novel hardly disengages Jewish identity from biblical discourse; in fact, M'Crie claims that Scott invokes the biblical Hebrews expressly to designate the Cameronians as a cult beneath civility and undeserving of civil rights. The contrast between Scott's ferocious Mucklewraths and his beneficent, noble Rebecca could not be more pronounced. Second, M'Crie seems to intuit Scott's hostility not only toward the Cameronians, but also toward the Hebrews. And he'd have been sensitive with good reason: For among Presbyterians defending their liberties against the established church, invoking the hebraic character of Presbyterianism was a time-honored way to evoke the austere purity of the Scottish church. M'Crie himself, in November of 1817, wrote a pamphlet accusing the Crown of suppressing Presbyterian liberties in the national mourning for the deceased Princess Charlotte, in which he praised the Jews' proscription of a funeral for Moses as an example for Presbyterians: "He who provided that Moses should be interred secretly so that 'no man knoweth of his sepulture to this day,' lest the Jews should have abused it to idolatry, wisely and graciously guarded against a practice which he foresaw would easily degenerate into superstition."[22] And, M'Crie implies, it was a Jewish Christ who was buried without a religious service. Third, M'Crie's pamphlet reminds us that England's religious tolerance could hardly have been perceived as the theme of a novel in which the Crown's intolerance of Presbyterians is so spectacular, violent, and unredeemed. England, after all, means different things to different people; not all readers understood Scott to speak for *their* nation.

What, then, is at stake in Scott's hebraizing representation of the Covenanters? First, if Scott's novel ironizes the Covenanters' perception of themselves as living out the conflict between mortal monarchs and Divine will, we can nonetheless see in this hebraic allegory a severe challenge not only to the Crown, but also to the Royalists' Christian value of civility. As I have already suggested, Scott's relentless equivocations about the motives and conduct of the English, in particular of the English General Claverhouse, unmasks the English worship of civility as idolatry. Hence, while M'Crie is no doubt right about the anti-Semitism and anti-Presbyterianism harbored in Scott's sources, Scott's use of a hebraic framework for the Covenanters' cause places a crippling burden on any endorsement of the established church.

So much for the hebraic *Presbyterians*. As for the Hebrews themselves, rather than ask this novel to resolve Scott's stance on the Jewish question, I want to isolate the one feature of Scott's hebraic Covenanters that sets them quite apart from both British and Continental Jewry: Despite the long arm of prelacy and the sweep of dragoons, Scott's Covenanters have always been, and remain, associated with land, albeit feudally organized. It is Scott's decisive achievement to invoke the Hebrews as a landed people negotiating between the sovereignty of their God and that of their earthly kings. In this respect, Scott more than outdoes contemporary millenarian gestures toward the "restoration of the Jews," a restoration that more often than not is complemented by a demand for a contrite conversion. Not only is conversion not at issue—the only convert (from Anglicanism to Presbyterianism) is Macbrier—but neither are the basic freedoms for which Morton finally enters the fray on behalf of the Presbyterians: the freedom of self-government, the right to property, the right to due process under law, the right to bear arms. This last right is not to be taken for granted; it is declared by every Covenanting musket fired in the novel, and there are many. Scott's identification of the Covenanters with fighting, warring, violent, sometimes idolatrous Jews has a certain visionary quality, far from what he might have perceived in the emancipated Jews of France. In short, I do not think it excessive to glimpse, in Scott's novel of seventeenth-century Scotland, a vision of a Hebrew state, triply embattled: by intractable enemies from without; by its own often uncivil treatment of aliens; and by protracted, internecine strife. And it was in the latter decades of Scott's century that such a vision would take political shape.

And as for Scott, we find that his much-debated historicism is oddly inflected by the hebraism of *Old Mortality*. Rather than massage that historicism for a post-Napoleonic politics—either on the left (the position of Lukács[23]) or on the right (the position best articulated by Alexander Welsh[24])—I would hazard that at the heart of Scott's "most historical" novel, lies a rich imagining of a strikingly unmodern historicism. The Covenanter's Bible-centered "reading" of contemporary events provides a haunting reminder that in many cultures, periods and pasts have been found far less compelling than continuities and repetitions. For Covenanters and pre-modern Jews alike, history is prophecy, the drama of the imminent against the matrix of the pre-ordained. That this quality endows the novel with a richer, stranger texture than *Waverley* or *Ivanhoe* hardly needs saying; but that Scott would only intermittently touch this bar in his subsequent career might. *Old Mortality* is a novel of living prophecy rather than historical realism. Its Romantic historicism links it more closely to Keats' *Fall of Hyperion*, Shelley's *Prometheus Unbound*, and Blake's *Four Zoas* than to *Ivanhoe* or *Daniel Deronda*. To read *Old Mortality* is not to take hold of the past, but to enter an alien world in which we wait, like history's unknowing strivers and sufferers, upon an outcome. David Lloyd George, reflecting in 1930 on his "contract with Jewry," wrote of his childhood, "I could tell you all the Kings of Israel. But I doubt whether I could have named half a dozen of the Kings of England and no more of the Kings of Wales."[25] *Old Mortality* gives strong evidence that British philo-Semitism—and very likely Zionism as well—received at least some measure of its impetus from those, like Scott, who refused to place "biblical discourse" in abjection.[26]

Notes

1. See David B. Ruderman, *Jewish Enlightenment in an English Key: Anglo-Jewry's Construction of Modern Jewish Thought* (Princeton: Princeton University Press, 2000), and Tom Segev, *One Palestine, Complete: Jews and Arabs under the British Mandate*, trans. Haim Watzman (New York: Henry Holt, 2000). A broader treatment of Anglo-Jewish history is offered by David S. Katz, *The Jews in the History of England, 1485–1850* (Oxford: Oxford University Press, 1994). A narrower purview, focused on the eighteenth century and the Romantic era, is found in Todd M. Endelman, *The Jews of Georgian England, 1714–1830: Tradition and Change in a Liberal Society* (Philadelphia: Jewish Publication Society, 1979; reprint, with new preface, Ann Arbor: University of Michigan Press, 1999).
2. For a discussion of the Hutchinsonians and the Jews, see Ruderman, 23–56; chapter four is devoted to Anglo-Jewish thought and dissent, both religious and political (see 135–83).
3. In his superb introduction to the Penguin edition, Angus Calder provides a historical overview of the period (see Angus Calder, Introduction to *Old Mortality*, by Sir Walter Scott [London: Penguin, 1975], 18–26). All references to *Old Mortality* are to the Calder edition, and are cited parenthetically in the text.
4. Calder discusses both points—the radicalism of the preachers and the dating of the violent peak of conflict—in his introduction, 27.
5. For a discussion of the English reception of *Old Mortality*, including a dissenting review published in *The Eclectic*, see Ina Ferris, *The Achievement of Literary Authority: Gender, History, and the Waverley Novels* (Ithaca: Cornell University Press, 1991), 140–60. Excerpts from reviews, including Scott's self-review in the *Quarterly Review*, are available in John O. Hayden, *Scott: The Critical Heritage* (London: Routledge and Kegan Paul, 1970), 106–45.
6. Thomas M'Crie, *A Vindication of the Scottish Covenanters: Consisting of a Review of the First Series of the "Tales of My Landlord"* (Philadelphia: James M. Campbell, 1843), 29. All subsequent references to M'Crie's review refer to this edition and appear parenthetically in the text.
7. See Calder, 17.
8. For a classic treatment of hebraic historicism and its vicissitudes, see Yosef Hayim Yerushalmi, *Zakhor: Jewish History and Jewish Memory* (Seattle: University of Washington Press, 1982).
9. Sir Walter Scott, *Miscellaneous Prose Works* (Edinburgh: Robert Cadell, 1841), 1:43.
10. Scott, *Miscellaneous Prose Works*, 1:45.
11. For a shrewd treatment of Scott's use of dialect jokes, see Alexander Welsh, *The Hero of the Waverley Novels* (Princeton: Princeton University Press, 1963; reprint, with new essays, 1992), 186–90.
12. Calder, 539 n19.
13. See Daniel Whitmore, "Bibliolatry and the Rule of the Word: A Study of Scott's *Old Mortality*," *Philological Quarterly* 65 (Spring 1986): 243–62.

14. See Beth Dickson, "Sir Walter Scott and the Limits of Toleration," *Scottish Literary Journal* 18 (November 1991): 56.
15. "[A]nd we now believe, upon the same authority, though it cost us, we confess, some pain to swallow it, that clocks or timepieces were then a common article of furniture in a moorland farm house" (see M'Crie, 13).
16. Quoted in Katz, 236.
17. See Katz, 145–89.
18. Quoted in Michael Ragussis, *Figures of Conversion: "The Jewish Question" and English National Identity* (Durham: Duke University Press, 1995), 266.
19. Ragussis, 89.
20. Ragussis, 2–3.
21. Ragussis, 7.
22. Quoted in Esther Schor, *Bearing the Dead: The British Culture of Mourning from the Enlightenment to Victoria* (Princeton: Princeton University Press, 1994), 215.
23. Georg Lukács, *The Historical Novel*, trans. Hannah and Stanley Mitchell (Lincoln: University of Nebraska Press, 1983), 30–63.
24. Welsh, 63–85.
25. Quoted in Segev, 36–8.
26. I am grateful to audiences at Haverford College, SUNY Buffalo, and the 2001 NASSR Conference in Seattle for their responses to earlier versions of this chapter.

Chapter 7

Maria Edgeworth's *Harrington*: The Price of Sympathetic Representation

Neville Hoad

In 1815, a young Jewish woman teaching in a girls' school set up by her father in Warrenton, North Carolina, initiated what was to be a life-long correspondence with Maria Edgeworth by raising the issue of Edgeworth's stereotypical and unjust representation of Jewish characters in her œuvre. Rachel Mordecai wrote:

> Relying on the good sense and candour of Miss Edgeworth, I would ask how can it be that she, who on all other subjects shows such justice and liberality should on one alone appear biased by prejudice, should even instill that prejudice into the minds of youth. Can my allusion be mistaken? It is to the species of character which wherever a Jew is introduced is invariably attached to him. Can it be believed that this race of men are by nature mean, avaricious and unprincipled?[1]

Harrington, written in 1816, is Edgeworth's extended reply.

In *Harrington*, a male, ruling-class, Anglican first-person narrator provides a retrospective account of the origin and development of his anti-Semitism and his final overcoming of it. As a young boy, Harrington is terrorized by his nursery maid, Fowler, into a deep fear of the Jews. This is encouraged by his mother as a sign of inspired genius and great sensitivity. His father perceives it as effete and foolish and attempts to convert his son's fear into contempt. At school, the vicious behavior of one of his aristocratic schoolmates (Mowbray) toward the son of a Jewish peddler induces a growing sympathy for the Jews. Harrington then goes to Cambridge where he meets a generous and scholarly Jew, who links him up with a wealthy Spanish Jew (Montenero), who has a beautiful daughter called Berenice. The virulently anti-Semitic schoolmate wants the Jewish heiress for himself and goes into competition with the narrator. During the Gordon Riots the narrator saves the house and honor of Montenero, as well as the mother and sister of the schoolmate, two notorious anti-Semites. However, the hero is told of some mysterious obstacle to his marriage with the beautiful Jewess. Her father has heard rumors of his insanity, which have been inculcated by an unholy alliance of the nursemaid and the schoolmate. This conspiracy is disclosed—the wicked schoolmate is killed in a dual over a dispute concerning the son of the Jewish peddler. Meanwhile, financial ruin threatens Harrington senior and Montenero offers him the necessary financial assistance. When the conspiracy between Fowler and Mowbray is discovered, the evil nursery-maid is banished to America, and it turns out that the beautiful Jewess is actually an English Christian Protestant in disguise. The parental objections to the marriage melt away and everyone lives happily ever after.

The narrative is thus a confession, a fairy-tale and proto-psycho-analytic cure. What is at stake in its weird mix of modes, its convoluted narrative twists and double-backings, its opposition between feminine sensitivity and male contempt in the figuring of anti-Semitism? Why does Edgeworth have to work so hard to produce a happy ending? What are the costs of Harrington and Berenice's union?

My bald narrative summary suggests that Edgeworth's avowal to create sympathetic representations of Jewish identity is framed by issues of social, economic, and most importantly national *incorporation* and *exclusion*. The terms of these exclusions and incorporations are riven by both class and gender (particularly a gendered opposition between reason and irrationality in the definition of the nation), making for a very complicated set of determinants in moving Jews into, out of, and around the English social spaces of the novel. The novel struggles to preserve Jewish difference while arguing for religious tolerance and the possibility of naturalization, battling to address the question of the possibility of such a creature as an English Jew.

In this sense, the narrative repeats many of the issues raised by the Jewish Naturalization Bill of 1753, and the narrative's concluding gesture of fully assimilating the daughter as Christian and English, while maintaining the father as Jewish and Spanish, needs to be understood against the backdrop of the first public debates over the legal status of the Jews since Readmission. However, the history of religious identity is not the only factor in Edgeworth's national romance, despite the concerted attempt to create sympathetic Jewish characters. I will argue that Jewish identity in relation to the nation is always over-determined. This literary representation of the historical relation of Jewish identity to the English nation is complicated by the novel's figuring of the nation as necessarily irrational and anti-Semitic and simultaneously as the secular vehicle for the building of religious tolerance. In the encounter with Jewishness in the novel, Englishness gets anxious. It is the difficulty in managing these over-determinations and contradictions that produces much of the narrative strain.

The conspiracy between Fowler, the evil nursery-maid, and Mowbray, Harrington's anti-Semitic schoolmate, offers the most striking incidence of the narrative buckling under the weight of its ideological labor. The conspiracy is evoked to explain retroactively certain events, which took place before Mowbray has ostensible motivation for conspiring against Harrington. Mowbray puts up for auction the picture "Dentition of A Jew" in order to produce one of Harrington's emotional collapses in front of Montenero, to be used later as evidence of Harrington's instability. However, Mowbray, as yet, has shown no interest, sexual or financial, in Berenice, so why would he produce this spectacle in the same way that he produced the spectacle in the synagogue? Why would he already be in league with Fowler before he has broken off with Harrington?

The chronology of the novel is thus undermined by the explanatory mechanisms of its plot. The re-introduction of Fowler, at the expense of chronological coherence, can be explained by the way it allows for the displacement of the anti-Semitism, which is shown to be rife throughout English society, onto the socially marginal figure of the maidservant. Fowler, as the disease of the national body, can be excluded and is sent to America on the very boat that was to take Berenice and her father away. (Miraculously, the ring of Sir Josseline, mysterious carrier of national anti-Semitism, passes from Lady de Brantefield to Fowler. We are never told how Fowler comes to be in possession of the ring.)

The terms of national incorporation and exclusion need to be seen through the novel's gendering of both the national and protagonist's body in relation to a shifting opposition between reason and passion. Why is anti-Semitism sometimes gendered as a hysterical female disorder, and how and why is this disorder associated with the mob? Harrington is very much a mommy's boy—highly imaginative, prone to raptures, and consequently vulnerable to imputations of insanity. Fowler, the instigator of his anti-Semitism in this female economy of prejudice, is punished, whereas the elder Harrington, the agent of effecting the conversion of Harrington's effeminate fear into manly contempt, is forced into the acceptance of Mr. Montenero by economic considerations. Working-class English women are irrational in their purported hatred of Jews. Sensible ruling-class men can realize that Jews are good for business. Through the differing treatment of the anti-Semites in the text, we see the terms of Edgeworth's tolerance. The novel conceives the English nation in contradictory ways. The nation needs to be both a community of irrational allegiance and the political site for the advancement of legal and economic rationality.

The action of the novel is framed by two crucial historical events—the Gordon Riots of 1780 and the furor over the 1753 Bill for the Naturalization of the Jews, which, to some significant extent, set up certain of the terms for the novel's representation of Jewish identity. Arguably, Edgeworth conflates the two incidents, for no records exist for the mob in the Gordon Riots deflecting their outrage against the Catholic Relief Act onto Jews in London in 1780, whereas sectors of the Jewish population were extensively harassed over the naturalization bill.[2] There is no record of damage to Jewish property. In 1780, the violence took place far from the Jewish quarters. Such a conflation on Edgeworth's part would only serve to confirm the political volatility of the extension of citizenship rights to religious minorities and suggest the mutually imbedded, if not interchangeable, nature of religious and national identities in the late eighteenth century. Edgeworth effectively denies the specificity of both Jewish and Catholic demands for assorted civil rights by deliberately or mistakenly presenting the Gordon Riots of 1780 as a consequence of the harassment of Jews in 1753. The conflation further indicates the struggle to think through the problem of creating national identity without having to rely on, and yet never being entirely able to repress, the irrational sentiments of the mob.

Edgeworth figures the Jews as a surplus of a constitutively English francophobia:

> The very day before Mr. Montenero was to leave town, without any conceivable reason, suddenly a cry was raised against the Jews: unfortunately Jews rhymed to shoes: these words were hitched into a rhyme, and the cry was "No Jews, no wooden shoes!" Thus without any natural, civil, religious or moral or political connexion, the poor Jews came in remainder to the ancient anti-Gallician antipathy felt by English feet and English fancies against the French wooden shoes.[3]

The depiction of Jewish identity as a national, as well as religious, *other* is an accurate reflection of the terms of the Naturalization Bill.[4] The bill was intended to help foreign-born Jews overcome certain trading obstacles, by alleviating the difficulties they faced in attaining naturalization. The conflict the bill induced ultimately led to the questioning of the already uncertain rights of English-born Jews, even though the bill did not claim to address these. The novel partially interrogates religious prejudice, acquiring some critical distance from religious bigotry, yet never interrogates the xenophobia, which is paradoxically shown to function in tandem, if not in confusion, with the demonizing of religious difference.

Most of these restrictions stemmed from the status of these Jews as aliens rather than as Jews as members of a religious minority. They included a prohibition against owning land or other real property, including a British vessel. Another significant restriction excluded aliens from colonial trade, and, in those areas of trade open to them, aliens were subjected to extra fees and custom duties. Finally, aliens were constantly subject to the possibility of expulsion.[5]

Harrington, with its different modes of incorporating and excluding the Jew, replicates the uncertainties of the legal incorporation of the Jew into the nation. British law allowed for two possibilities in acquiring some or all the rights of native-born subjects: one was to receive a royal letter of denization; the second and preferred path was to attain a Parliamentary act of naturalization, which allowed the alien to acquire the economic and property rights of native-born subjects. However, a Jew was not eligible for naturalization, for, according to a Parliamentary act of 1609: "The naturalizing of strangers ... have ever been reputed mere matters of grace and favor, which are not fit to be bestowed upon any others such as are of the religion now established in this realm."[6] The act specified that a petitioner must receive the sacrament within a month prior to his naturalization. *Harrington* neatly avoids a consideration of this problem in presenting Berenice as already Christian and in insisting on the retention of Mr. Montenero's foreign status. He is "my Spanish Jew," to Harrington, throughout the novel.

The sacrament requirement left alien Jews (and approximately half the Jews in England at the time were foreign-born) dependent on letters of denization from the king, which Jews faced no exceptional difficulties in attaining, and relieved certain of the trading restrictions, including the ban against trade with the colonies. The oath required for denization concluded with the phrase "So help me God," and so did not contradict the profession of Jewish faith and no sacrament was necessary. However, denization, unlike naturalization, was not retroactive. So a child born abroad prior to denization was unable to inherit property until he himself applied for and received denization. The 1753 bill sought to remove the sacrament requirement for the naturalization of Jews.

Given the considerable expense of achieving a Parliamentary act of naturalization, only wealthy Jews could be expected to benefit. Many proponents of the Jew bill tended to stress this. They argued that the bill would facilitate the immigration of a limited number of wealthy Jews, and the wealth they would bring would result in increased consumption, tax revenues, and investment capital. Proponents seemed unconcerned with the tension between the claims of great benefit to the nation of the influx of Jewish wealth and the concurrent argument that only a few Jews would be affected and that consequently the impact of the bill would be minimal. This peculiar logic places the Jew at both the economic center and the social margins, a move that Harrington's incorporation of Mr. Montenero will repeat. Harrington senior can take Montenero's money but Montenero must remain Spanish. The shunting of Jacob, a peddler victim of Mowbray's anti-Semitic incivility, from center to periphery, from London to Gibraltar and then back to London, also marks an anxiety about what to do with the poorer Jew. Jacob is more identifiably English; yet his place in the nation is revealed as tenuous.

The bill passed through both houses of Parliament with ease but met with vocal and organized opposition from city merchants and High Church leaders, though the uproar around the bill was clearly out of proportion to its possible consequences. Opponents of the bill mobilized the vocabulary of traditional religious bigotry. Anti-naturalization propaganda systematically named Jews as "crucifiers, professed enemies of Christianity, infidels, Antichrists, children of the devil" who frequented the "synagogues of Satan." These designations clearly underpin Fowler's anti-Semitism, but appear more submerged in the ostensibly more rational and masculine discourse of the elder Harrington, who claims that once a man begins dealing with Jews, he will soon go to the devil. Harrington means that such a man soon faces economic ruin, but revealingly couches this in the vocabulary of religious bigotry.

Although these representations undoubtedly sprung from authentic sentiments held by certain sectors of the population, they also masked or were made to carry other political interests. City merchants feared competition with Jews who had more extensive international brokerage contacts. Particular interests had already moved to exclude Jews from areas of trade where it was perceived that Jews could have some advantage. The attempted entry of Jews into Russian and Levantine companies earlier in the century had provoked exclusionary clauses and the city had traditionally denied its freedom to Jews, permitting only twelve licensed brokers and no Jewish retailers within its limits. Even before the bill was passed in the House of Commons, city interests petitioned for its repeal and were instrumental in the distribution of especially virulent anti-naturalization pamphlets of clergymen such as William Moraine.

The bill further acted as a synecdoche of wider political interests. To many contemporary observers, the frenzied Christian zeal that it provoked appeared politically motivated. Philo-Patriae, a pro-bill pamphleteer, argued that opposition to the bill proceeded "with a view to the future elections and not from Christianity, as the pretence is."[7] Another anonymous pamphleteer claimed that: "In the mouth of a Jacobite, Judaism is another name for the revolution of 1688, a limited monarchy, the Hanover legacy and the royal family. In the mouth of a pretended patriot and flaming bigot, Judaism is a Whiggish administration and House of Commons, Protestant bench of bishops, a liberty of conscience and an equitable toleration."[8] For Edgeworth in *Harrington*, the Jew, rather than masking these extra-religious strands, is thought through them. Edgeworth implicitly, if not unconsciously, recognizes the over-determined nature of Jewish identity, in her depiction of the constituting power of difference in the establishment of Englishness. The novel poses but cannot resolve a cluster of the following questions: How can England remain an Anglican nation and not discriminate against Jews and Catholics? On what terms can Jews be assimilated? If Englishness is no longer marked by any racial or religious essence, but by allegiance to a set of Enlightenment principles, what possible grounds can remain for the exclusion of the Jews?

Pro-bill factions pleaded for the bill in philo-Semitic terms, sometimes asserting that the system of government instituted by Moses had affinities with the English constitution, and that Judaism, unlike Roman Catholicism, which was perceived as proselytizing and intolerant, did not threaten the foundations of the English state. One pamphleteer went so far as to claim that Jews were more Christian (read Anglican) than Papists, and that Judaism was infinitely nearer to Protestantism. The appeal that Judaism held for patriarchal Christian authority is scrupulously avoided by Edgeworth. Paradoxically, her enlightened rationalist feminism is the locus for her most naked anti-Semitism.

Defenders of the bill frequently invoked the secular state as the authority in deciding such disputes, citing Locke's 1689 "Letter Concerning Toleration," with its claim that the state has no interest in examining the religious persuasion of its citizens, provided that they obey its civil laws. This re-figuring of the nation as a community of private individuals ruled by rational law rather than as a body united by a shared set of religious beliefs and symbolic allegiances connects with Edgeworth's educational philosophies and is played out in *Harrington*, in, for example, the denigration of Mowbray for his willingness to accept a synagogue on the lands he is to inherit, but not a dissenter's chapel. Consistency of rational legal principle and application, rather than personal favor, must provide the grounds for tolerance. The novel sets out an opposition between law and feelings in the following exchange:

> "Of that everybody's own feelings must be the best judge," said my mother, "the best and sole judge."
> "Thank Heaven! That is not the law of libel yet, not the law of the land yet." (59)

The law of the land must rise above personal feeling, religious or otherwise. The state must regulate the boundaries between the public and the private. This association of the government with reason, and the English nation with enlightened secular government, is a crucial line of argument in understanding the conflicts produced over national incorporation in *Harrington*.

Like the debates around the bill, *Harrington* centers around questions of national *incorporation* and *exclusion*, with religious identity operating as one over-determined variable among many. Though inflecting the debates selectively, the novel never moves beyond their *scope*. For despite the anti-Semitic outcry, the gains for Jews from the bill were minor, and not even the rhetoric of pro-bill defenders could broach the question of Jews being admitted to full civil rights, just as *Harrington* cannot permit Berenice to have Jewish children. Perceiving this as the real problem the narrative has to confront, as opposed to figuring the problem solely in terms of the sympathetic representation of Jewish identity, makes the two most jarring narrative maneuvers meaningful—the abrupt conversion of Berenice and the return of the maid Fowler. However, these trajectories of inclusion and exclusion are compounded by class and gender textual economies.

Berenice's conversion marks a recognition of the boundaries of tolerance, not a failure in Edgeworth's nerve or commitment to pro-Jewish representations. The conversion needs to be understood in terms of a reproductive economy (the nation reproduces itself through the family). The presentation of Berenice as always and already Christian, Protestant, and descended from the daughter of an English gentleman keeps the irrational threat of miscegenation on foreign soil—Spain—and outside the time-span of the novel. The moment of anxiety can be historically and spatially displaced; and Jewish capital rather than Jewish bodies and beliefs can be appropriated into the nation. In *Harrington,* as in the pamphlets of the proponents of the Naturalization Bill, tolerance is justified in terms of commerce.[9] Mr. Montenero, despite the acclaimed sympathetic portrayal of him as the humanized gentleman merchant, remains an alien. When Harrington cannot understand Montenero's cryptic reservations about a possible marriage to Berenice, he attributes this to a "foreign idiom" (147). The elder Harrington can only tolerate Montenero's Jewishness as long as it remains yoked to an alien nationality. Speaking of the encounter in the bank, he says: "I turned to look at the books, of which I knew I should make no head or tail, being no auditor of accounts, but a plain country gentleman. Your Jew, Harrington, came to me and with such a manner as I did not conceive a Jew could have—but he is a Spanish Jew—that makes all the difference, I suppose …" (179).

The prospect of holding respect for an English Jew remains unthinkable. As class difference becomes impossible to maintain, Harrington senior now being financially dependent on the generosity of a Jew, national affiliation must "make all the difference." The elder Harrington can take Montenero's money and expertise into the nation. They are a necessary supplement, for the "plain country gentleman" is clearly bewildered by the confounded ledger and day books. Montenero not only supports the Harrington family, but he bails out the entire bank when he intervenes on Harrington's behalf. For Harrington senior is well aware, "if I drew, I certainly ruined them; if I did not draw, I ran a great hazard of being ruined myself" (179). Montenero allegorically intervenes to save a class, not just an individual. This is clearly the condition for his incorporation into the national romance, which is *Harrington*. He hands over money and his daughter (as does Shylock!) to secure the happy ending of the narrative.[10]

As opposed to her father, Berenice can be truly naturalized. Hints at her impending Englishness come earlier in the novel. She assumes the appearance of an Englishwoman of her class upon overhearing the snide comments of Lady Anne Mowbray. (The unconscious granting of naturalizing agency to an anti-Semite of Lady Anne's caliber equally points to the problematic nature of inclusion in the novel.) As soon as Berenice finds that her "Spanish dress subjected her to the inconvenience of being remarked in public, she laid it aside" (132). Berenice, as the only potential agent of reproduction in the text, must be so fully naturalized that even her past *otherness* is to be retroactively forgotten.

The places that Harrington visits with the Monteneros resonate with the assumption of the rights and duties of citizenship—the Bank, the mint, the Tower of London; and the experiences of the characters in these places suggest much about the desired modes and extents of their assimilation. The visit to the tower particularly establishes what kind of identifications entry into the nation requires. This is apparent in the way the visits also serve symbolically to induct Harrington into the nation: "Though I had lived in London half my childhood, my nervous disease had prevented my being taken to see even the sights that children are usually shown. My object, of course, was now merely to have the pleasure of accompanying Berenice" (97). Harrington attempts to set up an opposition between the things children are usually shown—the Tower of London, etc.—and his "nervous disease" brought about by the things he was shown—Simon the Jew, as child-eater. However the narrative quickly confounds this opposition. Mowbray reminds Harrington of Sir Josseline and the tapestry chamber, instances of national public displays of anti-Semitism. The difference between anti-Semitism, as a nervous disease that prevents enjoyment of the spectacles of the nation, and anti-Semitism, as a very part of those spectacles, is collapsed. The irrationality of the community of nationhood is a problem that the narrative consistently encounters and then evades. Entering the nation requires that one simultaneously acquire the nervous disease anti-Semitism, and the means for effecting its cure.

The irrational, emotional identification that national identity requires emerges in Harrington's feminized swooning and ecstatic incanting in front of the Black Prince (the first indication he gives to Montenero of his imputed insanity). This is a fascinating incident. The child-murderer, who in Fowler's discredited account is Simon, the Jew, returns in the figure of an English historical king. The irrational violence within the nation is connected with Harrington's nervous disease. And it is Berenice's sympathetic quickness, and her shared feeling for poetry that attract Harrington to her, and explain her more extensive incorporation into the nation. For it is Berenice who can sympathize with Harrington's reveries in the Tower of London, entering into the national spirit, complicit as it is with irrationality and anti-Semitism.

This configuration of the nation as community produced by feminized and irrational currents of feeling is both supplemented and undercut by Edgeworth's Lockean rationalism, in which Englishness comes to signify enlightened secular rule of law. Mr. Montenero is the spokesman for this when he says: "But I hope and believe... that my Berenice is not disposed to form uncharitable judgments either of individuals or nations, especially not of the English, of whom she has from their history and literature, with which we are not unacquainted, conceived the highest ideas" (74). The difficulty of reading this quotation is apparent when we consider the self-conscious denigration of English literature and history in the novel itself. It is easy to read Edgeworth's response to the accusations made by Rachel Mordecai in Harrington's disclaimer that anti-Semitism is a disease of the English imagination and his acknowledgment that Jews in English literature are universally depicted in a vicious and uncharitable way. Combined with the invocations of English history from the story of the Black Prince to the recounting of the Gordon Riots, this suggests a history and literature of violence and prejudice, and consequently that Montenero's conceptions are a little optimistic. Harrington senior's response to the Gordon Riots clarifies this more rational conception of the nation, articulated in terms of a split between passion and principles:

> This ill-humour was increased by the perplexing situation in which he found himself, with his *passions* on one side of the question and his *principles* on the other, hating the Papists and loving the ministry. In his secret soul, my father cried with the rioters: "No papists!—No French!—No Jews!—No wooden shoes!" but a cry against government was against his very nature. (172)

The idea of the nation as ordered and rational is one that circulates among certain men in the novel; yet even so it is not strong enough to obliterate the participation in the passionate/irrational feminized economy of prejudice that appears to be essential to national identity.

In the above quotation, the mob with their cry against government is aligned with the kind of anti-Semitism associated with Fowler—emotional, uncontrolled, anarchist, yet also displaying a passionate sentimental investment in the nation. This xenophobia is shared by all the English characters in the novel, with the exception of Harrington, who reserves his original bigotry and subsequent adoration for Jews. This gendered anti-Semitism operates as a kind of social cement in the narrative in the way that it conceals class-cleavages and allows for a shared community between the Brantefields, the Harringtons, Fowler, and the mob.

Only when anti-Semitism threatens to expose and overturn class hierarchies is it punished. The conflict the elder Harrington experiences here is a result of anti-Semitism operating as the site of both class-conflict and national cohesion. In discussing his son's defense of the Monteneros, he develops this conflict more fully:

> I acknowledge that was a good hit you made, about the gun—but I wish it had been in the defence of some good Christian: what business has a Jew with a gun at all? Government knows best, to be sure; but I split against them once before, three and twenty years ago, on the naturalization bill. What is this cry which the people set up?—"No Jews! no

wooden shoes!"—ha! ha! ha!—the dogs!—but they carried it too far, the rascals!—When it comes to throwing stones at gentlemen's carriages, and pulling down gentlemen's and noblemen's dwelling houses, it's a mob and a riot, and the rioters deserve certainly to be hanged. (172)

The mob and Fowler are irrational and threatening, not only to the Jews, but to the ruling classes, persecuting and enslaving their representatives—Lady Brantefield and her daughter, and Harrington. The mob is dehumanized—"the dogs"—but is spoken of with a contemptuous affection. Dogs are all very well, provided that they do not turn against their masters. The nationality of the mob in *Harrington* is further ambiguous due to the historical hindsight on the French Revolution that the backdating of the novel permits. In 1817, the mob of 1780 has lost much of its Englishness, its representation filtered through the more successful mobs of its espoused "wooden shoes" (French) enemies. However, what is un-English in the above description of the mob is clearly not the virulence of its national and religious prejudices but the refusal to acknowledge proper class authority. Later, the irrationality of the mob is quickly forgotten in the ease of its conversion to reason, a conversion facilitated by a national predisposition. Harrington proclaims: "In England, the mob is always in favor of truth and innocence wherever these are made clearly evident to their senses" (170).[11] Implicit in this characterization is the other mob, one that will not listen to reason, that does not heed the master's voice. This mob is not English. The dependence of the category of the English nation on some *other*, in this case the French, is never interrogated by the novel, which can only problematically attempt to rescue Jewishness from a role as the term of difference in the constitution of the nation, or, as in the case of Montenero, substitute national difference for religious difference.

Having considered who can be incorporated into the narrative of the nation and the peculiar functioning of differently gendered and classed anti-Semitisms in that process, the question remains: Who is excluded at the close? Most obviously, Fowler and Mowbray are the two banished figures. Mowbray is never quite at home in England. The covering lie that Fowler tells to Montenero about Mowbray's whereabouts contains some truth—"his lordship had been abroad—was in the army—always on the move" (202). Mowbray moves around the peripheries of the nation—Gibraltar—and never remains long in the center. The narrative's yoking of the dissolute, corrupt, and bankrupt aristocrat with the demonized nursery maid marks a subversive alliance across class, gender, and generational boundary lines, for which the characters must be punished as much as for their anti-Semitism. In certain ways, both protagonists exist outside the circuits of anti-Semitism in the novel, even though they appear its prime instigators. They act out of neither principle nor passion, but out of a shifting and threatening amoral expedience. Neither of them is interested in the Jew as Jew. For Fowler, the story of Simon is simply the means to controlling an excited child, and for Mowbray, anti-Semitism can be assumed and dropped according to other social pressures—his desire for preeminence at school, his need for a wealthy heiress.

Their alliance is not thus the alliance of the true anti-Semites in the text, but an alliance of the only characters who refuse to play by the rules, that is, those who cannot understand the importance of the Jew in the changing composition of the nation. Mowbray's willingness to convert, his refusal to identify with any stable set of religious principles, along with his reneging on his class-responsibilities mark him as being dangerously unruly in the text's attempt to establish the terms for the naturalization of the Jews. The terms of naturalization are ultimately those of class and patriarchal consolidation.

Fowler is a similar agent of disruption. The representation of the act of looking in the opening scenario reveals a reversal of the Enlightenment trope that runs throughout the rest of the novel. The lamp-lighter flashes onto the face of Simon the Jew and the intervention of Fowler makes the moment of illumination the moment of the installation of prejudice, the bringing on of darkness, which subverts, this time metaphorically, Edgeworth's superficially cheerful narrative of national progress and exposes an underlying uncertainty about the tenability of the rational/irrational binary in the constitution of the nation. Fowler uses the stereotypical figure of the Jew to control the child and in doing so reverses hierarchical class and gender relations between Harrington and herself. Harrington himself acknowledges: "from that moment on, I became her slave" (10). The pinning of the crime of anti-Semitism on the most socially disruptive agent in the text reinforces Edgeworth's commitment to enlightened reform, but the narrative insidiously exposes the difficulties of religious tolerance as a national project, by reminding us of the imaginative and irrational leap national identification requires.

Issues of national incorporation and exclusion along the trajectory of the nation are not only apparent in the narratives of the characters in the novel, but also in the novel's own writing of the history of the nation. Parallel to the way the chronology within the novel is ruptured by the difficulties of finding a place for a sympathetic representation of Jewish identity within the narrative of the nation, Edgeworth's backdating of the novel produces some similarly revealing anachronisms. Edgeworth writes *Harrington* in 1816, having Harrington produce his narrative shortly after 1780. Yet *Harrington* explicitly refers to Edgeworth's *Moral Tales for the Young,* which was published in 1801. Thus both Harrington and Edgeworth attempt to locate anti-Semitism in the past:

> In our enlightened days, and in the present improved state of education, it may appear incredible that any nursery maid could be so wicked as to relate, or any child of six years old so foolish as to credit such tales; but I am speaking of what happened many years ago, nursery maids and children are very different now from what they were then; and in further proof of the progress of human knowledge and reason, we may recollect that many of these stories of the Jews, which we now hold too preposterous for the infant and the nursery maid to credit, were some centuries ago universally believed by the English nation, and furnished more than one of our kings with pretexts for extortion and massacres. (10)

Here the narrator presents both personal and national progress in terms of the successful eradication of prejudice. However the confidence in the nation's progress is undermined by the subsequent reference to *Moral Tales.* Nearly forty years later than the dark days described above, an educator and writer—Edgeworth herself in *Moral Tales for the Young* (1801)—is capable of producing the stereotypes of the evil and reprobate Jew that the child and nursery maid should find preposterous. Edgeworth, the libeler, tries to eat her own words before their historical moment of utterance. Moreover, the gently ironic invocations of the putative universals of nursery maids and children in this passage work to undermine the idea of progress by subtly reinstating such transhistorical stereotypes of incompetence and credulity. Even while the narrator shunts his (and Edgeworth's) anti-Semitism into the past, he suggests the naturalness of its continuance.

Harrington, the character, attempts to present anti-Semitism as something confined to his personal past but he cannot account for why it should thrive in the public present. Similarly, *Harrington,* the novel, tries to establish a psychological, private etiology of prejudice as a disease, which in itself marks an evasion of the historical, legal, economic, and social underpinnings of anti-Semitism. The proto-Freudian structure of the narrative privileges the primal scene as the originary moment of prejudice but the class and gender markers of the protagonists in this scene suggest a much wider and fraught national narrative.[12]

In other respects, Edgeworth's allegiance to the project of the nation as the instrument for the progress of human knowledge and reason emerges less problematically. *Harrington* emphatically approves the broadening of the intellectual avenues open to women:

> Female conversation, in general, was at this time very different from what it is in our happier days. A few bright stars had arisen, and shone and been admired, but the useful light had not diffused itself. Miss Talbot's and Mrs. Carter's learning and piety, Mrs. Montague's genius, Mrs. Vesey's elegance, and Mrs. Boscawen's "polished ease" had brought female literature in to fashion in certain favored circles; but it had not, as it has now, become general in almost every rank of life. Young ladies it is true had got beyond the Spectator and the Guardian: Richardson's novels had done much to opening a wider field of discussion. One of Miss Burney's excellent novels had appeared and had made an era in London conversation; but it was still rather venturing out of the safe course for a young lady to talk of books, even of novels, it was not, as it is now, expected that she should know what was going on in the literary world. The Edinburgh and Quarterly Reviews and varieties of literary and scientific journals had not allured to brighter worlds and led the way. (55)

Here, the schism between the past and the present is unequivocally asserted and the advancement of the present is indisputable. These are indeed "happier days." The tropes of light and illumination are used without complicating irony. However this liberatory gender tale is implicated in the narrative's anti-Semitism. Harrington's visit to the synagogue produces only one piece of anthropological information: "All I recollect are the men and women's thanksgivings. 'Blessed art thou, O Everlasting King! that thou hast not made me a woman.' The woman's lowly response is, 'Blessed art thou, O lord! that thou hast made me according to thy will'" (137). The representation of Judaism produced here is clearly informed by Edgeworth's nascent feminism embedded as it is in Enlightenment rhetoric and metaphors. Here, the rational, progressive narrative of the nation is what produces the irrational anti-Semitism.

Finally, the progressive thrust of women's historical trajectory runs counter to a conservative depiction of the historical movement of class-relations. In writing of the fraudulent Christian urban poor, who plague the young Harrington, the narrator displays a Romantic nostalgia for earlier class configurations and behaviors. Harrington's father is able to exert his authority in ridding the neighborhood of the nuisance of the "old clothes men":

> So he set to work with the beadles, and the constables and the parish overseers. The corporation of beggars were not in those days, so well grounded in the theory and so alert in the practice of evasion, by long

experience, they have since become. The society had not then, as they have now, in a certain lane, their regular rendezvous, called the Beggar's Opera; they had not then, as they have now, in a certain cellar, an established school... they had not even their regular nocturnal feasts, where they planned the operations of the next day... so they could not, as they do now, set at nought the beadle and the parish officers.... (19–20)

The rhetorical construction of this extract and the previous passages, outlining the progress of the nation in terms of the eradication of religious prejudice and women's greater access to learning, turns on the juxtaposition of then and now, history and the present. The favoring of one of the two dialectically opposed time-spans is particularly revealing in each case. The positing of anti-Semitism in the primal space of childhood trauma de-historicizes her national narrative here, not entirely permitting the comfortable relegation of anti-Semitism to the credulous and wicked past. In relation to women's intellectual currency, Edgeworth is clear in her preference for the present. However, in relation to class, the past relations are valorized. Informed by a nostalgia for days when the ruling class could impose its will without resistance, the passage of time is seen to bring about decay and degeneration in the social fabric, though the implications for a return to the old way for the approved gender and religious configurations is not considered. The faith in Enlightenment science and reason, which underpins the narrative of progress in the other two instances, is here confounded, for here the increased efficiency and resistance of the beggars is blamed upon "the means of conveying swift and secret intelligence, by telegraphic science" (20).

Thus the narrator's pointed asides on the changing nation contain a similarly problematic figuration of the history of the nation, as both progressive and reactionary, to the narrative's use of contradictory rational and irrational components in the constituting of the national identities of its characters. *Harrington* plays out the dramas of assimilation and difference in ways that reveal the limits of thinking about the politics of identity as simply a question of producing sympathetic representations.

Notes

1. Edgar E. MacDonald, ed., *The Education of the Heart: The Correspondence of Rachel Mordecai Lazarus and Maria Edgeworth* (Chapel Hill: University of North Carolina Press, 1977), 6.
2. Todd M. Endelman, *The Jews of Georgian England: Tradition and Change in a Liberal Society* (Philadelphia: Jewish Publication Society of America, 1979; reprint, with new preface, Ann Arbor: University of Michigan Press, 1999), 114.

3. Maria Edgeworth, *Harrington* (London: J. M. Dent and Co., 1893), 154. Subsequent references to *Harrington* will be indicated parenthetically in the text.
4. A more detailed discussion of the Jewish Naturalization Bill can be found in Alan H. Singer's "Great Britain or Judea Nova?: National Identity, Property, and the Jewish Naturalization Controversy of 1753," the first chapter of this volume (ed.).
5. For a detailed discussion of the changing legal position of Jews in England, see H. S. Q. Henriques, *The Jews and the English Law* (Oxford: H. Hart, 1908; reprint, Clifton, NJ: A. M. Kelley, 1974), 221–64.
6. R. Liberles, "The Jews and their Bill: Jewish Motivations in the Controversy of 1753," *Jewish History* 2, 2 (Fall 1987): 31.
7. Endelman, 91.
8. Liberles, 31.
9. Edgeworth espouses similar notions in relation to Ireland. In an 1825 letter to Rachel Mordecai, she writes: "We hope what is called Catholic Emancipation will be granted by the English parliament. If this be done, people will be contented and quiet. English capital now overflowing will flow here, set industry in motion all over this country, and induce habits of punctuality, order, economy, virtues and happiness that have been for centuries unknown to the despairing, oppressed Irish population" (MacDonald, 75).
10. Although I think Michael Ragussis may be right in arguing that Harrington self-consciously reworks *The Merchant of Venice,* Montenero is different from Shylock in the sense that he does not resent the cost of the comic ending. He is happily assimilated, even if it means giving up his money and his daughter. This, I would argue, renders him highly suspect as a sympathetic portrayal of a Jew ("Representation, Conversion, and Literary Form: Harrington and the Novel of Jewish Identity," *Critical Inquiry* 16 [Autumn 1989], 112–43).
11. The class paternalism of this remark is linked to Edgeworth's attitude toward the Irish: "There cannot be more generous spirits, more grateful dispositions to work upon, than those of the Irish, when they are kindly treated" (Macdonald, 75).
12. Ragussis is astute in his recognition of the psychological sophistication of Edgeworth's understanding of childhood trauma as the founding moment in psychological narratives. However, in accepting the narrative frame of anti-Semitism as psychological, he reproduces Edgeworth's evasion of history. In both the novel, and in Ragussis' reading of it, history is the repressed that returns with a vengeance. See *Figures of Conversion: "The Jewish Question" and English National Identity* (Durham, NC: Duke University Press, 1995), 65–76.

CHAPTER 8

IMAGINING "THE JEW": DICKENS'
ROMANTIC HERITAGE

Efraim Sicher

Fagin, in *Oliver Twist,* is usually read as an expression of the author's anti-Semitism or, alternatively, as an attempt to create a "representative" Jew,[1] while Riah, in *Our Mutual Friend,* is understood to be Dickens' attempt to correct the "bad" Jew in the earlier novel. From this perspective, Riah can be viewed as either an expression of contrition and atonement, or a reflection of changed attitudes toward the Jews and their improved socio-economic position in the period between the two novels.[2] This chapter attempts to avoid the fallacies of these approaches to the literary text by restoring the context of cultural discourse in nineteenth-century Britain in which the construction of "the jew" bolstered a class-determined ideology and contained response to the horrific conditions among the outcasts of London and other major cities at the height of triumphant capitalism. There were diverse and conflicting descriptions of the Jew, and these variously position "the jew" within racist and misogynist perceptions of the *other,* the female, the Irish, and the filthy disease-ridden inhabitants of "criminal" dens and promiscuous "sinks of iniquity." The figure of the Old Clothes Man in particular locates "the jew" within the larger anxieties of contamination of nationhood, class, and domesticity, but it is also associated with the legendary Wandering Jew, whose condemnation to eternal banishment is open to Romantic readings such as Coleridge's Ancient Mariner or Byron's Cain. The legend was highly assimilable to the figure of the wanderer prominent in the Romantic poets' creative consciousness and in their actual situation of exile and wandering.[3]

Dickens was drawing on mythical material rooted in English and Western culture that resounded with theological meaning and cultural memory. The satanic Jew's role as anti-Christ, for example, surfaced in "The Prioress' Tale," and Chaucer's story would have been remembered by readers of Dickens' "Parish Boy's Progress," which tells of the temptation by the Jew of an innocent Christian child. The reception of Shakespeare's Shylock, in particular, reflected historical debates over power politics, usury, equity, and money, for which "the jew" served variously as foil or scapegoat.[4] The Jew was the international, extra-territorial evil genius, like Marlowe's Barabas, capable of everything from poisoning wells to crooked brokering—the "trade" he teaches Ithamore—and therefore a suitable figure for the Machiavellian machinations of modern politics. In Fagin we recognize the stage Jew with his red hair, which traces his lineage to the satanic figure of Judas. The arch-villain of London's underworld, Fagin is a spendthrift Shylock who exerts a merciless hold on his victims. A Shylock brought to judgment, the warder questions him in the condemned cell and asks if he is a man. To consider the manliness of the circumcised Jew as more than a mere question of Fagin's imminent mortality is to recall the bawdy jokes at Shylock's expense.[5]

At the same time, besides Sir Walter Scott, whose figure of the Jew in *Ivanhoe* cannot entirely escape censure, Dickens was highly receptive to the Romantic influence of Wordsworth and Blake. The romance of a lost English pastoral makes the edenic haven of the Maylies particularly attractive as a refuge from the corrupt city and the wicked Jew who pursues the innocent parish boy.[6] Fagin is a malicious omnipresence who reflects Romantic hostility toward urban capitalism, a hostility that breeds a new kind of literary anti-Semitism in Du Maurier's *Trilby* and T. S. Eliot's "Gerontion." Rather than see Fagin as a single, stereotyped figure outside the discourse of the city, as Murray Baumgarten does,[7] I prefer to see Fagin as the alien outsider in the city discourse, who bears the guilt of the city. Thus, political and social emancipation might not necessarily erase an archetypal, global role for "the jew" but, on the contrary, might intensify anxieties about race and nationhood in a deterministic utilitarian or Marxist economic model.

On the other hand, Riah is as incredibly good as Fagin is irredeemably bad. He is a Wandering Jew, both cursed and blessed to wander the earth as a warning to mankind, who shows Victorian society to be failing its Christian principles of charity and humanity. That was a role Sheva played in Richard Cumberland's *The Jew* (1794), in the Enlightenment spirit of Lessing, and Dickens was familiar with Thomas Dibdin's *The Jew and the Doctor* (1798), which describes a similarly sympathetic Jew, Abednego.[8] Moreover, Riah's role fits Romantic interpretations of Shakespeare's Jew. Granted a humane compassion ("Hath not a Jew eyes..."), Shylock was in Kean's performance felt to be a wronged man. Riah becomes a foil for the wicked Christian, just as in

Shakespeare's play Shylock scorns Christians for the hardness they teach him, as well as exposing their hypocrisy when during his trial he mocks Christian husbands for their willingness to give up their betrothal rings.

Attempts such as Steven Marcus' explanation of Fagin in psychoanalytical terms as a projection of screen memory and transformation of the Blacking Warehouse episode[9] too often miss the surrounding cultural discourse and the complex Romantic reading of "the jew" as *other*.[10] It is not so much, I argue, that Dickens is in some way making up for Fagin in his depiction of Riah in *Our Mutual Friend,* but that, despite the changes in the narrative of the *other* between the 1753 Jew Bill and the emancipation of 1858, the Romantic reading of "the jew" was characterized by simultaneous and contradictory impulses of philo-Semitism and anti-Semitism. Romanticism thus tended to displace Jews into figures for conversion to a Christian eschatology while romanticizing the exiled state of wanderers from a destroyed Jerusalem.[11]

Nation, Race, Religion

The Jews were not only identified as the ancient foe of the Christian redeemer. They were also an Oriental race that was degenerate, according to the cultural paradigm of superiority in degree of geographical and cultural progress from East to West, from the Greeks to the English. When the Anglo-Irish journalist and contemporary of Dickens, John Fisher Murray, wandered into the Jewish quarter in London's East End, he imagined he had discovered the New Jerusalem, so strange did he feel among these aliens surrounded by shop signs in Hebrew and patriarchal beards. Like Robert Southey, he saw the Jews as a condemned race who were criminal—they received stolen silver ("no questions asked") and killed meat according to the "old dispensation." Their physiognomy betrayed them and, true to supposed racial phrenology, they were repulsively ugly. To emphasize the un-Christian criminality of the race, Murray declared that their one goal was lust for money and to this end they would stop at nothing to exploit the native Englishman and prostitute his daughter—the very charge Dickens brings in the figure of Fagin:

> ... we must candidly confess that when we see the daughter of a Christian man patrolling the streets, decorated in the trumpery properties of a Jewish brothel, while the devil's dam, in the shape of a hideous Hebrew hag, follows the poor unfortunate like the shadow of death to clutch the wages of her shame, we really think a Christian government might, without any hazard of public odium, string up at the doors of their own dens Mother Abrahams, Mother Isaacs and Mother Jacobs.[12]

In one stroke Murray then attributes prostitution to the Jew and absolves the English from this vice, for they have no more in common with the Jew than a weasel with its prey—an image of the bestial parasite that recalls Fagin, who has put Nancy on the streets, as well as Fledgeby's offensive "Catch a weasel at it, and catch a Jew!" *(OMF* III.1). Murray's conclusion that the Jew "will do you" puts into focus the racialized accusation that the Jew is behind the evil of urban capitalism.

Jewish involvement in crime, particularly among destitute Ashkenazim, who were conspicuous among peddlers and second-hand dealers, contributed to a criminalizing racial stereotype that was reinforced by the legend of Judas' betrayal and the collective guilt attributed to the Jews in the Christian scriptures. However, there were enlightened men like the Romantic poets Leigh Hunt and William Hazlitt who preferred to observe the truth with their own eyes and filter through a more humane sensibility their perception of the Jew. In his *Table-Talk,* Coleridge realized the injustice of the stereotype of the Jew-Old Clothes Man, who spoke good English but was forced to cry hoarsely all day "Ogh Clogh"; yet Coleridge could not help objecting to the smell of the Jew in a railway-carriage.[13] In *London Labour and the London Poor,* Henry Mayhew treats the Jews respectfully, as types of London's streetpeople pursuing occupations peculiar to the metropolis, not a criminal class at all, and other investigators of the slums of the East End such as Charles Bosanquet remarked that much could be learned from the Jews' charitable and educational institutions.[14] Yet prejudiced perceptions and ugly anti-Semitic caricatures persisted in *Punch* and *The Illustrated London News* or in the racist description of the Irish and the Jews in London's slum districts, found for example in Watts Phillips' *The Wild Tribes of London* (1855).

If "the jew" stands for the forces in the capitalist economy undermining natural virtue, pastoral innocence, and domestic bliss, the representation of *other* also foregrounds the instability of constructions of "Englishness" and Christianity. When Bill Sikes recognizes in Fagin the devil, he also identifies in him the anti-type and foe of the Englishman and the Christian. In chapter XV, Fagin comes between Sikes and his dog, who have been having a savage fight, and Sikes wishes Fagin were a dog so that he could murder him just as brutally. In boasting that his dog is as willing a Christian as any, however, Sikes is thinking more of manly qualities of ferociousness than any compassion. Charley jokes, "He's an out-and-out Christian," a "tribute" that elicits the narrator's remark that "there are a good many ladies and gentlemen, claiming to be out-and-out Christians, between whom, and Mr. Sikes' dog, there exist strong and singular points of resemblance" *(OT* XVIII.181–2), just as earlier in the novel, when the gentleman of the board inquired whether Oliver prayed like a good Christian for those who looked after him, the narrator commented with dry irony that it "would have been *very* like a Christian, and a marvellously good Christian, too, if Oliver had prayed for the people who fed and took care of *him*. But he hadn't, because nobody had taught him" *(OT* II.54).

Dickens hated xenophobic displays of "Englishness," and the joke, in *Our Mutual Friend*, about the marks of the constitution left in London's streets mocks Podsnap's national superiority just as false ideas of law and liberty were derided in *Oliver Twist*. The "Artful Dodger" has a particularly hilarious way of standing up for the rights of an Englishman when he confronts his judges: "I'm an Englishman, ain't I?" rejoined the Dodger. "Where are my priwileges?" *(OT* XLIII.394). Threatening a Parliamentary inquiry, he is carried off amid a carnival laughter that signals a radical challenge to the social hierachy by the subaltern and makes gentle fun of the Law, but it also undoes definitions of Englishness identified with class privilege and liberty. Fagin, however, is indelibly alien, and is almost lynched on the way to his trial.

Part of the impetus for reconsidering the removal of Jewish civil disabilities prior to emancipation in 1858 was a shift in the role of state religion as a defining factor in determining Englishness and hence the right to be considered part of the nation. If nominal adherence to the rites of the Church of England had barred Catholics and Dissenters from public office, what could justify the exclusion of the Jews from the body of the nation when this restriction was removed? Macaulay's defense, in *The Edinburgh Review* in January 1831, of removing civil disabilities from the Jews was based on a refutation of the very definition of Englishness, nation, and state. If the state religion is no longer integral to Englishness, then emancipation could not be imagined, as it was in the mid-eighteenth century, as a threat to the Englishman's nation and to his body (in fantasies of forced circumcision and the conversion of St. Paul's to a synagogue).

The Jews were an anomalous alien minority who had benefited since the Restoration from de facto residency status and benign toleration, but now they included a sizable proportion whose birth-place and language were English. As part of the reformulation of the electorate leading up to the Reform of 1867, the concept of nation came to be a community of shared national feelings, which required a common ancestry, origin, and culture.[15] To define the Jews as eligible for franchise was to class them as Englishmen and to redefine the nation whose religious differences were no longer a rational or expedient bar to civil rights. The Jews, however, did not quite fit the category of religious dissenters, from whom civil disabilities ought to be removed as an embarrassing anachronism, nor could they disclaim foreign ancestry and allegiance to a supra-national, extra-territorial community. Their detractors were quick to point to over-representation by mid-century of the Jews as owners of private wealth and as important international financiers dealing in war loans, an alien race whose toleration contradicted the national interest. The racial definition of the Jew speaks to perceived English cultural superiority, and the Oriental image conjures up suspicion of sly turbaned traders sneaking up behind the Jew-peddler to reveal a slimy Levantine deceitfulness and a degenerate descent from ancient Hebrews (the arch-betrayers of the Christians' savior). A cartoon at the time of the failed campaign for Jewish emancipation in 1830 mocks the ridiculous attempt of the Jew-Old Clothes Man to enter Parliament, and warns of the ominous Oriental character lurking behind his disguises. The Jew-Old Clothes Man is doubly suspect because of his crafty bargains and the danger of the old clothes carrying contagion into decent English homes. Significantly, Fagin learns of Oliver's whereabouts from another Jew who has bought Oliver's cast-off rags.

Race could determine physiological and cultural characteristics; physiognomy, for example, was closely connected in the Victorian mind with morality and character, national spirit and cultural heritage. Fagin would then be a representative of the ugly degenerate racial type, the Jew, who is reptilian, parasitic, and irredeemably wicked. How Dickens conceived the Jew as race/nation/religion may be judged from his correspondence with a Jewess, Mrs. Eliza Davis. Mrs. Davis' acquaintance with Dickens began when her husband purchased Dickens' London home, Tavistock House. Dickens thought this was a strange change of ownership, from a famous English novelist to a Jew-banker, but he was pleasantly surprised by the honest and businesslike manner in which the transaction had been completed. Building on that acquaintance, Mrs. Davis wrote on June 22, 1863, to solicit a contribution to the Lady Judith Montefiore Memorial Fund to support a Jewish convalescence home. It is in a letter soliciting a monetary contribution that Mrs. Davis accuses Dickens of encouraging in the portrayal of Fagin a "vile prejudice against the despised Hebrew"—in a land where "the liberty of the subject is fully recognized," unlike those where Jews were still oppressed, as demonstrated by the Damascus Affair, and "where the law knows no distinction of Creed." Dickens, she writes, has wronged a "whole though *scattered nation*" (emphasis in original), something which she apparently thinks should shame an author so celebrated for pleading on behalf of the oppressed of his own country and for contributing to social reform. Benevolence unlimited by "distinctions of Creed," Mrs. Davis is arguing, is the only way to atone.

Dickens had no choice but to submit to moral blackmail and send his contribution "to shew you that I have no feeling toward the Jewish people but a friendly one" and to "bear my testimony" to their "perfect good faith" in business transactions (letter to Mrs. Davis, July 10, 1863).[16] A similar accusation of anti-Semitic prejudice had been voiced in 1854 by *The Jewish Chronicle*, which asked "why Jews alone should be excluded from the 'sympathising heart' of this great author and powerful friend of the oppressed?" What is remarkable here is Mrs. Davis' manipulation of Dickens' national status and particularly her manipulation of Dickens' promotion of benevolence as a Christian ideal (in contrast to the mean Jews, in his *Life of Our Lord*, who hated the Christian savior and wished to have him killed). Charity, as in Mrs. Davis' example of Sir Moses Montefiore, knows no limits of religion. Dickens' response to one of the "wanderers from the Far East" (as Mrs. Davis rather exotically styles herself) is interesting because in its defense of Dickens' portrayal of Fagin it retroactively constructs "the jew" not as a religion (Mrs. Davis' definition of her Creed), but as a race whose "cruel persecution" under King John and Edward I Dickens had condemned in his *Child's History of England*.[17]

"Fagin, in *Oliver Twist*," wrote Charles Dickens in a letter of July 10, 1863, to Mrs. Davis, "is a Jew, because it unfortunately was true of the time to which that story refers, that that class of criminal invariably was a Jew." This oft-quoted self-defense against a charge of anti-Semitism in the portrayal of Fagin claims an objective truth for a fictional characterization—not that all Jews are criminal, but that, at that time, this "class of criminal invariably was a Jew," a libel that actually reverts to the racial criminalization of the Jews by alleging that fences were "invariably" Jews.[18] So Fagin is not to be thought of as "the Jew," as he was called in the novel, but as a bad Jew, because he is a fence.

Dickens offers two further defenses to mitigate Mrs. Davis' expression of deep offense at the portrayal of Fagin, and both are revealing in their ingenuity. First, he notes that the other villains are all Christians (Dickens seems to have forgotten Barney), a claim that would then reclassify Fagin as one of the dangerous classes of the metropolis. Second, Fagin is called "the Jew," not because of his religion, but because of his race: "To describe someone by his religion, like describing a Frenchman or Spaniard as 'the Roman Catholic,' I should do a very indecent thing; but I make mention of Fagin as the Jew because he is one of the Jewish people, and because it conveys that kind of idea of him, which I should give my readers of a Chinaman by calling him a Chinese." It would be offensive, that is, to brand a Frenchman by his religion, as "the Catholic"; however, Dickens seems to be reasoning, "the Jew" is not a definition of religion, but a definition of race. A racial stereotype of the Jew-fence is therefore defensible, for it is not a stereotype of Judaism! In this respect, Fagin's refusal to listen to the venerable rabbis before his execution reinforces the impression that Jewish wickedness was to be seen as a mark of race, not religion.

Mrs. Davis was delighted to read the seventh number of *Our Mutual Friend*, where Riah is introduced, and writes again to Dickens, on November 13, 1864, breaking "a promise" (she must have been aware of being a troublesome and inveterate letter-writer!). In her letter she thanks the author for "a great compliment paid to myself and my people," but then goes on to criticize the character of Riah for uttering the Tetragrammaton, something that no real Jew would do. She also objects that while Riah bears some resemblance to an "aged Hebrew" living not far from St. Mary Axe, his costume is quite untypical of English Jews, as is his habit of kissing his benefactor's hand, a gesture typical of Polish Jews—the perceived uncouth and unassimilated *Ostjude* who were fast outnumbering the assimilated *Sephardim* and from whom Mrs. Davis would presumably prefer to disassociate herself. This complaint of fallacious verisimilitude is accompanied by a further homily on showing kindness to strangers as a Jewish belief that cuts across religious divisions of faith. Dickens responds by admitting error and justifying himself on the grounds that dress and manners serve a picturesque effect, thereby placing Riah firmly in a Romantic tradition of the wanderer. "Picturesque" is how Riah is described in the novel, in contrast, we should note, to the melodramatic grotesque features of Fagin. Dickens concludes by reiterating once more that he wishes to be as ever "the best of friends with the Jewish people." Again, Mrs. Davis has defined the Jew in religious terms that are inseparable from race, and, since the Jew is still to some extent a stranger, despite the Jews' recent emancipation, the Jew is enjoined by religion to show charity because the Jews were strangers in the land of Egypt. Dickens has responded in racial terms by calling the Jews a people and has ingeniously distanced himself from stereotyping. Each of these different perceptions of the Jew reflects changing attitudes to race and nationhood in the middle of the nineteenth century.

Uriah, Maria, Riah

Fagin is a cold-blooded monster feigning "abject humility," like the slimy and hypocritical red-haired Uriah Heep; both are impervious to conversion. Fagin is a despicable villain, not just brutish like Sikes, and his villainy deserves vengeful hatred, whether one sees his portrayal as a scapegoat for capitalism or a transference of the psychic injury and social shame for his father's financial incompetence that Dickens felt in his days at the Blacking Warehouse and when unsuccessfully courting Maria Beadnall. The owner of a debtors' sponging-house, where Dickens' father was once arrested, is renamed Solomon Jacobs in "Passage in the Life of Mr. Watkins Tottle" (1835), included in *Sketches by Boz,* and Arthur is arrested in *Little Dorrit* (*LD* II.xxvi.784–5) by "an elderly member of the Jewish persuasion, preserved in rum," who lisped "'a tyfling madder ob bithznithz,' and executed his legal function." In that novel, Maria Beadnall was turned into Flora, who remarks on the Jews not eating ham, that these are "scruples of conscience which we must all respect though I must say I wish they had them equally strong when they sell us false articles for real that certainly ain't worth the money" (*LD* I.xxiv.328). The prejudiced caricature of "the jew" seems to carry some of the recurrent anxiety throughout Dickens' work that the shameful past will catch up with the author and shatter the hard-won bourgeois security. Amy Dorrit, for example, is as frightened by Rigaud, the red-haired bogey of the city in *Little Dorrit,* pursuing her in the Alps, as Oliver is when Fagin peeps in at the Maylies' pastoral haven. The transformation of a personal bogey of the city into other characters continues through Dickens' career. Jaggers might not be an evil genius like Fagin, but he belongs to the whole corrupt system of injustice and acts as a powerful manipulator in the world of "portable property"; interestingly, Jaggers is beset by a comical Jewish criminal trying to buy off the law and pleading for intercession in his case.

Riah, on the other hand, is an ideal type who only pretends to be a villain. It is Mrs. Davis who understood Riah to be a correction of Fagin when, on February 6, 1867, she sent Dickens a specially bound Hebrew Bible with English translation, presented by a Jewess, "in grateful and admiring recognition of his having exercised the noblest quality man can possess; that of atoning for an injury as soon as conscious of having inflicted it."[19] This is also the year Dickens eliminated Fagin's epithet "the Jew" in part, but not all of *Oliver Twist*—mainly and significantly in the final chapters and the trial scene. The fact that some twenty-six years had passed since the publication of *Oliver Twist,* during which time Dickens made no public apology for Fagin, makes less likely any such "atonement," but this did not deter Mrs. Davis from pursuing the notion, and in a note of February 6, 1867, Mrs. Davis assured Dickens how much she appreciated his "nobility" in depicting Riah "in contrast to Fagin." "Most gratefully," she wrote, "do my people accept the spirit of the work."[20]

Riah, of course, is no more a real Jew than was Fagin. He is, like Shylock, a Jew turned "gentle" when he embodies a Christian ideal of charity and is discovered to be only playing "the jew" as cover for the real usurer Fledgeby (the "gentle Jew" recalls Shakespeare's play on gentle/gentile). Appearances, however, are deceiving in the opposite sense to Shylock's goodly apple: Riah is, as Jenny puts it, a sheep in wolf's clothing. The old Jew, who conventionally stands for the exacting, vengeful Old Law, extends selfless love and charity to the stranger (in the spirit of Mrs. Davis' admonition), takes in a Christian virgin on the run from her suitor who attempts through perfidy to procure her, and showers benevolence on Jenny Wren. This is an Aaron, an Old Clothes Man, in Eugene's demeaning mockery, bidden go to his synagogue. Yet Riah performs altruistic good deeds as if he were Portia's candle lighting a naughty world (he could be another mutual friend).[21] The reversal of identity mocks prejudiced stereotypes of the Jew; yet, it is also part of a major pattern of such identity reversals in *Our Mutual Friend,* whose plot hinges on John Harmon's disguise and resurrection to test Bella, Boffin's disguise as a miser to fool Wegg and educate Bella, and the exposure of the Veneerings as wasteful parasites.

Riah is a minor figure in the novel, unlike Fagin, who is the arch-villain of *Oliver Twist;* yet Riah plays the mean Jew who feigns poverty and who must defer to his principal (as Shylock does to Tubal), a "convenient fiction" for the comic Machiavellan, Fascination Fledgeby, who himself cannot disbelieve that all Jews are wealthy and liars. This is one of Judah's "dodges" and Riah is the dodgerest of dodgers, as Fledgeby insinuates when wheedling out of Jenny Wren the information as to Lizzie's whereabouts. Riah is "Riah the Jew" or "the Jew" in the eyes of those whom he squeezes for payment of loans at Fledgeby's instigation, such as Lemmle and Twemlow; looking on at the extortion of Twemlow, Jenny Wren herself mistakes Riah for the Wolf who will sell and betray Lizzie like Judas. However, the Jew is not held totally blameless for the prejudice against him since he has acquiesced in playing the role of scapegoat:

> "It looked so bad, Jenny," responded the old man, with gravity, "that I will straightway tell you what an impression it wrought upon me. I was hateful in mine own eyes. I was hateful to myself, in being so hateful to

the debtor and to you. But more than that, and worse than that, and to pass out far and broad beyond myself—I reflected that evening, sitting alone in my garden on the housetop, that I was doing dishonour to my ancient faith and race. I reflected—clearly reflected for the first time—that in bending my neck to the yoke I was willing to wear, I bent the unwilling necks of the whole Jewish people. For it is not, in Christian countries, with the Jews as with other peoples. Men say, 'This is a bad Greek, but there are good Greeks. This is a bad Turk, but there are good Turks.' Not so with the Jews. Men find the bad among us easily enough—among what peoples are the bad not easily found?—but they take the worst of us as samples of the best; they take the lowest of us as presentations of the highest; and they say 'All Jews are alike.' If, doing what I was content to do here, because I was grateful for the past and have small need of money now, I had been a Christian, I could have done it, compromising no one but my individual self. But doing it as a Jew, I could not choose but compromise the Jews of all conditions and all countries. It is a little hard upon us, but it is the truth. I would that all our people remembered it! Though I have little right to say so, seeing that it came home so late to me." (*OMF* IV.IX.795)

Riah is not so much a good Jew in contrast to Fagin's bad Jew, as an anti-archetype of the Jew, only acting the anti-Christ/Usurer, "the monster of an Israelite," who allows himself to be taken for "quite a Shylock."

Riah's portrait is permeated by a Romantic reception of the figure of the biblical prophet, and he practices a romanticized Christian compassion missing in the materialist hedonist society of the Veneerings. Riah is a Wandering Jew from the East,

> an old Jewish man in an ancient coat, long of skirt, and wide of pocket. A venerable man, bald and shining at the top of his head, and with long grey hair flowing down at its sides and mingling with his beard. A man who with a graceful Eastern action of homage bent his head, and stretched out his hands with the palms downward, as if to deprecate the wrath of a superior. (*OMF* II.v.328)

His flowing dress, a "veritable gabardine," is as ancient and as old-fashioned (a significant word in Dickens' vocabulary of approval) as he is: his "rusty large-brimmed low-crowned hat" is "as long out of date as his coat; in the corner near it stood his staff—no walking-stick but a veritable staff" (*OMF* II.v.328). The gabardine, according to Mayhew in *London Labour and the London Poor,* was no longer characteristic of street Jews like the Old Clothes Man, while the beard that had made him distinctive fifty years before was now in fashion. Be that as it may, Riah's "graceful Eastern action of homage" orientalizes him, but he has also been Romanticized: "He made a little gesture as though he kissed the hem of an imaginary garment worn by the noble youth before him. It was humbly done, but picturesquely, and was not abasing to the doer" (*OMF* II.v.328–9). A little later, Fledgeby's "grateful servant—in whose race gratitude is deep, strong, and enduring—bowed his head, and actually did now put the hem of his coat to his lips: though so lightly that the wearer knew nothing of it" (*OMF* II.v.335). Rather than a figure of suspicion and intrigue lurking behind the Jew-Old Clothes Man, or the hem-kissing of Mr Jaggers' lisping Jewish supplicant, the picturesque portrait of Riah turns his Orientalism into a racial virtue.[22]

Who is the Christian here, and who the Jew? The money-lender who deals in rags, Riah looks shabby but not mean; Fledgeby does not look shabby but he does look mean. In a neat reversal of the Shylock plot, Riah defers to Fledgeby as "merciful" and a "generous Christian master" (*OMF* II.v.328), for he holds Riah in bond for debts to his late father. Riah meekly turns his cheek as good Christians should to their persecutors, and lets the lie of the Jewish stereotype rebound on the un-Christian Christian. Provoked by Fledgeby's anti-Semitic libel of "sweating a pound," Riah makes a humble protest, "Do you not, sir—without intending it—of a surety without intending it—sometimes mingle the character I fairly earn in your employment, with the character which it is your policy that I should bear?" (*OMF* III.i.482). In the exposure of anti-Semitic prejudice, the Jew is shown to be defenseless because he can never disprove the socio-economic identity that the Christian has invented for him—the deceitful money-lender and wealthy owner of a fancy business. The mean, deceitful, money-grubbing Jew is, of course, also the stereotyped figure at the butt of Sikes' entertaining mockery of Fagin. Fledgeby enjoys the extended joke until he is punished by Jenny Wren when she eventually learns the true identity of Pubsey & Co. As for Fledgeby, in his un-Christian Turkish attire, he warns his fellow-Christians that he will out-Jew them all. So the stereotype has not so much been corrected as reversed.

On the roof with Jenny Wren and Lizzie, Riah has been tasting an English Romantic pastoral above the roof-tops of the polluted Babylon and declaring the kingdom of the meek on earth. Books and the world of the spirit are too much for Fledgeby's poor head, for he cannot see heaven in city smoke. Jenny declares, "And you see the clouds rushing on above the narrow streets, not minding them, and you see the golden arrows pointing at the mountains in the sky from which the wind comes, and you feel as if you were dead." When asked how it feels to be dead, she replies, "And such a chain has fallen from you, and such a strange good sorrowful happiness comes upon you!" (*OMF* II.v.334). As in the gardens atop the Delectable Mountains after Christian and Hopeful leave Vanity Fair in *Pilgrim's Progress,* or the Arcadian bower enjoyed by Adam, Eve, and Raphael in *Paradise Lost,* this is a rural innocence unpolluted by Satan "long in populous City pent,/Where Houses thick and Sewers annoy the Air" (IX:445–6). The golden radiance of the child–woman's hair shines with the "Glory" of the divine clouds trailed by her soul, an intimation of immortality in a poor travesty of Wordsworthian nature, but that shares a Christian belief in the spiritual home that is in heaven (John 3). Riah, who is both the Wandering Jew and the Blakean prophet walking the midnight streets of the city of destruction, has gained this kingdom of heaven through a vision of innocence in experience. Jenny Wren fancied she "saw him come out of his grave! He toiled out at that low door so bent and worn, and then he took his breath and stood upright, and looked all round him at the sky, and the wind blew upon him, and his life down in the dark was over!" (*OMF* II.v.334). Fledgeby, like Milton's Satan, must go down in unredeemed and unenlightened darkness to the illegible streets of Mammon's City of Experience below, where (echoing Shylock) he can only urge Riah to fasten the house doors.

The Christian scriptural source of Riah's identity is no less apparent when Riah, true to his *racial* characteristic of charity to strangers (as distinct from Mrs. Davis's insistence on this virtue as a *religious* obligation), rescues Lizzie, who has been quarreling with her brother:

> "He is a thankless dog," said the Jew, angrily. "Let him go. Shake the dust from thy feet and let him go. Come, daughter! Come home with me—it is but across the road—and take a little time to recover your peace and to make your eyes seemly, and then I will bear you company through the streets. For it is past your usual time, and will soon be late, and the way is long, and there is much company out of doors to-night." (*OMF* II.xv.462–3)

Not only is he a Good Samaritan, but the Jew has found a beautiful daughter in the paradigm of the ugly Jewish father and his beautiful daughter who runs away and converts.[23] However, this time the Jew is saving her from the wicked Christian lover, the discontented loiterer, Eugene Wrayburn. Unlike Fagin slinking through the mud in search of offal, Riah is a patriarchal figure of Eternity who goes "his patient way; stealing through the streets in his ancient dress, like the ghost of a departed Time" (*OMF* II.xv.465). Riah's "perfect patience" and submission is a racial characteristic akin to Shylock's tribal badge of sufferance, and when he waits on Fledgeby's doorstep, it "was characteristic of his habitual submission, that he sat down on the raw dark staircase, as many of his ancestors had probably sat down in dungeons, taking what befell him as it might befall" (*OMF* III.i.480).

In contrast to Fagin's parody of the work ethic and his devilish trapping of innocent Oliver in the labyrinth of the city, the Paper Mill offers a vision of the Blakean New Jerusalem with its ideal working-conditions in a green and pleasant land blessed by the mutual benevolence of the Jews. The context of Betty Higden's Ascension, at the last station of her cross fleeing the cruel Poor Law and robbed by Rogue Riderhood, who has declared in mockery of John 11:25, "I am the Lock," underscores the symbolic place of the Jews in a redemptive plot that concludes the novel with the Romantic ideal of Harmony, in the rainbow-paradise the resurrected John Harmon builds for the new baby. These idealized Jews follow Puritan principles of thrift and industriousness and encourage those qualities in Lizzie—the best factory-worker Harriet Martineau could have wished for! Dickens disabuses the reader of a common misconception of Jews and dismisses the threat to Christianity common in anti-Jewish rhetoric, but in doing so he attributes to the Jews Christian virtues of charity and benevolence influenced by Romantic ideals of toleration and compassion, virtues that characterize Dickens' heroes, so lacking in the world of Dombey, Gradgrind, or the Veneerings.

Suffering, wise, deserving of grace, teaching patience in the face of hatred and cruelty, Riah is one more dissimulator in the novel, besides Boffin and John, who show what is wrong with a society of speculators and money-lenders, a society that does not do as it would be done by. Dickens' Riah points to shifts in the cultural representation of "the jew" since the admission of Rothschild to Parliament and paves the way for another ecumenical anti-type who presents England with a rather different Romantic ideal of race and nation, Daniel Deronda.

Notes

1. For the post-war debate on Dickens' anti-Semitism, see: Leslie Fiedler, "What Can We Do About Fagin?" *Commentary* 7 (1949): 411–18; Edgar Johnson, "Dickens, Fagin, and Mr. Riah," *Commentary* 8 (1950): 47–50; Lauriat Lane, "Oliver Twist: A Revision," *Times Literary Supplement,* July 20, 1951, 460. Lane continued the debate with "Dickens' Archetypal Jew," *P. M. L. A.* 73 (1958): 94-100, to which Harry Stone responded in "Dickens and the Jews," *Victorian Studies* 2 (1959): 223–53. Montagu Frank Modder takes an empirical approach in *The Jew in the Literature of England* (Philadelphia: Jewish Publication Society of America, 1939; reprint,

Cleveland: Meridian Books, 1960), 217–36. For a psychological standpoint on anti-Jewish prejudices in Dickens, see Anne Naman, *The Jew in the Victorian Novel* (New York: AMS Press, 1980), 57–95. See also Milton Kerker, "Charles Dickens, Fagin and Riah," *Midstream* 45, 8 (December 1999): 33–6; Deborah Heller, "The Outcast as Villain and Victim: Jews in Dickens' *Oliver Twist* and *Our Mutual Friend*," in *Jewish Presences in English Literature*, ed. Derek Cohen and Deborah Heller (Montreal: McGill-Queen's University Press, 1990), 40–60. A methodological discussion can be found in Mark H. Gelber, "Teaching 'Literary Anti-Semitism': Dickens' *Oliver Twist* and Freytag's *Soll und Haben*," *Comparative Literature Studies* 16, 1 (1979): 1–11. The following editions will be used for this chapter: *Little Dorrit*, ed. John Holloway (Harmondsworth: Penguin English Library, 1967); *Oliver Twist*, ed. Peter Fairclough (Harmondsworth: Penguin English Library, 1966); and *Our Mutual Friend*, ed. Stephen Gill (Harmondsworth: Penguin English Library, 1971). References to the novels will be indicated parenthetically in the text, with large Roman numerals indicating book, small Roman numerals chapter, and arabic numerals page numbers.
2. David Philipson, *The Jew in English Fiction*, 5th ed. (New York: Bloch, 1927), 88–106; see Stone also. Jonathan H. Grossman mounts a resistance to the mimetic fallacy in "The Absent Jew in Dickens: Narrators in *Oliver Twist*, *Our Mutual Friend*, and *A Christmas Carol*," *Dickens Studies Annual* 24 (1996): 37–57.
3. See G. K. Anderson, *The Legend of the Wandering Jew* (Providence, RI: Brown University Press, 1965).
4. See James Shapiro, *Shakespeare and the Jews* (New York: Columbia University Press, 1996); and Michael Ragussis, *Figures of Conversion: "The Jewish Question" and English National Identity* (Durham: Duke University Press, 1995).
5. On the femininity of Fagin and Riah, see Murray Baumgarten, "Seeing Double: Jews in the Fiction of F. Scott Fitzgerald, Charles Dickens, Anthony Trollope, and George Eliot," in *Between Race and Culture: Representations of "the Jew" in English and American Literature*, ed. Bryan Cheyette (Stanford: Stanford University Press, 1996), 52–3. On feminization of the Jew's body, see Sander Gilman, *The Jew's Body* (London: Routledge, 1991).
6. On Romantic constructions of nationhood, see Marlon B. Ross, "Romancing the Nation-State: The Poetics of Romantic Nationalism," in *Macropolitics of Nineteenth-Century Literature: Nationalism, Exoticism, Imperialism*, ed. Jonathan Arac and Harriet Ritvo (Philadelphia: Pennsylvania University Press, 1991), 56–85.
7. Baumgarten, 49–50.
8. Stone discusses the influence of this latter play on the portrait of Riah (236–7).
9. Steven Marcus, "Who is Fagin?" in his *Dickens from Pickwick to Dombey* (London: Chatto & Windus, 1965), 358–78.
10. I use the quotations marks of Jean François Lyotard, found in his *Heidegger et "les Juifs,"* trans. Andreas Michel and Mark S. Roberts (Minneapolis: University of Minnesota Press, 1990). Bryan Cheyette has adopted this usage for his studies of cultural anti-Semitism in modern Britain; see his

anthology, *Between Race and Culture: Representations of "the Jew" in English and American Literature.*
11. William Galperin, "Romanticism and/or Antisemitism," in *Between Race and Culture,* ed. Bryan Cheyette, 16–26.
12. John Fisher Murray, *The World of London* (Edinburgh: Blackwood, 1843), 1:255.
13. Excerpts from Robert Southey's *Letters from England* (1807) and William Hazlitt's essay in *The Tatler* (1831), as quoted in Modder, 324–9; Coleridge, *The Table-Talk and Omiana,* ed. T. Ashe (London: G. Bell, 1905), 101–2.
14. See Charles Bosanquet, *London: Some Account of its Growth, Charitable Agencies and Wants* (London: Hatchard & Co., 1868).
15. See David Feldman, *Englishmen and Jews: Social Relations and Political Culture, 1840–1914* (New Haven: Yale University Press, 1994), 72–82; and David S. Katz, *The Jews in the History of England, 1485–1850* (Oxford: Oxford University Press, 1994). For a survey of Victorian attitudes to race, see Robert Young, *Colonial Desire: Hybridity in Theory, Culture and Race* (London: Routledge, 1995). On the racialization of "the jew" in a later period, see Bryan Cheyette, *Constructions of "the Jew" in English Literature and Society: Racial Representations, 1875–1945* (Cambridge: Cambridge University Press, 1993).
16. *The Letters of Charles Dickens,* under the general editorship of Madeline House, Graham Storey, and Kathleen Tillotson (Oxford: Oxford University Press, 1965–2002), 10:269–70.
17. This was a point Dickens had made in responding in 1854 to an invitation to address an anniversary dinner of the Westminster Jewish Free School (Stone, 223). The Dickens–Davis correspondence has been discussed by Heller, Baumgarten, and others, but not usually in its political or cultural context.
18. In the entry on Ikey Solomons, the notorious Jewish criminal on whom Dickens supposedly modeled Fagin, in the second volume of *The New Newgate Calendar,* there is not the slightest suggestion that fences were predominantly Jews at this time, even though the author discusses trades of Jews in the East End and mentions their connection with Dutch Jews who handled stolen bank-notes. Nor does Henry Mayhew in volume four of *London Labour and the London Poor* identify Jews with the training of pickpockets. The "fact" that fences were invariably Jews was more likely a persistence of prejudice found, for example, in Watts Phillips' *The Wild Tribes of London.*
19. Dickens, *Letters,* 11:322 n7. The Davis–Dickens correspondence was partly published by Cecil Roth in his *Anglo-Jewish Letters (1158–1917)* (London: Soncino Press, 1938), 304–9; see also Stone, 249–50.
20. Dickens, *Letters,* 11:322 n6.
21. Murray Baumgarten (51) suggests Riah is named for the Hebrew *re'ah* ("friend, neighbor"), as in the biblical commandment "to love one's neighbor as oneself," but this seems to me doubtful considering Dickens' evident lack of familiarity with the Hebrew language.
22. Goldie Morgentaler, in *Dickens and Heredity: When Like Begets Like* (London: Macmillan Press, and New York: St. Martin's, 2000), points to

the confusion of racial definitions of the Jews as being of ancient Hebrew stock and of mixed Caucasian origins (152–3).
23. See Harold Fisch, *The Dual Image: The Figure of the Jew in English and American Literature* (London: World Jewish Library, 1971). One thinks of Abigail and Jessica, but also Scott's Rebecca; her father, like Shylock, stops to think (if only momentarily) of his ducats when his daughter is in danger.

Part III
Jewish Writers and British Romanticism

Chapter 9
British–Jewish Writing of the Romantic Era and the Problem of Modernity: The Example of David Levi

Michael Scrivener

The British–Jewish writing current during the Romantic era illustrates how British Jews negotiated the problem of modernity, which was quite differently than the Jews in Continental Europe. As explained by historians Todd Endelman, David Katz, and David Ruderman, British Jews accepted and adapted to modernity while at the same time they retained a Jewish identity.[1] Whether British Jews wrote in Hebrew, like Mordecai Schnaber Levison, Abraham Tang, and Jacob Hart, or in English, like David Levi, Isaac D'Israeli, Daniel Mendoza, Emma Lyon, Levy Alexander, and Hyman Hurwitz, or both English and Hebrew (Levison and Tang), they allowed themselves to be influenced by British and European currents of thought. Anglophone writers addressed both Jews and Gentiles, and when they defended the Jewish community, they did so forthrightly. In numerous texts by British Jews one finds a recurrent pattern: Jewish difference makes itself fit into already existing generic conventions in much the same way that British Jews became acculturated. Against Christian conversionist pressures, these texts affirm Jewish identity with varying degrees and strategies of defiance. Although Britain had no conventional *Haskalah*—modernizing Enlightenment movement of cultural renewal and reform led by an intellectual elite—which the German states did indeed have, Britain had a modernizing Jewry nevertheless, as well as reformist writers who tried to play the role of *maskil*, someone who was critical of traditional beliefs and practices and who adapted Jewish culture to modernity. British Jewry embraced modernity to such a high degree that there was anxiety over retention of Jewish tradition and maintenance of Jewish continuity, even if such modernism rarely took the form of Reform Judaism.

D'Israeli did indeed break with the Jewish community, but his writing, even before that, was not evidently constrained by his Jewishness. His exit from the Jewish community was neither inevitable nor total, reflected by his son's provocative self-fashioning as a religious Christian and an ethnic Jew.[2] Some of the writers were theologically adventurous, like the deistic Tang, while others, like Hurwitz and Joshua Van Oven, were moderate reformers. David Levi, whom this essay will concentrate on, was a fierce defender of orthodoxy, but the style of his defense—pugnacious, idiomatically English, courageous in its choice of antagonists (members of Parliament and Anglican notables, not just Dissenters and radicals)—was so fearless that his writing does not truly resemble comparable writings from the Continent. Moreover, Levi's writing illustrates a process of what David Ruderman has called the "Englishing" of British Jewry, the adaptation of Judaism to English ideas, language, and culture.

This Englishing process can also be seen in many other British Jewish texts, including Daniel Mendoza's memoir in which an established, conventional aspect of British culture—boxing—becomes transformed by Jewish innovation. Mendoza's Jewishness is not prominent in his memoir, but it is not repressed or muted, either. Indeed, there are several key parts of the narrative that turn on Jewishness: as a young man before he is a professional boxer he protects with his fists the greengrocer for whom he works and who is subject to harassment solely because of her Jewishness; he has numerous fights, early and late, with anti-Semitic bullies; and in virtually all representations of his fights he is known as "the Jew" Mendoza.[3] British boxing, because of Mendoza and other Jews, becomes Jewish, and the Jews become British. Mendoza's specific contributions to boxing—defensive tactics, scientific training, reliance on balance, quickness, and strategy rather than brute strength—transform the sport, thus marking a cultural hybridization. In the various prints of Mendoza at the time he is identified as Jewish but he is not caricatured as a stereotypical Jew, thus suggesting a level of cultural acceptance.[4]

Although Jews at the time did not enjoy full legal rights and were victims of snobbery, stereotyping, and occasionally worse forms of prejudice, another story of the British Jews is how they retained their Jewishness while at the same time appropriated British and European culture. Accordingly, a philo-Semitic play like Richard Cumberland's *The Jew* (London, 1794) lacks the centrality for British Jews that Gotthold Lessing's two philo-Semitic plays (*Die Juden,* 1749; and *Nathan der Weise,* 1779) possessed in the German states.[5] Lessing (1729–81) argued for the humanity of Jews; Jews in Britain had gone well beyond the point where they had to defend their humanity. British

Jewish writers embodied in their texts a sense of dual identity, which was not without its anxieties, of course, but it was more secure than the more problematic dual identity of the *maskilim* in Continental Europe. Present in Britain was a literary public sphere that permitted Jewish participation in a degree far in advance of political emancipation. The public sphere in Continental Europe was not nearly as powerful, hobbled as it was by a weaker middle class and stronger absolutist governments.[6]

To illustrate how modernity is worked out in British–Jewish writing, I will concentrate on David Levi, the theological controversialist. He illustrates perhaps better than anyone else how a British Jew could make use of the public sphere to "English" Judaism, defend the Jewish community, and effect a hybridization of British and Jewish cultures, however marked with ambivalence.

David Levi (1740–99) as Example

Of the unknown and barely known Jewish writers that David Ruderman has brought to our attention recently in his magnificent study, *Jewish Enlightenment in an English Key*, David Levi stands out as the exemplary figure for a number of reasons. First, unlike his friend and patron, Jacob Hart (Eliakim ben Abraham, 1756–1814), Levi wrote in English, not Hebrew. By writing only in Hebrew, Hart limited his audience to only the most literate Jews, few of whom resided in Britain, most of whom lived in the German states and eastern Europe. Levi and Eliakim were well acquainted, as Levi printed and sold Eliakim's books,[7] and Eliakim—a prosperous jeweler—established a philanthropic fund that supported Levi in his scholarly research on and writing of *Lingua Sacra* (5 vols.; London, 1785–87).[8] *Lingua Sacra* was a Hebrew language primer as well as Hebrew/English dictionary with extensive commentary on theological and rabbinic controversies. From Arthur Barnett's description of Eliakim's work, Eliakim seems to be something like a Jewish William Blake in several respects: he defends his religion against the Enlightenment logic of scientific materialism, targeting especially one of Blake's antagonists, Newton, and also like Blake linking political liberty with biblical prophecy. Cecil Roth characterizes Eliakim thus: "Strongly orthodox in feeling, [Eliakim's writings] are modern in conception, written in a lively and accurate Hebrew, tackle in an energetic fashion problems of the hour and show a remarkably wide knowledge of contemporary scientific literature in English and the European languages."[9] The example of Eliakim, a London-born Jew like Levi, his contemporary, suggests an option that only the most scholarly British

Jews could have taken, but such an option retains Jewishness at the price of limiting his audience to Jews only. Accordingly, British readers, Jewish and Gentile, were unaware of Hart's anti-modernist critique of Newton and Locke, *Milchamot Adonai* ("Wars of the Lord," London, 1794). Drawing upon the British Tory writers, Robert Greene and William Whiston, as well as the great Spanish rabbinical writer, Isaac Abravanel (1437–1508), Hart attacked what he felt were the metaphysical foundations of a modernity that threatened religious faith and identity.[10] By writing in English and only in English, Levi fused together a Jewish and a British cultural focus and enjoyed a readership of British Jews and Gentiles. On the Continent there was a sufficiently large number of literate Jews who worked in Hebrew and who could sustain a project like *Ha-Me'asef* (1784–97), a journal devoted to the grammatical and aesthetic study of Hebrew by followers of Moses Mendelssohn (1729–86),[11] but until the rise of Zionism at the end of the nineteenth century, Hebrew-language literature was for a small minority readership.

Levi was exemplary also in his courageous seizing of opportunities to defend the Jewish community at a time when the received wisdom was to stay out of arguments with Gentiles who were so much more numerous and more powerful. He read the cultural situation accurately, however, so that he could criticize harshly anti-Jewish writings without also at the same time bringing down on the Jewish community harsh treatment. In fact, Levi's combative writings helped raise tolerance for theological debate between Christians and Jews to a new level. A popular print of the day draws a parallel between the boxing victories of Daniel Mendoza and the debating victory of David Levi over their respective Gentile opponents. Both Mendoza and Levi were seen to have been battling and to have defeated Christians. Moreover, in both cases, the Jewish victory is not counteracted by Gentile retribution.[12] Levi rebutted what he deemed the anti-Jewish ideas of Anglican theologians like Henry Prideaux (1648–1724) and Anselm Bayley (d. 1794); radicals like the Unitarian Joseph Priestley (1733–1804) and the deist Thomas Paine (1737–1809); influential Christian scholars of Hebrew like Benjamin Kennicott (1718–83) and Bishop Robert Lowth (1710–87); and even members of Parliament like Nathaniel B. Halhed (1751–1830), defender of Richard Brothers (1757–1824).[13]

If one compares the debates between Moses Mendelssohn and his Christian opponents—Johann Casper Lavater (1741–1801) and Friedrich Heinrich Jacobi (1743–1819)—one is struck above all by the insecurity and anxiety of Mendelssohn and the pugnacious confidence of Levi. Just as German Jewry was much more vulnerable than British

Jewry, so the public sphere in which Mendelssohn operated was far less extensive and capacious, permitting far less room for negotiation. Lavater, who insisted that Mendelssohn defend Judaism or convert to Christianity, forced Mendelssohn to pay a price that Mendelssohn was in no position to circumvent, if he wished to continue writing as a philosopher in the European intellectual community. Mendelssohn's heroic example illustrated that a Jew could retain his religion and still participate in the most up-to-date discussions of philosophy, but his way of harmonizing modernity and Judaism was neither painless nor unproblematic.[14] Priestley, who invites Jews to convert to Unitarianism, does not exert the coercive power wielded by Mendelssohn's opponents. In fact, only Levi decided to respond to Priestley, and his response provided an extensive defense of Judaism and a critique of Priestley's theology. As a millenarian, Priestley assigns an important role to the Jews who are to be restored to Zion and whose conversion is an indispensable event in the apocalyptic drama of Jesus' second coming. The not-so-subtle subtext of Priestley's letter to the Jews, however, is that if they refuse even this most magnanimous offer, they will have illustrated once again their evil propensities that God has been punishing these many centuries since they killed and denied Jesus. Even so, the "enlightened" Christian is not supposed to harm the "wrongheaded" Jews; God will mete out the appropriate correction.[15] Levi, however, is not intimidated and exploits the opportunity to cite Jewish survival as a sign of Divine favor.[16]

For the Jew fully within modernity, "Jewishness forms only a portion of his total identity." According to Michael A. Meyer, "Jewish identity becomes segmental and hence problematic" only in the second half of the eighteenth century.[17] In Britain, however, as Todd Endelman describes, Jews had an easier transition from pre-modern traditionalism than did the Jews in the German states and Continental Europe. In the eighteenth century British Jews started to act in many respects like other British people, and "adopted the habits of Englishmen because they wanted to feel at home there. They quietly abandoned the ways of traditional Judaism, whose practices set them apart from other men and interfered with their pursuit of pleasure and success."[18] Yet they retained enough Judaism to maintain a Jewish identity, thus illustrating that modernity did not necessarily doom Jewish continuity, even if it did produce inevitable changes.

The final exemplary aspect of Levi I want to discuss is his effective use of the literary public sphere. An accomplished Hebraist and a religiously knowledgeable Jew, but not an ordained rabbi, Levi was a largely self-taught shoemaker, hatter, and finally printer who reached Jewish and Christian readers. As an artisan autodidact, Levi was a publishing author a generation before such shoemaker writers in the self-taught tradition became commonplace in nineteenth-century Britain.[19] That Levi does not make his first appearance in print until he is forty-three years old indicates a long literary apprenticeship and limited opportunities, not unusual for a working artisan. Shoemaking was, according to the historian Jacques Rancière, the path taken by the most intellectually ambitious artisans because the job allowed more opportunity for reading and writing than most other trades. Levi's friendship with Henry Lemoine (1756–1812), son of a Huguenot refugee, started in 1780 when they met at Lemoine's Bishopsgate bookstall, thus giving Levi an opening to the world of print culture and the literary market. With Lemoine and others, Levi dined at the home of publisher George Lackington, who formed a lower-middle-class salon to assist the popular publisher in stocking the most marketable books for sale. Just as Joseph Johnson, the successful Dissenting publisher, was at the center of an intellectual hub of advanced middle-class thinking, hosting parties and providing literary patronage for writers like Mary Wollstonecraft and William Godwin,[20] so Lackington sponsored his own literary circle that was much more modest in its philosophical ambitions, more plebeian in its social style, but also more aggressively popular and commercial.[21] The importance of these literary circles in constituting, sustaining, and reproducing a literary public sphere cannot be exaggerated. Writers met one another, exchanged ideas, tested arguments, and formed collaborative relationships. For example, Lemoine helped Levi get various theological texts he might not have gotten otherwise. Similarly, Lemoine's Jewish contacts were indispensable when he collaborated with Levy Alexander on the sketch of Abraham Goldsmid's life.[22] These collaborative efforts, however valuable, did not prevent Lemoine in certain instances from expressing anti-Semitic bias,[23] but this less-than-perfect cultural situation was in advance of the cultural opportunities available to Jews on the Continent. Heine and Börne believed that they had to pay the price of baptism to participate fully in the literary public sphere of Europe. No such price was demanded in Britain.[24]

Levi as Writer

Levi's first book, *A Succinct Account of the Rites and Ceremonies of the Jews* (London, 1783), mediates between Jewish knowledge and, according to the preface, both Gentile and Jewish ignorance. The "rites and ceremonies of the Jews" was an established genre in Christian histories of the

Jews. In Jacques Basnage's history, for example, all of Book Five is devoted to "Rites and Ceremonies."[25] Levi targets for criticism some of the descriptions of Jewish belief found in Humphrey Prideaux's immensely popular history of the Jews from the first temple to the time of Jesus.[26] Levi, who disputes specifically Prideaux's account of the Jewish doctrines of resurrection, predestination, and free will,[27] chooses to refute Prideaux rather than some other commentator perhaps because by 1783 Prideaux's text was the standard. Levi might not have known Basnage's history at that time for there are no references to it; he seems to have depended on his friend Henry Lemoine for getting research materials, but the Huguenot Lemoine probably would have known about his fellow Huguenot Basnage's very famous book and by 1787 Levi is citing Basnage.[28] Levi does not seem to know Abraham Mears's Jewish "rites and ceremonies" that was published in English for an English audience forty-five years earlier.[29] According to one scholar, Levi's account must have been successful because there was no other "rites and ceremonies" by a Jewish writer to appear for another fifty years.[30] Notable in Levi's text is an absence of defensiveness. Although he refutes Prideaux's misrepresentations, he otherwise provides straightforward, unapologetic descriptions of Jewish religious culture, including long sections on the history of the *Mishnah* and the rabbinic sages. He does not defer in any manner to Christian and Deist anti-Talmudic prejudices.

If his target audience was Jews who were ignorant of their religion or who had been misinformed by conversionist Christians, why use English? Levi states in the preface that many Jews did not know Hebrew and were fluent instead in English. He never mentions Yiddish but at that time many British Jews were *Sephardim*—Jews from Spain and Portugal—who did not know Yiddish. Indeed, the wealthiest Jews were Sephardim, so that the low prestige of Yiddish would have been even lower in London at that time. The synagogues in the early nineteenth century tried to banish Yiddish altogether but too many working-class *Ashkenazim*—Jews from Europe—knew only Yiddish, so the battle against Yiddish had to be restrained.[31] Nevertheless, Yiddish was hardly an unproblematic option for Levi.

We do not know if Levi was tempted to write in Hebrew like Eliakim but we do know Levi wrote a capable English prose. Indeed, he was chosen by London's Great Synagogue to translate into English several Hebrew texts in 1790.[32] As an artisan and tradesman with much contact with English-speaking customers, and as a London-born Jew, Levi used a prose that reflects the model of the Puritan plain style—Defoe—rather than the Augustan periods of Johnson. Levi's translations of the liturgy, his writing that undoubtedly had the greatest influence, having been reproduced many times in nineteenth-century daily and holiday prayer books, are either dependent on the King James Version when passages are biblical, or cautiously literal otherwise, producing not great poetry but retaining somewhat the dignity of the original, but at times being also a little stilted. Levi's first line of the *mah nishtannah,* which introduces the four questions chanted by the youngest child during the Passover *seder* service, for example, reads: "Wherefore is this night distinguished from all other nights?" Perhaps Levi got this from an earlier translation, but if he is the first to have phrased it thus, he would have been pleased to know that the North American "Maxwell House *Haggadah*" used by millions of Jews retains that same phrasing in its translation.[33] Even if he did not originate the translation, his choice to retain the earlier translation rather than change it to the less stilted English he was fully capable of writing indicates the stylistic claims to dignity that Scripture possessed for Levi. According to one of the few scholars who have studied English translations of the Jewish liturgy, Levi's translations became "part of the religious outfit of almost every Anglo-Jewish family," Ashkenazi or Sephardi, throughout the nineteenth century.[34]

Levi's influence is not necessarily a sign of translation skill but is rather a sign of British Jewry's deference to British Protestant culture. Levi's "translations" of the *Torah* are almost always identical with the King James Version. His commentary on the opposite page frequently and forthrightly quarrels with the King James translation on theological and grammatical grounds, but there is no attempt to rework the English prose of the Pentateuch to reflect a specifically Jewish perspective. To take just one of many examples, he quarrels with the King James Version of Exodus 24:5 but offers his alternative translation only in the commentary, not in the text proper: "This I think, should be translated thus:—'And he sent the ministers of the children of Israel, and they offered burnt-offerings, &c.' I must likewise, observe, that Scripture generally calleth upper servants lads, or young men, though they be aged."[35] It is anachronistic but heuristically useful to compare the innovative way Martin Buber and Stefan Rosenzweig translated the *Torah* into German; one sees how Buber and Rosenzweig succeeded in producing a decidedly hebraic German translation. That would be one pole, then, of a translation reflecting a genuine dialogue between the two languages that marks the cultural specificity of the Jewish experience with the German language. Levi's translations are very much at the other pole, of mirroring the already existing dominant culture while at the same time acknowledging that the already existing "translation" is not adequate. Levi's deference to the King James Version vies with his knowledge of its inadequacy but neither British Jewry nor Levi himself at this time has the desire to produce a uniquely different English to accommodate Jewish specificity. Although the English translations played no role in the synagogue service—even the Reform services that began many decades after Levi's death were mostly in Hebrew—they are significant in this context in reflecting cultural identity by betraying an ambivalence about English. The holy language is of course Hebrew, but the retention of an "Old Testament" style of translation suggests a tension that has not been fully resolved between Judaism and British identity.

Levi as a Controversialist

Cultural identity, not just theology, governs the logic of Levi's replies to Priestley and other Christian critics of Judaism. In David S. Katz's summary of the Priestley-Levi controversy, he concludes that this "storm of controversy" was so important that it generated texts even after Levi's own death.[36] Open questions were the degree of toleration and acceptance British Gentiles would grant Jews and the degree of acculturation and Britishness Jews wanted to claim. Todd Endelman was the first to capture nicely the tone of the controversy when he cited a contemporary print linking Daniel Mendoza's boxing victory in 1788 with Levi's theological victory over Priestley.[37] One cannot discount an element of ethnic pride in the theological debate. Levi responded to Priestley in the first place against the received wisdom of the Jewish community whose posture was cautious, especially after the vehement repudiation of Jewish rights during the "Jew Bill" controversy of 1753. The Jewish community blamed Levi for risking persecution of Jews by debating publicly with a prominent Christian.[38] Despite these expectations, many Christians "of all denominations" approved of Levi's initial answer to Priestley's challenge.[39] Only one of the published counter-responses to Levi was abusively hostile. "Anti-Socinus," the alias of Anselm Bayly, even threatened to "tear" Levi to "pieces" if he mentioned Jesus Christ again in any of his subsequent writings. Levi is so confident of his public position that he is able to mock Bayly and sarcastically display a feigned dread at what Bayly might do to him.[40] (The pugilistic parallels seemed to be obvious to everyone at the time.) More indicative of public opinion than Bayly's coarse rant is James Bicheno's polite and respectful address, to which Levi responds with amicable disagreement in the spirit of enlightened debate.[41] Even one of the latest responses to Levi, written a decade after Levi's death by the theologically reactionary William Cunninghame, who rehearses the charge of

Jewish deicide for which Jews have properly suffered for centuries, did not pose any threat to the Jewish community.[42] Rather than intimidating Jews, this commonplace rebuttal of Levi was followed seven years later by John "Jew" King republishing Levi's *Dissertations on the Prophecies of the Old Testament*.[43] King, on the margins of the Jewish community, was a figure in the ranks of the political radicals.[44] That Levi was usable by someone like King at a time of great political turmoil when there also did not seem to be any fear of anti-Semitic scapegoating suggests that Jews enjoyed a surprisingly high degree of security and freedom of expression that exceeded their technically legal "rights." According to Endelman, King used the re-publication of Levi's book as an opportunity to announce publicly King's return to Judaism.[45]

The controversy suggests that the public sphere, well ahead of the political institutions and law, acknowledged Jews as full citizens, equal to Christians, even to Protestants. The harsh exchanges between Bayly and Levi, which might appear upon first glance to be almost violent, are in fact just the opposite. As Ruderman explains, "Christians and Jews felt free to verbally assault each other and their faith." One-time friend of Levi's, Bayly is no bigot but a passionate partisan of his religious perspective.[46] Yet another indication of the quality of the public sphere is that Levi, despite his long and bitter conflict with Priestley, was the printer of Priestley's *Inquiry into the Knowledge of the Antient Hebrews Concerning a Future State* (1801). As Ruderman comments: "Levi, the proud and unrepentant Jew," finds nevertheless "common ground with his former antagonist."[47] Enlightenment norms such as the authority of the strongest argument, the impersonality of rational debate, and reliance on evidence and logic in fact sustained the public sphere within which Levi influenced British culture and British culture influenced him.

Levi's polemics are moderately conservative theologically, but they project a vigorously assertive posture in terms of cultural politics. Levi never comes close to making the elegant connections between Judaism and natural religion that Mendelssohn made so famous, but Mendelssohn also never came close to the combative rhetoric Levi uses as a matter of course, such as this from the reply to Thomas Paine: "Surely Sir, you must have considered your readers as no better than *heads* of onions."[48] The *Aufklärer* from Berlin was more personally deferential to his opponents, and stylistically he did not use Yiddish-like phrases about the heads of onions. On the issue that mattered most in the public debates between Jews and Christians—the prospects of Jews converting to Christianity—Levi is provocatively bold: "I am free to assert, that there is scarcely an instance of a Jew ever having embraced

Christianity on the pure principles of religion."[49] He illustrates this point by recalling someone who had converted five separate times and "got a pretty sum of money."[50] The locution "pretty sum of money" is a colloquial turn of phrase one would not find in Mendelssohn either; such diction is a sign of comfort with an urban English of trade and commerce, not just scholarship. Levi's style does not betray the awkward bookishness of some autodidacts. Returning to the content of his statement, one takes note of its uncompromising indictment of Christian coercion. Mendelssohn had to be more careful in his public statements because the political culture and the Christian political authorities in the German states were more malevolent and Mendelssohn played a representative role that Levi plays to a far lesser extent.

One notices something quite new in Levi's 1796 book on prophecy and his 1797 answer to Paine's *Age of Reason*. Levi displays a knowledge of writers—Morgan, Tindal, Bolingbroke, Hume, Voltaire, Spinoza, Lowth, Basnage, Kennicott, Newton—far broader than what he had available in his responses to Priestley. As a consequence he can contest Christian writing on prophecy with more authority and show where Paine gets his Deistic ideas to identify what is new with Paine. There is also a breadth of overall knowledge, almost as if he took Priestley's gibe about being ignorant of secular knowledge to heart.

Levi began his *Dissertations on the Prophecies of the Old Testament* in 1793, at a time of tumultuous political conflict in London. As Jon Mee has illustrated, during the 1790s secular Enlightenment and revolutionary writing mingled often harmoniously with religiously inspired millenarian writing.[51] Perhaps thinking of the revolutionary emancipation of French Jewry, Levi in the preface gives a recapitulation of British Jewish history, highlighting many of the atrocities and injustices the English had inflicted on the Jews.[52] These eight pages are significant because they are a rare reminder by Jew or Gentile of how badly the English had treated the Jews in the medieval period. Although couched in an ambiguous context—the atrocities are both historical and religiously semiotic, signs of Divine displeasure—the short history assigns historical guilt. The book as a whole is not just Jewish theology critical of Christian theology; the book is political in nature and it suggests, if tentatively and hesitantly, issues for a Jewish political agenda. When, for example, Levi discusses the resurrection of the dead, he insists that all Jews, even the ones who have fallen from the faith, those who either pretended to be Christian or converted to Christianity, will enjoy a new birth.[53] The political understanding behind such a theological judgment is that Christian coercion has been so harsh for centuries that Jews are not wholly responsible for apostasy. Apropos a passage in Isaiah, Levi says that "Christianity cannot be the Peaceable kingdom of the Messiah"; all one has to do is look at the history of Christian mistreatment of Jews.[54] However undeveloped, the use of history and the appeal to history point toward a rationalistic theology informed by secular politics.

The logic Levi uses in his critique of Paine is even more insistently secular. Levi defends the Old Testament not just as the word of God, as Divine Revelation, but as literature and history. He makes use of Bishop Lowth's discussion of biblical literature to praise the different literary genres in the Bible.[55] Echoing to some extent the *Haskalah,* Levi also defends the basic precepts of Judaism in terms of its secular influence on morality, from loving the stranger to generous treatment of the poor and socially powerless.[56] Moreover, Jewish law embodies enduring insights into socio-economic justice, as the laws of land distribution, including the Jubilee, prevent concentrations of wealth and mitigate against poverty by institutionalizing God's morality over private property rights.[57] Levi's defense of a favorite Deistic target, the conquest of Canaan, relies largely on a secular logic: the Mosaic sexual morality was superior, and extermination of the residents came only after the resident tribes were offered a peaceful settlement.[58] Notable here is the secular logic. Revelation, even if authentic and definitive in the eyes of an observant Jew, has to be defended as consistent with universal morality.

Another area that Levi develops in his reply to Paine is philological. Paine makes the mistake in *The Age of Reason* of discussing Ibn Ezra— Abraham ben Meir (1092–1167), the great Spanish rabbinical commentator, scientist, and poet—and the meaning of some Hebrew words, something about which Paine knew almost nothing, but Levi a great deal. Levi shows no mercy in illustrating Paine's ignorance.[59] Even here Levi's logic is secular: Paine is wrong not because he does not believe in Torah; he is wrong because he is ignorant of Hebrew. Levi had, in three volumes of *Lingua Sacra,* produced a capable Hebrew grammar, dictionary, and miscellaneous commentary; his level of Hebrew knowledge was far higher than any of his non-Jewish opponents', and whenever he could make the debate one of philological analysis, he was at a great advantage. Indeed, Levi's was the only philologically accurate Hebrew grammar available in English in the late eighteenth century because the Hutchinsonian distortions had for decades interfered with the serious study of Hebrew.[60]

Conclusion

The Mendelssohn friendship with Lessing, which symbolized the unity between Jewish *maskil* and Gentile *Aufklärer,* promised a more tolerant

Europe in the future. Levi's debates with Priestley and others also promised a more tolerant world, but not because of elegant arguments; rather, the vigor of the public sphere that can sustain sometimes coarse and vehement polemic suggests that important issues can be debated between Jews and Gentiles non-violently. In Europe, where the public sphere was more fragile, an apparent politeness concealed Jewish vulnerability. Although the Mendelssohn-Lessing circle was able to maintain such an amicable sub-culture, because the idea of natural religion provided discursive openings for Jew, Christian, and Deist, Mendelssohn and his fellow Jews really needed the assistance of philo-Semitic Gentiles such as Lessing to act as a buffer against the hostile Christian culture. Levi and the Jews in Britain were not in desperate straits at all. As I mentioned earlier, Richard Cumberland's philo-Semitic play, *The Jew* (1794), did not have anything close to the impact of Lessing's *Die Juden* (1749) and *Nathan der Weise* (1779) because anti-Semitism was so much stronger in the German states, which lacked a democratic culture, a strong middle class, and a powerful public sphere. In his famous review of *Die Juden,* Johann David Michaelis (1717–91) remarked on the play's lack of realism because of the portrayal of a virtuous Jew; such a Jew was not conceivable for the Göttingen professor.[61] It is not that Britain lacked raw anti-Semitism, such as William Cobbett's and the High Church Anglicans', but that Jews only infrequently had to experience it. As Endelman suggests, one contributing factor is that Britain had other scapegoats, namely the Irish and Catholics, who took the pressure off Jews.[62]

If we insert Levi into this frame of analysis, we find a mixed situation characteristic of deep ambivalence. Levi affirms Jewish difference in a bold way when he debates Christian critics of Judaism, but he defers to a dominant British Protestantism in his use of the King James Version of Scripture; however, Levi's combative commentary on the inadequate King James Version subverts the deference toward Protestantism. One way to look at the Jewish embrace of the King James Version is to see it as a strategic move: the English translation is Protestant, but the text behind it is Jewish, thus linking together Jew and Briton. The edition of the Torah with Levi's translations and notes published by Levy Alexander is a good example of acculturation with a vengeance. Instead of *Torah* or *Ḥumash,* it is entitled "The Holy Bible." Especially telling are the numerous colored plates that illustrate the narrative; none of them, without exception, makes any attempt to represent the actual Middle Eastern environment in which the events took place. Instead, Jerusalem and Beersheva look like London and Windsor. The plate illustrating the birth of Esau and Jacob shows a huge, lush, regal interior, something like the inside of Windsor Castle. The plate illustrating Abraham entertaining the three angels looks more like something from the set for a BBC production of an Austen novel, more like Abraham the dapper squire getting ready for tea than a desert nomad taking care of visitors. These plates reflect a defensiveness about Jewish identity that is rarely present in Levi's writings.

Levi himself, who had nothing to do with these plates, is best represented perhaps by *Lingua Sacra*, which was published initially in weekly numbers. The early work, which was subsidized to some extent, required sixteen-hour days, six days a week. After he lost his subsidy, he was relieved finally by a fund already mentioned. Levi does not identify Eliakim or any other benefactor by name, but we know it was prosperous Jews who granted him the eighteen shillings a week. He complains of a lack of fellow scholars with whom to consult. The picture one gets from Levi's address "To the Public" (vol. 3) is of a somewhat isolated scholar who knows nevertheless that he is appreciated by the most knowledgeable Jews and who realizes he is performing a useful task by making Hebrew lessons available to the uninstructed and by making Hebrew more accessible to those Jews who need help. Levi says that most of the Jews he knows are not fluent in Hebrew. The Hebrew-to-English dictionary includes not just meanings of words but long notes about rabbinic commentary and biblical scholarship (some of which is Christian), including biographies of the most prominent rabbinical writers. For one man—without *yeshiva* training—to have written such a work is truly remarkable. One can acquire much unsystematic learning by reading around in the dictionary. The commentator to whom Levi turns more than any other is Isaac Abravanel (1437–1508), a favorite as well with Eliakim. For example, Levi takes Abravanel's side in the dispute with the more rationalistic Moses Maimonides (1135–1204) over the Book of Daniel. For Maimonides it is a lesser text within the *Tanakh*—the Hebrew Bible—because Daniel was not a prophet. The more messianic Abravanel, with whom Levi agrees, makes Daniel a prophet and takes seriously the prophetic content of the book in a way that traditional Judaism ordinarily does not. The Book of Daniel, of course, was a favorite Christian text for millenarian prophecy, including the prophetic writing of Priestley. In this one instance Levi is slightly heterodox but the overall commentary is not theologically adventurous. Perhaps we see here in the example of interpreting the Book of Daniel the influence of Protestant millennialism that was so strong during the French Revolution. In Levi's voluminous notes there is no equivalent to Mendelssohn's critique of the rabbinic *ḥerem* (excommunication) or the

Haskalah's neo-Karaite tendencies that elevated the authority of the Hebrew Bible over the Talmud.[63] Several aspects of his revered Abravanel were consistent with a modernizing trend, Abravanel's historical understanding of Scripture, and his willingness to comment on and use Christian scholars, especially the humanists.[64] Despite the centrality of Abravanel, the dictionary has much on and by Maimonides, so that it is not a narrowly focused study.

Lingua Sacra is a textbook with a strong personality. The hand of the autodidact is everywhere, but Levi's passion for learning compensates many times over for the lack of philosophical polish. That someone like Levi was sponsored by the Jewish community to do the work of *Lingua Sacra* tells us that the community would support traditional learning, at least at sixteen shillings a week. Several things are interesting about the subscription list for *Lingua Sacra*. The "Learned Society" in Berlin and Königsberg ordered fifty copies, more than any single British patron. An important goal of the *Haskalah*, of course, was to make Hebrew an object of scholarly study and literary use. The fifty copies suggests that Levi's level of Jewish learning was deemed fairly serious and also accessible. Another thing stands out: although the overwhelming majority of the subscribers have names that seem Jewish, some subscribers are obviously Christian, such as the Reverend W. B. A. Grant of Walworth and John McNair, printer of Edinburgh. Somehow Levi had tapped into a community of scholars, however small, that was interested in his work. Unlike the anachronistic prints in the Levy Alexander "Holy Bible," *Lingua Sacra* has intellectual and cultural integrity. Gentiles and Jews who were reading that text experienced something quite other than Anglicized and Protestant versions of Judaism.

Notes

1. Todd M. Endelman, *The Jews of Georgian England 1714–1830: Tradition and Change in a Liberal Society* (Philadelphia: Jewish Publication Society of America, 1979; reprint, with a new preface, Ann Arbor: University of Michigan Press, 1999); David S. Katz, *The Jews in the History of England 1485–1850* (Oxford: Clarendon Press, 1994); and David B. Ruderman, *Jewish Enlightenment in an English Key: Anglo-Jewry's Construction of Modern Jewish Thought* (Princeton: Princeton University Press, 2000).
2. See Todd M. Endelman, "'A Hebrew to the end': The Emergence of Disraeli's Jewishness," in *The Self-Fashioning of Disraeli, 1818–1851,* Charles Richmond and Paul Smith, ed. (Cambridge: Cambridge University Press, 1998), 106–30. (On Isaac D'Israeli, see "Not for 'Antiquaries,' but for 'Philosophers': Isaac D'Israeli's Talmudic Critique and His Talmudical Way with Literature," Stuart Peterfreund's contribution to this volume-ed.)

3. Daniel Mendoza, *Memoirs of the Life of Daniel Mendoza*, Paul Magriel, ed. (1816; reprint, London and New York: Batsford, 1951), 16; 23–4; passim.
4. There are prints included in the Magriel edition of Mendoza's *Memoirs*.
5. The British Library has a 1781 French translation by J. H. Eberts of *Die Juden—Les Juifs*—and a 1781 translation of *Nathan der Weise* into English by R. E. Raspe (London: J. Fielding). These translations, the earliest I have found, were perhaps provoked by the death of Lessing in 1781.
6. For the public sphere, see Jürgen Habermas, *The Structural Transformation of the Public Sphere: An Inquiry into a Category of Bourgeois Society*, trans. Thomas Burger and Frederick Lawrence (Cambridge, MA: MIT Press, 1989).
7. Arthur Barnett, "Eliakim ben Abraham (Jacob Hart): An Anglo-Jewish Scholar of the Eighteenth Century," *Transactions of the Jewish Historical Society of England* 14 (1935–9): 207–20.
8. Cecil Roth, "The Haskalah in England," in *Essays Presented to the Chief Rabbi Israel Brodie on the Occasion of his Seventieth Birthday*, H. J. Zimmels, J. Rabinowitz, and I. Finestein, ed., 2 vols. (London: Soncino Press, 1967), 1:372–3.
9. Roth, 372–3.
10. Ruderman, 196–9.
11. Michael A. Meyer, *The Origins of the Modern Jew: Jewish Identity and European Culture in Germany, 1749–1824* (Detroit: Wayne State University Press, 1967), 115–18.
12. The front cover of David Ruderman's *Jewish Enlightenment in an English Key* reproduces the 1789 print.
13. For the discussions of Levi's critiques, see Ruderman, chs. 2 and 4; also, Richard H. Popkin, "David Levi, Anglo-Jewish Theologian," *Jewish Quarterly Review* 87 (1996): 79–101.
14. For Mendelssohn's statement on Judaism and modernity, see his *Jerusalem, Or On Religious Power and Judaism*, trans. Allan Arkush (Hanover & London: University of New England Press, 1983). The secondary literature on Mendelssohn is voluminous but I will mention the important biography, Alexander Altmann, *Moses Mendelssohn: A Biographical Study* (Tuscaloosa: University of Alabama Press, 1973). (For a comparison of Mendelssohn's and Blake's *Jerusalems*, see "'What Are Those Golden Builders Doing?': Mendelssohn, Blake and the (Un)Building of *Jerusalem*," Leslie Tannenbaum's contribution to this collection-ed.)
15. Joseph Priestley, *Letters and Addresses to the Jews* [1787–99], in *The Theological and Miscellaneous Works of Joseph Priestley*, J. T. Rutt, ed., 25 vols. (1817–32; reprint, New York: Kraus Reprint, 1972), 20:227–300.
16. Popkin, 79–101.
17. Meyer, 8.
18. Todd M. Endelman, "The Englishness of Jewish Modernity in England," in Jacob Katz, ed., *Toward Modernity: The European Jewish Model* (New Brunswick and Oxford: Transaction Books, 1987), 229. See also his *Radical Assimilation in English Jewish History, 1656–1945* (Bloomington: University of Indiana Press, 1990).

19. For the self-taught tradition of artisan writers, see Jacques Rancière, "The Myth of the Artisan: Critical Reflections on a Category of Social History," *International Labour and Working Class History* 24 (1983): 1–12; Brian Maidment, ed., *The Poorhouse Fugitives: Self Taught Poets and Poetry in Victorian Britain* (Manchester: Carcanet, 1987); Michael Scrivener, "Shelley and Radical Artisan Poetry," *Keats-Shelley Journal* 42 (1993): 22–36; John Goodridge, ed., *The Independent Spirit: John Clare and the Self-Taught Tradition* (Tyne and Wear: Peterson Printers, 1994); Anne F. Janowitz, *Lyric and Labour in the Romantic Tradition* (Cambridge: Cambridge University Press, 1998).
20. Gerald P. Tyson, *Joseph Johnson, A Liberal Publisher* (Iowa City: University of Iowa Press, 1979). It is interesting to note that Joseph Johnson's imprint is on Levi's critique of Thomas Paine (1797).
21. See the *DNB* entry for Henry Lemoine and George Lackington. Also, see Lemoine's "Elegiac Verses, To the Memory of the late learned David Levi, Author of *Lingua Sacra*, &c," *Gentleman's Magazine* 71 (Oct. 1801): 934–35. In his memoirs, he writes of his origins in the laboring classes and spectacular business success with "cheap" literature that appeals to the poor. James Lackington, *Memoirs of the First Forty-Five Years of the Life of James Lackington,* rev. ed. (London: Lackington, 1792), 381–9.
22. See the *DNB* entry for Lemoine. Levi Alexander (d? 1834), son of Alexander Alexander (d? 1807), was a Jewish printer like his father; the Alexander printing family focused their business on the British–Jewish literary market. Abraham Goldsmid (1756–1810), like his brother Benjamin (1755–1808), was a financier specializing in government loans; both brothers, who gave generously to Jewish philanthropies, committed suicide. (On the Goldsmids, see "Abraham Goldsmid: Money Magician in the Popular Press," Mark Schoenfield's contribution to this collection-ed.)
23. Endelman, *Jews of Georgian England,* 264.
24. For Heine and Börne, see Sander L. Gilman, *Jewish Self-Hatred: Anti-Semitism and the Hidden Language of the Jews* (Baltimore and London: The Johns Hopkins University Press, 1986), 148–88.
25. Jacques Basnage, *The History of the Jews,* trans. Thomas Taylor (London, 1708).
26. *The Old and New Testaments Connected in the History of the Jews and Neighbouring Nations,* 4 vols. (Charlestown, 1815). Prideaux (1648–1724), Dean of Norwich, had many editions of his *Connection*; I counted thirty-six separate editions from the first in 1716–18 to 1871. Levi is using the 1779 edition.
27. Levi, *A Succinct Account,* 261–7.
28. Endelman, *The Jews of Georgian England,* 263; Levi cites Basnage in his writings beginning with the reply to Priestley in 1787.
29. Abraham Mears (Gamaliel ben Pedahzur), *The Book of Religion, Ceremonies, and Prayers of the Jews, as Practiced in their Synagogues and Families* (London, 1738). See the brief discussion of Mears in Endelman, *The Jews of Georgian England,* 250.
30. S. Singer, "Early Translations and Translators of the Jewish Liturgy in England," *Transactions of the Jewish Historical Society of England* 3 (1896–8): 59.

31. Endelman, *The Jews of Georgian England*, 124.
32. Charles Duschinsky, *The Rabbinate of the Great Synagogue, London, From 1756 to 1842* (1921; reprint, Westmead: Gregg International, 1971), 98–9.
33. One of the few who have studied comparatively and historically the various translations of the Jewish liturgy into English is S. Singer, 36–71. Because the Maxwell House Haggadah has been offered free of charge since 1934 in North American supermarkets, several generations of Jews have been using it for their *sedarim*; there are 40 million copies in print, and it is in English and Hebrew.
34. Singer, 66–7.
35. *The Holy Bible, In Hebrew... English Translation [and] Notes of the Late David Levi*, rev. Levy Alexander, 5 vols. (London, 5582 [1822]).
36. Katz, 296–300. Katz also provides a useful bibliography on Priestley.
37. Endelman, *The Jews of Georgian England*, 220.
38. David Levi, *Letters to Dr. Priestley, In Answer to His Letters to the Jews, Part II* (London: David Levi, 1789), 3.
39. Levi, *Letters to Dr. Priestley, Part II*, 5.
40. Levi, *Letters to Dr. Priestley, Part II*, 155.
41. Levi, *Letters to Dr. Priestley, Part II*, 127–34. Bicheno, a Baptist and millenarian, is interesting in his own right. See Mayir Vreté, "The Restoration of the Jews in English Protestant Thought 1790–1840," *Middle Eastern Studies* 8 (1972): 7–9. Bicheno was rare among millenarians to declare that Jews could return to Zion without converting to Christianity first.
42. William Cunninghame, *Remarks Upon David Levi's Dissertations on the Prophecies Relative to The Messiah* (London: Black, Parry, and Kingsbury, 1810).
43. Alfred Rubens, "Portrait of Anglo-Jewry: 1656–1836," *Transactions of the Jewish Historical Society of England* 19 (1955–59): 36–9.
44. See Todd M. Endelman, "The Chequered Career of 'Jew' King: A Study in Anglo-Jewish Social History," in *From East and West: Jews in a Changing Europe, 1750–1870*, Frances Malino and David Sorkin, ed. (Oxford: Basil Blackwell, 1990), 151–81.
45. Endelman, "The Chequered Career of 'Jew' King," 179–80.
46. Ruderman, 40.
47. Ruderman, 177.
48. David Levi, *Defence of the Old Testament* (London: David Levi and Joseph Johnson, 1797), 201.
49. David Levi, *Dissertations on the Prophecies of the Old Testament* (London: David Levi, 1796), 2:117.
50. Levi, *Dissertations on the Prophecies of the Old Testament*, 2:117n.
51. Jon Mee, "Apocalypse and Ambivalence: The Politics of Millenarianism in the 1790s," *South Atlantic Quarterly* 95 (1996): 671–97; *Dangerous Enthusiasm: William Blake and the Culture of Radicalism in the 1790s* (Oxford: Clarendon Press, 1992).
52. Levi, *Dissertations on the Prophecies*, 1:xxvi–xxxiii.
53. Levi, *Dissertations on the Prophecies*, 1:40.
54. Levi, *Dissertations on the Prophecies*, 1:40.

55. Levi, *Defence of the Old Testament,* 56.
56. Levi, *Defence of the Old Testament,* 59–77.
57. Levi, *Defence of the Old Testament,* 99–106.
58. Levi, *Defence of the Old Testament,* 116–26.
59. Levi, *Defence of the Old Testament,* 154–95.
60. Sheila A. Spector discusses eighteenth-century Hebraism in "Blake as an Eighteenth-Century Hebraist," in David V. Erdman, ed., *Blake and His Bible,* Locust Hill Literary Studies No. 1 (West Cornwall, CT: Locust Hill Press, 1990), 179–229. See also the first chapter of Spector's *"Glorious incomprehensible": The Development of Blake's Kabbalistic Language* (Lewisburg, PA: Bucknell University Press, 2001), and David S. Katz's "The Hutchinsonians and Hebraic Fundamentalism in Eighteenth-Century England," in Katz and Jonathan I. Israel, ed., *Sceptics, Millenarians and Jews,* Brill's Studies in Intellectual History, vol. 17 (Leiden: E. J. Brill, 1990), 237–55.
61. Meyer, *The Origins of the Modern Jew,* 17.
62. Endelman, "The Englishness of Jewish Modernity," 238. (On Cobbett's anti-Semitism, see Schoenfield's chapter-ed.)
63. The Karaites, a Jewish sect dating from the eighth century of the Common Era and surviving into the modern period, denied the authority of the rabbinic tradition, rejecting the Divine origin of the *Mishnah* and the *Gemara.* See the *Encyclopedia Judaica,* 16 vols. (Jerusalem: Judah Magnes, 1972).
64. Levi's essay on Abravanel is remarkably similar to what one will find in standard Jewish encyclopedias such as the *Encyclopedia Judaica,* and the *Jewish Encyclopedia,* 12 vols. (New York and London: Funk and Wagnalls, 1901).

Chapter 10

Not for "Antiquaries," but for "Philosophers": Isaac D'Israeli's Talmudic Critique and His Talmudical Way with Literature

Stuart Peterfreund

Although Isaac D'Israeli (1766–1848), father of the more generally recognized and illustrious politician and novelist Benjamin Disraeli (1804–81), is not at present widely known as a figure who was part of the literary scene during the years more or less comprising English Romanticism (ca. 1789–ca. 1832), he was widely known as such during his lifetime. James Ogden, the author of the only book-length literary life of D'Israeli to date, reminds his reader that "from about 1790 to 1840 D'Israeli generally had a book in the press. At first he aspired to being an imaginative writer, and published two tentative volumes of poetry, a collection of 'Romances,' and three novels. These are by no means without interest, but it is to his credit that after 1811 he confined himself to giving the public the results of his literary and historical research."[1]

As Ogden observes, there was an avid readership for the published fruits of such research. "The Romantic sensibility," he notes, exhibited an "intense interest in the psychology of literary genius, and [an] enthusiasm for literary history." D'Israeli gratified this interest and this enthusiasm: "*The Curiosities* is a first-rate browsing book; *The Literary Character* is an original work that deserves to be better known; and the *Amenities* contains some excellent criticism of medieval and sixteenth-century literature."[2]

But D'Israeli himself does not describe his project as being that of a historian or literary historian per se. In one instance he describes his project as being in part that of a literary commentator who makes use of literary history in undertaking the allied tasks of popularizer and leveler of intellectual inequities arising from distinctions imposed by class and/or occupation. In the three-volume first series of *Curiosities of Literature* (1817), one of the texts cited by Ogden, D'Israeli observes that he has found that "literary history afforded an almost unexplored source of interesting facts" of use in raising the level of English cultural literacy, but he makes no claim to be writing literary history in his own right (1:v). His design is plainly otherwise: "Every class of readers requires a book adapted to itself; and that book which interests, and perhaps brings new information to a multitude of readers, is not to be contemned, even by the learned," situating *Curiosities* culturally by likening it to the Roman *varia eruditio* and the Oriental miscellany (1:vi). D'Israeli then states that "the design of this work is to stimulate the literary curiosity of those, who, with a taste for its tranquil pursuits, are impeded in their acquirement. The characters, the events, and the singularities of modern literature, are not always familiar even to those who excel in classical studies. But a more numerous part of mankind, by their occupations, or their indolence, both unfavourable causes to literary improvement, require to obtain the materials for thinking, by the easiest and readiest means. This work has proved useful" (1:vi–vii).

Throughout his œuvre, including his imaginative, historical, and critical writing as well as his popular miscellanies, D'Israeli repeatedly makes the point that he is not writing history—above all, not literary history—as that genre is commonly understood. Interestingly enough, although he is proposed by Ogden as a literary historian among other things, D'Israeli himself never uses the word *history* in any of his book titles, not even the titles of his novels, which present the life histories of fictive individuals, and not even the titles of his book-length historical works.[3] For example, the full title of his novel *Vaurien* is *Vaurien: or, Sketches of the Times, Exhibiting Views of the Philosophies, Religions, Politics, Literature, and Manners of the Age* (1797).[4] The full title of *Flim-Flams*, which owes a good many of its comedic moments to *The History of Tom Jones, a Foundling* (1749), as well as to *The Life and Opinions of Tristram Shandy, Gent.* (1759–67) is *Flim-Flams! Or, the Life and Errors of My Uncle, and the Amours of My Aunt* (1805).[5] And the full title of his study of England heading toward Civil War and the Commonwealth during the second quarter of the seventeenth century is *Commentaries on the Life and Reign of Charles the First, King of England* (1828).[6]

The word *history*, and the common understanding of what that word denotes, are simply not definitive or even accurate descriptors of D'Israeli's larger literary or cultural project. In fact, he was uneasy with the implication that history of a certain kind was a part of that project. In *The Genius of Judaism* (1833), for example, in a discussion of the lot of European Jewry since the rise of the Inquisition and the expulsion of the Jews from Spain (1492), D'Israeli regards being a historian as attesting to a failure of his sponsoring culture. "I once might have been a prophet," he writes, "whom am now only an historian."[7] But D'Israeli resists the implications of this falling off when he attempts to clarify what that cultural project is. "I am not writing the history of the Jews, for antiquaries," he observes, "but the Genius of Judaism for philosophers" (239). And in the preface to *Amenities of Literature,* although D'Israeli concedes that "a history of our vernacular literature has occupied [his] studies for many years," he is careful to note, with an almost Shelleyan note of urgency, that "it was [his] design not furnish an arid narrative of books or of authors, but following the human mind through the wide track of Time, to trace from their beginnings the rise, the progress, and the decline of public opinions, and to illustrate, as the objects presented themselves, the great incidents in our national annals" (1:3). D'Israeli's purpose in so doing is nothing less than to render the genius of English literature for philosophers. As he continues, "literary history, in this enlarged circuit, becomes not merely the philological history of critical erudition, but ascends into a philosophy of books, where their subjects, their tendency, and their immediate or gradual influence over the people, discover their actual condition." D'Israeli clearly has both a strong sense of his project's philosophical ambitions and an equally strong sense of how those ambitions distinguish that project from the antiquarian's or the narrative historian's. That said, it remains to identify the intellectual and conceptual basis of that project and to make a start at understanding how that basis informs the project's operations and its outcomes.

At first glance, given what D'Israeli has to say about philosophers and philosophy in general, he seems ill-suited to engage the philosophical tradition as it is commonly understood. In fact, D'Israeli apparently conceives his project as a corrective for what has gone before—all the way back to the origins of Western philosophy. In the article "Aristotle and Plato," for example, D'Israeli, although he clearly evinces some admiration for Plato, has some unkind things to say about both of the pillars of classical philosophy, stating in part that Aristotle's "diction, pure as it is, has something uncommonly austere; and his obscurities, natural or affected, disgust and fatigue his readers. Plato is equally delicate in his thoughts and expressions. Aristotle, though he may be more natural, has not any delicacy: his style is simple and equal, but close and nervous; that of Plato is grand and elevated, but loose and diffuse. Plato always says more than he should say: Aristotle never says enough, and leaves the reader to think more than he says" (*Curiosities* 1:198).

Nor does the Neo-Platonism that emerged during the Renaissance and after come off very well. Of Henry More (1614–87), D'Israeli, in the article "Modern Platonism," states that "Dr. More, the most rational of our modern Platonists, abounds, however, with the most extravagant reveries, and was inflated with egotism and enthusiasm, as much as any of his mystic predecessors. He conceived that he held an intercourse with the divinity itself! that he had been shot as a fiery dart into the world, and he hoped he had hit the mark. He carried his self-conceit to such extravagance, that he thought his urine smelled like violets.... These visionaries indulge the most fanciful vanity" (*Curiosities* 1:293).

In *Vaurien* and *Flim-Flams,* D'Israeli satirizes contemporary philosophy and philosophers point blank. And the satire extends to include political and natural philosophers and philosophy as well. Early in the former novel, the speaker presents the philosopher Mr. Subtile, of whom he says, "Subtile gives a reason for the most unreasonable thing; for he distinguishes between probabilities, possibilities, what is evidence, what is equivalent to evidence. He has constructed tables, physical and metaphysical, moral and political, where, with precision, are marked different degrees of probability, and consequently, the quantity of belief, which may be assigned to every opinion." Lest Subtile seem a creature entirely of D'Israeli's own invention, he contextualizes Subtile in a footnote, adding, "this jargon is curiously indulged by Helvetius" (*Vaurien* 1:137–38 and n.). Subsequently, when Subtile proclaims as a tenet of his philosophy, "no man can confer on me a *favour,* but only do me a *right*" (1:77 and n.), D'Israeli is quick to note that both the idea and the language expressing it come from William Godwin's *Political Justice* (1:137).[8]

Flim-Flams takes as the butt of its satire what D'Israeli derisively refers to as "philos"—that is, philosophers of all kinds. One of the novel's principal characters is "Caco-Nous, Metaphysician" (1:103). The name, Greek for "bad-mind," would seem to be in part a slyly satirical allusion to Philonous, the lover of mind, who appears opposite Hylas, the proponent of the material world, in *Three Dialogues between Hylas and Philonous* (1713), by George, Bishop Berkeley (1685–1753), and in part a satire of Godwin.[9] Nor is Caco-Nous' name the only reference to Berkeley in *Flim-Flams.* As the unnamed nephew-narrator subsequently laments, "my honoured uncle...lost himself in the ideal system of Berkeley! By that system he considered himself authorized to declare that I, his affectionate nephew, with his learned apothecary...were no more than *two bundles of ideas* labeled Nephew and Apothecary" (2:155).

Immanuel Kant (1724–1804) is also a prime target in *Flim-Flams,*[10] along with the post-Kantian idealist Johann Gottlieb Fichte (1762–1814). The nephew-narrator explains, "I have told you Professor Fichte is a Kantian; but I don't know if I mentioned that he sent over ... Mr. *Kant's Glossary,* for the due understanding of Mr. *Kant's philosophy.* It seems that, the divine Kant employs *certain terms* in his own *peculiar sense*—which, with great fatigue of mind and body, you are first to get by rote (no trifle), and afterwards are to be understood, as Mr. Kant, and the devil shall bless you!" (2:171–2).

And Kant is sent up in an extended footnote that sounds more like D'Israeli *in propria persona* than the nephew-narrator, and is in effect a great satiric conflagration of philosophers that also engulfs Berkeley, David Hume (1711–76),[11] Gottfried Wilhelm von Leibniz (1646–1716), and Scots Common-sense philosopher Thomas Reid (1710–96):

> After all, what is the system of Kant? In the Critical Philosophy (say the Edinburgh Reviewers, vol. I, p. 279) the *egotism* of Berkeley and Hume is largely incorporated and combined with the *opposing tenets* of Dr. Reid. If to the *common sense* of that school we add the *minute susceptibilities* of Leibnitz [*sic*], and the denial by Hume of *necessary connexion in causation,* and of the *reality of external perception*—we bring before us the *theory of cognition* of Kant .... So the whole amounts to this *Tincture of Solar Extract* [i.e., moonshine]—Berkeley, Hume, Reid, and Leibnitz, all mingled together in the perfume pot! Enough to stink out fifty devils and to exorcise a whole legion. (2:175–6n.)

Experimental, natural, and political philosophers fare no better. In attempting to account for his uncle's most striking physiognomical feature, a small, thin, and rather pointy head, the nephew-narrator reviews the theories of the reproductive physiologists Lazzaro Spallanzani (1729–99), Johann Friedrich Blumenbach (1752–1840), and Georges, Comte de Buffon (1707–88), as to whether appearance is determined by the male or the female complement at fertilization. The nephew-narrator opts for Buffon and the male complement, inferring that his Uncle Jacob is descended from a long line of pointy heads (1:34). Naturally enough, Uncle Jacob is himself a "philo" of the experimental school. As his nephew relates, with a wink in the direction of the iatrochemist Hermann Boerhaave (1668–1738), "my uncle evinced the most *exemplary patience!* In all kinds of experimental philosophy—as all experimenters ought. He would repeat a distillation one thousand times, as Boerhaave did" (1:80). And as noted above, Godwin comes in for his share of satiric ridicule, as does Thomas Robert Malthus (1766–1834), who appears as Mr. Toomany (3:237).

Philo Judaeus (ca. 20 BCE–ca. 50 CE) the ancestor and putative namesake of all the "philos" in *Fim-Flams,* does not escape D'Israeli's satirical scrutiny. But in his comments on Philo, D'Israeli does at least begin to offer some sense of what he means in his remarks about his intended audience of "philosophers" rather than "antiquaries," and the project of articulating "a philosophy of books." As the nephew-narrator characterizes him, "Philo, that learned Jew who was so happy an imitation of Plato, that it is said of him, Philo *platonises,* or Plato *philonises*—in his curious life of Moses, the great legislator of the Jews, giving an account of his education, pourtrays him as *an universal genius*" (1:71–72).

Although the nephew-narrator subsequently sends up Philo, literally reducing Moses to a skilled tradesman by adding the socially loaded aside that "the Royal Institution could not have done much more for him!" (1:72), D'Israeli recuperates an important moment not to be lost sight of amid the laughter. The recuperation, moreover, points toward an understanding of what D'Israeli means by philosophers and philosophy, and what he has in mind when he comments positively on them.

The comment attributed to Philo captures the spirit of his age—the age in which the Hebrew Pentateuch was translated into the Greek Septuagint. It was a moment in which a recognition dawned—as Emmanuel Levinas notes, the recognition that "a certain 'assimilation to Europe' [was] not rejected by the Talmudic doctors as purely negative."[12] (Whether this moment gave rise to a sustained process of recognition will be considered below.) The moment in question is in part the subject of the commentary in the Talmudic tractate *Megillah* (8b–9b), written five or six centuries later, which raises the question of which religious texts may be translated: the Pentateuch may be; *tefillin* (phylacteries), *mezuzot* (doorpost scrolls), and the *megillah* (the Book of Esther) may not be.

The translatability of the Pentateuch (Torah), according to the Talmud—and here and in the discussion to follow, the Talmud intended is the Babylonian Talmud (*Bavli*), not the Jerusalem Talmud (*Yerushalmi*)—is in large measure owing to the ability of Moses, held by Judaism to be the author of the entire Torah, to render the word of God. According to Rav Yehuda, the author of a *baraita*[13] concerning the tractate *Ptolemy,* after He had installed each of "*seventy-two elders*" in "*seventy-two little houses,*" commanded each of them, "'*Write for me [in Greek] the Torah of Moses, your master.' The Lord inspired each one, and they found themselves in the same thought, and wrote for Him.*"[14] As Levinas elsewhere notes, "according to these same learned doctors, nothing is worse for a believer than to make a distinction, in the Pentateuch, between the 'Mosaic' and the 'divine': so strong is the principle according to which the prophetic intervention of Moses is the concreteness of the Revelation without mediation."[15]

To the extent that Moses speaks "without mediation" for an omniscient God, then, he himself is omniscient, "*an universal genius*" as the nephew-narrator reports that Philo characterized him, and a figure to be emulated by the learned, Philo included. The translation into Greek proceeded on the assumption that the Mosaic text would convey the unmediated Divine inspiration necessary to the task at hand, thereby making the translators at least temporarily capable of rendering what Levinas calls "the Word of the Most High," that is, the Torah. Indeed, as Levinas notes, one of the requirements of the Talmudic doctors who would sit in the "high judicial assembly" known as the Sanhedrin is universal knowledge, expressed as the ability "to understand seventy languages." As Levinas observes, "this is a metaphor that in the Talmudic manner of speaking, in the oral Torah, designates all mankind surrounding Israel; mankind taken as a whole, in its entirety, although split up by differences that group men into nations."[16]

The kind of learning of which Levinas speaks, as well as the resultant wisdom, has the potential to nullify the contingencies of space and time—above all, time. As Jacob Neusner argues, Rabbinic Judaism, by which he means the Judaism that gives rise to such documents as the *Mishnah* and the *Gemara*, is a religion of paradigms, not history, notwithstanding the fact that the Torah "set[s] forth Israel's life as history, with a beginning, a middle, and end; a purpose and a coherence; a teleological system."[17] Neusner explains as follows:

> Rabbinic Judaism formulates its conception of social order—of the life of its "Israel" and the meaning of that life through time and change—in enduring paradigms that admit no distinction between past, present, and future. All things take form on a single plane of being; Israel lives not in historical time, moving from a beginning, to a middle, to an end, in a linear plan. Nor does it form its existence in cyclical time, repeating time and again familiar cycles of events. Those familiar modes of making sense out of the chaos of change and the passage of time serve not at all. Rather, Israel lives in accord with an enduring paradigm that knows neither past, present, nor future. Appealing to a world of timeless myth, that Judaism accounts for how things are not by appeal to what was and what will be, but by invoking the criterion of what characterizes the authentic and true being of Israel, an idea or ideal defined by the written Torah and imposed upon the chaos of time and change.[18]

Loving the God of Abraham, Isaac, and Jacob, in the sense intended by the Torah, means loving "the Word of the Most High," and to the extent that that "Word" comprises linguistically all that is knowable and known, such love is the unmediated love of wisdom: *philos sophia,* as practiced by the *philosophoi.* D'Israeli would seem to concur, and he goes so far as to locate this love of that word in the history of Israel. As he states in *The Genius of Judaism,* "the Deity designed his Hebrews as a human instrument to recover knowledge of the Creator; a knowledge which had been lost by worshippers of the heavenly bodies or statues, the rude symbols of the divinity; by sensual corruptions, which had disguised the celestial origins of religion" (33–4).

D'Israeli's intended audience of philosophers—those who will look kindly upon his philosophy—are secularized versions of this ideal. They are, above all, lovers of language uttered in an enlightened if regular manner, as well as of the laws and truths that such language expresses. Such philosophers are epitomized by Moses Mendelssohn (1729–86), who, "rejecting the Talmudical dreamers ... caught a nobler spirit from the celebrated Maimonides [1135–1204]," and whose "effort to master the living languages, and chiefly the English, that he might read his favourite Locke in his own idiom," according to D'Israeli, resulted in the self-fashioning of "a great genius for language and metaphysics" (*Literary Character* 63). D'Israeli himself, while not being the master of seventy languages or their literatures, was a student of a number of languages and/or literatures, including his native Italian, liturgical Hebrew, probably Ladino (the Hispanic counterpart of Yiddish), and his adopted English.[19] To these may be added "small Latin and less Greek," Spanish, Portuguese, French, "some Dutch," and at least "a smattering of German."[20] And D'Israeli evinces a concern for correctness of spelling and pronunciation, as well as copiousness of comprehension. In the article "Orthography and Orthoepy," found in *Amenities,* D'Israeli reflects on the consequences of the fact "that our written language still remains to the utter confusion of the eye and ear of the baffled foreigner, who often discovers that what is written is not spoken, and what is spoken is not written" (2:31).

It is important to note why the philosophers that D'Israeli intends as his readers and the philosophy that he wishes to introduce them to are secularized: D'Israeli does not subscribe to the authority of Rabbinic Judaism in general, or to the authority of the Talmud in particular, for he sees the practices of that institution and textual study as these evolved even prior to the Diaspora as being at odds with principles such as those set forth above. Commenting on the events that transpired during the historical epoch surveyed by 1 and 2 Samuel, which begin roughly with the Lord revealing himself to Samuel, chronicle the rise of kingship, and end with the old age of King David, D'Israeli observes, "the Israelites deposed their God, for their God was their sovereign. The menace of Heaven was the future silence of the Lord, when, hereafter they should call on him" (*Genius* 55).

In that silence, Israel undertook to speak for its absconded God, or at least for Moses, the bearer of his unmediated word. Of the supposed authority of the laws, which inhere in the "twelve folios of the Babylonish Talmud, or 'the Doctrinal'" (77), D'Israeli notes the following practice: "Whenever they [i.e., the Israelites] refer to a Talmudical authority, they exultingly exclaim, 'This comes from Moses and Mount Sinai'" (79). And yet D'Israeli himself sees in operation none of the knowledge and wisdom that Levinas sees as a prerequisite for sitting in that "high judicial assembly" known as the *Sanhedrin*. He remarks on the "holy ignorance of geography and chronology in the rabbinical histories" (93). He takes the side of the Karaites (scripturists) who opposed the Talmudists in Babylon (103–4). In *The Literary Character* D'Israeli deplores the early Talmudic education of Moses Mendelssohn in particular and the culture of the *shtetl* (a small Jewish town or village formerly found in eastern Europe) in general. Although D'Israeli is wrong about Yiddish—it is a dialect of Old High German—he says of the *shtetl*-dwellers in general and of Mendelssohn in particular, "they employ for their common intercourse a barbarous or *patois* Hebrew; while the sole studies of their young rabbins are strictly confined to the Talmud, of which the fundamental principle, like the Sonna [the body of Islamic custom and practice based on the prophet Muhammad's words and deeds] of the Turks, is a pious rejection of every species of profane learning" (*Character* 62). And in his appeal at the close of *The Genius of Judaism* to implement a course of action that anticipates the rise of Reform Judaism, D'Israeli "would implore the Jews to begin to educate their youth as the youth of Europe, and not the youth of Palestine; let their Talmud be removed to an elevated shelf, to be consulted as a curiosity of antiquity, and not as a manual of education" (*Genius* 265).[21]

Yet despite this critique of Talmudic Judaism, D'Israeli, no less than his hero Moses Mendelssohn, reveals the informing influence of the means, if not the object, of Talmudic studies. In the case of Mendelssohn, the problem was not the method, but the text itself. D'Israeli states that as the result of his studies, Mendelssohn came to view the Talmud as a composite of "voluminous legends" (*Literary Character* 62). But one might hasten to add that it is precisely through his careful, continuous, and systematic study of what Neusner characterizes as the Talmud's "ongoing discourse of continuous, intimate commentary, magisterial code, and concrete niggling application"—through using the method against the text, in other words—that Mendelssohn found the text lacking.[22] Mendelssohn may have been, as D'Israeli characterizes him in an article in the *Monthly Magazine* for July 1798, "the Jewish Socrates,"[23] that is, the consummate dialectician. *Phaedon, or on the Immortality of the Soul* (1767), his first philosophical work is, in fact, a dialogue. But it must be remembered that Mendelssohn's chief philosophical influence was Locke, not Plato, and that the intra-textual discourse of the Talmud—"the Aramaic voice of applied reason and practical logic—applied to, practiced upon, the Hebrew-language writings (or statements orally formulated and orally transmitted) of the *Mishnah* and comparable sources"[24]—is by its nature dialectical.

What is characteristically Talmudical about D'Israeli's way with literature, and how does this way manifest itself in the text itself? To begin with, like commentators and students of the Talmud, and like Levinas' "Talmudic doctors," D'Israeli displays—indeed, he all but flaunts—a love of learning in general and of languages in particular, the more abstruse the learning and the more exotic the language, the better. He spent a good deal of his time conducting his research at the British Museum. It was there that Washington Irving (1783–1859), recording the encounter in *The Sketch Book of Geoffrey Crayon, Esq.* (1819; 1834), observed D'Israeli making "more stir and show of business than any of the others; dipping into various books, fluttering over the leaves of manuscripts, taking a morsel out of one, a morsel out of another."[25] As Ogden notes, the mature D'Israeli himself possessed a "considerable library."[26]

In *Mejnoun and Leila, the Arabian Petrarch and Laura*, the longest of the three works comprising *Romances* (1799),[27] for example, D'Israeli retells a traditional romance still current today, but he also showily displays his attainments as an Orientalist. Many of the pages of this 208-page work, with its copious metacommentary, in fact look like the pages of the *Bavli*, divided into *Mishnah* ("'Repetition,' i.e., 'learning'") and *Gemara* ("Completion"—"The commentary on the Mishnah by the *amoraim*, or sages").[28] The orientalist works that D'Israeli cites include: "Bell's Travels to China" (*Romances* 57)—actually, *Travels from St. Petersburgh in Russia to Various Part of Asia* (1788), by John Bell (1691–1780); *Constantinople* (1797), by James Dallaway (1763–1834); *Grammar of the Persian Language* (3rd ed., 1783), by Sir William Jones (1746–94); *A Collection of Late Voyages* (1797), by Carsten Niebuhr (1713–95); *Persian Miscellanies* (1795), by Major William Ouseley (1767–1842); and *A Dictionary,*

Persian, Arabic and English (1777–80), and *A Grammar of the Arabic Language* (1776), both by John Richardson (1741–1811).[29] The discussion in the footnotes is as exotic as the citations themselves. Kais, a youthful poet and son of the Yemeni Bedouin chieftain Ahmed, has been driven to distraction as the star-crossed lover of Leila, the daughter of "an Emir, distinguished by a green turban, [who] claims his descent from Fatima wife of Mahomet" (*Romances* 7n.). After the emir refuses to permit Leila to marry Kais, he flees to the wilderness, where he is sighted as a *mejnoun:* "The surname, in Arabic, means a manic; but sometimes an *enthusiast,* and a *man inspired*" (80n.). Prior to this tragic turn of events, Kais gains access to Leila's quarters by stealth: "To attract the attention of her slaves, he whirled himself with great velocity on one foot, and held a red hot iron between his teeth; and sometimes the *Neh,* or transverse flute, so musically warbled his wild and enthusiastic notes, that the slaves soon approached him." D'Israeli glosses the narrative in part as follows: "The Mevleheh Dervises perform a public worship, which consists of dancing and turning on one foot with incredible rapidity, whilst a red hot iron is held between the teeth.... In this they are accompanied with the softest music, &c. — Dallaway's 'Constantinople,' p. 129" (*Romances* 42 and n.).

Having gotten the slaves' attention, Kais rapidly makes his way toward the inner sanctum, where Leila is to be found. Kais bribes the one slave left between him and his beloved with rose water: "Unlucky boy! She softly murmured, sighing as the full and fragrant incense crept over her senses; her bulky body sank gently to the earth, half-closing her swimming eyes, her quivering lips yield the feeble cry of a fainting voluptuary." D'Israeli glosses the narrative in part as follows: "The orientals are particularly susceptible to all aromatics, but OTTAR-GUL [essence of roses] is their passion. Major Ouseley, with his accustomed elegance, writes:—'So fond of aromatic and highly-fragrant ointments were the ancient [Persians and Assyrians], that many writers made their excessive indulgence in the use of these perfumes the subject of learned dissertations'" (*Romances* 48–49 and n.). A few pages thereafter, when Kais' suit has been rejected, and he has fled into the wilderness, his former poetry teacher, Effendi Lebid, appears on the scene—in *mufti,* as it were. He "was distinguished by a tuft of plaited hair.... What was remarkable, it was not his own hair, but formed of the relics of his friends, from every one of whom he had affectionately collected a handful of hair, which he had interwoven with his own. It was in this manner that the traveler had memorised their affections." D'Israeli glosses the narrative as follows: "This singular form of expressing the sensibility of friendship is recorded in Bell's travels in China, and was employed by an old and virtuous Bramin" (*Romances* 57).

Nor are the sesquipedalian footnotes restricted to arcane subject matter. In "Shakespeare," a fifty-four-page article found in *Amenities* (186–240), D'Israeli glosses his statement that "the life of our poet remains almost a blank, and his very name a subject of contention" (189–90) with a note twenty times the length of the observation, sounding once again his recurrent plea for a uniform orthography and orthoepy. The note is not without its share of hyperbole, beginning with the observation that "posterity is even in some danger of losing the real name of our great dramatic poet. In the days of Shakespeare, and long after, proper names were written down as the ear caught the sound, or they were capriciously varied by the owner" (190n.). A few pages later, D'Israeli finds it necessary to gloss rather showily a passage from Robert Greene's (1558?–92) *Groats-worth of Wit Bought with a Million of Repentaunce* (1596). Greene's deprecating characterization of Shakespeare to his fellow playwrights proposes Shakespeare in part as one who "is as well able to *bombast out a blank verse* as the best of you." D'Israeli responds by observing, "*bombast* is not used here in the present application of the term, in a depreciating sense, but is a simile derived from the cotton used in stuffing out or quilting fashionable dresses" (*Amenities* 194 and n.). D'Israeli may have gotten his historical provenance right, but the term is used as a metaphor, and Greene's intent is clearly to imply that Shakespeare pads his pentameter to make his verses tally.

As showy as it may sometimes appear, D'Israeli's love of learning has its purpose in parallel with the purpose of Talmudic erudition: the discernment, discussion, and application of the law—not civil or religious law in his case, but the laws of human nature in general, and of the literary temperament in particular. D'Israeli parts company with those who would draw a ready if facile analogy between the polity and the republic of letters. As he says of the former, "the three great functions of a commonwealth, are the proposing—the debating—and the resolving of the laws; functions which, in all the governments which man ever planned, are divided among different orders of society, but whose clashing interests no human wisdom can ever adjust" (*Genius* 49–50).

However, on the level of "brotherhood" if not of "commonwealth," D'Israeli is less pessimistic about the possibility of a common cause. "All that I assert," he says in *The Literary Character*, "is, that every man of genius will discover, sooner or later, that he belongs to the brotherhood of his class, and that he cannot escape from certain habits, and feelings, and disorders, which arise from the same temperament and sympathies, and are the necessary consequence of occupying the same position, and passing through the same moral existence. Whenever we compare men of genius with each other, the history of those who are no more will serve as a perpetual commentary on our contemporaries" (3–4). D'Israeli's understanding is that the word *character,* here and elsewhere— for example in the article "Self-Characters" found in *Literary Miscellanies* (295–7)—means *life* or *biography.*

It should also be noted that D'Israeli views the "brotherhood" in question as being organized along lines that, culturally, if not geopolitically, are national. As he argues in *Amenities,* "whoever imagines that he may safely lay aside all of the successive efforts of the English mind, as fashions out of date, contracts his faculties within his own day, and can form no adequate conception of that ample inheritance of the intellectual powers bequeathed to us from age to age" (v).

What is ultimately Talmudical about D'Israeli's larger literary or cultural project is its engagement with identifying and elaborating the paradigms by which literature generally, and the literary imagination in particular, may be understood. It may at first glance seem as though D'Israeli undertakes his task as a way of "passing," of de-emphasizing his outsider status through flaunting his peculiarly English and European book-learning, making reference to a "brotherhood," and incorporating himself into the tradition of English letters through the use of the first-person plural pronouns "we" and "our." But notwithstanding his Anglophilia and desire to be thought of as an English man of letters above all else—Ogden soberly observes that "Isaac D'Israeli did not achieve his place in the aristocracy of literature without a struggle," largely because "its members were suspicious of 'lively foreigners' and said so in their reviews"[30]—D'Israeli is engaged in something far more significant than cultural affiliation.

As Ogden observes of D'Israeli, "out of the books with which he surrounded himself, he may be said to have created facts; and he passed them on to the literary world in a manner that defied imitation."[31] The creative activity that Ogden describes has a good deal in common with Talmudic paradigm formation:

> Paradigms derive from human invention and human imagination, imposed on nature and on history alike. Nature is absorbed, history recast, through time paradigmatic; that is, time invented, not time discovered; time defined for a purpose determined by humanity (the social order, the faithful, for instance), time not discovered by determined and predetermined, time that is not natural or formed in correspondence to nature, or imposed upon nature at specified intersections; but time that is defined completely in terms of a prior pattern or the determined

paradigm or fabricated model itself: time wholly invented for the purposes of the social order that invents and recognizes time.[32]

What, ultimately, is the significance of D'Israeli's contribution to English literature? To make a start at answering this question, one might note that in this era of canon recuperation and expansion, the satirical novels *Vaurien* and *Flim-Flams* are still pointedly funny and are most certainly worth re-issuing in scholarly editions. As for D'Israeli's literary scholarship, while the line of descent to modern letters is not entirely clear, there are some striking parallels worth noting.

To unearth these parallels, one might begin with an observation seemingly unrelated to much of what has gone before. Of D'Israeli, Ogden notes, "his tastes in contemporary poetry were those of the average cultivated reader of the time, except that he was one of the first to discern the genius of Blake."[33] In fact, as Ogden notes, "apart from Blake's few close friends, D'Israeli seems to have been the earliest collector for the illuminated books. His collection consisted of *The Book of Thel, The Marriage of Heaven and Hell, Songs of Innocence and of Experience, Visions of the Daughters of Albion, Europe, a Prophecy,* and *The First Book of Urizen.*"[34] In a letter to a friend, D'Israeli writes of Blake admiringly, noting "an infinite variety of these wondrous deliriums of his fine and wild creative imagination," and compares Blake to the very precursors with whom Blake seeks to be compared: "Sometimes playful, as in the loveliest arabesques of Raffaelle, Blake often breaks into the '*terribilitá*' of Michael Angelo, and we start amid a world too horrific to dwell in. Not the least extraordinary fact of these designs is, their colouring, done by the artist's own hand, worked to his fancy; and the verses, which are often remarkable for their sweetness and their depth of feeling."[35]

Blake scholars have made little of this intersection—it is annotated in Geoffrey Keynes' Blake bibliography, and noted, for example, by S. Foster Damon and Mona Wilson.[36] But D'Israeli's paradigmatic approach to literature seems to have found a subsequent parallel, if not a descendant outright, in another Blakean: Northrop Frye.

Whether Frye read any of D'Israeli's texts seems to be an open question. Frye does not mention D'Israeli in *Fearful Symmetry*, his study of Blake;[37] yet it seems clear that Frye knew something about Jewish law in general, and perhaps about the Talmud in particular. He studied theology at Emmanuel College (Canada) and was an ordained minister in the United Church of Canada before he went to Oxford to earn his M. A. with the thesis that would become that book. Frye mentions "the myth of a primeval giant," which "has been preserved by the Cabbala in its conception of Adam Kadmon."[38] And Frye's characterization of the intervention of Jesus in the life of Judaism, as that intervention is described in *The Marriage of Heaven and Hell* (1790-93), reads a good deal like D'Israeli's strictures against studying the Talmud. Jesus, according to Frye, "found the Jews worshipping their own version of Nobodaddy, a sulky and jealous thundergod who exacted the most punctilious obedience to ceremonial law and moral code."[39]

But there is no mention of D'Israeli in "The Problem of Spiritual Authority in the Nineteenth Century," or in any of the other essays in *The Stubborn Structure,* or throughout *Anatomy of Criticism.*[40] Yet in this last work Frye begins to generalize from some of the insights already latent in *Fearful Symmetry,* and to develop a system of paradigms that provides for the same activity of creating facts that Ogden ascribes to D'Israeli. "There is a place for classification in criticism," Frye argues in *Anatomy of Criticism,* "and in any other discipline which is more important than an elegant accomplishment of some mandarin caste. The strong emotional repugnance felt by many critics toward any form of schematization in poetics is ... the result of a failure to distinguish criticism as a body of knowledge from the direct experience of literature, where every act is unique and classification has no place."[41] If Frye's seems to be a formalist's paradigmatic classification of literary modes, symbols, myths, and genres rather than D'Israeli's narrational "philosophy of books," with its amenities, calamities, and curiosities, both are nevertheless monumental acts of erudition and paradigmatic classification that attempt to see the world of letters as a whole. And if one consults Frye's *The Great Code,*[42] s/he begins to see the two paradigmatic systems merge—to see that for Frye as well as for D'Israeli, form has its narrative implications no less than narrative has its formal ones.

Notes

1. James Ogden, *Isaac D'Israeli* (Oxford: Clarendon, 1969), 1.
2. Ogden, 2. Ogden's references are to *Curiosities of Literature, in Three Volumes* (1817; Boston: Lilly, Wait, Colman and Holden, 1833); *The Literary Character; or the History of Men of Genius, Drawn from Their Own Feelings and Confessions; Literary Miscellanies; and an Inquiry into the Character of James the First* (1840; London: Routledge, Warne, and Routledge, 1862); *Amenities of Literature, Consisting of Sketches and Characters of English Literature*, 3 vols. (London: E. Moxon, 1841); 2nd ed., 2 vols. (1841; Boston: William Veazie, 1864). Subsequent references to works by D'Israeli will be indicated by parenthetical citations in the text.
3. Titles of individual articles sometimes contain the word *history*—for example, "The History of Gloves" (*Curiosities* 1:318-23), or "The Secret History of Charles I and His Queen Henrietta" (3:317-33).

4. Isaac D'Israeli, *Vaurien: or, Sketches of the Times, Exhibiting Views of the Philosophies, Religions, Politics, Literature, and Manners of the Age*, 2 vols. (London: T. Cadell, 1797).
5. Isaac D'Israeli, *Flim-Flams! Or, the Life and Errors of My Uncle, and the Amours of My Aunt* (London: John Murray, 1805). Of his Uncle Jacob's toad, the narrator of *Flim-Flams* observes, "It was a foundling, a Tom Jones, which my all-worthy uncle had found constantly haunting 'the steps before the hall-door'" (3:111).
6. Isaac D'Israeli, *Commentaries on the Life and Reign of Charles the First, King of England*, 2 vols. (London: Henry Colburn, 1828).
7. Isaac D'Israeli, *The Genius of Judaism* (London: Edward Moxon, 1833), 178.
8. *Enquiry Concerning Political Justice and Its Influence on Morals and Happiness*, 2 vols. (London: G. G. J. and J. Robinson, 1793). Ogden, taking D'Israeli at his word, characterizes *Vaurien* as "an attack on what he calls the 'romantic absurdities' of Godwinian philosophy." Ogden goes so far as to identify Godwin as the original of Subtile (Ogden, 60–1), although D'Israeli's reference to Helvetius suggests that the identification may not be absolute.
9. Caco-Nous is also associated with D'Israeli's arch-antagonist Godwin. At one point Caco-Nous proclaims, "in whatever sense a great genius understands a particular expression, we are certainly at liberty to apply it *in the sense that we think proper!!!*" D'Israeli's note refers the reader to Godwin's *Political Justice* (1:151–2 and n.).
10. Ogden reports that D'Israeli, commenting on William Lisle Bowles's review of Joseph Spence's *Anecdotes* (1820), finds Bowles's contention "that while Pope's style is excellent, his subjects are 'not poetical'" to be "as incomprehensible as Kant" (Ogden, 92).
11. In *Calamities of Authors; Including Some Inquiries Regarding Their Moral and Literary Characters*, 2 vols. (1812; New York: Johnson Reprint Corporation, 1971), D'Israeli begins by characterizing Hume as "an Author so celebrated, a philosopher so serene, and a man so extremely amiable, if not fortunate, that we may be surprised to meet his name inscribed in a catalogue of Literary Calamities" (2:224). While this characterization may at first glance appear to be entirely positive, D'Israeli cannot resist the impulse to satire, even in the context of a tale of woe recounting the hostile reception accorded Hume's major texts upon their first publication. Recalling Hume's categorical denial of an afterlife, D'Israeli remarks that near the end of his life, Hume began to receive positive recognition. D'Israeli concludes, "what a provoking consolation for a philosopher, who according the result of his own system, was close upon a state of annihilation!" (2:227).
12. Emmanuel Levinas, *In the Time of Nations*, trans. Michael B. Smith (Bloomington: Indiana University Press, 1994), 48.
13. A *baraita* is an "external" Mishnah, that is, an opinion or teaching of *Tannaim* (a group of Jewish authorities on the oral law), not included in the *Mishnah* (Levinas, x, xii).
14. As quoted by Levinas, 34.
15. Levinas, 112.
16. Levinas, 2, 1.

17. Jacob Neusner, *The Presence of the Past, the Pastness of the Present: History, Time, and Paradigm in Rabbinic Judaism* (Bethesda, MD: CDL Press, 1996), 1.
18. Neusner, 19–20.
19. "As late as 1823 a reviewer suggested that he wrote English as an acquired language" (Ogden, 14). Throughout his career, despite his immersion in English letters, D'Israeli continued to display signs of not being a native speaker. In the account of Hume discussed in a previous note, for example, D'Israeli invites the reader to examine Hume's "literary life, and you will discover that the greater portion was mortified and angried" (2:224). In the *Commentaries on the Life and Reign of Charles the First*, D'Israeli repeats the error, writing, "Charles, under the influence of angried feelings, hastily dissolved the second Parliament" (1:340). Earlier in the same volume D'Israeli speculates, "it might seem dubious, had Charles been a converted Romanist, whether the Minister who offered to remain equally zealous, might not have slided over like his son" (1:319–20).
20. Ogden, 9–10.
21. The harsh judgment of the Talmud and Talmudists is relatively constant throughout D'Israeli's works. See, for example, the articles "The Talmud" and "Rabbinical Stories" in *Curiosities* (1:60–69; 69–77). His own solution to the problem of separation versus assimilation was a good deal more radical than the one he proposed in *The Genius of Judaism*. D'Israeli's four children—Ralph, James, the future Prime Minister and novelist Benjamin, and Sarah—were all baptized during the summer of 1817 (Ogden, 201–2). Ogden also observes that D'Israeli's "admiration for [Moses] Mendelssohn shows that he was sympathetic to the ideas which were to lead to the establishment of Reform Judaism in England" (197). (On Mendelssohn's and Blake's two *Jerusalem*s, see Leslie Tannenbaum's "'What Are Those Golden Builders Doing?': Mendelssohn, Blake and the (Un)Building of *Jerusalem*," in this volume; and on *Alroy* as Benjamin Disraeli's apologetic for his conversion, see my "Alroy as Disraeli's 'Ideal Ambition,'" also in this volume [ed.].)
22. Jacob Neusner, *Talmudic Thinking: Language, Logic, Law* (Columbia: University of South Carolina Press, 1992), 7.
23. Quoted in Ogden, 196.
24. Neusner, *Talmudic Thinking*, 39.
25. Quoted in Ogden, 115. The reference is to Washington Irving's *The Sketch Book of Geoffrey Crayon, Esq*, 2 vols. (1819; London: John Murray, 1834).
26. Ogden, 162. For an abbreviated idea of the D'Israeli library, see "Judaica from the Disraeli library sold in October 1881," the appendix to Todd M. Endelman's "The Emergence of Disraeli's Jewishness," in *The Self-Fashioning of Disraeli: 1818–1851*, ed. Charles Richmond and Paul Smith (Cambridge: Cambridge University Press, 1998), 128–30.
27. *Romances by I. D'Israeli* (London: Cadell and Davies, 1799).
28. Levinas, xi, x.
29. John Bell, *Travels from St. Petersburgh in Russia to Various Parts of Asia. Illustrated with Maps* (London: W. Creech, 1788); James Dallaway, *Constantinople Ancient and Modern, with Excursions to the Shores and Islands of the Archipelago and to the Troad* (London: Cadell and Davies, 1797);

William Jones, *Grammar of the Persian Language* (1771), 3rd ed. (London: J. Murray, 1783); Carsten Niebuhr, *A Collection of Late Voyages and Travels... Concerning the Present State of Society and Manners, of Arts and Literature, of Religion and Government, the Appearances of Nature, and the Works of Human Industry in Persia, Arabia, Turkey, &c* (London: J. Hamilton, 1797); William Ouseley, *Persian Miscellanies: An Essay to Facilitate the Reading of Persian Manuscripts with Engraved Specimens, Philosophical Observations, and Notes Critical and Historical* (London: Richard White, 1795); John Richardson, *A Dictionary, Persian, Arabic and English, by John Richardson, to Which There Is Prefixed a Dissertation on the Languages, Literatures, and Manners of Eastern Nations*, 2 vols. (Oxford: Clarendon, 1777–80), and *A Grammar of the Arabic Language, in Which the Rules Are Illustrated by Authorities from the Best Writers, Principally Adapted for the Use of the Honourable East India Company* (London: J. Murray, 1776).
30. Ogden, 207.
31. Ogden, 207, 209.
32. Neusner, *Presence,* 51.
33. Ogden, 207.
34. Ogden, 43.
35. Quoted in Ogden, 44.
36. See Geoffrey Keynes' *Bibliography of William Blake* (New York: Grolier Club, 1921), 18–19; S. Foster Damon's *William Blake: His Philosophy and Symbols* (New York: Grolier Club, 1924), 243; and Mona Wilson's *The Life of William Blake* (London: Nonesuch, 1927), 236.
37. Northrop Frye, *Fearful Symmetry: A Study of William Blake* (1947; Princeton: Princeton University Press, 1969).
38. *Fearful Symmetry,* 125.
39. *Fearful Symmetry,* 79.
40. Northrop Frye, "The Problem of Spiritual Authority in the Nineteenth Century," in *The Stubborn Structure: Essays on Criticism and Society* (Ithaca: Cornell University Press, 1970), 241–56; *Anatomy of Criticism: Four Essays* (1957; Princeton: Princeton University Press, 1971).
41. Frye, *Anatomy of Criticism,* 29.
42. Northrop Frye, *The Great Code: The Bible and Literature* (New York: Harcourt, 1982).

Chapter 11

Hyman Hurwitz's *Hebrew Tales* (1826): Redeeming the Talmudic Garden

Judith W. Page

Two years before he became the first Jewish Professor of Hebrew Language and Literature at University College, London, in 1828, Hyman Hurwitz published the first collection of Hebrew literature in English, an anthology entitled *Hebrew Tales*.[1] The volume is composed of tales and aphorisms from rabbinic literature, including the Talmud and *midrash*. As Hurwitz's preface and essay make clear, he intended the volume to counter negative and uninformed assumptions about this literature in much Christian writing, and to educate British Jews in their own rich traditions. More fundamentally, he wanted to show the compatibility of traditional Jewish wisdom and contemporary British culture. Inspired by his friend Coleridge, Hurwitz set out to redeem the Talmud and to cultivate a new tradition that would make Jews more at home in Britain and Britain more hospitable to Jews and Jewish culture.[2] The historian David Ruderman, who sees the project of translation as a major part of the *Haskalah* or Enlightenment in England, believes that Hurwitz's project, like that of Jewish biblical translators of the period, "constructed a radically new image of what they thought Judaism meant to their age. This image was so formidable and pervasive that, to the readers of their prodigious translations, the reality on which their new image was based was virtually displaced." According to Ruderman, in attempting to make the rabbis and Judaism palatable to English men and women, Hurwitz deprived the tradition of its "unique idiom and cultural perspective."[3]

    I will argue, however, that Hurwitz did maintain certain elements of rabbinic wisdom even as he crossed the linguistic and cultural border into English and into the world of Romantic literature and theory. Hurwitz rejected the belief that the Talmud was inspired, the word of God, a position that distances him from the tradition. But in choosing to focus on narratives, *aggadot,* from the Talmud and other rabbinic sources, Hurwitz deflected attention from both the Law itself and the commentary. Therefore, he focused on that part of rabbinic teaching linked to ancient Jewish popular culture and avoided direct debate about the Law and its status. In doing so, he transmitted the narrative traditions and wit of rabbinic literature without attempting to make sense of the entire Talmud, although he did outline his theory for the project in an appended essay. In this sense Hurwitz's project bears resemblance to Wordsworth and Coleridge's *Lyrical Ballads,* particularly to the way that Wordsworth theorized the project in the Preface and transmitted a literary version of traditional folk narratives in the poems. Because of Hurwitz's desire to redeem Judaism from scorn and to reconcile it with contemporary English culture, his goal was even trickier than Wordsworth's. The comparison of the two authors is revealing, however, because Hurwitz thought of his project as a contribution to English readers, whose preferences and tastes were susceptible to influence.

Literary Theory

> If a man attaches much interest to the faculty of taste as it exists in himself and employs much time in those studies of which this faculty ... is reckoned the arbiter, certain it is his moral notions and dispositions must either be purified and strengthened or corrupted and impaired. How can it be otherwise, when his ability to enter into the spirit of works in literature must depend upon his feelings, his imagination and his understanding, that is upon his recipient, upon his creative or active and upon his judging powers, and upon the accuracy and compass of his knowledge, in fine upon all that makes up the moral and intellectual man. What is true of individuals is equally true of nations.
> —Wordsworth, "Essay on Epitaphs II"

Hurwitz takes great care with the selection and arrangement of his volume, but he does not simply let the tales speak for themselves. Instead, he prefixes a theoretical essay to *Hebrew Tales,* placing his work in various contexts and assuring that his readers do not miss his polemical points. In the essay, Hurwitz is careful to acknowledge that he is presenting the collection with a particular function in mind. He calls this function "moral improvement" (5), but his agenda is both broader and more specific than that: He acknowledges that he intends to refute influential misreadings of Talmudic literature and to provide a framework in which English readers can appreciate the tradition anew. He does this by explaining the rabbinic method of storytelling, which includes a metaphorical imagination of the world, by drawing comparisons between rabbinic and other intellectual traditions, and by arguing that the diversity of opinion found in the Talmud is an asset rather than a detriment. Although collections of tales or poems were common during the period,[4] the one that most closely resembles *Hebrew Tales* in its didactic and moral purpose is the *Lyrical Ballads*. In Hurwitz's years of close conversation with Coleridge, he no doubt spoke with his friend about Coleridge's various literary ventures, including his early collaboration with Wordsworth. Whatever the source of the link, however, Hurwitz thought of his anthological project in similar terms to those Wordsworth outlines in his Preface. Both men were sophisticated literary thinkers who articulated their ideas in polemical prefaces to their volumes and who also appealed to "simple" traditional materials. In his Preface, Wordsworth argues that the poet must create the taste by which readers can enjoy and appreciate his work. Wordsworth sees himself writing in a time of crisis. He wants to forge a new contract with readers, to woo them away from sensational literature and to cultivate the taste for his "simple" tales, for the folk and rural traditions that many of his tales represent. He also makes an urgent plea for the power of his own literary style in a poem such as "Tintern Abbey," to continue the tradition of Shakespeare and Milton— his version of "the language of men."[5] As if to emphasize the ideological function of the collection, Wordsworth underscores the various problems besetting the world in 1800: growth in urban life and industrial production, rapid changes in media, communication, transportation, and the continuing threat of war. In response to these alienating circumstances of life, Wordsworth proposes a literature that promotes human warmth and sympathy by combining the pleasures of reading with high moral purpose. Like so many of his Romantic contemporaries, Wordsworth centers his project on the interplay of sympathy and pleasure: "We have no sympathy but what is propagated by pleasure" (140), an idea implicit in Hurwitz's arrangement of *Hebrew Tales*.

Hurwitz outlines a similar rhetorical and theoretical strategy as the basis for his anthology. Hurwitz wants to create a collection of pleasurable tales, but he also has clear ideological goals. His volume, he hopes, will educate the public and dispel anti-Semitic attitudes about the Talmud and other rabbinic literature. In selecting tales from Hebrew literature, Hurwitz emphasizes the imaginative, fictive, and folk elements of the tradition, the *aggadot*, rather than the portion of the Talmud and rabbinic teaching that interprets *halakhah*, the Law. He also denies that Jewish tradition values the Talmud above the Bible (a common charge), making it clear that he views all rabbinic literature as "uninspired," or not the direct word of God. Hence, too, he takes liberties with his translations, in his attempt to package the tales for his time and place. Furthermore, the folksiness of the tales helps to "naturalize" them into English traditional culture like other collections of tales, ballads, and melodies.

Hurwitz responds to what he sees as a crisis for contemporary Jews at a moment when they are seeking to establish themselves both as English men and women and as Jews. Like Wordsworth in the Preface, he writes with a sense of the urgency of his message and with the hope that his volume will have a direct effect on a specific cultural problem: he writes with a purpose. Most important, he seeks to elicit sympathy for Jews and Jewish tradition by finding common ground: "the Reader may assure himself that in the little volume here offered to him, it is the fervent wish, and has been the constant aim of the Writer, to enforce the religious and moral truths on which the best interests of all men of all names and persuasions find their common basis and fulcrum, and with scarcely less anxiety to avoid every invidious reference to the points on which their opinions are divided" (x). Like Wordsworth's idea of "the Poet," Hurwitz's role as translator and anthologist brings together disparate elements. In Wordsworth's words,

> [the poet] is the rock of defence of human nature; an upholder and preserver, carrying every where with him relationship and love. In spite of difference of soil and climate, of language and manners, of laws and customs, in spite of things silently gone out of mind and things violently destroyed, the poet binds together by passion and knowledge the vast empire of human society, as it is spread over the whole earth, and over all time. (141)

Sharing this liberal humanist view of humanity and of art, Hurwitz believes that tales have the power to bring about change for the good by binding together "men of all names and persuasions."

Like other Romantic theorists, Hurwitz thinks of writing in organic terms. He presents his *Tales* not as specimens from an exotic foreign garden but as adaptable to an English linguistic and cultural climate. Hurwitz, in fact, uses organic imagery when he articulates his intentions in his polemical essay:

> Indeed, the proceedings of these Talmudical detractors can only be compared to the conduct of a person, who being admitted into an extensive garden, should, instead of regaling himself with its variegated productions, deliberately walk about, and busy himself with picking up every worthless pebble, withered fruit, and noxious weed; and having loaded himself with as much "Look, Sir! Look at the precious productions of your garden!"—Might not the proprietor with justice reply, "Sir, that weeds

grow in my garden may be true; for in what garden planted by human hands do they not grow? But, surely, that is no enviable taste, which, amidst the many and various fruits and flowers produced here, leads you to notice these alone; even though they were indeed what you suppose them to be. This, however, is by no means the fact. In that plant, which your hasty and undiscerning prejudice regards as a weed, there is a hidden virtue, which strikes every beholder. Of this apparently withered fruit, you need but remove the external covering, and you will find it delicious. These pebbles, too, require only a little polishing, and their genuine luster will soon appear." (17–18)

Hurwitz makes his point in the essay by inventing a metaphorical tale, not unlike the *aggadot* that he translates for the collection. He thus defends the Talmud with a tale that itself demonstrates the narrative tradition he so admires. But his metaphor also makes it clear that he wants to acknowledge the need for a discerning reader to find the sweetness and luster in this garden that, at least to an unsympathetic eye, contains some "rubbish." Rather than claim that Talmudic detractors have completely falsified the Talmud, Hurwitz argues that detractors have distorted the tradition by focusing on questionable passages, wrenching others out of a context that might reveal a hidden beauty, and reading a highly metaphorical literature as literalists. Furthermore, these detractors ignore that the Talmud was compiled over many years by different authors, and therefore represents different perspectives. Predictably, some of the authors reveal greater wisdom or artistic sensibility than others. Hurwitz justifies his collection by pointing out "Several selections have also been made by Writers of different denominations; but these have not even the merit of good intention. For (to judge from the collected articles) the sole aim of these Writers appears to have been to throw an odium on the ancient Hebrew works, as well as on their learned authors and their unfortunate descendants; and thus to nourish the worst feelings of human nature" (vi). Such volumes, Hurwitz implies, propagate no pleasure and hence no sympathy.[6]

Hurwitz's strategy in the polemical essay is, then, to acknowledge problems in the rabbinic writings for contemporary readers, both Jews and non-Jews, and also to enlarge the context for understanding rabbinic Judaism. Hurwitz acknowledges that some of the tales are extravagant and exaggerated—they are "idle tales, borrowed most probably from Parthians and Arabians, to whom the Jews were subject before the promulgation of the Talmud" (35n.). He goes on to explain that "[a]nother fertile source of misconception originated in that natural fondness for the marvelous—so common to undisciplined minds—of which the Ancient Rabbis sometimes availed themselves with the sole view of exciting the attention of their respective audiences" (35n.).

Hurwitz's continued rejection of "the marvelous" is particularly interesting in relationship to Wordsworth's and other literary theories of the period. Hurwitz's prejudice echoes Wordsworth's rejection of the gothic in his Preface to *Lyrical Ballads*—of "idle and extravagant tales in verse" or "sickly and stupid German Tragedies" (129). In place of gothic, Hurwitz invents the category I shall call the "rabbinic marvelous," which he links to the less talented rabbis with "undisciplined minds" who fall back on nonsense and exaggeration in order to command the attention of their audiences (who, no doubt like Wordsworth's mythical countrymen, crave "outrageous stimulation" [131]). Like Wordsworth, Hurwitz hopes to elicit responses from his audience from the more simple pleasures of homey tales, folk traditions, and domestic scenes. Hurwitz rejects the marvelous because it is just what the detractors of the Talmud focus on in presenting Jewish writing as "primitive" and wildly irrational. For Hurwitz, the literature is filled with the "feelings of human nature," but also with the voice of wisdom and reason. Hurwitz's general practice is to tone down the marvelous or to identify it clearly as metaphorical.

Hurwitz also implies that rabbinic tales include the marvelous because they have roots in oral sermons,[7] in which rabbis had free rein to show their originality and ingenuity in reaching their audience.[8] No doubt many accomplished this goal. Their use of exaggeration, superstition, and marvelous events is compatible with folk culture and traditions, whereas the commentary on the Law (*halakhah*) is usually more academic in content and dry in rhetorical style.[9] Hence, in creating and transmitting the tales, the rabbis hoped to reach a broader, more diverse audience of Jews. An interesting parallel exists with the *Lyrical Ballads*, literary ballads based on old folk traditions, contemporary rural legends, and superstitious tales. While Hurwitz wants to temper and contain the marvelous altogether, Wordsworth incorporates the psychological and cultural effect of such narratives into the framework of the tale itself, as in "The Thorn," "Goody Blake and Harry Gill," and "Lucy Gray," to name a few.[10]

In his attempt to bring the *Hebrew Tales* in line with mainstream thought, Hurwitz compares rabbinic ideas with such writers as Plato, Aristotle, Pythagoras, and Aesop. He also alludes to Shakespeare and Milton in order to show a harmony between British and rabbinic literature. Hurwitz's main point in alluding to ancient philosophers is to argue that the same critics who condemn certain ideas in the Talmud do not do so in these other contexts. For instance, Hurwitz argues that the rabbis were interested in "the perfectibility of human nature" so "they justly concluded, that an *idea* of that perfectibility must have existed in the Divine mind" (26). Hurwitz concludes that "These sentiments, worthy of *Plato,* have yet been decried as rabbinical reveries, and their authors even arraigned of impiety!—on no better grounds than what the detractors themselves supplied, by wantonly imposing their own literal sense on expressions evidently, and (but by motive or dullness) *unmistakably,* figurative" (26). This is, once again, part of Hurwitz's desire to find common ground between rabbinic Judaism and other philosophical and religious systems, and to convince English readers to grant the same capacity for metaphor to the rabbis as they grant to a thinker such as Plato.

In the same vein, Hurwitz notes that Coleridge's description of the "luminous appearance of the sea" (27) in Letter I of "Satyrane's Letters" is comparable to the rabbinic tale: "Those that travel on the sea have told me, that on the head of the wave which threatens destruction to the ship, there appear sparks of white fire: that they beat it (the sea) with sticks, on which is written the name of the Almighty, and it rests, or is subdued" (27; attributed to the Talmudic tractate *Bava Batra*). Hurwitz singles out the passage from Coleridge to demonstrate the same kind of imagination before the wonders of God: "A beautiful white cloud of foam, at momently intervals, coursed by the side of the vessel with a roar, and little stars of flame danced and sparkled and went out in it: and every now and then light detachments of this white cloud-like foam, darted off from the vessel's side, each out of sight like a Tartar troop over a wilderness" (27n.).[11] In the context of Letter I, the narrator, traveling on board a ship, has just rebuffed "the Dane" who assumes that the narrator is "un philosophe" and thus "commence[s] an harangue on religion" (167). After professing himself a believer, the narrator wraps himself in a coat and looks out at the divine beauty of the water. Hurwitz implies that Coleridge, like the rabbis, sees the name of the Almighty.

Hurwitz portrays the contradictions and "diversity of opinion" (38) in the Talmud as evidence of its vitality. He reminds his readers that the authors were "thousands of learned men, of various talents, living in a long series of ages, in different countries, and under the most diversified conditions. And how, in the name of truth, can perfect agreement be expected under such circumstances?" (37). Hurwitz explains that disagreement on "philosophical and speculative subjects" (i.e., not on "the essential parts of religion") is a strength of the Talmud and of Jewish thought because it leaves the "mind unfettered" (37), in something akin to a Keatsian state of "negative capability." In assessing the Talmud, readers should consider its history, composition, and status as a mixed genre. Diversity of opinion also makes for a living text, a position in line with later theorists of the Talmud's anthological and encyclopedic qualities and organic, evolutionary process. As Jonathan Rosen summarizes in *The Talmud and the Internet*, "Theirs [the Rabbis'] was a system that made a virtue of ambivalence and built uncertainty into bedrock assertions of faith. No wonder fundamentalists and fascists have hated it so."[12] For readers like Rosen, the "unlikely joinings" of the Talmud present "an invitation to openness."[13]

Diversity can contribute to balance. For instance, Hurwitz responds to the charge that the Talmud is vengeful because it includes passages cursing the "idolatrous heathen" (50). Hurwitz acknowledges that such passages appear in the Talmud and mean what they say (in this case) literally. Hurwitz warns his readers to consider this before passing judgment:

> Let us not forget that they were the implacable enemies of the Hebrews—that they polluted the holy sanctuary—desolated the country—slaughtered its inhabitants, and covered the land with mourning. Let the reader, of whatever persuasion he may be, read the books of the Maccabees—then let him for a moment suppose himself to be one of those unfortunate Israelites, who were made to drink the bitter cup of affliction to the very dregs. (51)

Hurwitz asks his readers to consider the context in which Jews uttered these curses and to have sympathy for their suffering under oppression. He also goes on to note that expressions of charity for the heathen poor balance the condemnation of heathen oppression in the Talmud. Furthermore, Hurwitz quotes Rabbi Moshe as distinguishing between the ancient idolaters who oppressed the Jews and righteous gentiles who protected the Jewish people: "the nations amongst whom we live, whose protection we enjoy, must not be considered in this light; since they believe in a creation, the divine origin of the law, and many other fundamental doctrines of religion" (53n., attributed to Beer Hagoleh Chosen Hamishpat,[14] no. 425). Hurwitz implies that generosity and gratitude balance expressions of harshness, although bigots will only see the latter. In other words, Hurwitz must depend, like Wordsworth's writer of epigraphs, on the moral and intellectual makeup of the recipient.

Storytelling

> O reader! Had you in your mind
> Such stores as silent thought can bring,

O gentle reader! You would find
A tale in everything.
—Wordsworth, "Simon Lee, the Old Huntsman" (*Lyrical Ballads*)

Hurwitz arranges *Hebrew Tales* so that positive values and perspectives receive the most emphasis: Hurwitz's gentle reader, like Wordsworth's, should find a moral in every tale. Hurwitz conveys meaning both through the thematic content and through the framework of the tale, never losing sight of his moral purpose as a translator and anthologist. The predominant themes of his selected tales are charity, the holiness of life, familial relationships, and faith in the after-life, all rabbinic values that would resonate with both his Jewish and Christian readers.

Hurwitz takes some pains to show that such seemingly universal moral teachings as the Golden Rule originate in Jewish thought. He translates the Talmudic tale of the heathen who asked the great rabbi Hillel to teach him the entire law "whilst I stand upon one leg" (60 *Tales*). Unlike the proud Shammai who pushes the man away, Hillel responds: "*Remember, whatever thou dislikest thyself, do not unto thy neighbors.* This is the substance of the law; every thing else is but its comment; now go and learn" (60 *Tales*).[15] Hurwitz's rendition of this familiar tale conveys a universal moral, but it also preserves the rabbinic spirit by embedding the kernel of truth in another didactic narrative—that of the contrast between the humble brilliance of Hillel and the learned but proud and morose Shammai. Hillel proves to be the better teacher because he meets the questioner on the questioner's terms (even though the challenge seems riddle-like and absurd) and his efforts lead the heathen to become "a good and pious man" (60 *Tales*). Thus, Hurwitz's translation conveys both Hillel's distillation of the moral purpose of the law and its effect on his life. As Jonathan Rosen explains, "In a sense Hillel outwitted the lazy man by teaching him that one of the principles of Judaism, in addition, of course, to kindness, is study. The man is caught in the web and, in the timeless manner of the Talmud, is probably still studying to this day."[16]

Hurwitz's organization of his collection is also revealing. Following a brief preface and his polemical essay, Hurwitz opens the collection with a *midrashic* story of "Moses and the Lamb," one of many in rabbinic literature that imaginatively embellish biblical accounts:

> Our wise Instructors relate, that whilst Moses was attending Jethro's flock in the wilderness, a lamb strayed from the herd. Moses endeavoured to overtake it, but it ran much faster than he, till it came near a fountain, where it suddenly stopped, and took a draught of water. "Thou little dear

innocent creature," said Moses, "I see now why thou didst run away. Had I known thy want, on my shoulders would I have carried thee to the fountain to assuage thy thirst. But come, little innocent, I will make up for my ignorance. Thou art no doubt fatigued after so long a journey, thou shalt walk no further." He immediately took the little creature into his arms, and carried it back to the flock. (4 *Tales*)

This story, which Hurwitz attributes to "Medrash Shemoth Rabah,"[17] suggests that God chose Moses as his great prophet because Moses showed himself to be compassionate in his respect for all life. It implies that God valued Moses' capacity to sympathize and knew that he would extend this sympathy to "the children of men" (4 *Tales*). Thus, the very first tale in the collection sets the tone for what follows and emphasizes that a respect for life and a sympathetic heart are central to the rabbinic conception of God's purpose in giving the Torah. Hurwitz begins with this tale, too, to counter the Christian assumption that a Jewish emphasis on law and justice comes at the expense of love and mercy. Contrary to this common position, which has fostered anti-Semitism, Hurwitz wants to establish that love in fact is the essence of the Law, not its opposite.

Following the main body of tales, which includes a wide variety of themes and narrative structures, Hurwitz adds "Facetiæ" and "Aphorisms and Apophthegms" in the final sections to make the volume as a whole "as entertaining, as it is hoped, it will be found instructive" (vii). The "Facetiæ" are interesting in their focus on smart (some might say smart-alecky) children and less wise adults, a set-up familiar to readers of *Lyrical Ballads*. In fact, the Wordsworthian parallels continue. Structurally, most of these tales involve questions and answers, as do the ballads. For instance, take "The Wise Child," a tale involving Rabbi Joshuah (an adult, in this case, willing to learn):

"More than a mile-stone must be consulted in deciding which is the shortest way." Once on my travels, I came near a town where the road separated to right and left. Not knowing which to take, I enquired of a little boy who happened to be there, which of the two led to the town. "Both," replied he; "but that to the right is *short* and *long*—that on the left is *long* and *short*." I took that on the right; but had not far advanced, when my progress was stopped by a number of hedges and gardens. Unable to proceed, I returned, and asked the little fellow, how he could be so cruel as to misdirect a stranger? "I did not misdirect thee," replied the boy. "I told thee what is true. But art thou a wise man amongst Israel, and canst not comprehend the meaning of a child?—It is even as I said. This road is the nearest, but still the longest, on account of the many obstructions. Unless thou wouldest trespass on other people's ground, which I could hardly suppose from so good a man. The other road is, indeed, more distant, but it is, nevertheless, the shortest, being the public road; and may, therefore, be passed without encroaching on other people's property."—I admired his wit, and still more his good sense, and went on. (*Tales* 182–3)

This tale may not teach a profound moral, but it does illuminate the relationship between adults and children, and it implicitly admonishes adults to listen carefully to the wisdom of a child, even if mischievous. It also tells the reader something particular about Judaism—that questioning, interpretation, and attention to details are important, that prominent rabbis do not know everything, and that sometimes the sources of knowledge are unexpected. Hurwitz's ideal reader would enjoy the child's wit as well as admire the wisdom of the great rabbi. Because the reader too takes pleasure in the tale, the reader feels a sympathetic connection to the tradition.

The final entry in the volume begins with a translation of one of Hillel's best-known sayings: "If I am not for myself," says the pious Hillel, "who is to be for me?—If I am for myself only—what am I then?—And if not now, when then?" (207 *Tales*). In his essay on the "Jewish" Wordsworth, Lionel Trilling noted the affinity between Hillel's brilliant formulation of the balance between self and community and Wordsworth's poetic faith, variously expressed over the years, that "the mind is fitted to the world."[18] Hurwitz ends with this aphorism, I think, because he wants to show the efficacy of rabbinic thought in the contemporary world—the need to acknowledge this kind of balance in moral as well as epistemological terms. Hurwitz is so concerned to convey this moral that he does not let Hillel's words speak for themselves. Instead, he includes a lengthy series of footnotes for various parts of his last entry, beginning with this explanation of Hillel:

> Man as a social being has various duties to perform; some relating to his individual welfare, others to the welfare of society. If he neglect the former, how can he expect that others, less interested, will perform them for him. If he neglect the latter, and studies only his own interest, he becomes a *selfish* creature, scarcely deserving the name *man*. A good man will neglect neither: and this is what the pious Rabbi wished to inculcate. (207n. *Tales*)

Hurwitz implies that this rabbinic wisdom is consistent with the best moral philosophy in advocating a balance between self-respect and benevolence, not unlike the morality of Wordsworth's Pedlar at the end of *The Ruined Cottage,* who urges the young poet, distraught over the fate of Margaret: "My Friend, enough to sorrow have you given,/The purposes of wisdom ask no more" (509–10).[19]

Hillel's injunction balances and to some extent qualifies the call for sympathy in the tales, best exemplified by the first tale involving Moses. The narrative framework, therefore, represents a progression of sorts, from noble but naïve expressions of love for the lamb (and thus for all of God's creation) to a more sophisticated statement of how one's love and sympathy work in the human community, in the here and now. This coincides with the "ultimate object" of the publication, "moral improvement" (vii). It is paradoxical that whereas Hurwitz claims the later tales and aphorisms to be more entertaining, he actually encases many of them in the mechanism of scholarship: lengthy explanatory footnotes that make sure the reader absorbs the moral of the story. This practice also demonstrates that the collection works on different levels, as if many of the footnotes are for the more advanced reader or the teacher.

Audience

> Monday, 26th December [1825]: I may class this as one of the happiest days of my life in the serene and obliging society of my dear Mon[tefiore], blessed with health and cheerfulness and an unremitting desire to please for which I cannot sufficiently thank the Almighty.... The evening passed delightfully reading Hurwitz's *Hebrew Stories*, and Montefiore getting up his new journal.
>
> —Judith Montefiore[20]

Who read this volume? *Hebrew Tales* was immediately popular with the Jewish community when it came out a few months in advance of its publication date in 1826 (as Judith Montefiore's diary hints) and it did contribute to the teaching of Jewish children. The work was a best seller in England and America throughout the nineteenth century and was also translated into several languages, including German, as early as 1828.[21] But Hurwitz's influence seems mainly to have been limited to Jewish audiences, particularly to school children, and that influence diminished in the twentieth century. Hurwitz did not succeed, then, in bringing rabbinic wisdom into the mainstream of British literary culture. Nevertheless, Coleridge continued to praise Hurwitz's work for the years remaining in his life (he died in 1834), urging it on his friends and readers. And *Hebrew Tales* enjoyed at least one mainly positive and impressively knowledgeable twenty-eight-page unsigned review—in the *Quarterly Review* in 1827.[22]

In this long, scholarly review, the reviewer praises the tales as an entertaining selection, but objects to Hurwitz's attempt to bowdlerize the Talmud and present the rabbinic texts as less problematic than the reviewer finds them: "The books abound with precepts, which are still more plain than those which Mr. Hurwitz has exercised so much ingenuity in softening; they distinctly consign those who neglect the rabbinical writings to *eternal immersion in boiling dung* in the other world" (97). But even though he makes this argument and supports it with examples from the Talmud, the reviewer acknowledges the value of Hurwitz's project and writes passionately about the oppression of the Jews in history and the need for Britain to remove disabilities and bestow "well-deserved favour on a loyal and industrious body of men" (95). The Christian reviewer, in other words, transforms the review into an occasion for making a strong statement about the place of Jews in the nation and their potential as British subjects, implicitly one of Hurwitz's goals in publishing the collection to begin with.

In the midst of a long critical explanation of the Talmud itself and a more sympathetic history of the Jews, the reviewer urges his readers that

> it must not be imagined that the great rabbinical repository does not contain better things. In spite of its trifling, and of other objections that might be urged against it, few works are better worth the attention of the antiquary, the philologer, the philosophic historian, and the theologian. It presents the most curious picture of the modes of thinking and acting of the most singular people that ever existed, under circumstances altogether unparalleled. (91)

The reviewer takes up Hurwitz's defense of the Talmud as unkind to heathens and challenges head-on the additional charge that the Talmud is anti-Christian. He reminds readers that the Talmud was meant for the Jews themselves, and that they were entitled to speak slightingly of other sects. Furthermore, with irony directed against the oppressors, the reviewer endorses Hurwitz's defense: "The poor Jews had indeed much reason to be civil. After being persecuted, hunted like beasts, robbed, reviled, trampled upon, in every Christian country in the world, it might surely be pardoned them that they were occasionally disrespectful to that faith, the abuse of which exposed them to such calamities" (99). The reviewer is also particularly critical of the oppression of Jews by a succession of popes, many of whom were the most vociferous critics of the Talmud.

The reviewer makes the point that the very fact that the Talmud contains stories interspersed with text of the Oral Law (*Mishnah*) and the commentary (*Gemara*) has been one reason why bigots have slandered the Talmud. He quotes one critic as charging that its authors are the "most impudent patchers together of old wives' stories" (103). In response to such objections to the mixed genre and folk qualities of the

Talmud, the reviewer reminds readers that "These critics did not sufficiently attend to the oriental origin of the work which they were reviling, and reflect that, in all the nations of the East, it was customary to mix up such narrations with graver matters" (103). Hurwitz himself chose not to emphasize the Eastern connections, but the reviewer is perceptive in seeing the implicit connection between the Talmudic tales and such framed narratives as the *Arabian Nights*.[23] In fact, the reviewer comments on an allegorical tale involving a Talmudic bird and wittily concludes that "The Talmud and the Arabian Nights Entertainment drew from the same systems of ornithology" (108).

Furthermore, the reviewer reminds his Christian readers that "our Saviour sanctified the principle of applying stories (some of them drawn, in all probability, from a common source with many of those in the Talmud) to the elucidation of affairs of the most sacred importance" (103). That said, the reviewer does object to what he sees as Hurwitz's over-allegorizing material that might well have been meant literally, thus questioning Hurwitz's foundational idea that the tales are almost always metaphorical. But, according to the reviewer, "Such will always be the case, where philosophical generations are called on to believe in the fancies of poetical antiquity, and to interpret the dreams or wisdom, as the case may be, of mystic or superstitious predecessors" (103). The reviewer implies that Hurwitz has been unfaithful to the original in allegorizing away too much of the rabbinic marvelous. In closing, the reviewer calls for Hurwitz to continue his researches in and translations of the Talmud, urging the author to see *Hebrew Tales* as an opening act: "He well knows that there is much for him to glean there, and he has only to guard against painting things better than they are. What man of sense is there who is not prepared to find fable, and nonsense, and indelicacy, and intolerance, occasionally mixed with the better matter of a work composed at such a time, and under such circumstances?" (113).

Hurwitz did not translate another Talmudic volume, but as an educator he continued to emphasize the importance of a proper knowledge of Hebrew for an accurate understanding of both Hebrew Scriptures and rabbinic literature. *Hebrew Tales* was an attempt to popularize rabbinic literature in English, to cross the border from Hebrew into English language and culture.[24] As André Lefevere has commented, "Translators are the artisans of compromise.... Since they are at home in two cultures and two literatures, they also have the power to construct the image of one literature for consumption by the readers of another."[25] Hurwitz conflated the roles of anthologist and translator. For Hurwitz, the two processes of selection of tales or portions of tales and their translation were linked by his desire to create the taste for this consumption, to present readers with an inviting image of Hebrew culture in English. He rejected both the translations of detractors as well as Yiddish translations: "Selections from [the Talmud and *midrashim*] have, indeed been made by several Jewish writers, with the laudable view of imparting moral instruction to the illiterate portions of their respective communities; but they are written in a language—if at all it deserves the name—so low and corrupt, and they are, besides, interwoven with so many false opinions and glaring absurdities, that they have deservedly sunk into oblivion" (v). By this negative example, Hurwitz emphasizes the cultural importance of presenting *Hebrew Tales* in his English version of Wordsworth's "language of men."

In denying the value of Yiddish, the lingua franca of other European Jews, Hurwitz also rejected the notion that English Jews should have a completely separate cultural identity from other Britons. Hurwitz, himself a Polish-born Jew who learned English as an adult, embraced the Englishness of English as both a cultural and a linguistic legacy. By translating rabbinic tales into the King's English, Hurwitz demonstrated that the *otherness* of Judaism could fit into and make sense within the larger culture. As the 1827 reviewer implicitly recognizes, Hurwitz was in a catch-22: he would alienate both Christian readers and Reform-minded Jews if he did not package the tales for the modern world; but he risked compromising the tradition in the transformation. The popularity of the volume with Jews for over a hundred years proves that he connected with Jewish readers. I have here tried to show that Hurwitz succeeded in conveying the narrative spirit of ancient Jewish thought even as he transplanted it in England's green and pleasant land.

Notes

1. Hyman Hurwitz, *Hebrew Tales; Selected and Translated from the Writings of the Ancient Hebrew Sages: To Which is Prefixed, an Essay, on the Uninspired Literature of the Hebrews* (London: Morrison and Watt, 1826). The essay is numbered separately from the *Tales;* when indicated specifically, the pagination refers to the *Tales* and appears parenthetically in the text.
2. The most complete introduction to date on Hurwitz is still Leonard Hyman, "Hyman Hurwitz: The First Anglo-English Professor," in *Transactions of the Jewish Historical Society of England, 1962–67,* 21 (London: The Jewish Historical Society of England, 1968), 232–41. Ina Lipowitz includes some interesting comments in relation to Coleridge in "Inspiration and the Poetic Imagination: Samuel Taylor Coleridge," *Studies in Romanticism* 30 (Winter 1991): 605–31. Finally, David B. Ruderman devotes some pages in his final chapter of *Jewish Enlightenment in an English Key: Anglo-Jewry's Construction of Modern Jewish Thought* (Princeton: Princeton University Press, 2000), to Hurwitz. See "Translation and Transformation: The Englishing of Jewish Culture," 261–73.

3. Ruderman, 268.
4. See Neil Fraistat, *The Poem and the Book: Interpreting Collections of Romantic Poetry* (Chapel Hill: University of North Carolina Press, 1985).
5. "The Preface to *Lyrical Ballads*," *The Prose Works of William Wordsworth*, ed. W. J. B. Owen and Jane Worthington Smyser, 3 vols. (Oxford: Clarendon Press, 1974), 1:131. My references are to the "1850" edition (which incorporates the 1802 changes), and appear parenthetically in the text.
6. Because of their own prejudices, bigoted Talmudic critics do not understand that the collection or anthology is central to Jewish literary tradition. As David Stern explains in attempting to define the significance of the anthology, "The definition of the form itself is open to alteration, and in addition to conventional anthologies, we have included such works as the Talmud—which may resemble an encyclopedia more than an anthology—precisely because it was a collaborative project that programmatically preserved and systematically collated the traditions of earlier generations. In fact, for such works as the Talmud—which are generically 'problematic' precisely because they do not fit neatly into any of our familiar literary genres—the category of the anthology provides an extraordinarily useful heuristic tool for defining literary identity" ("Introduction: The Anthological Imagination in Jewish Literature," *Prooftexts,* Special Issue: The Anthological Imagination in Jewish Literature, Part 1, 17 [January 1997]: 2).
7. See Joseph Heinemann, "The Nature of Aggadah," in *Midrash and Literature,* ed. Geoffrey H. Hartman and Sanford Budick (New Haven: Yale University Press, 1986), 41–55.
8. See Judah Goldin, "The Freedom and Restraint of Haggadah," in *Midrash and Literature,* ed. Geoffrey H. Hartman and Sanford Budick (New Haven: Yale University Press, 1986), 57–76.
9. Heinemann argues that the *aggadot* were responses to a time of crisis and were created by rabbis as a way to reach "the simple folk" (47).
10. I address this in "Style and Rhetorical Intention in Wordsworth's *Lyrical Ballads,"* *Philological Quarterly* (Summer 1983): 293–313.
11. I thank Professor Anthony Harding for helping me with this reference. "Satyrane's Letters," first written during Coleridge's trip to Germany in 1798–99, were subsequently published in *The Friend* (nos. 14, 16, and 18; 1809), and then published with the second volume of the *Biographia* (Hurwitz's reference). See *Biographia Literaria*, Bollingen Series LXXV, ed. James Engell and W. Jackson Bate (Princeton: Princeton University Press, 1983), 160n.
12. Jonathan Rosen, *The Talmud and the Internet: A Journey Between Two Worlds* (New York: Farrar, Straus and Giroux, 2000), 61.
13. Rosen, 91.
14. The reference is to *Be'er ha-Golah,* a commentary written by Moses b. Naphtali Hirsch Rivkes (d. c. 1671/72), to the *Shulan Arukh,* a legal code written by Joseph Caro (1488–1575).
15. Hillel, a rabbi who lived from the end of the first century BCE to the beginning of the first century CE; Shammei, his contemporary, lived from approximately 50 BCE to 30 CE.

16. Rosen, 31.
17. An *aggadic midrash* on the Book of Exodus.
18. See Lionel Trilling, "Wordsworth and the Rabbis," in *The Opposing Self: Nine Essays in Criticism* (New York: Viking, 1955), 127.
19. For the rabbinic context, see Trilling, especially 128–31.
20. Taken from Montefiore's "honeymoon diary," December 26, 1825 (in Lucian Wolf, "Lady Montefiore's Honeymoon," in *Essays in Jewish History*, ed. Cecil Roth [London: The Jewish Historical Society of England, 1934], 256).
21. See, for instance, Ruderman, 261.
22. The anonymous review was published in *The Quarterly Review* 35 (January and March, 1827): 86–114. All subsequent references will be cited parenthetically in the text.
23. In "The Hebrew Narrative Anthology in the Middle Ages," Eli Yassif analyzes the influence of Eastern tales on Jewish anthological literature (*Prooftexts,* Special Issue: The Anthological Imagination in Jewish Literature, Part 2, 17 [May 1997]: 157).
24. Ruderman notes J. Hillis Miller's use of this metaphor in Miller's "Border Crossings, Translating Theory: Ruth," in *The Translatability of Cultures: Figurations of the Space Between,* ed. Sanford Budick and Wolfgang Iser (Stanford: Stanford University Press, 1996), pp. 208–23.
25. André Lefevere, *Translating Literature: Practice and Theory in a Comparative Literature Context* (New York: Modern Language Association of America, 1992), 6.

CHAPTER 12

GRACE AGUILAR: REWRITING SCOTT
REWRITING HISTORY

Elizabeth Fay

I apprehend domestic and private affections inseparable from the nature of man, and from what may be styled the culture of the heart.
—William Godwin, *St. Leon*[1]

In this chapter I will use a reading of Grace Aguilar's *Vale of Cedars; or, The Martyr* (posthumously published 1850) and Walter Scott's *Ivanhoe* (1819) to center a discussion of Aguilar's uses of Jewish identity to construct a literary and authorial identity.[2] My reading will begin with the observation that Aguilar's Jewish heroine not only bears the Catholic name "Marie," but in contrast to Scott's Orientalized Rebecca, is also unmarked physically, culturally, or behaviorally by her Jewishness.[3] Indeed, the secret of being Jewish presents a captivating mysteriousness for the unsuspecting English hero, Arthur Stanley, but it is only decipherable through Marie's essentializing spirituality, an unstigmatized resource that is the only inheritance from Scott's Rebecca that Aguilar allows. I want to begin with the steps leading up to this point of departure, and end with an assessment of the complex literary negotiations Aguilar makes.

Border Raids: Cultures of the Heart

Grace Aguilar (1816–47) belongs to that group of women writers sometimes called "bridge writers," whose publications during the 1830s and 40s bridged the gap between the Romantic and Victorian eras and ideologies in much the same fashion as those women poets who turned out verse in such quantity at the end of the eighteenth century bridged the gap between the Enlightenment and Romantic movements. But Aguilar bridges another, more significant gap, that between the Anglo and the Jewish communities, Anglo and Jewish readerships. Significantly, she began publishing in the vein of Mary Shelley, Letitia Elizabeth Landon, and other women Romantics, writing for the keepsake annuals, books that targeted the Christmas gift market. Her first book was a volume of poems with a keepsake-style title, *The Magic Wreath* (1835), which met with praise in the secular press so that she began contributing poems to annuals and women's magazines such as the *Keepsake, La Belle Assemblée,* and *Chamber's Miscellany,* as well as to Jewish periodicals. She wrote twelve books in the twelve years of her life remaining after the publication of *The Magic Wreath,* of which six were published posthumously.

But Aguilar is more than a bridge writer; as a progressive, she understood that Jewish emancipation necessitated both reform within the community and the development of a culture of exchange between the Anglican and the Jew. Aguilar saw that rigid community borders not only blinded those within to the need for reform, which she desired as the only route to bettering the traditional role for Jewish women, but that impermeable boundaries between the dominant culture and the Jewish community meant continuing the possibility for persecution and expulsion. It is just such borders that caused her to be labeled an "inauthentic Jew" by some because of the adolescent years spent outside the Jewish community due to her father's health, and her resultant reliance on Christian friends and Christian tools of worship during that period. Not just a bridge writer but a borderer, she was a woman sitting on the edges of things. And yet she was not a border writer like Scott, bleeding at the edges because desiring resolution out of national and cultural conflict, but a woman writing "tales from the heart," writing from the heart outward into the world, writing in order to demonstrate the permeability of edges even if it required her heart to "bleed at every pore."

What distinguishes Aguilar's historical romances, domestic romances, short stories, and prose writing from that of other bridge writers, then, is her distinctly Jewish emphasis. With the exception of her Scott imitation, *Days of Bruce* (published posthumously in 1851), a romance of the Scottish surge for independence that analogically comments on the Jewish community's struggle for political recognition and equity, all of Aguilar's works, whether written for Christian or Jewish readerships, focus on aspects of Jewish history, culture, and religion. Much of her work is historically oriented, seeking ways to reconcile present concerns of reform and emancipation with racial and cultural history. As a Sephardic Jew, Aguilar looked on the Spanish Inquisition, the experience of becoming crypto-Jewish, as a pseudo-conversion survival tactic, and the expulsion from Spain, as an allegory of racial history. This period of Jewish history reads as both a re-inscription of the Egyptian habitation and flight, and as a predictor of Jewish experience if no alterations in identity, tradition, and inter-cultural exchange take place. Such changes would transform the normative interpretive practice of dominant culture to misread Jewish presence, not by acculturating that presence but by making its own practices more familiar and acceptable to the nation.

Scott's medieval romance *Ivanhoe*, as an exemplary mis-reading, proposes a fiction of the cultural formation of Englishness occurring at the expense of Jewish identity. Yet the novel is historically more or less coincidental with the Golden Age of Spain in which Muslims and Catholics, like the Saxons and Normans in Scott's story, used Jews to define insider–outsider relationships. The Jews in each case become expenditures, their complicity in the insider–outsider dynamic usually defined in terms of mis-acculturation: usury (a practice denied to Christians), or passing as Christian to gain access to the public sphere. Scott's medievalism highlights the Jew's misplacement as it rejects the possibility for Jewish participation in nation formation, silencing and forgetting by exiling Isaac and Rebecca back to a Spain where they will become lost from view. There they will be forgotten objects, lost in a way that Ivanhoe's crusader memories and Oriental desire, which had attracted him to Rebecca, will never quite be. In revising Shakespeare's more equivocal *Merchant of Venice*, *Ivanhoe* provided Jewish women writers like Aguilar with an important fictional model to respond to: the exclusion and exile of Isaac and Rebecca, necessary to Scott's anxiety over national identity and disruptive desire, needed to be answered in strictly historical terms so that the exile of Jews would no longer serve as the terminal mechanism for nationalized tensions. Aguilar does so in her early and Romantic *Vale of Cedars* (written between 1831 and 1835), but in a sense continues to do so throughout her career. For Aguilar, exclusionary strategies predict inquisitory practice; for exile to be the predictable solution, then the legalized unmasking of Jews and the inquisition of their hearts and minds becomes necessary. To secrete the cross-boundary traffic in desire and knowledge by refuting and exiling it is to install at the level of the word a legalistic interpretation and evaluation of form that knows no difference. The essentialist binary of spirit and form held to be what separates Christianity from Judaism, and Jews from Christians, is in inquisitory practice re-inscribed on the body to extract from that body false words of conversion. By force it silences Jewish formalism, which in speaking from the margins could not fail to point out the formalism resurrected in the Catholic Church, a formalism the

Church at all costs wished to deny in the name of spirit. Rebecca could have offered a new England much in the nature of formal supplement; instead she was silenced. This is a point to which I will return.

Aguilar and other Jewish women writers of the new age of emancipation refused to be silenced by conversionist pressures, at least during the effusion of their productivity in the mid-nineteenth century.[4] But if Aguilar positions herself in relation to Scott, she equally strongly positions herself relative to women's narratives. The distinguishing characteristic of Aguilar's fiction beyond its Jewish identity, and what aligns it with the work of contemporary Christian women writers like Mary Shelley and Felicia Hemans, and with prior writers like Mary Wollstonecraft and Mary Hays, is that it revolves around the problem of maternity, a problem Scott does not treat with any complexity or centrality. In part, her concern with maternity participates in the larger focus on mothering in women's literature toward the end of the Romantic period, and in part it is predetermined: in the Sephardic tradition, women during the crypto-Jewish period maintained cultural identity through oral history, telling tales from the heart in order to assure the continuance of the religio-cultural identity.

The encryption of political, religious, and cultural history and identity as narratives of heart and home, or as Aguilar's posthumous volume of short stories and *midrashim* phrases it, *Home Scenes and Heart Studies* (published in 1852), opens her œuvre up to the very figures that she herself worries: textual silence versus textual commentary. It is biblical exegesis—*midrash* (as a supplemental narrative that helps interpret the primary narrative) being its accessible form intended for the community rather than preserved for scholars—that grounds the Judeo-Christian interpretive critical tradition, and that tropes for readers a way of delving beneath the semantic surface, of making words speak their silences.[5] Biblical commentary as much as historical and domestic romance are the shared concerns inhabiting the Judeo-Christian borders, and it is no accident that these are the genres in which Aguilar specializes. Frank Kermode identifies biblical exegesis and *midrash* as "the genesis of secrecy," that is, a secondary level of silence or secretness and privileged knowledge that doubles the problem of silence inherent in the semantic level: what can a text mean when it speaks only the words that it does speak?[6] Who can know the real meaning of those words, and who can supply the words that are lacking? Decryption gives authority and power to the interpreter, signals his insider status as it is derived from a prior belonging and knowing outside the text. This belonging and prior knowing or education are ritualistically and historically the domain of the male. Yet, Michael Galchinsky argues, the crypto-Jewish Sephardic tradition—passing narratives of Jewish history and experience on to new generations in disguised, allegorical, encrypted forms—begins at home and belongs to the woman.[7] Aguilar would have experienced these narratives of the expulsion, Inquisition, and other events from her mother, Sarah Aguilar, whose use of the Sephardic "matriarchal role of story-teller" Grace adopted. It is fundamentally a *midrash*-like narrative tradition, except that instead of clarifying and legalizing Talmudic texts, it encrypts history and religion to secrete it from outsiders, thereby establishing the insider/outsider borders of belonging based not on power and interpretive authority, but on danger and identity. In using *midrashim*, Aguilar turns the woman's tradition against itself and toward decryption, clarification, and speaking silences. Yet without the proper authority, and without access to the proper texts, she can only claim to do so from the textually silenced, complementary rather than competing, maternal spaces of heart and home.

Aguilar's fiction and exegesis, viewed in this way, conform to encryption to decryption, making the act of secreting, and the redoubled act of interpreting so as to install secrecy, a maternal act. Unlike Scott, who used history to re-read the current times—imposing current history on the past in an anachronistic method that typified Romantic-period popular attitudes to history, Aguilar used history both in her romances and her re-telling of Talmudic narratives, to look to the present in order to change the future. In this way Aguilar could open up concealed histories to Christian perusal, extending the crypto-Jewish transmission of oral histories and traditions to the Anglo culture at large. By proffering *midrash* to the masses, Aguilar politicizes the textual level of narrative. This is followed by the religious meditations in *Spirit of Judaism* (1842),[8] and the Talmudic and biblical commentaries in her two-volume *Women of Israel* (1844), works that reveal the logic of her *midrashic* activity, that is, as both a hermeneutic act of reading secrecy in order to undo it, and a transformative act of re-figuring biblical or historical women for contemporary identity appropriation. This second act re-writes Scott's anachronism of the Jewish heroine in *Ivanhoe* away from that of ethical monotheism, and thus a kind of Jewish Protestant—which is how Scott wants to see contemporary Anglo-Jews assimilate and disappear into Anglo culture—and back toward the historical reality of Jewish womanhood and heroism.

In *Women of Israel*, Aguilar is also participating in the tradition of female biography, a genre that gained popularity in the eighteenth century ranging from George Ballard's *Memoirs of Several Ladies of Great*

Britain (1752), Mary Scott's *The Female Advocate* (1774), John Duncombe's *The Feminiad* (1754), Mary Hays' *Female Biography* (6 vols., 1803), and Matilda Betham's *Biographical Dictionary of the Celebrated Women of Every Age and Country* (1804) to the more literary versions by Lucy Aikin, *Epistles on Women* (1810), Mary Russell Mitford, *Narrative Poems on the Female Character* (1813), and Felicia Hemans, *Records of Woman* (1828). The female biographical sketch as practiced through to Hays' relatively exhaustive work usually focused on women writers, and served two purposes: to demonstrate the utility and constructive nature of women's literary activities; and to provide didactic examples of women who combined domestic affections and domestic duty with their unorthodox pursuits.[9] Hemans, like Aikin and Mitford, extends this characterization from the literary woman to various women, both celebrated and ordinary, who must confront their own frustrated creativity and affective desires. It is this aspect of the domestic affections, so important to female biography, which Aguilar reads into the gaps and silences of the biblical texts. Aguilar's contemporaries, still scripted into the same tradition-bound roles as their medieval predecessors, were taught that while the Old Testament recorded the deeds of heroic women, these were exceptional rather than generative individuals. The woman's domain was the home not the heroic, her tasks defined by family not politics, repetition not interpretation, relapse not reform.

Yet Aguilar's vision of the religious domestic sphere was not highly radicalized, differing from that of the men reformers mostly in that she lamented the lack of religious education available to women, particularly their lack of Hebrew. She makes this case specifically in *Women of Israel*, where she claims that her own knowledge deficits have prevented her from offering a comprehensive history of Jewish women. She lays the blame for her inability to tell a full story on her lack of access to the realm of knowledge: not factual history, but sacred texts, sacred language, and commentaries. Factual history is clearly not the problem, as her many forays into historical romance and historical narrative reveal. Aguilar appears convinced that women's history is conveyed in these male domains of knowledge, or that women's place in history can be fully understood without the aid of imaginative intervention once the domains of knowledge are debarred. Her chapters on Talmudic and biblical women bear this out. In one such commentary (Genesis 29:17), attempting to reconcile the comparative situations of the ordinary Leah and her beautiful sister Rachel, beloved of Jacob, the man with whom Leah was in love, Aguilar interprets the mystery of God's treatment of the two women by explicating the Hebrew phrases as well as the English used to describe their persons, feelings or utterances:

> That Leah was much less beautiful than her sister is evident from the words of the text, but it does not appear that she was as plain and homely as some commentators declare her. The Hebrew word translated "tender," "And the eyes of Leah were tender...," does not signify *weak* only, as is generally supposed, but soft and delicate, and leads me to suppose that the soft and tender eyes of Leah were her only good feature, whereas her younger sister was "very beautiful and of exceeding beauty," which is the literal meaning of the Hebrew expression ... though even such translation is far from possessing the force of the original. This difference of appearance occasioned, as would appear by the sequel, a complete difference of character. (1:110)[10]

Aguilar asserts her authority by showing she can read the original text, which allows her to correct male commentary through her authoritative knowledge of the domestic and private sphere of affect, appearance, religiosity, and self-interest. She asserts not only a better, because more femininely astute, interpretation of the biblical text, but corrects both the hebraic hermeneutic product and the interpretative uses of the English translation. Her hermeneutic adopts the male approach of reading parable into the text: she takes this passage to be indicative of the whole. The physical comparison between Leah and Rachel as the text voices it, will reveal the differences in their spirits and psyches, as well. Moreover, Jacob, who serves as the wedge that opposes one sister to the other, is specifically analyzed in terms of the chivalric romance: in explaining why Jacob would have bound himself to serve Rachel's father for love of her, Aguilar comments that:

> We think much of those tales of chivalry where man performs some great and striking deed—conquers his own passions—becomes a voluntary wanderer—all to win the smile and love of woman. And we do right, for the motive is pure and the moral good. But such high-wrought volumes should not blind our hearts and eyes to this exquisite narration, wherein the same truth, the same moral is impressed, with equal force and beauty, only in the simple language of the Bible.... His was no service to call upon distant lands and far-off ages to admire. Nothing for FAME, that brilliant meteor, which, equally with love, divided the warrior's heart in the middle ages.... And it was for this end love was so mercifully given. (1:111)

As this rehearsal of the romance paradigm indicates, the historical and domestic romance genres that Aguilar herself exploits have no place in the history of real women. Furthermore, her reference to the chivalric romance indicates that she intended her history of Jewish women to be read by a larger audience than that of contemporary Jewish women, and indeed, this "more than any other of her works, achieved lasting popularity."[11] Her commentary continues by comparing the two different orders of love, Divine and human:

> As the word of God disdains not to portray the extent of love borne by one mortal for another, we trust we may be pardoned if we linger a moment on that emotion, the very name of which is generally banished from the education of young females, as if to feel or excite it were a crime, forgetting that, in banishing all idea of its *influence,* we banish also the proper means of regulating that influence, and subject our young charge unguarded to the very evil that we dread. (1:111)

Recollecting Wollstonecraft's and Hemans' empathetic treatments of female desire, as well as Scott's ambivalence toward it, Aguilar shows how Rachel's beauty leads her to self-love and to an inability to rely on her husband's God, while Leah is able to devote herself both to Jacob and to Jacob's God and is therefore the happier and more truly beautiful woman. Although clearly a *midrash* for a contemporary domestic homily, this interpretation of the Leah and Rachel narrative also indicates that the patriarchal text does not reveal all it knows: "And she called the name of her eldest son Reuben: for, she said, 'Surely the Lord hath looked upon my affliction; now therefore my husband will love me.' What a volume of woman's deepest feelings and the compassionating love of the Eternal do these brief lines reveal!" (1:115). Reading between the lines, Aguilar is able to untangle the seeming paradox of God's gift of sons to Leah versus Rachel's barrenness: "And even for those bitter griefs, which from their nature, their seeming selfishness, woman shrinks in trembling from bringing before her God, and buries them in her own heart till it bleeds at every pore—Leah's history proves that He will grant peace and healing" (1:115). It is for this reason that women's history must be retold, made new and relevant, because the human heart continues to bleed at every pore.

At the same time, such history reveals the lack at the center of the male hermeneutic's apparent knowingness: "We will not linger on the affairs narrated in Genesis xxix, from the 21st to the 30th verse, because they belong so strictly to the manners and customs of the Eastern nations, that it is quite impossible to comment upon them with any justice, prejudiced, as birth and education cannot fail to make us, in favor of the manners and customs of modern Europe" (1:114). These are the verses that treat Leah's unrequited love and her "compelled agency in her father's fraud," and Aguilar and her reader must not make ungrounded interpretive assumptions when they begin from a ground of bias and ignorance; this is not a question of lacking access to spheres of knowledge, but of the spheres themselves being assessed as partial. The supplement to this partiality, of course, is women's domestic and affective knowledge, specifically Aguilar's ability to read Leah's and Rachel's character aright. However, the supplement's job in reading the heart is to show the heartlessness of the center: Laban sold his daughters to Jacob in return for servitude; Jacob preferred Rachel to Leah for the younger sister's beauty; Leah is recompensed only by the birth of her sons.

As Galchinsky notes, Aguilar's *Spirit of Judaism* expands "on the power and importance of maternal storytelling for the continuation of Judaism," and in doing so, "provide[s] a detailed instruction manual for mother-instructors" to mediate the inherent disability mother-instructors faced through lack of access to Talmudic and Hebrew studies and commentaries. These are not just tales from the heart; they are mother's milk. In her introduction to the first volume, she encourages mothers to re-narrate sacred stories in the form of "interesting tales," an expansion on what her own œuvre, at large, achieves: "In this moment, women's storytelling—especially if it includes 'simple, domestic, highly moral tales'—becomes a defense against conversion, and a primary means of infusing Jewish identity."[12] Curiously, she begins this introduction with the figure of chivalry, which she had used to compare with Jacob's behavior regarding Leah and Rachel, and then transfigures the field of contest to that of harvest: "Among the many valuable works relative to woman's capabilities, influence, and mission, which in the present age are so continually appearing, one still seems wanting. The field has, indeed, been entered ... but all the fruit has not been gathered." Not chivalric warfare and/as love but harvest, the field is thus open to women's labor. Moreover, young women should be encouraged to read Scripture, which they should do in order to become good mothers to their children, because it offers "a true and perfect mirror of themselves" (*Women of Israel* 2).

This is the lesson, then, of hermeneutic reading: it offers not a centrist vision of power and authority, not a *midrash* for the purpose of law and containment, not even a vindication of the knowing silences of Divine words, but a reflection of the self as it is. This is the truth of sacred texts, and this is why conversion offers only falsity. For what the sacred text has reflected from the beginning has been the true nature of the heart, and it is this that now must be held sacred.

Young England and *The Days of Bruce*

Leah's maternalism, her recompense for the wrongs suffered through patriarchal servitude and the purity of her heart, make her one of the mother models of Jewish history. Such models must be understood in light of Scott's Rebecca, who offers a very different, eroticized model for Jewish womanhood. They must also be understood in terms of the political movements surrounding the London Jewish community, particularly those concerned with Jewish assimilation.[13] Such debates must certainly be the fodder for women's chivalric labor, their entering of the field of contest and transforming it into a field of corn. In order for it not to become a tale of Ruth amid the alien corn—that is, exile and cultural loss—the contest must be rigorously focused on the problem of assimilation versus religio-cultural tradition and Jewish identity, Englishing versus isolationism. These provide the limits of the field, and anything beyond that, such as the problem of authorial gender, female textual authority, and Jewish authorial identity must be treated as distractions to the central issues, sidebars and not jousting lanes.

What is significant about Aguilar's figuration of the field as one of both contest and harvest, is that its central metaphor of the field is a medieval one. In this she combines the Jewish history in Spain with Scott's historical fiction to anticipate the spirit of chivalry that produces the Young England Party, a reform party that rises anew out of the matter of old. It is a movement, not insignificantly, associated with Benjamin Disraeli who, by embodying the pressure of Anglo desire for Jews to assimilate into Anglican normalcy, is an ideal figure. Popularizing his views through authorship, Aguilar's own field of choice, and through politics—the only field that really matters—Disraeli offers Aguilar an interesting alternative to Scott.

The leading conceit of Romantic and Victorian medievalism was that the Middle Ages represented an ordered and well-led community founded on imagination and faith, which stands in direct contrast to Victorian mechanization, laissez faire, and a surrender of the imaginative facility to the supremacy of capitalism. In the Jewish community, medievalism signified calcification and stagnation. At the same time, medievalism was being used impressively to restore dignity to Catholicism, through the work of Kenelm Digby, a converted Catholic, Aubrey de Vere (friend of Tennyson, and a poet himself), and the Oxford Movement. Significantly, the proponents of this counter-religious thrust to the pressures on Jews to assimilate were for the most part themselves converts away from Anglicanism. Disraeli stands in relief against both interpretations of the medieval in his participation in the Young England Party.

An offshoot of the Oxford Movement, Young England began as a small group of aristocrats (Lord John Manners, George Smythe, Alexander Baillie-Cochrane, whose interest in Catholicism was sparked by the Wordsworth enthusiast "poet-priest" Frederick Faber) and those associated with the group, from Peter Borthwick, William Busfield Ferrand, to Disraeli. The party was devoted to dandyism, Byronism, and "a deeply serious romanticism," in conjunction with a desire to reform social ills through paternalistic sympathy as an essential political agency as the "new chivalry."[14] Kenelm Digby's *Broad Stone of Honour* (1822) was their bible as these young and ambitious men sought to define their neo-feudalism into a political program. The party was active in Parliament only between 1842 and 1845, but with lasting influence, and while its neo-feudalism served to enfranchise Disraeli in a political arena, where he most fully explored its chivalric ideals was not politics but fiction. In his trilogy, *Coningsby* (1844), *Sybil* (1845), and *Tancred* (1847), Disraeli uses the imaginative field to strategically position this program. Overtly, however, Disraeli's political reform focused on larger social issues and did not press for the Jewish community until the 1870s.[15] And it was this Anglicized aspect of Disraeli's nationalism, the doubled conversionist force of Anglicans to Catholicism in the Oxford Movement and of Anglicans attempting to convert Jews, that Aguilar shows herself to be sensitive to and even anticipating in her own fiction.

Aguilar's *Days of Bruce,* published posthumously but written prior to *The Vale of Cedars,* was in imitation of Scott's historical novels but anticipates the neo-feudalism of the Young England Party, and poses a strong maternality against Catholic paternalism. Aguilar may also have been influenced by Hemans' prize-winning *Wallace's Invocation to Bruce* (1820) when choosing her subject matter for her novel of the Scottish struggle for emancipation. What is significant about her novel, in relation to Disraeli's modernizing of feudalism as a model for the captains of industry, is that she insists on the value of analogy over identity. She uses Scottish medieval history as an analogy of Jewish medieval history, and Scottish emancipation from England as an analogic model for Jewish separatism. In this Aguilar is adopting Scott's allegorical comparative between past and present to juxtapose and ameliorate nationalisms. Aguilar imitates this approach, providing a new crypto-history by allegorizing Jewish struggles for autonomy and identity as Scottish ones. The Bruce becomes a synecdoche that can replace Shylock with an explicitly political rather than mercenary or mercantile force, but in a *midrashic* manner that is too easily missed if he is not read cryptically. *Days of Bruce,* with its Scott-like heroes and heroines, can be read by

Anglo and Jewish readers alike, each taking something different from it according to need.

The Vale of Cedars as Ivanhoe

As *Days of the Bruce* is an adaptation of Scott's literary politics, *The Vale of Cedars* is quite specifically a revision of his politicized Jews in *Ivanhoe*. Taking place in the Spain of 1479, the story's telling is motivated by the exile of the noble Arthur Stanley from England by King Edward. His given name indicates both his representative Englishness and *Broad Stone*-style chivalry.[16] The novel begins when, having taken a leave from the court of Ferdinand, Stanley re-encounters Marie Henriquez (whose name secrets her identity, allowing her to pass for Catholic) in the Vale of Cedars, a secreted valley he finds on his wanderings like a true knight-errant. Earlier, Stanley had fallen in love with Marie at the court of Castile, but she was unofficially betrothed to her cousin, Ferdinand Morales; one day she mysteriously disappears, and the bewildered Stanley and the court itself remained ignorant of both Ferdinand's and her Jewish identity.

As the novel discovers the mystery of Marie's identity and her disappearance from the court and from Stanley, we begin to understand the Protestant Stanley as Scott's Ivanhoe, and Marie as Rebecca. Ivanhoe's rival for Rebecca, the rapacious Templar Bois-Guilbert, becomes the stalker and Inquisitor Don Luis. Marie's father Manuel Henriquez displaces the disturbing and xenophobic stereotype of Isaac, while the tightly knit Jewish family that inhabits the "vale of cedars" rewrites Rebecca and Isaac's English isolation and concluding exile. Because *The Vale of Cedars* deals with the crypto-history of Jews in the years leading up to the Spanish Inquisition,[17] and the reality of being under the sentence of death, Aguilar's focus on the bleak conclusion to the Golden Age of Sephardic Jewish history, with its Spanish and Jewish co-habitation, makes an ideal analogy to Scott's focus on Anglo-Saxon and Norman co-habitation in England. Aguilar specifically positions the edenic valley— centered by the private temple that organizes family life, and the temporary ritual bower of palm and cedar that even further habituates us to an edenic reading—as an allegorical space of biblical prehistory layered over Spanish medieval history, of originary power over sustained loss. That space, which is safe only because entirely secret and therefore invisible, directly opposes the public spaces of England that for Aguilar are dangerous, and for Scott are both dangerous and highly marked as anti-Semitic.

The issue of visibility becomes the ground of border transgression. If in Aguilar's story it is possible for Jewishness to be unseen—unwritten on the body and signaled only by clothing and architecture—in Scott this is utterly impossible, for Jewishness is bodily inscribed, and such visibility an absolute necessity. Medieval Christianity depends on seeing Jewishness for its very identity, for its construction of the pure/impure binary by which it understands and empowers itself. Impurity is always already a reason for aggression, torture, theft, and other acts of violence that are figurations of inquisitorial practice: it is how Templars such as Bois-Guilbert and the Church itself can remain pure despite barbarity. It is also the sign of comedy, for both impurity and barbarity are the common discourses of comedy. Scott takes advantage of the impurity of Jewish identity to position his comic relief—Isaac as farce—against the politically dangerous seriousness of Ivanhoe's and Rebecca's emotional entanglement. Isaac's torture scene at Front-de-Boeuf's castle is farcically divested of narratorial concern or sympathy for Isaac's emotional and bodily well-being at the same time that this is the primary focus of narratorial vision for the would-be lovers. The voyeuristic scenes of Rebecca nursing the wounded knight enmesh the distraught body with love's dangerous and wounding emotions, even as they are deliberately weighted against the torture of Isaac for his money, as well as the scenes foreshadowing this that allow the novel to imagine that torture as an expected, and even necessary, wounding.

That necessity, predicated on Isaac's inability to hide his identity to protect himself, and the obverse of Ivanhoe's wounding as a masked and unidentified knight, is what grounds Anglo identity in *Ivanhoe*. Isaac's provision of Ivanhoe's armor for the tournament positions this necessary connection. For Scott, it is Saxon identity that can be secreted as Norman, and that can be dangerous for Ivanhoe to reveal. But, I would argue, Scott can set up disguise as necessary only because Isaac's identity as Jewish is already foreknown through facial appearance, exotic clothing, and stereotypical mannerisms. For Aguilar, however, Marie is by name and appearance any English woman, her Jewishness both secreted and invisible, a matter of inner light rather than outward darkness: "the very perfection of each feature, the delicate clearness of the complexion— brunette when brought into close contact with the Saxon, blonde when compared with the Spaniard.... Truth, purity, holiness, something scarcely of this nether world ... had rested there [in Marie's face], attracting the most unobservant" (*Vale* 7). Marie's holiness elevates her above Rebecca's mysterious, Orientalized beauty by making her indescribable ("To attempt description of either face or form [of Marie] would be useless"), and therefore secured from stereotypes.[18] In contrast to Scott's farcical use of the usurer Jew, Aguilar examines the subjective and existential experience of living under the penalty of death for a crime of identity—a criminal birth—and portrays the psychological conditions for an individual's willingness to tempt that fate, as well as the consequences of crossing undue boundaries. Marie's real crime of identity, Aguilar makes clear, is not really that of having been born Jewish, but rather of having been tempted to pass as Christian, to secret her Jewishness.

Rebecca, however, is never allowed to be invisibly Jewish.[19] Her crime of identity is the one used by Templars and others who view impurity as a gate to violation: Rebecca, like Jewish money, is an object of rapine. It is this criminality of being, exposing the bearer to violation and torture, that Scott exploits in the case of Isaac and other peripheral Jewish characters; but he tentatively suggests Rebecca is either sensitive to its psychological extenuations, and/or heroically resists its pathos. Aguilar, by contrast, represents her Jewish characters as fully sensitized, but squarely centers the overt representation of such inner turmoil on Marie, its dire consequences for personal happiness dominating the novel as a thematic device that explains Marie's plot-motivating actions. The main action for which we need such motivation is Marie's decision to reject all suitors in order to remain single, which she views as the only possible course after her twofold deception: Stanley believes her to be Catholic, and Ferdinand has not been told about her love for Stanley. Although her father marries her to Ferdinand anyway, deciding to secrete her love for the other man, Marie's original claim—"could I not be true, I would not wed" (28)—haunts her marriage and her public life with Ferdinand, beginning with the Catholic wedding that literally translates Marie into a proper subject. Her thwarted wish for a constant singleness, and the unintended consequences of secreting truth as a version of secreting identity, define the novel and both align her with Rebecca and position her against heroism.

The singleness Marie desires has two consequences. First, it suggests that her medieval story should have been a hagiographic narrative of a sainted virgin heroically resisting her unwanted sexuality for a higher devotion. However, her martyrdom, teasingly implicit in the novel's subtitle *The Martyr*, is not a death but a giving up of the heart in order to preserve the home—an inversion of the maternalistic emphasis in Aguilar's later writings whose significance lies in the home's contradictory power.[20] This would-be Catholicization of Rebecca's-cum-Marie's story, installed into the reader's expectations so that martyrdom is re-directed from the Catholic to the Jewish subject, deserves further attention. Second, Marie's flight from Stanley prior to her marriage to Ferdinand—which equals the time spent in the edenic valley where chastity and paternal duty rule—is a singleness that distills Rebecca's sacrifice of self for the care of her father into Marie's paternal caretaking as an act of mothering. Placing family over self, Marie represents the ideal of mothering by giving up the possibility of love and marriage with Stanley, something Rebecca was never truly able to expect from Ivanhoe. Marie's reverse mothering, caring for her father *because* she was born Jewish, becomes a reverse generating, a displacement of the mixed-identity babies she might have produced with Stanley. Marie is not allowed to pursue this course, for if Manuel's prime purpose in marrying his daughter to his nephew is reproduction, the consequences of the crime of identity are anti-reproductive, stopping generation.

Let me return to the Catholicization of Rebecca's/Marie's story. Disraeli's Young England Party establishes two divergent perspectives already implicated by the group's name. "Young England" implies the medieval past of England's youth, and so, that which is historically purer, yet also alluding to the invigorated youthfulness of muscular Christianity exhorted in Digby's *Broad Stone of Honour*. But hovering over "Young" is the meaning "new." Here "new" is in the sense of a new Englishness produced by the joining of Catholic and Jewish identities within the Party. While Catholicism as an idea represents the medieval form of Christianity, so that both it and Judaism pose an "old" against the "new," their conjoining—both as the product of conversion to Catholicism and desertion from Jewishness—offers a renovation of the Anglo identity. This is a new Englishness that builds on the Oxford Movement's revival of medieval Catholicism and concurrent effort to de-politicize the Anglican Church. The ironies involved—using Catholicism to effect separation of church and state, and converting to Catholicism as a part of a party identification—contained alarming potentialities for the Jewish community. The return to Catholicism could provoke a renewed anti-Semitism, or the new conversionism from Anglicanism to Catholicism could re-inforce the pressures from Anglicans on the Jewish community. Marie's hagiographic story, as the medieval story of virginal resistance, is a directed response to the pressures of Catholicization, and the social pressures to convert to Catholicism and away from Jewishness. Her stand, after experiencing the dangers of temptation and transgression, is a formal one—the embracing of Jewish religion and Jewish life as Christian chastity—that takes the form of a simple utterance with elocutionary force: "No." In this refusal, the mystery of identity, and the secret spaces of the Jewish home as represented by the hidden valley—normally translated into the secrets of sacred texts that need de-cryption and *midrash*—need no clarification. It is this resistance that Scott elided in Rebecca, and that Aguilar explores on a cultural level in *Days of Bruce* by focusing on the Scottish heroic resistance to England's colonialization. Significantly, Scotland is associated with a Protestantism that is not Anglicanism, not a white-washed version of Catholicism, and so not the form without a revised content that is the paradoxical inversion of Catholicism's use of Jewish conversion in the Spanish Inquisition. Scotland can formulate a truer model for the problem of conversion/assimilation/identity that kept being proposed to the Jewish community of the mid-nineteenth century as a solution to their bordered existence. And, it can provide resistance to the hypocritical solution of the Jew passing as Anglo, which is its own parody of the inquisitorial practice of writing on the body.

Finally, Aguilar's achievement has another aspect that derives from the two functions of virginal singleness, but in a reverse direction. Instead of one metaphor splitting into two interpretations, this last achievement is the conjoining of two ethnic identities into one: not Scott's Saxon and Jewish identities, but his Saxon and Norman into Anglo-English identity, which Aguilar translates as not Anglo and Jewish but English. It is Englishness that allows borders to be freely traversed without transgression. This is the singularity of identity that Aguilar begins to imagine so early in her career, and distributes throughout her writing as a politicized dialectic and dialectical resolution to the problem of borders, the problem of bleeding, the problem of identity. It also begins to be a resolution to the problem of gender in that she sees this resolution as being gender neutral—Marie as much as her father, Stanley as much as Marie. It is a very different solution from inquisitory practice because it makes political and national identity the priority even while religious and ethnic identities are prior and not preempted. There is no need for conversion—the alarming characteristic of the new Oxford Movement—but there is a need for the Jewish and Anglo communities to view each other as adequate members of the dominant culture. If Aguilar had lived to witness Disraeli's political career as England's Prime Minister, she would have viewed its major flaw, I think, as his need to be English at the expense of being Jewish. This is the very crime of identity Marie committed at the Queen's court, and for which she must do penance the rest of her life. It is the very crime Aguilar was accused of committing as an adolescent in attending Anglican churches and having Anglo friends, and she was sensitive to the political and personal implications of such identity crisis in her writing, both as an author who saw herself as bridging rather than isolating Jewish from Anglo communities, and as one doing penance through a constant bleeding from the heart.

Notes

1. Preface to William Godwin, *St. Leon: A Tale of the Sixteenth Century*, 4 vols. (1799; reprint New York: Garland Publishing, 1975), ix.
2. This essay is dedicated to my student Ilene Weismehl, whose fascination with Aguilar kindled my own. This study will refer to the following works by Aguilar: *The Days of Bruce* (London, 1851); *Home Scenes and Heart Studies* (London, 1853); *The Magic Wreath* (published anonymously in Devon, 1835); *The Spirit of Judaism*, ed. I. Leeser (Philadelphia, 1842); *The Vale of Cedars; or, The Martyr*, 2 vols. (New York, 1850); and *The Women of Israel; or, Characters and Sketches from the Holy Scriptures and Jewish History*, 2 vols. (London, 1845). All references to these texts will be cited parenthetically in the text.
3. At the tournament at Ashby-de-la-Zouch, Scott describes Rebecca's luxurious dress as highly oriental: "Her form was exquisitely symmetrical, and was shown to advantage by a sort of Eastern dress, which she wore according to the fashion of the females of her nation. Her turban of yellow silk suited well with the darkness of her complexion ... [her hair] fell down upon as much of a lovely neck and bosom as a simarre of the richest Persian silk, exhibiting flowers in their natural colours embossed upon a purple ground, permitted to be visible." Rebecca also wore "golden and pearl-studded clasps, which closed her vest," a diamond necklace "with pendants of inestimable value," and the "feather of an ostrich, fastened in her turban by an agraffe set with brilliants" (Walter Scott, *Ivanhoe*, ed. Ian Duncan [Oxford: Oxford University Press, 1996], 93–4). Rebecca is thus described as both the Oriental *other*, and a version of the nouveau riche whose taste is overdone. Moreover, in so ostentatiously advertising her father's wealth, Rebecca draws attention to herself, and sets herself up to be the object of avaricious and sexual desire.
4. Michael Galchinsky analyzes Scott's role in particular in relation to the pressure on the Jewish community to convert to Anglicanism (*The Origin of the Modern Jewish Woman Writer: Romance and Reform in Victorian England* [Detroit: Wayne State University Press, 1996], 39–58). The apparent tolerance of conversionist writers like M. G. Lewis (*Jewish Maiden*, 1830), Amelia Bristow (*Rosette and Miriam*, 1837), Edward Bulwar Lytton (*Leila*, 1837), and Thackeray (*Rebecca and Rowena*, 1843) was, Galchinsky argues, a masquerade for the pressure to convert, a masquerade Aguilar clearly intends to uncover (39). Other Jewish women who also wrote against conversionist pressures included Marion Hartog, Charlotte Montefiore, Anna Maria Goldsmid, Maria Polack, Celia and Marion Moss. See also: Cecil Roth, *A History of the Jews in England*, 3rd ed. (London: Oxford University Press, 1964); David S. Katz, *The Jews in the History of England, 1485–1850*

(Oxford: Oxford University Press, 1994); and Todd M. Endelman, *The Jews of Georgian England, 1714–1830: Tradition and Change in a Liberal Society* (Philadelphia: The Jewish Publication Society of America, 1979; reprint with a new preface, Ann Arbor: University of Michigan Press, 1999). For a discussion of the principal activist bodies for conversion—the London Society for Promoting Christianity among the Jews (founded 1809) and the British Society for the Propagation of the Gospel among the Jews (founded 1842)—see Michael Ragussis' chapter "The Culture of Conversion" in *Figures of Conversion: "The Jewish Question" and English National Identity* (Durham: Duke University Press, 1995), esp. 15–26. For Ragussis' discussion of Scott, *Ivanhoe*, and conversionism, see 89–116.

5. For my understanding of *midrash*, I have relied on Geoffrey Hartman and Sanford Budick, eds., *Midrash and Literature* (New Haven: Yale University Press, 1986); Sander Gilman, *Self-Hatred: Anti-Semitism and the Hidden Language of the Jews* (Baltimore: The Johns Hopkins University Press, 1986), and Geoffrey Hartman, "On the Jewish Imagination," *Prooftexts* 5 (September 1985): 201–20.

6. Frank Kermode, *The Genesis of Secrecy: On the Interpretation of Narrative* (Cambridge: Harvard University Press, 1979), 2–5, and 16–17.

7. Galchinsky, 23, 136–7.

8. "*The Spirit of Judaism*, her meditation on the humanistic spirit that underlay the formal rituals of Judaism, was written as an aid in her brothers' education. Isaac Leeser agreed to publish it in 1840, but it was lost in transit to America and had to be rewritten. It appeared in print in 1842, with Leeser's editorial comments and refutations, and nonetheless achieved an enormous success... [and was] reprinted well into the 1880s" (Galchinsky, 138). Philadelphia publisher Isaac Leeser played an important role in promoting Jewish women writers, and was the publisher of Aguilar's *Spirit of Judaism*, as well as, interestingly, of works written by Aguilar's great-grandfather.

9. See Jeanne Wood, "'Alphabetically Arranged': Mary Hays's *Female Biography* and the Biographical Dictionary," *Genre* 31 (1998): 117–42; Paula McDowell, "Consuming Women: The Life of the 'Literary Lady' as Popular Culture in Eighteenth-Century England," *Genre* 26 (1993): 219–52; and Gary Kelly, *Women, Writing, and Revolution, 1790–1827* (Oxford: Clarendon Press, 1993), 236–46.

10. The eleventh-century commentator Rashi, says that Leah's eyes were "weak" from crying at the prospect of being forced to marry Esau; Rashi's grandson, Rashbam (twelfth century) says that the normative meanings of the word are "soft" and "beautiful" (*The Soncino Chumash: The Five Books of Moses with Haphtaroth*, ed. A. Cohen [New York: Soncino, 1983], 170). Aguilar's printed version transposes the first and last three words of the Hebrew text.

11. Galchinsky, 138.

12. Galchinsky, 141.

13. Linda Gertner Zatlin discusses Aguilar's emphasis on the similarity in spirit between Christians and Jews, which is the fundamental principle, I would

argue, on which Aguilar's maternalism rests (see *The Nineteenth-Century Anglo-Jewish Novel* [Boston: G. K. Hall, 1981], 35–7).

14. Alice Chandler, *A Dream of Order: The Medieval Ideal in Nineteenth-Century English Literature* (Lincoln, NE: University of Nebraska Press, 1970), 159–60; Richard Faber, *Young England* (London: Faber and Faber, 1987), 106–21.

15. For instance, the Carlton Club credited *Coningsby* ("Young England's 'manifesto,'" Faber 188) and Disraeli for Sir Robert Peel's defeat as Prime Minister. Disraeli's work at this point was an extension of the party's paternalism (efforts to shorten factory hours, oppose the New Poor Law, and support Corn Law reform), and then to mediate the Catholic-Anglican controversy surrounding Irish Home Rule. On Disraeli and the Irish Question, see Richard Shannon, *The Age of Disraeli, 1868–1881: The Rise of Tory Democracy* (London: Longman, 1992), 87–97. But Alice Chandler sees even Disraeli's work to help de Rothschild assume his contested seat in Parliament in 1858 as limited, his attention not shifting to the Jewish community until later (181). In *Tancred*, however, Disraeli is already shifting focus from Young England to Jerusalem and the Semitic heritage. Contemporary reviews noted this emphasis, commenting that Disraeli is obsessed by "the essential and unalienable prerogative of the Jewish race, to be at once the moral rule and the political master of humanity" (R. M. Milnes, in *The Edinburgh Review* 86 [July 1847]), that he "would make us believe that the Jewish mind still governs the world, through the medium of prime-ministers, bankers, and actresses" (J. R. Lowell, in *The North American Review* 65 [July 1847]), and that he is obsessed with "a Mosaic Parliament, sitting in Rag Fair" (*Punch* [April 10, 1847]: 145). The reviews are collected in R. W. Stewart, ed., *Disraeli's Novels Reviewed, 1826–1968* (Metuchen, NJ: Scarecrow Press, 1975), 224, 227, 231. These responses show the care Disraeli needed to take politically to present himself as Anglican and English. But his biographer Stanley Weintraub views Disraeli's identity—Anglican by religion, Jewish by race—as further conflicted by his fascination with Catholicism, and his next novel *Lothair* (1870) as "a host of heresies that were a clue to the real Disraeli beneath the politically necessary fiction" (*Disraeli, A Biography* [New York: Truman Talley Books/Dutton, 1993], 489).

16. "His physiognomy told truth. Arthur Stanley was, as his name implied, an Englishman of noble family" (*Vale of Cedars* 4).

17. Aguilar takes great pains to explain that although Ferdinand and Isabella have not yet instituted the Spanish Inquisition, inquisitorial practice actually already existed in Spain. Marie's grandfather, Julien Henriquez, had built the family refuge in the Vale of Cedars after having miraculously escaped from their prison.

18. On literary uses of Jewish stereotypes, see Frank Felsenstein, *Anti-Semitic Stereotypes: A Paradigm of Otherness in English Popular Culture, 1660–1830* (Baltimore: The Johns Hopkins University Press, 1995); Edgar Rosenberg, *From Shylock to Svengali: Jewish Stereotypes in English Fiction* (Stanford: Stanford University Press, 1960); and Bryan Cheyette, *Construction of "The Jew" in English Literature and Society* (Cambridge: Cambridge University Press, 1993).

19. Interestingly, Ivanhoe is at first unable to read her body as Jewish, and she must tell him "her father's name and lineage" despite the fact that he could see her "turban'd and caftan'd" body, and hear her speak Hebrew to her servant (299, 298). By serving in the Crusades, Ivanhoe had developed a tolerance for Easternized appearance that made Rebecca's Jewishness invisible to him despite their present location in England. But his reaction, which allows the love plot to develop, is anomalous in the novel. Marie's costume in the Vale is unusual but not Oriental: Stanley cannot read its cultural signs, and it serves to signal her mysterious identity rather than her Jewishness.
20. Marie's martyrdom has all kinds of resonance to the martyrdom of the Templars already foreshadowed in *Ivanhoe* by Bois-Guilbert's defeat, and the relation between the Church's execution of Jews, the execution of the Templars, and the Templars' fantastic rapine of Jerusalem in the name of Christianity. As Ragussis notes, the main connection between Marie's Jewishness and Inquisitorial practice is rape: "Raping Marie and converting her are part of a single desire, a single mission.... The bodily torture that the Inquisitor subsequently inflicts on her serves concurrently as the substitute for his passion and the instrument of his proselytism" (144).

Chapter 13
Alroy as Disraeli's "Ideal Ambition"
Sheila A. Spector

Identified by Cecil Roth "as one of the earliest, and perhaps indeed the earliest, of Jewish historical novels," Benjamin Disraeli's *The Wondrous Tale of Alroy* has been criticized for its historical inaccuracies.[1] Based on the failed messianic movement led by David Alroy in the twelfth century,[2] the novel traces the archetypal cycle prevalent in Jewish culture of the rise and fall of an anointed king whose personal shortcomings, coupled with external exigencies, prevent his restoring the Jewish people to their homeland, where they are to rebuild the Temple and reestablish the ancient biblical cult.[3] Instead, the novel ends where it began, with the Jews in their Eastern diaspora, paying tribute to their Muslim oppressors. In creating what he called a "dramatic romance," Disraeli exercised a great deal of poetic license, some acknowledged, some not.[4] He altered historical events, anachronistically relocated real individuals from their own epochs, and introduced not necessarily accurate portrayals of Jewish rites and ceremonies, including an elaborate overlay of kabbalistic machinery that, despite his assertion to the contrary, does not particularly reflect the mystical practices of the Jews, thus provoking the critical response to his only Jewish novel. Yet, to measure what the author would eventually call his "ideal ambition" against the standard of factual accuracy distorts the larger implications of the novel, limiting its fictional relevance to a narrowly defined Jewish context. Rather, as a "Jewish" work written by a practicing Anglican of Jewish ethnicity, *Alroy* is neither a "Jewish novel," nor, as Disraeli's early reviewers would testify, a popular work of fiction.[5] Rather, as the only Jewish novel written by a baptized Jew, *Alroy* can more properly be viewed as a Christian apologetic, a fictionalized defense of Disraeli's own apostasy.

Psychologically, converts have frequently felt constrained to justify in writing their reasons for abandoning Judaism. Although, in contrast to Disraeli's, their literary works are usually hostile, for the most part they serve two purposes. First, given the political realities of the diaspora, the apologetics are used to ingratiate converts with their new co-religionists, often by revealing to the public Jewish "secrets" that eventually would be turned against the Jewish populace. Second, these treatises serve an evangelical purpose. Possibly to rationalize their own choice, possibly to please their new spiritual advisors, apostates often feel compelled to persuade others to join them in their move from one faith to the other. As a result, some of the most virulent forms of anti-Semitism have emanated from those who experienced for themselves the effects of such religious discrimination.

Such was not the case with Disraeli. Having been baptized at the age of twelve, by parents who themselves remained Jewish, Disraeli was technically part of both worlds, and consequently, felt he belonged in neither. While there is no evidence that his Anglican faith was anything other than sincere, he still retained an ethnic connection with what he called the Jewish race, believing that "Christianity is Judaism for the multitude."[6] Yet, he also recognized that his conversion, which gained him access to the political career he was about to embark upon when he published *The Wondrous Tale of Alroy* in 1833, would likely generate accusations of opportunism, that he had abandoned his faith for the sake of secular success. However, as the son of a second-generation Englishman with Mendelssohnian sympathies, Disraeli was historically a man out of his time. Internally, a separatist reformed synagogue would not be organized until 1840, while externally, English Jews would not gain full emancipation until 1871, when they would be permitted to take degrees at Oxford and Cambridge.[7] Consequently, as Isaac D'Israeli was persuaded in 1817, it would be best to have his children baptized.

In contrast to its Continental counterparts, the Anglo-Jewish community was slow to institute the kinds of reforms that might have dissuaded D'Israeli.[8] Externally, instead of granting the Jews full citizenship, ever since the failed Jewish Naturalization Bill of 1753, England had followed a process of incremental emancipation,[9] gradually eliminating civil disabilities until, in 1858, Baron Lionel de Rothschild could take his seat in Parliament, and in 1871, the Universities Tests Act would be passed. Existing in an amorphous state in which they were neither granted full privileges of citizenship nor forced to suffer the extreme hardships of anti-Semitism, English Jewry was bifurcated into two completely different groups. The older Sephardic community, some of whose members had been in England for centuries, had assimilated to the extent that they could, their knowledge of the modern European languages providing access to the intellectual world of post-Enlightenment England; yet, because of public prejudice and civil disabilities, they were still looked down upon as Jews. Basically, they had the sensibilities of Reformed Jews, though without any internal institutional support. In contrast, the newer Ashkenazic community, which for the most part lacked the educational background and linguistic facility of the Sephardim, required the security of a traditional synagogal hierarchy, maintained through a strict adherence to biblical rites and customs. Hence Isaac D'Israeli's dilemma. While neither he nor his father believed in the tenets of rabbinic Judaism, both felt an emotional tie to their heritage, maintaining membership in the London Congregation of Spanish and Portuguese Jews. Yet, after his own father's death, when embroiled in a controversy with the Wardens at the Bevis Marks Synagogue, Isaac formally broke with a community whose theology had always conflicted with his own.[10] Still, despite his criticism of Anglo-Jewry, Isaac seems never to have come to terms with his decision to have his children baptized, publishing anonymously *The Genius of Judaism* in 1833, the same year Benjamin published *Alroy*. For his part, Benjamin seems to have accepted the necessity of his conversion, in *The Wondrous Tale of Alroy* satirizing a panorama of Jewish types found throughout the history of the diaspora, suggesting that as an "ideal ambition," Alroy might be the hero of some sort of sentimental romance, but that as a whole, the traditional Jewish community constituted an unviable religious establishment for the modern world.

In the novel, Disraeli uses David Alroy's failed messianic movement as the vehicle for illuminating the shortcomings of the contemporary Anglo-Jewish community, with the backdrop of the medieval Muslim-Turkish world as the vehicle for displacing contemporary criticism onto a neutral culture. Within that context, Alroy, as the scion of the House of David, attempts to accommodate his personal desires with his social obligations, all within the exigencies of the real world. To that end, in the first half of the novel, he interacts with all of the disparate types found in a traditional Jewish community, including the secular leader, the virtuous woman, the rabbi, the kabbalist, the prophetess, and the *maranno,* or crypto-Jew, so that in the second half, he can try to consolidate their ultimately contradictory attitudes toward Judaism into a viable theocracy. As is to be expected, he will fail. However, Alroy's experience provides Disraeli with what was apparently the necessary rationalization for his apostasy. Yet, in contrast to more conventional apologetics, he does not evangelize his Jewish readers but, instead, he seems to suggest that internal reform—along with civil emancipation—might help others avoid being forced to make the choice he and his father had to confront.

Providing the context for the action are the male and female symbols of stability within the Jewish social structure: the lay leader, and the virtuous woman, that is, the secular head of the community and the female head of the household. Because, historically, Jews had been ghettoized into their own communities, they established their own internal political structure, a leader being required both to maintain order among the Jews and to intercede among the Christians of the larger community. By identifying Bostenay as the "exilarch" of his novel, Disraeli associates the action with the entire history of the Jewish diaspora, the title *Resh Galuta,* as an exilarch with hereditary ties to the House of David, dating back to the Second Temple era.[11] Consequently, Bostenay's official functions, including the protection of orphans like David and his sister Miriam, and the payment of tribute to the Turkish overlords, are historically authentic, reflecting the exilarch's primary duties; but they also project the obligations to be imposed on their later Western manifestation, the *parnas,* who, like the official of the Bevis Marks Synagogue, imposed a fine on Isaac D'Israeli for refusing to serve as warden. Significantly, by naming his character Bostenay (or Bustenai), the name of the first exilarch, Disraeli not only associates the secular head of the community with the full history of Jewish exile, but more specifically, introduces the concept of inter-marriage, Bustenai supposedly having been married to the Persian emperor's daughter. Applying the corrective of historical reality, Disraeli uses the actual Bustenai's inter-marriage to undermine the pretext used by the fictional Jabaster and Esther for plotting against Alroy at the climax of the novel, implying that the former was actually more interested in restoring the biblical cult, and the latter in avenging a perceived sexual rejection. Within the novel, Bostenay is not really part of the action per se, but represents the Jewish community at large, literally interceding on its behalf, symbolically living at the mercy of external forces over which he has no control. In periods of prosperity, the exilarch lived like a prince, though when the novel opens, Bostenay undergoes the indignity of paying tribute to the Turks. When the nephew triumphs, his uncle prospers; at Alroy's death, Bostenay is again degraded to the level of servant.

As Alroy's female counterpart, his sister Miriam is the virtuous Jewish woman whose piety and valor are celebrated in folklore. In the beginning of the novel, she provides the impetus for the action, Alschiroch's attack symbolizing the eternal condition of the Jew in exile, being vulnerable to some form of rape by the sultan's brother. In defending Miriam, Alroy assumes his obligations as messiah-king; his ensuing exile to the wilderness, like Moses' before him, initiates the process of revelation as he accepts his larger obligations to his people. Symbolically,

Miriam, as the archetypal Jewish woman, embodies the historical goal of Jewish messianism, to restore the Jewish nation. Consequently, she must die when Alroy is executed: the failure of the movement signifies the death of the traditional (i.e., pre-Reform) Jewish community.

Within the context established by Bostenay and Miriam, the core of traditional Judaism emerges as the real object of Disraeli's satire. Focusing on what he portrays as a rigid, irrational rabbinate, trapped by the combination of a superstitious adherence to archaic rites and customs, and a preference for revealed, as opposed to natural, religion, Disraeli implies that traditional Jews are incapable of adapting to the exigencies of the contemporary world. Personifying these non-rational Jewish archetypes are Zimri, the chief rabbi of Jerusalem; Jabaster, the kabbalistic zealot; and Esther, the prophetess.

The most extensive satire is directed against the Talmudic sophistry of an unenlightened rabbinate, as portrayed by Zimri, Chief Rabbi of Jerusalem, presumably the religious authority to whom Alroy must prove himself before he can be anointed the messiah-king. But by locating the rabbinic examination in medieval Jerusalem, Disraeli conveys the impotence of an institution supposedly designed to regenerate the Jewish community. As the embodiment of rabbinic Judaism, Zimri is physically old, intellectually constricted, and, consequently, spiritually blind. When they first meet, Alroy mistakes the "old man, in shabby robes, who was passing" (77), for a doddering derelict:

> "Fellow, I see thou art a miserable prattler. Show me our quarter, and I will pay thee well, or be off."
> "Be off! Art then a Hebrew? to say 'be off' to any one. You come from Bagdad! I tell you what, go back to Bagdad. You will never do for Jerusalem."
> "Your grizzled beard protects you. Old fool, I am a pilgrim just arrived, wearied beyond expression, and you keep me here listening to your flat talk!"
> "Flat talk! Why! what would you?"
> "Lead me to the Rabbi Zimri, if that be his name."
> "If that be his name! Why, every one knows Rabbi Zimri, the chief rabbi of Jerusalem, the successor of Aaron. We have our temple yet, say what they like. A very learned doctor is Rabbi Zimri."
> "Wretched driveller. I am ashamed to lose my patience with such a dotard." (78)

More than comic, the scene undermines the basic tenets of rabbinic Judaism. Taking place in a Jerusalem controlled by "Franks" who do not deign to speak to Jews, the setting provides a constant reminder of the central contradiction inherent in the messianic myth. Despite the facts that Jews live in Israel, that remnants of the temple exist—"We have our temple yet," as Zimri boasts—and that the ancient Jewish rituals are adhered to, still, the majority of Jews live in exile. Significantly, the putative intellectual leader of the Jews is a silly old man who makes no sense, speaking "flat talk." Even more important, though, the rabbi fails to recognize the future messiah, telling Alroy, "You will never do for Jerusalem." Ironically, the rabbi is right. Alroy will not become the traditional messiah of rabbinic belief.

The next chapter satirizes Talmudic learning for being ahistorical and circular. In the scene, Rabbi Zimri discusses Talmud with his elder, the 109-year-old Rabbi Maimon:

> "No one reasons like Abarbanel of Babylon," said Rabbi Zimri.
> "The great Rabbi Akiba, of Pundebita, has answered them all," said Rabbi Maimon, "and holds that they were taken up to heaven."
> "And which is right?" inquired Rabbi Zimri.
> "Neither," said Rabbi Maimon.
> "One hundred and twenty reasons are strong proof," said Rabbi Zimri.
> "The most learned and illustrious Doctor Aaron Mendola, of Granada," said Rabbi Maimon, "has shown that we must look for the Tombs of the Kings in the south of Spain."
> "All that Mendola writes is worth attention," said Rabbi Zimri.
> "Rabbi Hillel, of Samaria, is worth two Mendolas any day," said Rabbi Maimon.
> "'Tis a most learned doctor," said Rabbi Zimri; "and what thinks he?"
> "Hillel proves that there are two Tombs of the Kings," said Rabbi Maimon, "and that neither of them are the right ones."
> "What a learned doctor!" exclaimed Rabbi Zimri.
> "And very satisfactory," remarked Alroy.
> "These are high subjects," continued Maimon, his blear eyes twinkling with complacency. "Your guest, Rabbi Zimri, must read the treatise of the learned Shimei, of Damascus, on 'Effecting Impossibilities.'"
> "That is a work!" exclaimed Zimri.
> "I never slept for three nights after reading that work," said Rabbi Maimon. "It contains twelve thousand five hundred and thirty-seven quotations from the Pentateuch, and not a single original observation."
> "There were giants in those days," said Rabbi Zimri; "we are children now."
> "The first chapter makes equal sense, read backward or forward," continued Rabbi Maimon. (80–1)

In addition to mixing up historical names and titles of treatises, the two rabbis turn basic logic topsy turvy. They accept contradictory precepts—"'Hillel proves that there are two Tombs of the Kings,' said Rabbi Maimon, 'and that neither of them are the right ones'"; they praise oxymoronic concepts, like Shimei's "Effecting Impossibilities"; they laud triteness—"and not a single original observation"; and basically, they strive for the irrational: "The first chapter makes equal sense, read backward or forward."

The synagogue scene that follows depicts the moribund nature of Zimri's religion. Located in a dark cemetery, which they must descend to enter, the synagogue is actually the inner chamber of a claustrophobic tomb that leaves the congregants essentially brain dead. After prayers, when Rabbi Zimri expounds the law, he poses a riddle that none of the Jerusalem Jews can solve: "it is written, that he took a rib from Adam when he was asleep. Is God then a robber?" (83). It takes an outsider, an African pilgrim, to respond: "Rabbi, some robbers broke into my house last night, and stole an earthen pipkin, but they left a golden vase in its stead" (83). The scene and the solution both reflect the need for new blood in the congregation, the riddle clearly indicating the need for change, the earthen pipkin symbolizing the old, moribund tradition, and the golden vase its evolution into a modern vessel whose use and beauty far surpass the original object.

For his part, the African then poses a riddle about a laughing girl and dreaming boy who marry, which he must solve himself:

> "Now hear the interpretation," said the African. "The youth is our people, and the damsel is our lost Sion, and the tomb of Absalom proves that salvation can only come from the house of David. Dost then hear this, young man?" said the African, coming forward and laying his hand on Alroy. "I speak to thee because I have observed a deep attention in thy conduct." (84)

More than simply the intellectual limitations of the congregation, the riddle turns back on the messianic prayers just uttered in the synagogue. Not only do the congregants not understand that the solution to the riddle is the basic tenet of their faith, but more important, they fail to recognize that Alroy is quite literally the answer to their prayers. Yet, even after the African compliments Alroy, Zimri keeps talking, preventing Alroy from accompanying the African out of the synagogue. In the next chapter, Alroy must leave Jerusalem to find the Tomb of the Kings, where he will be made messiah.

Rabbi Zimri is not only ineffectual, but his bumbling idiocy prevents the achievement of the messianic dream he espouses. He never recognizes, much less acknowledges, Alroy as messiah; instead, he buries himself in the ancient lore that makes equal sense backward and forward. Consequently, Alroy, in order to complete his obligations to the Jewish community, must leave both Jerusalem and its chief rabbi, symbols of a moribund rabbinate that inhibits the evolution of modern Judaism.

Unlike his satiric approach to the rabbinate, Disraeli's treatment of revealed religion is far more complex. Without actually attacking the possibility of either mysticism or prophecy, he confuses the issue, portraying Jabaster, the mystical zealot, and Esther, the prophetess, as fully human beings whose personal ambitions and drives are so intertwined with their Divine revelations that it becomes impossible to differentiate between the two.

Jabaster, Alroy's spiritual advisor, embodies the contradictions inherent in the question of revelation in the modern world. On the surface, he is depicted like the archetypal mystical ascetic, a Bar Kokhba living in the wilderness where he will be free to practice his ritualistic beliefs. Before the time of the novel, he had been Alroy's teacher who, having recognized early on young David's messianic potential, educated him in the supernatural lore associated with his Divine mission. At the beginning of the novel, Jabaster prepares Alroy for the quest in search of Solomon's scepter, providing him with both the talisman that controls access to the Tomb, and the ring that will protect him from the Muslims. Then, immediately after Alroy locates the scepter, he is transported back to Jabaster's cave, from where they will begin the proto-messiah's miraculously successful campaign against the Turks.

Interlaced with the mystical signs, however, are indications of a frustrated man, hoping to fulfill his own ambitions through the agency of his student. In an early soliloquy, Jabaster admits that in his own youth, he had attempted to lead his own crusade, but lacking Divine sanction, he had failed. Then, during Alroy's early messianic wars, Jabaster's Jewish troops falter, requiring the assistance of Scherirah and his band of multi-cultural mercenaries. Yet, after their success, Jabaster attempts to persuade Alroy to impose a rigid theocracy on the empire, permits his own troops to desecrate Muslim holy places, and resists Alroy's wish to include on the council representatives of all of the empire's disparate peoples. Then, when Alroy marries Schirene and chooses Bagdad over Jerusalem, Jabaster plots against the putative messiah, intending himself to slay the scion of the House of David.

The point is less Jabaster's human weaknesses than the ambiguity of the situation as a whole. Because the supernatural and purely human are so thoroughly mixed in Jabaster, it is impossible to know which of his demands are Divinely sanctioned, and which result from his own prejudices. Obviously, from an orthodox perspective, Alroy's inter-marriage could be interpreted as anathema, some biblical antecedents, such as

Samson and Solomon, providing evidence of a religious prohibition. Similarly, the choice of Bagdad over Jerusalem could also be interpreted as the kind of violation that resulted in the diaspora. Yet, Jabaster's troops would have died like the Zealots of Masada had Scherirah not saved them; and as the extensive scene with Rabbi Zimri suggests, any attempt to restore the biblical cult in the Jerusalem of the twelfth century (itself modeled after the Jerusalem of the nineteenth century that Disraeli visited while writing the novel) would have been absurd. Most significant, though, Jabaster's messianic ideology caused him to violate its most basic tenet—he was actually prepared to kill the messiah-king, thus privileging his own supposed revelation, which had already been proven unreliable, over that of the man who had been given Solomon's scepter.

Like Jabaster, Esther the prophetess embodies the same confusing mixture of Divine revelation and human desire, her prophecies directly paralleling her emotional state. That is, as long as she felt that she might have a chance with Alroy, her interpretations of his mission were positive. When first introduced in Part VII, she is overcome with her vision of the messiah's imminent success, as "foaming and panting, she rushed to Alroy, threw herself upon the ground, embraced his feet, and wiped off the dust from his sandals with her hair" (104). But once he announces his engagement to Schirene, Esther's prophecies grow increasingly more antagonistic; she endorses the plot against Alroy and the plan to murder Honain; and finally, she attempts to assassinate Alroy herself. As she says, "An irresistible impulse hath carried me into this chamber!... The light haunted me like a spectre; and wheresoever I moved, it seemed to summon me" (183). While the subconscious wish-fulfillment seems obvious, Disraeli leaves open the question of Esther's visionary prowess. After all, Alroy's decisions to marry Schirene and turn to Bagdad do cause Jabaster to set in motion the dastardly plot. Consequently, even though the prophecy does come true, we do not know whether it is a coincidence caused by human machinations, part of Divine providence, or possibly even both.

Just as Disraeli questions the validity of the mystic and prophet, he similarly undermines the integrity of the *maranno*, historically the crypto-Jew who pretended to convert to Christianity in order to escape punishment by the Inquisition. Although Disraeli would later romanticize the *maranno*, even going so far as to create for himself a pseudo-genealogy in which he claimed to have been descended from crypto-Jews, in *Alroy*, he portrays the anachronistic *moranno*, Honain, as a hypocrite, no better than the self-serving pragmatic utilitarian of nineteenth-century England.

In his first appearance, Honain projects the impression of a *maranno* who chose to go underground because even though the contemporary Jewish community could not fulfill his intellectual needs, he still wished to retain ties with his people, possibly even to help them from the outside. He first enters when Alroy is embroiled with a merchant in an argument about the ownership of Jabaster's ring. In sharp contrast to Alroy who, as a Jew, had been vilified by all who saw him, Honain conveys the impression of an urbane, cosmopolitan, international intellectual, eliciting the respect of everyone present. Immediately recognizing the ring as the token he had given his brother, Honain knows that Alroy is Jewish and, through a Solomonic judgment, retrieves the ring and saves its bearer, whom he brings to his home. But once they are in private, Honain reveals his hypocrisy:

> "Listen to me, Alroy," said Honain in a low voice, and he placed his arm around him, "I am your friend. Our acquaintance is very brief: no matter, I love you; I rescued you in injury, I tended you in sickness, even now your life is in my power, I would protect it with my own. You cannot doubt me. Our affections are not under our own control; and mine are yours. The sympathy between us is entire. You see me, you see what I am; a Hebrew, though unknown; one of that despised, rejected, persecuted people, of whom you are the chief. I too would be free and honoured. Freedom and honour are mine, but I was my own messiah. I quitted in good time our desperate cause, but I gave it a trial. Ask Jabaster how I fought. Youth could be my only excuse for such indiscretion. I left this country; I studied and resided among the Greeks. I returned from Constantinople, with all their learning, some of their craft. No one knew me. I assumed their turban, and I am, the Lord Honain. Take my experience, child, and save yourself much sorrow. Turn your late adventure to good account. No one can recognise you here. I will introduce you amongst the highest as my child by some fair Greek. The world is before you. You may fight, you may love, you may revel. War, and women, and luxury are all at your command. With your person and talents you may be grand vizir. Clear your head of nonsense. In the present disordered state of the empire, you may even carve yourself out a kingdom, infinitely more delightful than the barren land of milk and honey. I have seen it, child; a rocky wilderness, where I would not let my courser graze." (60)

Devoid of principles, Honain has become the deaf-mute eunuch he has Alroy pretend to be. He lies, panders, and even kills his own brother, all for the sake of power and wealth. Motivated strictly by self-interest, Honain manipulates Alroy, during the period of Jewish ascendancy, into replacing Jabaster with him as chief advisor. But after the Turks begin to rally, he negotiates Alroy's capture, to the last minute trying to persuade

Alroy to accept Islam, not out of any religious conviction, but to curry favor with Alp Arslan. Contrary to the more usual Jewish interpretation, Disraeli portrays the *maranno* as being far worse than the convert, who at least retains some semblance of religious principle.

Within this context, Alroy emerges as a Romantic hero doomed to failure. Descended from David, he accepts his obligation to lead the messianic wars, though once he triumphs, there is no way to establish himself as a messiah-king over a Jewish nation that can reclaim Jerusalem, rebuild the Temple and restore the biblical cult. Rather, the rabbinate, as represented by Rabbi Zimri, is moribund. The conquest of Jerusalem would require another war, this one against the Western Europeans, and given Jabaster's military inadequacies in the crusade against the Turks, not to mention his subsequent discrimination against Muslims, there is no reason to believe that his forces alone would triumph against all of the non-Jews in Palestine. Finally, even if Alroy did regain Jerusalem, he still would not be certain which elements of the newly revealed religion reflected Divine Will, and which were projections of human wish-fulfillment. The only other alternative open to him, the push toward Bagdad, is motivated by the utilitarian self-interest of the morally vacuous Honain, whose lack of principles could guarantee only the survival of the slyest.

Unavailable to Alroy—and to Disraeli—were the prerequisites for Reform Judaism, an evolved theology adapted to the exigencies of the contemporary world. Internally, the leaders of both the fictional Jewish community of twelfth-century Asia, and the historical community of early nineteenth-century England, adhered to tradition and opposed change, both religious establishments preventing the Jews from substituting newer forms of worship for what some considered to be archaic rites and ceremonies. Externally, constitutional restrictions against religious freedom forced the Jews to choose between the possibility of worshiping as they chose or participating in the secular world. Consequently, modern-thinking Jews who had been exposed to post-Enlightenment learning had no viable options. Unable to practice Judaism in the way he saw fit, the ideal hero, David Alroy, chose death. In contrast, Benjamin Disraeli, the real man living in the real world, accepted the necessity of conversion, working from the outside to remove the last disabilities against the Jews in Victorian England.[12]

Notes

1. Cecil Roth, *Benjamin Disraeli* (New York: Philosophical Library, 1952), 61. Published in 1833, *The Wondrous Tale of Alroy,* as it was originally entitled, was

intended primarily for a Christian audience, its anti-theocratic, anti-utilitarian theme anticipating the contemporary debate about dis-establishing the constitutional relationship between the Church of England and Great Britain. By the twentieth century, however, the focus had shifted, the Jewish content of the novel having taken precedence over its Christian theme. In "A Masterpiece for the Week: Disraeli's 'Alroy,'" (*The Jewish World,* No. 3005 [11 Tamuz 5673/16 July 1913], 9–10), Israel Abrahams explicitly associates *Alroy* with the Anglo-Jewish community, and now, as can be seen from John Vincent's assertion that "*Alroy* is important because of its Jewishness" (*Disraeli* [Oxford and New York: Oxford University Press, 1990], 68), the Christian significance has been effectively erased. Parenthetical references in this paper are to the standard 1871 Longmans edition of *Alroy,* itself based on the revised version of 1846, and the last overseen by Disraeli. The title of this chapter derives from a passage quoted in Disraeli's earliest biography: "In *Vivian Grey* I have portrayed my active and real ambition; in Alroy my ideal ambition" (William Flavelle Monypenny and George Earle Buckle, *The Life of Benjamin Disraeli Earl of Beaconsfield,* 6 vols. [London: Murray, 1910–20], 1:185). As will be seen from this chapter, the word *ideal* can be subject to much interpretation.
2. The primary source for information about David Alroy is Benjamin of Tudela's twelfth-century diary account (see *Jewish Travellers in the Middle Ages: 19 Firsthand Accounts,* ed. Elkan Nathan Adler [New York: Dover, 1987; reprint of 1930 ed.], 50–2). A spurious account, attributed to Maimonides, is included in the *Chronologia Sacra-Profana A Mundi Conditu ad Annum M.5352 vel Christi 1592, dicta [ẒemahDavid]* of David ben Solomon Gans (1541–1613), as derived from the *Shevet Yehudah* (1553) of Solomon ibn Verga (second half of the fifteenth–first quarter of sixteenth century). Despite its lack of authenticity, Disraeli was attracted to this version, a portion of which he included (in Latin) in his last footnote. Salo Baron straightens out the historical record in *A Social and Religious History of the Jews,* particularly in Volume III: *Heirs of Rome and Persia,* and Volume V: *Religious Controls and Dissentions* (New York: Columbia University Press, and Philadelphia: The Jewish Publication Society of America, 1957), part of which is reprinted in *Essential Papers on Messianic Movements and Personalities in Jewish History,* ed. Marc Saperstein (New York: New York University Press, 1992), 238–40. See also Abraham N. Poliak's entry, "Alroy, David," in the *Encyclopædia Judaica* (Jerusalem: Keter, 1972), 2:750–1.
3. On Jewish messianic movements, see Saperstein's anthology, especially his introduction (1–31), and the overviews by R. J. Zwi Werblowsky, "Messianism in Jewish History" (35–52), and Eliezer Schweid, "Jewish Messianism: Metamorphoses of an Idea" (53–70).
4. The first edition of *The Wondrous Tale of Alroy* was accompanied by an extensive polemical introduction, in which Disraeli defended his choice of genre and style, as well as by eighty-two footnotes, which supplement the text with information gleaned from his personal experiences and extensive reading. Interestingly, while he included background information about Jewish history and culture (usually from Christian sources), he never clarified the liberties he took with Muslim history.

5. Daniel R. Schwarz believes that "Alroy represents Disraeli's own dreams of personal heroism and political power in the alien British culture" (*Disraeli's Fiction* [New York: Macmillan, 1979], 42–51). The six-volume Monypenny–Buckle biography has been superseded by Robert Blake's *Disraeli* (New York: St. Martin's Press, 1967). Roth's *Benjamin Disraeli*, the first to deal with the Jewish heritage, has been superseded by Stanley Weintraub's *Disraeli: A Biography* (New York: Truman Talley Books/Dutton, 1993).
6. The quotation is from Disraeli's 1847 novel *Tancred, or The New Crusade* (London: Longmans, Green, and Co., 1870–1), 427.
7. The standard, if somewhat dated, source for Anglo-Jewish history is Roth's *A History of the Jews in England*, 3rd ed. (Oxford: Oxford University Press, 1964). Todd M. Endelman's *The Jews of Georgian England, 1714–1830: Tradition and Change in a Liberal Society* (Philadelphia: The Jewish Publication Society of America, 1979; reprint, Ann Arbor: University of Michigan Press, 1999), deals with the period leading up to the publication of *Alroy*. On Isaac D'Israeli, see James Ogden's *Isaac D'Israeli* (Oxford: Clarendon Press, 1969), especially the tenth chapter, "D'Israeli and Judaism" (192–206), and Stuart Peterfreund's "Not for 'Antiquaries,' but for 'Philosophers': Isaac D'Israeli's Talmudic Critique and His Talmudical Way with Literature," in this volume.
8. See Michael A. Meyer, *Response to Modernity: A History of the Reform Movement in Judaism* (New York and Oxford: Oxford University Press, 1988), especially the first two chapters, "Adapting Judaism to the Modern World" (10–60), and "Ideological Ferment" (62–99).
9. On the emancipation of English Jews, in contrast to other European communities, see David Vital, *A People Apart: The Jews in Europe, 1789–1939* (Oxford: Oxford University Press, 1999), especially 177–83. On the Jew Bill in particular, see Alan H. Singer, "Great Britain or Judea Nova? National Identity, Property, and the Jewish Naturalization Controversy of 1753," in this volume.
10. In *The Jews in the History of England, 1485–1850*, David S. Katz notes that as a result of the D'Israeli incident, the Anglo-Jewish community began instituting some of the changes that would eventually consolidate into a Reform Movement: "While this is probably wishful thinking along, certainly the Reform Movement went some way towards achieving the ideals expressed by Isaac d'Israeli. Had it existed in 1817, it is likely that the entire family would have stayed within the fold" ([Oxford: Clarendon Press, 1994], 334).
11. According to tradition, the exilarch (*Resh Galuta*), scion of the House of David, was, among other things, guardian of orphans and illegitimate children (H. H. Ben-Sasson, ed., *A History of the Jewish People* [Cambridge: Harvard University Press, 1976], 281). If not technically allegorical, most of the names used in the novel are at least evocative of Jewish or Muslim history. In addition to biblical references, like Miriam and Esther, Disraeli incorporates a broad range of Jewish allusions. From the post-biblical period, there are Rabbi Hillel (first century BCE to beginning of the first century CE) and Rabbi Shammei, his contemporary (approximately 50 BCE to 30 CE). Rabbi Akiva (c. 50–135 CE), one of the greatest scholars of his age,

is frequently associated with the zealots who, under the leadership of Bar Kokhba (d. 135 CE) defended Masada. From later history, Pumbedita is the location of an academy established in the mid-third century. Shimei, of Damascus, supposed author of *Effecting Impossibilities,* might be a reference to Joseph ben Judah ibn Shim'on (twelfth–thirteenth centuries), physician, poet, and philosopher. Rabbi Maimon is a possible allusion to the Maimon family—Maimon ben Joseph (d. 1165/1170) and his son Moses ben Maimon (Maimonides; 1135–1204). Similarly, Disraeli's Abarbanel seems based on Abrabanel or Abravanel, the family name of prominent Jews in fifteenth-century Spain who, during the time of the Forced Conversion of 1497, were baptized, but in the seventeenth century, reverted to Judaism and revived the name. Aaron Mendola, of Granada, may be a play on Raphael Meldola (1754–1828), one of the rabbis involved in the dispute between Isaac D'Israeli and the Jewish community. Not a historical figure, Rabbi Zimri might have derived from either of two biblical figures. The first (Numbers 25) became a symbol of the worst rebellion against God and his Word; the second Zimri, who reigned as king for only seven days (1 Kings 16), symbolized the slave who turned against his master.

The other names derive from the Eastern diaspora or from Islamic history. Bostenay seems named after Bustenai ben Ḥaninai (c. 618–670), the first exilarch under Islam, and supposedly married to Izdundad, one of the captive daughters of Chosroes II, king of Persia. Scherirah is possibly based on Sherira ben Ḥanina Gaon (c. 906–1006), head of the academy at Pumbadita from 968–1006, who believed that the exilarchs all descended from Bustanai, from whom he claimed descent. Honain is a possible allusion either to Hunayn (d. 873), a multi-lingual Syrian who translated a number of Greek scientific works into Arabic, or to Hunayn ibn Ishaq (d. 874), the first physician to translate Greek medical works into Arabic. Alschiroch seems to be an ironic allusion to Shīrkūh I b. Ayyūb Abū Ṣalāh al-Din (Ayyūbīd[e], "the lion of the mountain"; c. 1169), uncle of Saladin. Schirene, or Shereen, was the beloved of royal chieftains. Alp Arslan (r. 1063–72) was a Turkish sultan whose dynasty, the Seljuks, reigned from 1038–1157. The only name for which there seems no biblical or historical antecedent is Jabaster, a possible neologism based on the root *yavash,* "dry up, make ashamed."

12. This is not to imply that conversion was an easy choice. As Harold Fisch points out in his essay "Disraeli's Hebraic Compulsions," Disraeli never really reconciled the two parts of his identity: "Here, very accurately stated, is the betrayal of selfhood from which Disraeli suffered—the betrayal of his innermost Jewish selfhood from which he had partially, but nonetheless effectively, alienated himself. But such betrayals cannot go unnoticed in a man of imagination. They will reveal themselves in fantasy, emptiness and sentimentality, the spiritual ills of the dreamer from whom the true source of his dream is hidden" (in *Essays Presented to Chief Rabbi Israel Brodie on the Occasion of his Seventieth Birthday,* ed. H. J. Zimmels, J. Rabbinowitz and I. Finestein, Jews' College Publication, New Series, No. 3, 2 vols. (London: Soncino, 1967), 1:94.

CHAPTER 14
HAROLD'S COMPLAINT, OR ASSIMILATION IN FULL BLOOM
David Kaufmann

> Bloom appears to be a representative figure who resists representing any one major critical movement or school of thought consistently: his constituency seems to be everyone and no one at the same time.
> —Orrin N. C. Wang, *Fantastic Modernity*[1]

It has been more than a quarter century since the first publication of *The Anxiety of Influence,* and both the scandal it provoked and the influence it exerted have generally been forgotten. This was not, in itself, inevitable. It is easy to imagine that the late 1970s feminist appropriation of Bloom's notions of agonistic identity construction could have been extended to illuminate the narratives of struggle for authority and symbolic capital that have been such an important part of literary criticism since the late 1980s. But Bloom's own success and his self-presentations have militated against the re-tooling of his theory in this way. Part of the relative oblivion into which *The Anxiety of Influence* has fallen can be attributed to the victory of its insistent, if covert, polemic against the New Criticism. If the New Criticism is no longer a significant force, neither is the opposition that lined up against it. Furthermore, while Bloom's theory went to great pains to differentiate itself from its immediate forebears, it also defined itself against the other modes of theory that it competed against at the time. Like "French theory" of the early 1970s, *The Anxiety of Influence* takes as its touchstones Nietzsche and Freud, but sets up in opposition to the French a Nietzsche untouched by the later Heidegger and a Freud unrevised by Lacan. Instead of basing his theoretical language in either the neologisms of philosophy or the technical terms of the human sciences, Bloom derives his own outlandish vocabulary from the arcana of Gnosticism and the ancient mysteries. While these moves created a place for Bloom within the genre of theory, it was destined to be a place only he could fill, because the mix turned out to be too idiosyncratic and thus too stifling for younger academics. And finally, and no less important, the figure that Bloom has come to assume—a monstrously productive and campy version of Samuel Johnson, a self-appointed conservator of literary values against younger, more politically oriented academics—has made him a hard act to want to follow. Perhaps it is only now that *The Anxiety of Influence* no longer presents an enticement or a threat that we can begin to see what was at stake in its claims in the first place.

Bloom, like his friend Geoffrey Hartman, used the considerable authority he had gained as a Romanticist[2] to introduce Jewish forms of hermeneutics into theory.[3] I am less interested in this aspect of *The Anxiety of Influence* (which is not explicitly Jewish) than in the way the theory imagines the Romantic tradition in order to allegorize the place of Jews in the literary academy. I will argue in the course of this chapter that not only does Bloom imagine himself into the great low-church Protestant line of poets that extends from Milton to Ashbery, but he imagines those poets as occupying in a significant sense the position of Jews. Of course, Bloom can only mount such an argument through patience and cunning. So we will need to trace it by looking at the odd turns the argument takes, especially in its peculiar treatment of Freudian thought.

Adorno once quipped that in psychoanalysis, nothing is true except the exaggerations.[4] Given Bloom's reliance on Freud, we might want to pay close attention to some of the more scandalous and exaggerated aspects of Bloom's theory: to his contention that poetry and criticism are born of aggression, to his radical notion of subjective freedom (a freedom so extreme that the subjectivity it renders is apparently without content), and to his idiosyncratic elision of the mother from the family romance. If we take Bloom's equation of criticism and poetry ("all criticism is prose poetry"[5]) as a hint from Bloom himself, then we have to ask what motivates all this. To locate Bloom's theory in its richness and particularity, I will set the abstractions of his book against the anxieties and compulsions that drive the character of Alexander Portnoy, and brace Bloom's flight into the academically privileged realms of poetry and theory against Philip Roth's furious descent into the demotic.

My choice of Roth's novel is not arbitrary. *Portnoy's Complaint* and *The Anxiety of Influence* are both Freudian fantasies and both ring changes on the notion of the family romance. But Roth's novel, by locating its fierce play with Jewish stereotypes within the context of psychoanalytic discourse, reminds us that psychoanalysis has always been marked as a "Jewish" science and the extent to which—through the 60s and 70s—secular (and non-Zionist) Jewish culture was defined by the twin poles of standup comedy and psychoanalysis. In the end, my thesis is quite simple. Like Roth's novel, Bloom's theory uses a Freudian frame to meditate on the promise and the costs of assimilation. I suspect, in the end, that the fortunes of *The Anxiety of Influence* have waned as the ideal of assimilation has.

Like many successful works of literary theory, *The Anxiety of Influence* is based on a bold analogy—in this case, that poetic tradition looks more like the Freudian notion of the family romance than it does like the post-Arnoldian religious model of the inter-generational transmission of values.[6] For Freud, the pressures of the Oedipus complex lead the (male) child to fantasize an alternative history for himself: he is a changeling, the bastard son of royalty or perhaps his siblings are bastards. In the rawest version of this fantasy—the version that ultimately most interests Bloom—the son usurps the father's place in the mother's bed. The point of the family romance is that it is a fantasized tale of patrimony that relieves not only the strains of incestuous desire, but also the pains of fraternal jealousy and the severe disappointment of being caught in the bosom of a family whose social position never conforms to one's grandiosity.[7] Rather than submit to one's own history, one conjures a more gratifying genealogy. The (male) poet, in Bloom's revision, is summoned into poetry—which for Bloom is both the sense and expression of solipsistic power—by the strong poems of the past, by the works of the mighty dead. Poetry, Bloom's paradigm of self-creation, is thus both a yearning within the poet and a ravishment that originates outside the poet. Influence, the sense of the strength of the poets of the past, seems to stand in the way of self-creation, of poetry. And so the "strong" but belated poet gives himself over to fantasy. He misreads his precursor's poetry, sees it as weaker than it is, or (better still), as having been written by himself. For Bloom, the precursor poet takes the place of Freud's father. The poet, as Oedipal son, imagines a re-configured poetic patrimony, one that will allow him the full glory of his narcissism.

It is scandalous that in Bloom's version, the family romance of the poet lacks that essential component—the mother. At best, and then only half-heartedly, Bloom posits the Muse as the third point of the poetic Oedipal triangle. To see the degree of Bloom's misprision of Freud, one need only look at a place where he actually quotes Freud: "The mother gave the child his life and it is not easy to replace this unique gift ... all the instincts, the loving, the grateful, the sensual, the defiant, the self-assertive and independent—all are gratified in the wish to be the *father of himself*" (64; emphasis in original).

In Freud's account, the son expresses his tender emotions toward the mother through displacement. He repays her by replacing his father. In Bloom's cover version of all this, however, the psychic substitution disappears as the mother drops out completely: "If this is to serve as model for the family romance between poets, it needs to be transformed, so as to place the emphasis less upon phallic fatherhood, and more upon *priority*...." (64; emphasis in original).

In Freud, the emphasis on phallic fatherhood marks the child's way of coming to terms with his tenderness for his mother. It was not the main event, but a sideshow that made that main event more tolerable. But in Bloom's book, the sideshow, the fight with and for paternity is everything. Not surprisingly, then, the Muse, who unconvincingly comes in to take the place of the mother, does not feature prominently in Bloom's vision of what turns out to be an exclusively masculine struggle for mastery. The Muse is only a pale figure for the self's narcissistic investment. For Bloom it is the fight that constitutes identity that matters. Poetry is thus a question of survival, not desire.

Bloom's Freud is of course the "late Freud," the dark theoretician of *Beyond the Pleasure Principle* and *Totem and Taboo*. The *eros* of Bloom's account is pitched against death and has less to do with libido than with sheer *conatus*. He is worried about the survival of the poet's "aboriginal" identity. When Bloom follows Freud and sees poetry as a form of sublimation, he singles it out as a sublimation of *aggression,* not sex. Poetry is thus another twist in the self's defensive turning-around of the death drive:

> Whether sublimation of sexual instincts plays a central part in the genesis of poetry is hardly relevant to the reading of poetry, and has no part in the dialectic of misprision. But sublimation of aggressive instincts is central to writing and reading poetry, and this is almost identical with the total process of poetic misprision. (115)

The poet's freedom is won through the re-direction of the death drive. A radical Cartesian and certainly no Hegelian, Bloom's strong poet maintains an absolute split between the unimpeded liberty of "unextended thinking spirits" and the inescapable causality of "a huge mathematical machine extended in space" (39). The strong poet/critic tries to fight his way to an absolute discontinuity, a completely unmediated break between freedom and necessity. He dreams that he is not determined by his past, or by his position in the history of the world, or even by the existence of the world itself. Such an extreme notion of freedom is an important and impossible fantasy (perhaps even for God, hence the

Kabbalah's sometimes very uncomfortable flirtation with Gnosticism) and from this impossibility, no less than from its importance, stems the punch-line of Bloom's grand joke. One cannot *really* beget one's father or one's self. The poet's family romance, his quest to overcome time, is ultimately quixotic. Nevertheless, the quest and the battle are necessary, for without this delusion of freedom, Bloom's extreme, almost contentless dream of self-created identity, such as it is, is impossible. (Conversely, without this extreme ideal of identity, such a notion of freedom— complete self-determination—would be unnecessary.)

Sublimity, Nietzsche felt, smacked of *ressentiment,* the refusal to accept temporality. Bloom's revision of Nietzsche turns this *ressentiment* into the force behind any truly great literary quest. It is precisely "strong" poetry's inauthenticity in relation to time that makes it authentic poetry in the first place. For Bloom, the delusion of self-creation is in fact a sign of the poet's strength. Perhaps one of the most bracingly consistent aspects of *The Anxiety of Influence* is that, for all its aestheticism, it refuses to read poetry in terms of edifying truths or of redemption: "... the living labyrinth of literature is built upon the ruin of every impulse most generous in us. So apparently it is and must be—we are wrong to have founded a humanism directly upon literature itself, and the phrase 'humane letters' is an oxymoron" (86). Because for Bloom what is at stake in poetry is the always abstract identity of "the aboriginal poetic self," poetry is about nothing "higher," nothing more ideal or moral than the sheer preservation of that identity.

Given the fact that the poet's dream of absolute self-creation is ultimately a delusion, we might want to question Bloom's bracketing of all interest in the empirical poet or critic. His desire to be seen as nothing more than an "aboriginal poetic self" might be an authentic sign of strength, but the poet, like the critic, is condemned to live in a world of determinations, of extension, of causality. What impulses drive Bloom's defense of this delusion? Against what is Bloom defending? In a synopsis of *The Anxiety of Influence,* Bloom writes: "We read to usurp, just as the poet writes to usurp. Usurp what? A place, a stance, a fullness, an illusion of identification or possession, something we can call our own or even ourselves."[8] The metonymic play in this quotation is fascinating, because it indicates that the poet and the reader quite literally steal their identities from others. That thing we can call our own—our self, our identity—is not rightfully ours. Let us apply this back to Bloom. Whose place has Bloom stolen? An immediate answer to this is obvious. *The Anxiety of Influence* is dedicated to William Wimsatt, perhaps the sharpest theoretician among the New Critics and Bloom's beloved teacher and antagonist at Yale. Thus *The Anxiety of Influence* can be read as an antithetical assault on Wimsatt. While Bloom's rather stringent definition of tradition as a body of poems (rather than say a body of thought or religious beliefs) maintains Wimsatt's equally stringent attempts to establish literature as an autonomous realm of study, he breaks with Wimsatt and the other New Critics by rejecting the idea that the autonomous literary work is the repository of edifying doctrine or humane values.

Compare Bloom's view of poetry with the following statement from Wimsatt's "Concrete Universal":

> If it be granted that the "subject matter" of poetry is in a real sense the moral realm, human actions as good or bad ... all the thought and imagination that goes with happiness and suffering ... then the rhetorical structure of the concrete universal, the complexity and unity of the poem, is also its maturity or sophistication or richness or depth, and hence its value. Complexity of form is sophistication of content. The unity and maturity of good poems are two sides of the same thing.[9]

Wimsatt is famously not interested in either the poet's or the reader's intents or desires. He takes it for granted that the subject of poetry is not the poem or the poet's self, but the "moral realm," that is, the evaluation of human action. He also assumes that the particular structure of poetry, the self-contained formal unity of the individual work that draws together its apparent diversity of detail, the poem's ability to render generalizable abstractions through the play of its particulars, is the measure of its aesthetic worth and its moral sophistication. Bloom takes none of this for granted. Poetry and criticism as the usurpation of identity are beyond good and evil. What is more, Bloom, in good Longinian fashion, quotes passages, not poems. Not for him careful formal analyses of the unity of individual works. Rather, his version of close reading charts the flow of tropes and stances, echoes and resistances across poems, not within them. Wimsatt equates moral and aesthetic value with formal unity. Bloom rejects the equation. When Wimsatt claims psychological interest for literature, he appeals to the universals of a humanistic psychology, not the dark conflicts of Freud:

> ... a criticism of structure and of value is an objective criticism. It rests on facts of human psychology (as that a man may love a woman so well as to give up empires), facts, which though psychological, yet are so well acknowledged as to lie in the realm of what may be called public psychology—a realm one should distinguish from the private realm of the author's psychology and from the equally private realm of the individual reader's psychology.[10]

Note that Wimsatt's example of a psychological fact—that the plot of *Anthony and Cleopatra* is indeed credible—comes from dramatic literature and not lyric poetry (although he would read the lyric as a dramatic work). The theatrical analogy allows him to bracket off the psychology of both the empirical reader and writer as "private" and unknowable. Bloom, by concentrating on the individual, but not the biographical poet (that is, by looking at the "aboriginal poetic self"), is able to fashion a psychological realm that is surmisable, if only through a speculative appropriation of Freudian topoi.

That Bloom would signal his own *agon* with a critical father by dedicating his book to him is hardly surprising nor is it really news that *The Anxiety of Influence* was in some part a meditation on Bloom's own relations to the New Critics who were his teachers at Yale. Given the High Church orientation of Yale's English Department (Wimsatt was a Catholic) and given the fiercely though ambivalently anti-Semitic construction of "culture" in what Jonathan Freedman has called "literary Anglo-America," it is hardly surprising that even as combative and unrepentant a Jew as Bloom might declare his independence by coming up with a fantasy of radical self-fashioning.[11] What is surprising, though, is that he would claim Wimsatt as his father in this family romance (and not Abrams, or Trilling, or Frye), and that this romance of freedom would completely occlude the figure of the mother. What is more, in taking Wimsatt as his Oedipal father, he seems to leave his other father, Freud, relatively intact. Can we hear resonances in *The Anxiety of Influence* that go beyond Blake's struggle with Milton or Bloom's with individual teachers? Is the staged battle with Wimsatt a feint, masking something else?

There are several reasons why we should view the apparently contentless abstraction of Bloom's Gnostic notion of identity and the subtraction of the mother from the poetic family romance as evasions, if only because they seem, on the surface at least, so unmotivated. The Gnostic dream of a complete freedom from nature is extreme (even among the Romantics) and doubly odd in that Bloom shows it to be impossible. Bloom's revision of the family romance is, as we have noted, peculiar to him. Bloom's insistence on Freud and on psychoanalytic categories begs us to look at such moves as elegant bobbings and weavings. I want to see in these moves a defensive response to Bloom's identification as a Jew, but I am caught in a dilemma, because I need an account of American Jewish anxieties in the late 1960s, an account that will invoke the family romance in all its rich complications while revealing their concrete, social determinations. *Portnoy's Complaint*'s deep ambivalence about the costs of assimilation is particularly useful here because it casts an interesting and revealing light on Bloom's emphasis on aggression, identity, and masculinity. Like Bloom's strong poet, Alex Portnoy has fantasies of self-creation, of absolute freedom. Enmeshed comically, if painfully, in the Oedipal investments of a lower-middle-class Jewish family, Alex imagines a different life and so the book is framed as a family romance. Most famously, Portnoy's dreams of flight play out as sexual hedonism. During his adolescence, this hedonism takes the form of extraordinarily inventive, if not athletic, masturbation. In no small part, Portnoy's notorious capacity for self-abuse is a strong reaction to—a rebellion against—the asceticism he associates with Judaism: "Renunciation is all, cries the koshered and bloodless piece of steak my family and I sit down to eat at dinner time. Self-control, sobriety, sanctions—this is the key to a human life, saith all those endless dietary laws."[12]

But sex (as always) means more than transgressive pleasure, even if Portnoy finds it hard to transgress and to find pleasure in it: "Because to be *bad*, Mother, that is the real struggle: to be bad—and to enjoy it!... LET'S PUT THE ID BACK IN YID!" (123–4). Alex's fantasies about *shikses* are fantasies about being somehow *American*, which is to say, free from the debilitating ethnic marker of being Jewish, as well as the communal and family responsibilities that seem to go with Judaism: "No, no, these blond-haired Christians are the legitimate residents and owners of this place.... America is a *shikse* nestling under your arm whispering love love love love love!" (145–6).

The tragic-comedy of his sexual adventures—with the Midwestern Pumpkin, the New England WASP Pilgrim, the *shikse*-goddess model, the Monkey—charts his attempt to gain this America, this new-found land: "What I'm saying, Doctor, is that I don't seem to stick my dick up these girls, as much as I stick it up their backgrounds—as though through fucking I will discover America. *Conquer* America—maybe that's more like it...." (234). Of course, the grim joke is that Portnoy does not become more assimilated or any less marked by his Judaism for all his sexual success with the *goyim*. Rather, he is more surely and securely marked precisely by that success, or really, by the desire for conquest that lies behind it. And this desire stems from the particular gender relations of the Portnoy family.

As readers have recognized from the start, *Portnoy's Complaint* is structured like a stand-up monologue, a series of riffs on Jewish stereotypes, particularly of overbearing, phallic Jewish mothers, weak fathers, and their guilty sons. As Portnoy says, he is living in the middle of a

Jewish joke (31; see also 110). But the joke shows to what extent the Oedipus Complex is itself (within certain family configurations) a compensatory fantasy.[13] Alex Portnoy's father is hardly a castrating tyrant. Rather, as a hystericized man, rendered harmless by his constipation and anxiety, he presents much less of a threat than Alex's omnicompetent, phallic, and knife-wielding mother. In the face of the son's disrespect for the father, it is the mother who chastises him. This leads Alex to ponder the gender reversals in his family: his mother avenges the father's honor while the father is overcome by tenderness (40). But the etiology of this role reversal is social, not biological. Alex goes on: "Pregnable (putting it mildly) as his masculinity was in this world of *goyim* ... between his legs (G-d bless my father!) he was constructed like a man of consequence, two big healthy balls such as a king would be proud to put on display...." (41).

Given his regal genitalia, it is clear that Alex's father's fragile masculinity, manifested as it is by his furious constipation, is the result of his dead-end position as an insurance salesman in the ghetto, kept back from promotion by religion and education.[14] Jack Portnoy's rage—rendered comic by his epic incapacity to relieve himself—is the expression of the conflict between his commitment to what he does for a living and his firm understanding that he will never be recognized, either by his children or by the insouciant anti-Semitism of "The Company." In other words, Roth shows that what appears to be a pathological gender reversal in Alex's family is the result of very specific socio-historical pressures. What is more, we can now recognize, thanks to the work of Daniel Boyarin, that the assertive, competent Jewish woman and her mate, the "weak" sissy Jewish scholar—common types in Eastern European Jewish culture—only become "pathological" when analyzed in terms of the gender norms of Western European (and of course, American) modernity.[15] Roth's debt to the naturalistic tradition of American fiction has thus allowed him a rich and deadly historical precision. He shows exactly how Jack and Sophie Portnoy are caught quite neatly between the norms of their immigrant old-world parents and their assimilated son, between an older tradition of female worldly agency and the American ideal of the male breadwinner, between the practical failure of the ideology of the melting-pot and the renewed promise of its success. The revised family romance of *Portnoy's Complaint,* with its downtrodden father and its unrepentantly libidinized mother, reveals that its hyperbolic dreams of potency and freedom stem from the difficult negotiations that the fantasy of assimilation requires. The fierce humor of the book, as well as its pessimism, both derive from the fact that like the "strong" poet's Gnostic fantasy of pure self-determination, such potency, such freedom, such assimilation are all an illusion. Alex Portnoy ends the book derided by *sabras* (native-born Israelis) for being an effeminate, self-hating, Diaspora Jew, and—irony of ironies!—impotent.

Let me bring my two texts together, to make my argument as clear as possible. I am suggesting that, like Roth's revisionary family romance, *The Anxiety of Influence* is, among other things, a meditation on the psychic price of assimilation. It reveals that the drive to join a community to which you do not belong, or to which you come "too late," is in the end tantamount to a form of usurpation. Accordingly, it shows quite clearly how this drive is marked by both sheer aggressive rage and what seems like inevitable, ironic failure. I am suggesting that Roth's novel lends local specificity to the abstractions of Bloom's argument—that Bloom's poetic usurper is in no small part a Jew, and the idealized kingdom of the spirit to which he aspires is in no small part an alien, Protestant America (troped in Bloom's theory as the great Protestant line that leads from Milton to Ashbery and in his career as the WASP domain of culture and "lit. crit.").

Roth anatomizes the dream of being completely assimilated, of being unmarked by one's Jewishness. This helps us understand Bloom's elision of the mother from the family romance. After all, Judaism is matrilineal and Yiddish is the *mamma-loshen* ("mother tongue," as opposed, of course, to Hebrew, which was taught to the men). The Jewish mother as stock figure of polemic and humor is closely linked to the "effeminate" Jewish man (the "mamma's boy" par excellence). Perhaps we can take a lead from *Portnoy's Complaint* and align the occlusion of the mother in Bloom's poetic Oedipal struggle with his rather hyperbolic appropriation of the Nietzschean ideal of strength. We might want to recognize them less as part of a phallic protest against the castrating threat posed by the Jewish mother than as an equally phallic protest against the "castrated" position the Jewish father seems to assume in gentile culture. Of course, through a sad, but evidently common short-circuit, it is the Jewish mother who is presented as the problem (and not the culture that pathologizes the "effeminate" Jewish man). In many ways, and for a number of reasons, then, the Jewish mother defines the son as a Jew. It seems to be her fault that he is "belated," the one who does not fit in. I am suggesting that for Bloom (as well as for 60s American Jewish culture), the Jewish mother is a ready scapegoat and a potent stereotype (even as her sociological reality fades[16]) because she sums up in a rather tidy figure the communal pulls, gender identifications, and emotional demands that seem to stand in the way of full assimilation. It might be that Bloom's most brilliant evasion is the ultimately delusional promise that we can constitute our identities by rebelling against the *goyishe* fathers of our choice—be they Milton or Wimsatt—and not the Jewish mothers of our birth.

But this claim, which brings the full scandal of Bloom's motives to the fore, only tells part of the story. I would also argue that Bloom, like Alex Portnoy, is trying not merely to get away from his Jewish mother and rewrite his paternity, but also, and just as importantly, trying to vindicate his Jewish father. Here Freud serves two important functions—he is both an example of and a weapon in this vindication. In the section on infantile material in *The Interpretation of Dreams*, Freud ruminates on his bid to become *Professor Extraordinarius* and on his fiercely ambivalent desire to go to Rome (both of which bring up the central tension in that book between Freud's ambitions and the realities of Viennese anti-Semitism). He remembers a conversation from his childhood in which his father spoke of the advances that Jews had made in the Hapsburg Empire. Freud's father recounted an incident in which a Christian had shouted at him to get off the sidewalk and had knocked his new fur hat into the street. Freud's father reacted mildly and merely retrieved his hat from the gutter. Freud continues:

> This struck me as unheroic conduct on the part of the big, strong man who was holding the little boy by the hand. I contrasted this situation with another which fitted my feelings better: the scene in which Hannibal's father, Hamilcar Barca, made his boy swear before the household altar to take vengeance on the Romans. Ever since that time Hannibal had had a place in my fantasies.[17]

This story, of course, fits Bloom's revisionary notion of "the family romance" quite nicely, for the object of desire is not the mother but the child's idealized vision of the father, which the father cannot maintain. Freud, faced with his father's lack of heroism, imagines another, historically more potent father, and thus imagines himself as the great Punic general. Bothered by his father's resignation, he imagines himself as the revenger of his father's honor, and what is more, as having been called on by his father to fill that role. In the web of aggression and desire that is described by *The Anxiety of Influence*, Bloom has recast Freud as both Hannibal and Hamilcar, and himself as Hannibal, laying siege to the seat of both the empire and the seat of the Church. Freud is the model of the fantasizing son. He is also the idealized Jewish father whose authority Bloom invokes in order to slay the Oedipal (Christian) father.

(In the drama of *The Anxiety of Influence* this role is filled by the shadowy figure of Wimsatt.) Of course, Freud's Punic fantasy is poignant precisely because Hannibal does not win, does not destroy Rome. The reality principle kicks in even here to trim Freud's dreams, much as Bloom has to admit that his dream of absolute freedom is nothing more than a delusion, or much as Portnoy has to admit that the more he flees his Jewish identity, the more he is defined by it.

Bloom and Roth were born within a year of each other, the one in the Bronx and the other in Newark. Like Bloom, Roth's earlier career was marked by the desire to enter into and be accepted in that elite corner of America that Jonathan Freedman has called "the temple of culture." (In this regard, Roth's *My Life as a Man* is a brilliant and chilling reflection on that desire.) While their careers might show interesting parallels (including their shared remarkable gift for mimicry and parody), the later Bloom, as Freedman has shown, has attacked younger, politically motivated critics using the very terms that were once used to ban Jews from the domain of culture. Freedman has been careful to argue that Bloom's shrill rejection of recent academic trends is born of a "disturbing recognition," that "the faith in the Western literary canon ... as a way of interpreting and so entering 'America' no longer exists."[18] In other words, Bloom's anger derives from the fact that the model of authority on which he banked everything he had, no longer holds. And in Bloom's anger, one can hear something of the psychic price that attaining such authority demanded in the first place.

I have thus argued that *The Anxiety of Influence* meditates on and is driven by the furious ambivalences of assimilation. Part of its genius lies in its ability to cast the Romantics in the role of Jewish aspirants to culture while hiding the particularly Jewish anxieties that undergird this account of Romantic aspiration. Is this merely an example of Bloom's ability to project his own situation onto the Romantics, a remarkable act of *chutzpah* on his part? Or does this tell us something about the Romantics? If we bracket, for the moment, Bloom's identification of the line that extends from Milton to Ashbery with "the American sublime" (which thus makes Romanticism essentially American and America Romantic), we can ask if Bloom's theory does not also provide a trenchant analysis of the "Romantic Ideology" by showing us the social anxieties that sustain it. I have come to suspect that Marjorie Levinson's great *Keats's Life of Allegory: The Origins of a Style* is in no small part motivated by this realization.[19] The Romantic Ideology had real effects, especially on those it interpellated, and its costs could be told on their pulses as well as on our scholarship. Bloom's theory (as well as its enactment in

The Anxiety of Influence) provides us with an index of those costs. That critics have not wanted to use it for this purpose is due, most probably, to the fact that assimilation is no longer the model that drives our interpretations. Bloom's dream of freedom seems vitiated because it entails belonging, not resisting, although the aggression it champions is marked by rage and resistance all the way. *The Anxiety of Influence* tells us a good deal about the mechanisms and the costs of assimilation. That it has managed to hide both its own mechanisms and costs—while showing us exactly how to find them—is a measure of its potential worth.

Notes

1. Orrin N. C. Wang, *Fantastic Modernity: Dialectical Readings in Romanticism and Theory* (Baltimore: The Johns Hopkins University Press, 1996), 147. My understanding of Bloom's Gnosticism owes an important debt to Wang's account and my argument has been greatly improved by his suggestions for this paper. My thanks are also due to Sheila A. Spector for her comments and to Sharon Squassoni for her relentless precision. All mistakes and excesses are of course my own.
2. The British Romantics, having been denigrated by Eliot and demoted by the New Critics (although it should be remembered that both Brooks and Wimsatt wrote well and respectfully on the Romantics) presented an attractive subject for Jewish academics after the Second World War. The low-church prophetism of the Romantics brought them closer to Jewish interests and knowledge and at the same time allowed Jewish scholars to assert themselves, however surreptitiously, against the not-always-so-genteel anti-Semitism of Eliot and his followers. In this as in so much else, my argument owes much to the insights in Jonathan Freedman, *The Temple of Culture: Assimilation and Anti-Semitism in Literary Anglo-America* (New York: Oxford University Press, 1999). On Jews and Romanticism, see pp. 182–5. On Bloom's assertive re-definition of the Romantics in the early 1960s, see p. 184.
3. As will become clear, I am arguing that Bloom is a theorist of assimilation and in this way, he can be usefully compared to Hartman. Bloom and Hartman were extraordinary Romanticists early in their careers and they used the capital they gained as Romanticists to leverage what we could call the Judaizing of theory. Hartman, of course, assumed a more normative approach to Jewish hermeneutics, by taking *Midrash* as his model, and this proved to be in keeping with his construction of a mild Romanticism and a humanized sublime. Hartman, true to his German background, seems to maintain an allegiance to the German-Jewish assimilative ideal of cosmopolitan *Bildung*, of cultivated play and a well-earned distaste for the dangers of *Schwaermerei*. So when he sees in Wordsworth a "humanizing of imagination," a "marriage of heaven and earth ... *despite* apocalypse," he is recasting Wordsworth in terms of his own cultural allegiances. *Midrash* and an "unremarkable Mr Wordsworth," these are both powerful emblems for the émigré scholar in the wake of the

horrors of the Second World War. If his magisterial work on Wordsworth enables him to be a Jewish intellectual, his position as a Jewish intellectual informs his recuperation of Wordsworth. Bloom, home-grown in the Bronx, presents a different set of allegiances. His Wordsworth is as much a projection of his condition as Hartman's is of his own.
For *Bildung* as a model for assimilation for German Jews, see George L. Mosse, "Jewish Emancipation: Between *Bildung* and Respectability," *The Jewish Response to German Culture*, ed. Jehuda Reinharz and Walter Schatzberg (Hanover: University Press of New England, 1985), 1–16; David Sorkin, *The Transformation of German Jewry, 1780–1840* (New York: Oxford University Press, 1987), 15–33; Steven E. Ascheim, "German Jews Beyond *Bildung* and Liberalism," in *The German-Jewish Dialogue Reconsidered: A Symposium in Honor of George L. Mosse*, ed. Klaus L. Berghahn (New York: Peter Lang, 1996), 125–8. The Hartman quotations come from Geoffrey H. Hartman, *Wordsworth's Poetry* (New Haven: Yale University Press, 1971), xi, 69.
4. Theodor W. Adorno, *Minima Moralia: Reflections from Damaged Life*, trans. E. F. N. Jephcott (London: New Left Books, 1974), 49.
5. Harold Bloom, *The Anxiety of Influence: A Theory of Poetry* (New York: Oxford University Press, 1973), 95. All further references to this book will be included parenthetically within the body of the text.
6. It is worth noting that by the early 1980s, Bloom had come to question his reliance on the family romance as a model. See "Agon: Revisionism and Critical Personality," in *Agon: Towards a Theory of Revisionism* (New York: Oxford University Press, 1982), 44.
7. Sigmund Freud, "Family Romance," in *The Standard Edition of the Complete Psychological Works of Sigmund Freud*, ed. James Strachey (London: Hogarth Press, 1953–73), 9:237. My phrasing purposefully echoes J. Laplanche and J.-B. Pontalis, *The Language of Psycho-analysis*, trans. Donald Nicholson-Smith (New York: Norton, 1973), 160.
8. Bloom "Agon: Revisionism and Critical Personality," 17.
9. W. K. Wimsatt, Jr., "The Concrete Universal," in *The Verbal Icon: Studies in the Meaning of Poetry* (Lexington: University of Kentucky Press, 1954), 82.
10. Wimsatt, 82.
11. Freedman, 155–223. See also Suzanne Klingenstein, *Enlarging America: The Cultural Work of Jewish Literary Scholars, 1930–1990* (New York: Syracuse University Press, 1998), 407–18.
12. Philip Roth, *Portnoy's Complaint* (New York: Random House, 1969), 79. Hereafter, all references to this work will be included parenthetically within the body of the text.
13. My brother, Peter Kaufmann, a clinical psychologist in New York, has pointed out to me that in certain Jewish families, the father gives up on the Oedipal struggle from the get-go. This leads one to wonder whether the son's Oedipal fantasies might not be an attempt to constitute the father as the rival he never was.
14. "If he squeezed blood from a stone, wouldn't The Company reward him with a miracle of its own ... get wind of his accomplishment and turn him overnight from an agent at five thousand a year to a district manager at

fifteen? But where they had him they kept him. Who else would work such barren territory with such incredible results? Moreover, there had not been a Jewish manager in the entire history of Boston & Northeastern (Not Quite Our Class, Dear, as they used to say on the *Mayflower*), and my father, with his eighth-grade education, wasn't exactly suited to be the Jackie Robinson of the insurance business" (5–6).

15. Daniel Boyarin, *Unheroic Conduct: The Rise of Heterosexuality and the Invention of the Jewish Man* (Berkeley: University of California Press, 1997).
16. And to a certain extent, she had already faded, generationally, by the late 1950s—hence perhaps her availability as material for humor in popular (and therefore not specifically Jewish) culture in the 1960s. See Martha Wolfenstein, "Two Types of Jewish Mothers," in *The Jews: Social Patterns of an American Group*, ed. Marshall Sklare (New York: Free Press, 1958), 520–34; and also Riv-Ellen Prell, *Fighting to Become Americans* (Boston: Beacon Press, 1999), 111–13.
17. *The Standard Edition of the Complete Psychological Works of Sigmund Freud*, 4:230.
18. Freedman, 215.
19. Marjorie Levinson, *Keats's Life of Allegory: The Origins of a Style* (New York: Blackwell, 1988).

GLOSSARY

Adam Kadmon—the kabbalistic "primordial man."
Adam Rishon—the kabbalistic "first man"; created or protoplastic man; the biblical Adam.
aggadah (s.; *aggadot*, pl.)—lit. "homiletic narrative"; that portion of rabbinic teaching not concerned with religious laws or regulations.
amoraim—scholars active from the period of the completion of the *Mishnah* (c. 200 CE) until the completion of the Babylonian and Jerusalem Talmuds (roughly the end of the fifth century).
Ashkenaz—designation of Jewish community in northwest Europe, originally on the banks of the Rhine; Jewish culture originating in Germany.
Ashkenazi (s.; *Ashkenazim*, pl.)—descendant of German Jews.
baraita (s.; *baraitot*, pl.)—every *halakhah*, halakhic *Midrash*, and historical or *aggadic* tradition not included in the *Mishnah*.
bat kol—lit. "daughter of the voice"; a heavenly or Divine voice that revealed God's will, choice, or judgment to man.
Bava Batra—lit. "last gate"; tractate of the *Mishnah* with *Gemara* in the Jerusalem and Babylonian Talmuds.
Be'er ha-Goleh—revision of the *Shulḥan Arukh*, by Moses ben Naphtali Hirsch (d. c. 1671/72), a Lithuanian Talmudist.
Gemara—lit. "completion" or "tradition"; generally applied to the Talmud as a whole, or more particularly to the discussions and elaborations by the *amoraim* in the *Mishnah*.
goy (s.; *goyim*, pl.)—lit. "nation, people"; generally used to mean Gentile, sometimes derogatory.
goyishe—adj. form in Yiddish.
Haggadah—lit. "telling"; set form of benedictions, prayers, *midrashic* comments and psalms recited at the *seder* ritual on Passover.
halakhah (s.; *halakhot*, pl.)—from the root "to go"; legal side of Judaism, as distinct from *aggadah*; embraces personal, social, national, and international relationships, and all the other practices and observances of Judaism.
Ḥasid (s.; *Ḥasidim*, pl.)—pietist; historically used to refer to those who maintained a higher standard in observing the religious and moral commandments.
Ḥasidism—popular religious movement of the later eighteenth century, characterized by ecstasy, mass enthusiasm, close-knit group cohesion, and charismatic leadership.

Haskalah—Hebrew term for the Enlightenment movement and ideology that began within Jewish society in the 1770s and lasted to the 1880s.

ḥerem—the status of that which is separated from common use or contact either because it is proscribed as an abomination to God or because it is consecrated to Him; excommunication.

Ḥumash—lit. "five"; Pentateuch.

Karaites—Jewish sect of the eighth century, characterized primarily by a rejection of the Talmudic-rabbinical tradition.

luz of the spine—bone that, according to rabbis, is to be found at the base of the spine, in addition to the eighteen vertebrae; said to be indestructible and the source of a future resurrection of the body.

mah nishtannah—lit. "What is different?"; the first words of the four questions asked at the Passover *seder* service.

mamma-loshen—lit. "mother tongue"; usually refers to the Yiddish language.

maranno—crypto-Jew, usually referring to Jews hiding from the Inquisition.

maskil (s.; *maskilim*, pl.)—adherent of the *Haskalah*.

mazah (s.; *mazot*, pl.)—unleavened bread, the only bread permitted during Passover.

megillah—lit. "scroll"; refers to the five scrolls of the Bible: Ruth, Song of Songs, Lamentations, Ecclesiastes, and Esther. When the name of the scroll is not specified, the word *megillah* usually refers to Esther.

mezuzah (s.; *mezuzot*, pl.)—parchment scroll affixed to the doorposts of rooms in a Jewish home.

midrash (s.; *midrashim*, pl.)—designation of a particular genre of rabbinic literature constituting an anthology and compilation of homilies, consisting of both biblical exegesis and sermons delivered in public, as well as *aggadot* or *halakhot*, and forming a running *aggadic* commentary on specific books of the Bible.

Mishnah—etym. "to repeat"; Oral law, including *Midrash, halakhot* and *aggadot*.

mitnagged (s.; *mitnaggedim*, pl.)—lit. "opponent"; those who opposed *Ḥasidism*.

mizvah (s.; *mizvot*, pl.)—etym. "to command, ordain"; commandment, precept, or religious duty; commonly used to mean a good deed.

parnas— lay leader; head of the community.

Resh Galuta—exilarch with hereditary ties to the House of David.

Sabra—native-born Israeli.

Sanhedrin—the Great *Sanhedrin*, supreme political, religious, and judicial body in Palestine during the Roman period, both before and after the destruction of the Temple, until the abolishment of the patriarchate (c. 425 CE).

seder (s.; *sedarim*, pl.)—lit. "order"; used to indicate the order of prayers, especially in the Passover service conducted according to the order of the *Haggadah*.

Sepharad—Jewish community originating in Spain before the expulsion of 1492.

Sephardi (s.; *Sephardim*, pl.)—descendant of Spanish Jews.

shikse—Yiddish for gentile woman, usually derogatory.

shtetl (s.; *shtetlakh*, pl.)—Yiddish diminutive for *shtot*, town or city, to imply a small community; in Eastern Europe, a unique socio-cultural communal pattern.

Shulḥan Arukh—lit. "the prepared table"; code of law written by Joseph Caro (1488–1575).

Sunna—the body of Islamic custom and practice based on the prophet Muhammad's words and deeds.

Talmud—lit. "study" or "learning"; refers to opinions and teachings that disciples acquire from their predecessors in order to expound and explain them. Babylonian Talmud (*Bavli*)—interpretation and elaboration of *Mishnah* as carried on in the great academies of Babylon from the first half of the third century to the end of the fifth. Jerusalem Talmud (*Yerushalmi*)—elaboration of *Mishnah* compiled in Palestine.

Tanakh—Hebrew term for the Bible, composed of an acronym for *Torah* (Pentateuch), *Nevi'im* (Prophets), and *Ketuvim* (Hagiographa).

Tanna (s.; *Tannaim*, pl.)—sage from the period of Hillel to the compilation of the *Mishnah*, i.e., the first and second centuries CE.

tefillin—two black leather boxes containing scriptural passages, bound by black leather straps on the left hand and on the head, worn for morning services.

yeshiva (s.; *yeshivot*, pl.)—institutes of Talmudic learning.

Works Cited

Abrahams, Israel. "A Masterpiece for the Week: Disraeli's 'Alroy.'" *The Jewish World*, no. 3005 (11 Tamuz 5673/16 July 1913): 9–10.
Abrams, M. H. *Natural Supernaturalism: Tradition and Revolution in Romantic Literature*. New York: Norton, 1971.
Addison, Joseph, and Richard Steele. *The Spectator*. Edited by Donald Bond. 4 vols. Oxford: Clarendon Press, 1965.
Adler, Elkan Nathan, ed. *Jewish Travellers in the Middle Ages: 19 Firsthand Accounts*. London: G. Routledge, 1930. Reprint, New York: Dover, 1987.
Adorno, Theodor W. *Minima Moralia: Reflections from Damaged Life*. Translated by E. F. N. Jephcott. London: New Left Books, 1974.
Aguilar, Grace. *The Days of Bruce*. London, 1851.
———. *Home Scenes and Heart Studies*. London, 1853.
———. *The Magic Wreath*. Published anonymously in Devon, 1835.
———. *The Spirit of Judaism*. Edited by I. Leeser. Philadelphia, 1842.
———. *The Vale of Cedars; or, The Martyr*. 2 vols. New York, 1850.
———. *The Women of Israel; or, Characters and Sketches from the Holy Scriptures and Jewish History*. 2 vols. London, 1845.
Alexander, Levy. *Memoirs of the Life and Commercial Connections, Public and Private, of the Late Benj. Goldsmid, Esq. Of Roehampton, Containing A Cursory View of the Jewish Society and Manners, Interspersed with Interesting Anecdotes of Several Remarkable*. London, 1808.
Altmann, Alexander. *Moses Mendelssohn: A Biographical Study*. Tuscaloosa: University of Alabama Press, 1973.
Anderson, Benedict. *Imagined Communities: Reflections on the Origin and Spread of Nationalism*. London: Verso, 1983.
Anderson, G. K. *The Legend of the Wandering Jew*. Providence, RI: Brown University Press, 1965.
Andreades, Andreas Michael. *History of the Bank of England, 1640 to 1903*. Translated by Christabel Meredith. Preface by H. S. Foxwell. 4th ed. Reprints of Economics Classics. New York: A. M. Kelley, 1966.
Anonymous. *A Collection of the Best Pieces in Prose and Verse, Against the Naturalization of the Jews*. London, 1753.
———. *The Crisis, or an Alarm to Britannia's True Protestant Sons. In Two Parts, With an Appendix in each of them. Among a Variety of Things, An Address to King George*. London, 1754.

Anonymous. *A Letter from a Gentleman to his Friend Concerning the Naturalization of the Jews*. London, 1753.

———. *A Modest Apology for the Citizens and Merchants of London, who petitioned the House of Commons against Naturalizing the Jews*. London, 1753.

Arkin, Marcus. *Aspects of Jewish Economic History*. Philadelphia: Jewish Publication Society, 1975.

Arnold, Mathew. "Hebraism and Hellenism." In *Culture and Anarchy*. Edited by J. Dover Wilson. Cambridge: Cambridge University Press, 1961.

Ascheim, Steven E. "German Jews Beyond *Bildung* and Liberalism." In *The German-Jewish Dialogue Reconsidered: A Symposium in Honor of George L. Mosse*, ed. Klaus L. Berghahn, 125–40. New York: Peter Lang, 1996.

Barnett, Arthur. "Eliakim ben Abraham (Jacob Hart): An Anglo-Jewish Scholar of the Eighteenth Century." *Transactions of the Jewish Historical Society of England* 14 (1935–39): 207–20.

Baron, Salo. *A Social and Religious History of the Jews*. Volume III: *Heirs of Rome and Persia*. Volume V: *Religious Controls and Dissensions*. New York: Columbia University Press, and Philadelphia: The Jewish Publication Society of America, 1957.

Basnage, Jacques de Beauval. *The History of the Jews, from Jesus Christ to the Present Time: Containing their Antiquities, their Religion, their Rites, the Dispersion of the Ten Tribes in the East, and the Persecutions this Nation has Suffer'd in the West. Being a Supplement and Continuation of the History of Josephus*. Translated by Thomas Taylor. London: T. Bever and B. Lintot, 1708.

Baumgarten, Murray. "Seeing Double: Jews in the Fiction of F. Scott Fitzgerald, Charles Dickens, Anthony Trollope, and George Eliot." In *Between Race and Culture: Representations of "the Jew" in English and American Literature*, ed. Bryan Cheyette, 44–61. Stanford: Stanford University Press, 1996.

Beddoes, Thomas Lovell. *Selected Poems*. Edited by Judith Higgens. Manchester: Carcanet Press, 1976.

———. *The Works of Thomas Lovell Beddoes*. Edited, with an introduction by H. W. Donner. London: Oxford University Press, 1935. Reprint, New York: AMS Press, 1978.

Bell, John. *Travels from St. Petersburgh in Russia to Various Parts of Asia. Illustrated with Maps*. London: W. Creech, 1788.

Ben-Sasson, H. H., ed. *A History of the Jewish People*. Cambridge, MA: Harvard University Press, 1976.

Bentley, G. E., Jr. *Blake Records*. Oxford: Clarendon Press, 1969.

Berkeley, George, Bishop. *Three Dialogues between Hylas and Philonous*. London: G. James for H. Clements, 1713.

Bermant, Chiam. *The Cousinhood: The Anglo-Jewish Gentry*. New York: Macmillan, 1971.

Blake, Robert. *Disraeli*. New York: St. Martin's Press, 1967.

Blake, William. *The Complete Poetry and Prose of William Blake*, newly rev. ed. Edited by David V. Erdman. New York: Doubleday, 1988.

Bloom, Harold. "Agon: Revisionism and Critical Personality." In *Agon: Towards a Theory of Revisionism*. New York: Oxford University Press, 1982.

———. *The Anxiety of Influence: A Theory of Poetry.* New York: Oxford University Press, 1973.
Bosanquet, Charles. *London: Some Account of its Growth, Charitable Agencies and Wants.* London: Hatchard & Co., 1868.
Boyarin, Daniel. *Unheroic Conduct: The Rise of Heterosexuality and the Invention of the Jewish Man.* Berkeley: University of California Press, 1997.
Bradshaw, Michael. *Resurrection Songs: The Poetry of Thomas Lovell Beddoes.* Burlington, VT: Ashgate, 2001.
Braham, John. "Song." Printed in *The Englishman,* no. 167 (August, 1806). FC 46 in Archive at Morden Lodge.
Brewer, John. *The Sinews of Power: War, Money, and the English State, 1688–1783.* Cambridge, MA: Harvard University Press, 1990.
Britain, Ian. "Education." In *An Oxford Companion to The Romantic Age: British Culture 1776–1832,* gen. ed. Iain McCalman, 161–70. Oxford: Oxford University Press, 1999.
Britannia. *An Appeal to the Throne against the Naturalization of the Jewish Nation: In which we are Exposed Those practices for which the Jews were expelled out of England: and the fatal Consequences that may follow, should the Act of their Naturalization take Place.* London, 1753.
Burke, Edmund. *A Letter From Mr. Burke To A Member Of The National Assembly In Answer To Some Objections To His Book On French Affairs.* London, 1791. Smartboard Website, http://www.ourcivilisation.com/smartboard/shop/burkee/tonatass, 2000.
———. *Reflections on the Revolution in France.* Edited by J. C. D. Clark. Stanford: Stanford University Press, 2001.
Butler, Marilyn. "Antiquarianism (Popular)." In *An Oxford Companion to The Romantic Age: British Culture 1776–1832,* gen. ed. Iain McCalman, 328–38. Oxford: Oxford University Press, 1999.
Bynum, Caroline Walker. *The Resurrection of the Body in Western Christianity, 200–1336.* New York: Columbia University Press, 1995.
Calder, Angus. Introduction to *Old Mortality,* by Sir Walter Scott. London: Penguin, 1975.
Cambridge History of the Bible: Volume 1: *From the Beginnings to Jerome.* Edited by P. R. Ackroyd and C. F. Evans. Volume 2: *The West from the Fathers to the Reformation.* Edited by G. W. H. Lampe. Volume 3: *The West from the Reformation to the Present Day.* Edited by S. L. Greenslade. Cambridge: Cambridge University Press, 1963–70.
Centlivre, Susanna. *Bold Stroke For a Wife.* Edited by Nancy Copeland. New York: Broadview Press, 1995.
Chandler, Alice. *A Dream of Order: The Medieval Ideal in Nineteenth-Century English Literature.* Lincoln: University of Nebraska Press, 1970.
Chavel, Charles B. "Shneyur Zalman of Liady." In *Understanding Rabbinic Judaism: From Talmudic to Modern Times,* ed. Jacob Neusner, 317–35. New York: Ktav Publishing House, 1974.
Cheyette, Bryan. *Constructions of "the Jew" in English Literature and Society: Racial Representations, 1875–1945.* Cambridge: Cambridge University Press, 1993.

———, ed. *Between Race and Culture: Representations of "the Jew" in English and American Literature*. Stanford: Stanford University Press, 1996.

Christensen, Jerome. *Lord Byron's Strength: Romantic Writing and Commercial Society*. Baltimore: Johns Hopkins University Press, 1993.

Cobbett, William. *Cobbett's Paper against gold: containing the history and mystery of the Bank of England, the funds, the debt, the sinking fund, the bank stoppage, the lowering and the raising of the value of paper-money*. 2nd ed. London, 1817.

Cole, G. D. H. *The Life of William Cobbett*. New York: Harcourt, Brace and Co., 1924.

Coleridge, Samuel Taylor. *Biographia Literaria*. Bollingen Series LXXV. Edited by James Engell and W. Jackson Bate. Princeton: Princeton University Press, 1983.

———. *The Table-Talk and Omiana*. Edited by T. Ashe. London: G. Bell, 1905.

Colley, Linda. *Britons: Forging the Nation 1707–1837*. New Haven: Yale University Press, 1992.

Complete Newgate Calendar. London: Navarre Society Ltd., 1926. Reprint, Tarlton Law Library – Law in Popular Culture Collection Web Site Reproduction. http://tarlton.law.utexas.edu/lpop/etext/completenewgate.htm.

Cope, S. R. "The Goldsmids and the Developing of the London Money Market during the Napoleonic Wars." *Economica* 9 (1942): 160–206.

Cumberland, Richard. *The Jew*. London, 1794.

Cunninghame, William. *Remarks Upon David Levi's Dissertations on the Prophecies Relative to The Messiah*. London: Black, Parry, and Kingsbury, 1810.

Dallaway, James. *Constantinople Ancient and Modern, with Excursions to the Shores and Islands of the Archipelago and to the Troad*. London: Cadell and Davies, 1797.

Damon, S. Foster. *William Blake: His Philosophy and Symbols*. New York: Grolier Club, 1924.

Davies, J. G. *The Theology of William Blake*. Oxford: Clarendon Press, 1948.

Davies, Lloyd. "'Home at Grasmere,' or Romantic Contentment." *Prism(s): Essays in Romanticism* 9 (2001): 109–20.

Dickens, Charles. *Letters*. Edited by Madeline House, Graham Storey, and Kathleen Tillotson. 12 vols. Oxford: Oxford University Press, 1965–2002.

———. *Little Dorrit*. Edited by John Holloway. Harmondsworth: Penguin English Library, 1967.

———. *Oliver Twist*. Edited by Peter Fairclough. Harmondsworth: Penguin English Library, 1966.

———. *Our Mutual Friend*. Edited by Stephen Gill. Harmondsworth: Penguin English Library, 1971.

Dickson, Beth. "Sir Walter Scott and the Limits of Toleration." *Scottish Literary Journal* 18 (November 1991): 46–62.

Dickson, P. G. M. *The Financial Revolution in England: A Study in the Development of Public Credit, 1688–1756*. New York: St. Martin's Press, 1967.

Disraeli, Benjamin. *Alroy*. London: Longmans, Green, and Co., 1870.

———. *Tancred, or The New Crusade*. London: Longmans, Green, and Co., 1870–1.

D'Israeli, Isaac. *Amenities of Literature, Consisting of Sketches and Characters of English Literature*. 2nd ed. 2 vols. 1841. Boston: William Veazie, 1864.

---. *Calamities of Authors; Including Some Inquiries Regarding Their Moral and Literary Characters*. 2 vols. 1812. Reprint, New York: Johnson Reprint Corporation, 1971.

---. *Commentaries on the Life and Reign of Charles the First, King of England*. 2 vols. London: Henry Colburn, 1828.

---. *Curiosities of Literature, in Three Volumes*. 1817. Boston: Lilly, Wait, Colman and Holden, 1833.

---. *Flim-Flams! Or, the Life and Errors of My Uncle, and the Amours of My Aunt*. London: John Murray, 1805.

---. *The Genius of Judaism*. London: Edward Moxon, 1833.

---. *The Literary Character; or the History of Men of Genius, Drawn from Their Own Feelings and Confessions; Literary Miscellanies; and an Inquiry into the Character of James the First*. 1840. London: Routledge, Warne, and Routledge, 1862.

---. *Romances by I. D'Israeli*. London: Cadell and Davies, 1799.

---. *Vaurien: or, Sketches of the Times, Exhibiting Views of the Philosophies, Religions, Politics, Literature, and Manners of the Age*. 2 vols. London: T. Cadell, 1797.

Donner, H. W. *Thomas Lovell Beddoes: The Making of a Poet*. Oxford: Basil Blackwell, 1935. Reprint, Folcroft, PA: Folcroft Library Editions, 1970.

Duschinsky, Charles. *The Rabbinate of the Great Synagogue, London, From 1756 to 1842*. London: H. Milford, 1921. Reprint, Westmead: Gregg International, 1971.

Edgeworth, Maria. *Harrington*. 1817. London: J. M. Dent and Co., 1893.

Emden, Paul. "The Brothers Goldsmid and the Financing of the Napoleonic Wars." *Transactions of the Jewish Historical Society of England* 14 (1935–39): 225–46.

Encyclopædia Judaica. 16 vols. Jerusalem: Judah Magnes, 1972.

Endelman, Todd M. "The Chequered Career of 'Jew' King: A Study in Anglo-Jewish Social History." In *From East and West: Jews in a Changing Europe, 1750–1870*, ed. Frances Malino and David Sorkin, 151–81. Oxford: Basil Blackwell, 1990.

---. "The Englishness of Jewish Modernity in England." In *Toward Modernity: The European Jewish Model*, ed. Jacob Katz, 25–46. New Brunswick and Oxford: Transaction Books, 1987.

---. "'A Hebrew to the end': The Emergence of Disraeli's Jewishness." In *The Self-Fashioning of Disraeli 1818–1851*, ed. Charles Richmond and Paul Smith, 106–30. Cambridge: Cambridge University Press, 1998.

---. *The Jews of Georgian England, 1714–1830: Tradition and Change in a Liberal Society*. Philadelphia: The Jewish Publication Society of America, 1979. Reprint, with a new preface, Ann Arbor: University of Michigan Press, 1999.

---. "Judaica from the Disraeli library sold in October 1881." Appendix to his "The Emergence of Disraeli's Jewishness." In *The Self-Fashioning of Disraeli: 1818–1851*, ed. Charles Richmond and Paul Smith, 128–30. Cambridge: Cambridge University Press, 1998.

---. *Radical Assimilation in English Jewish History, 1656–1945*. Bloomington: University of Illinois Press, 1990.

Erinaceus. *Remarks on the Present State of Public Credit and the Consequences Likely To Result from the Decease of Mr. A. Goldsmid & Sir F. Baring: In A Letter To William Manning, Esq. M. P. Deputy-Governor Of The Bank.* London: J. Johnston, 1810.
The European Magazine and London Review 58 (October, 1810).
Faber, Richard. *Young England.* London: Faber and Faber, 1987.
Feldman, David. *Englishmen and Jews: Social Relations and Political Culture, 1840–1914.* New Haven, CT: Yale University Press, 1994.
Felsenstein, Frank. *Anti-Semitic Stereotypes: A Paradigm of Otherness in English Popular Culture, 1660–1830.* Baltimore: The Johns Hopkins University Press, 1995.
Ferris, Ina. *The Achievement of Literary Authority: Gender, History, and the Waverley Novels.* Ithaca, NY: Cornell University Press, 1991.
Fiedler, Leslie. "What Can We Do About Fagin?" *Commentary* 7 (1949): 411–18.
Fisch, Harold. "Disraeli's Hebraic Compulsions." In *Essays Presented to Chief Rabbi Israel Brodie on the Occasion of his Seventieth Birthday,* ed. H. J. Zimmels, J. Rabbinowitz, and I. Finestein, 1:94. Jews' College Publication, New Series, No. 3. London: Soncino, 1967.
———. *The Dual Image: The Figure of the Jew in English and American Literature.* London: World Jewish Library, 1971.
Fraistat, Neil. *The Poem and the Book: Interpreting Collections of Romantic Poetry.* Chapel Hill: University of North Carolina Press, 1985.
Francis, John. *Chronicles and Characters of the Stock Exchange.* London: Willoughby and Co., 1849.
Freedman, Jonathan. *The Temple of Culture: Assimilation and Anti-Semitism in Literary Anglo-America.* New York: Oxford University Press, 1999.
Fretwell, Katie and Judith Goodman. "The Fete of Abraham Goldsmid: A Regency Garden Tragedy." London: The National Trust website, www.ntenvironment.com/environment/html/gardens/_fspapers/fs_gold1.htm, 2000.
Freud, Sigmund. "Family Romance." In *The Standard Edition of the Complete Psychological Works of Sigmund Freud,* ed. James Strachey. Vol. 9. London: Hogarth Press, 1953–73.
———. *The Interpretation of Dreams.* In *The Standard Edition of the Complete Psychological Works of Sigmund Freud,* ed. James Strachey. Vols. 4–5. London: Hogarth Press, 1953–73.
Frye, Northrop. *Anatomy of Criticism: Four Essays.* Princeton: Princeton University Press, 1957. Reprint, 1971.
———. *Fearful Symmetry: A Study of William Blake.* Princeton: Princeton University Press, 1947. Reprint, 1969.
———. *The Great Code: The Bible and Literature.* New York: Harcourt, 1982.
———. *The Stubborn Structure: Essays on Criticism and Society.* Ithaca, NY: Cornell University Press, 1970.
Galchinsky, Michael. *The Origin of the Modern Jewish Woman Writer: Romance and Reform in Victorian England.* Detroit: Wayne State University Press, 1996.
Galperin, William. "Romanticism and/or Antisemitism." In *Between "Race" and Culture: Representations of "the Jew" in English and American Literature,* ed. Bryan Cheyette, 16–26. Stanford: Stanford University Press, 1996.

Gans, David Ben Solomon. *Chronologia Sacra-Profana A Mundi Conditu ad Annum M. 5352 vel Christi 1592, dicta [Ẓemaḥ David] German Davidis*. Translated by Guilielmum Henric Voustium. 1644.
Gelber, Mark H. "Teaching 'Literary Anti-Semitism': Dickens' *Oliver Twist* and Freytag's *Soll und Haben*." *Comparative Literature Studies* 16, 1 (1979): 1–11.
Genesis Rabbah: The Judaic Commentary to the Book of Genesis, A New American Translation. Translated by Jacob Neusner. 3 vols. Atlanta: Scholars Press, 1985.
Gilman, Neil. *The Death of Death: Resurrection and Immortality in Jewish Thought*. Woodstock, NY: Jewish Lights, 1997.
Gilman, Sander L. *Jewish Self-Hatred: Anti-Semitism and the Hidden Language of the Jews*. Baltimore: The Johns Hopkins University Press, 1986.
———. *The Jew's Body*. London: Routledge, 1991.
Godwin, William. *Enquiry Concerning Political Justice and Its Influence on Morals and Happiness*. 2 vols. London: G. G. J. and J. Robinson, 1793.
———. *St. Leon: A Tale of the Sixteenth Century*. 4 vols. 1799. Reprint, New York: Garland Publishing, 1975.
Goldin, Judah. "The Freedom and Restraint of Haggadah." In *Midrash and Literature*, ed. Geoffrey H. Hartman and Sandord Budick, 57–76. New Haven, CT: Yale University Press, 1986.
Goodridge, John, ed. *The Independent Spirit: John Clare and the Self-Taught Tradition*. Tyne and Wear: Peterson Printers, 1994.
Green, Ian. "Anglicanism in Stuart and Hanoverian England." In *A History of Religion in Britain: Practice and Belief from Pre-Roman Times to the Present*, ed. Sheridan Gilley and W. J. Sheils, 168–87. Oxford: Blackwell, 1994.
Greene, Robert. *Groats-worth of Wit, Bought with a Million of Repentaunce. Describing the Folly of Youth, the Falsehoode of Makeshift Flatterers, the Miserie of the Negligent, and Mischiefes of Deceiving Courtezans. Written before before* [sic] *His Death and Published at His Dying Request*. London: Richard Olive, 1596.
Grossman, Jonathan H. "The Absent Jew in Dickens: Narrators in *Oliver Twist, Our Mutual Friend*, and *A Christmas Carol*." *Dickens Studies Annual* 24 (1996): 37–57.
Guttmann, Julius. *Philosophies of Judaism: The History of Jewish Philosophy from Biblical Times to Franz Rosenzweig*. New York: Holt, Rinehart and Winston, 1964.
Habermas, Jürgen. *The Structural Transformation of the Public Sphere: An Inquiry into a Category of Bourgeois Society*. Translated by Thomas Burger and Frederick Lawrence. Cambridge, MA: MIT Press, 1989.
Hagstrum, Jean H. "Christ's Body." In *William Blake: Essays in Honour of Sir Geoffrey Keynes*, ed. Morton D. Paley and Michael Philips, 129–56. Oxford: Clarendon Press, 1973.
Hanway, Jonas. *Letters Admonitory and Argumentative from J. H———y, Merchant to J. S———r, Merchant. In Reply to Particular Passages and the General Argument, of a Pamphlet, entitled Further Considerations on the Bill, &*. London, 1753.
———. *A Review of the Proposed Naturalization of the Jews: Being an Attempt at a dispassionate Enquiry into the present State of the Case, with some Reflections on General Naturalization*. London, 1753.

Hartman, David. *A Living Covenant: The Innovative Spirit in Traditional Judaism.* New York: The Free Press, 1985.
Hartman, Geoffrey. "On the Jewish Imagination." *Prooftexts* 5 (September 1985): 201–20.
———. *Wordsworth's Poetry.* New Haven, CT: Yale University Press, 1971.
Hartman, Geoffrey and Sanford Budick, eds. *Midrash and Literature.* New Haven, CT: Yale University Press, 1986.
Hayden, John O. *Scott: The Critical Heritage.* London: Routledge and Kegan Paul, 1970.
Heinemann, Joseph. "The Nature of Aggadah." In *Midrash and Literature,* ed. Geoffrey H. Hartman and Sanford Budick, 41–55. New Haven, CT: Yale University Press, 1986.
Heller, Deborah. "The Outcast as Villain and Victim: Jews in Dickens' *Oliver Twist* and *Our Mutual Friend.*" In *Jewish Presences in English Literature,* ed. Derek Cohen and Deborah Heller, 40–60. Montreal: McGill-Queen's University Press, 1990.
Henriques, H. S. Q. *The Jews and the English Law.* Oxford: H. Hart, 1908. Reprint, Clifton, NJ: A. M. Kelley, 1974.
Hill, Christopher. *The English Bible and the Seventeenth-Century Revolution.* 1993. New York: Penguin, 1994.
Horner, Francis et al. *Report, Together with the Minutes of Evidence and Accounts from The Select Committee on the High Price of Gold Bullion.* London: J. Johnson, 1810.
Horner, Leonard. *Memoir and Correspondence of Francis Horner.* London: John Murray, 1853.
Hughson, David [Edward Pugh]. *London; being an accurate History and Description of the British Metropolis and its Neighbourhood, to Thirty Miles Extent, from an Actual Perambulation.* 6 vols. London: J. Stratford, 1805–9.
Hurwitz, Hyman. *Hebrew Tales; Selected and Translated from the Writings of the Ancient Hebrew Sages: To Which is Prefixed, an Essay, on the Uninspired Literature of the Hebrews.* London: Morrison and Watt, 1826.
Hyman, Leonard. "Hyman Hurwitz: The First Anglo-English Professor." *Transactions of the Jewish Historical Society of England, 1962–67,* 21:232–41. London: The Jewish Historical Society of England, 1968.
Irving, Washington. *The Sketch Book of Geoffrey Crayon, Esq.* 2 vols. 1819. London: John Murray, 1834.
J. M. "Poem." *The European Magazine and London Review* 58 (October, 1810): 244.
Jackson's Oxford Journal, September 1, 1753.
Jamilly, Edward. "Anglo-Jewish Architects, and Architecture in the 18th and 19th Centuries." *Transactions of the Jewish Historical Society of England* 18 (1953–5): 127–141.
Janowitz, Anne F. *Lyric and Labour in the Romantic Tradition.* Cambridge: Cambridge University Press, 1998.
Jewish and Christian Self-Definition: Volume 1: *The Shaping of Christianity in the Second and Third Centuries.* Edited by E. P. Sanders. Volume 2: *Aspects of Judaism in the Greco-Roman Period.* Edited by E. P. Sanders, with A. I. Baumgarten and Alan Mendelson. Volume 3: *Self-Definition in the*

Greco-Roman World. Edited by Ben F. Meyer and E. P. Sanders. Philadelphia: Fortress Press, 1980–2.
Jewish Encyclopedia. 12 vols. New York and London: Funk and Wagnalls, 1901.
Johnson, Edgar. "Dickens, Fagin, and Mr. Riah." *Commentary* 8 (1950): 47–50.
Johnston, Kenneth R. *The Hidden Wordsworth: Poet, Lover, Rebel, Spy.* New York: Norton, 1998.
Jones, D. W. *War and Economy in the Age of William III and Marlborough.* Oxford: Blackwell Ltd., 1988.
Jones, G. Lloyd. *The Discovery of Hebrew in Tudor England: A Third Language.* Manchester: Manchester University Press, 1983.
Jones, William. *Grammar of the Persian Language.* 1771. 3rd ed. London: J. Murray, 1783.
Jospe, Alfred. "Introduction" to *"Jerusalem," or On Religious Power and Judaism.* In *"Jerusalem" and Other Jewish Writings.* Translated and edited by Alfred Jospe, 1–8. New York: Schocken, 1969.
"Judaism." *Encyclopedia Britannica.* 15th ed., 22: 402–79. Chicago, 1992.
Katz, David S. "The Hutchinsonians and Hebraic Fundamentalism in Eighteenth-Century England." In *Sceptics, Millenarians and Jews,* ed. Katz and Jonathan I. Israel, 237–55. Brill's Studies in Intellectual History, vol. 17. Leiden: E. J. Brill, 1990.
———. *The Jews in the History of England, 1485–1850.* Oxford: Clarendon Press, 1994.
———. *Philo-Semitism and the Readmission of the Jews to England, 1603–1655.* Oxford: Clarendon Press, 1982.
Kelly, Gary. *Women, Writing, and Revolution, 1790–1827.* Oxford: Clarendon, 1993.
Kerker, Milton. "Charles Dickens, Fagin and Riah." *Midstream* 45, 8 (December 1999): 33–6.
Kermode, Frank. *The Genesis of Secrecy: On the Interpretation of Narrative.* Cambridge: Harvard University Press, 1979.
Keynes, Geoffrey. *Bibliography of William Blake.* New York: Grolier Club, 1921.
Klingenstein, Suzanne. *Enlarging America: The Cultural Work of Jewish Literary Scholars, 1930–1990.* New York: Syracuse University Press, 1998.
Lackington, Lackington. *Memoirs of the First Forty-Five Years of the Life of James Lackington,* rev. ed. London: Lackington, 1792.
Lamm, Norman. *Torah Lishmah: Torah for Torah's Sake in the Works of Rabbi Hayyim of Volozhin and his Contemporaries.* Hoboken, NJ: KTAV Publishing House, 1989.
Lane, Lauriat. "Dickens' Archetypal Jew." *P. M. L. A.* 73 (1958): 94–100.
———. "*Oliver Twist:* A Revision." *Times Literary Supplement,* July 20, 1951, 460.
Laplanche, J. and J.-B. Pontalis. *The Language of Psycho-analysis.* Translated by Donald Nicholson-Smith. New York: Norton, 1973.
Leask, Nigel. "Mythology." In *An Oxford Companion to The Romantic Age: British Culture 1776–1832,* gen. ed. Iain McCalman, 338–45. Oxford: Oxford University Press, 1999.
Lefevere, André. *Translating Literature: Practice and Theory in a Comparative Literature Context.* New York: Modern Language Association of America, 1992.

Lemoine, Henry. "Elegiac Verses, To the Memory of the late learned David Levi, Author of *Lingua Sacra*, &c." *Gentleman's Magazine* 71 (October 1801): 934–5.

Lessing, Gotthold Ephraim. *Die Juden, ein Lustspiel in einem Aufzuge*. 1749.

———. *Nathan der Weise, ein dramatisches Gedicht in fünf Aufzügen*. Berlin, 1779.

Levi, David. *A Defense of the Old Testament, in a Series of Letters, Addressed to Thomas Paine*. London, 1797.

———. *Dissertations on the Prophecies of the Old Testament, Containing All Such Prophecies as are Applicable to the Coming of the Messiah, the Restoration of the Jews, and the Resurrection of the Dead*. 3 vols. London, 1796–1800.

———. *The Holy Bible, In Hebrew... English Translation [and] Notes of the Late David Levi*. Revised by Levy Alexander. 5 vols. London, 5582 [1822].

———. *Letters to Dr. Priestley, in Answer to Those He Addressed to the Jews; Inviting Them to an Amicable Discussion of the Evidences of Christianity*. London, 1787; 2nd ed. 1787.

———. *Letters to Nathaniel Brasser Halhed, M. P. in Answer to his Testimony of the Authenticity of the Prophecies of Richard Brothers, and his Pretended Mission to Recall the Jews*. 1795.

———. *Lingua Sacra*. 5 vols. London, 1785–87. London, 1803.

———. *A Succinct Account, of the Rites, and Ceremonies, of the Jews... In which, their religious principles, and tenets, are clearly explained: particularly, their doctrine of the resurrection, predestination and freewill: and the opinion of Doctor Prideaux concerning those tenets, fully investigated, duly considered and clearly confuted. Also an account of the Jewish calendar, to which is added, a faithful and impartial account of the Mishna...* London, 1782.

Levinas, Emmanuel. *Difficult Freedom: Essays on Judaism*. Translated by Seán Hand. Baltimore: The Johns Hopkins University Press, 1990.

———. *In the Time of Nations*. Translated by Michael B. Smith. Bloomington: Indiana University Press, 1994.

———. *Nine Talmudic Readings*. Translated with an Introduction by Annette Aronowicz. Bloomington: Indiana University Press, 1994.

———. *Of God Who Comes to Mind*. Translated by Bettina Bergo. Stanford: Stanford University Press, 1998.

Levinson, Marjorie. *Keats's Life of Allegory: The Origins of a Style*. New York: Blackwell, 1988.

Liberles, Robert. "The Jews and their Bill: Jewish Motivations in the Controversy of 1753." *Jewish History* 2, 2 (Fall 1987): 29–37.

Lipowitz, Ina. "Inspiration and the Poetic Imagination: Samuel Taylor Coleridge." *Studies in Romanticism* 30 (Winter 1991): 605–31.

Lukács, Georg. *The Historical Novel*. Translated by Hannah and Stanley Mitchell. Lincoln: University of Nebraska Press, 1983.

Lyotard, Jean François. *Heidegger et "les Juifs."* Translated by Andreas Michel and Mark S. Roberts. Minneapolis: University of Minnesota Press, 1990.

MacDonald, Edgar E., ed. *The Education of the Heart: The Correspondence of Rachel Mordecai Lazarus and Maria Edgeworth*. Chapel Hill: University of North Carolina Press, 1977.

Maidment, Brian, ed. *The Poorhouse Fugitives: Self-Taught Poets and Poetry in Victorian Britain*. Manchester: Carcanet, 1987.

Marcus, Steven. "Who is Fagin?" In *Dickens from Pickwick to Dombey*. London: Chatto & Windus, 1965.

Martin, Bernard. *A History of Judaism*. Vol. II: *Europe and the New World*. New York: Basic Books, 1974.

Mayhew, Henry. *London Labour and the London Poor*. 4 vols. London: Griffin, Bohn, and Company, 1861–62.

McCalman, Iain, gen. ed. *An Oxford Companion to The Romantic Age: British Culture 1776–1832*. Oxford: Oxford University Press, 1999.

McDowell, Paula. "Consuming Women: The Life of the 'Literary Lady' as Popular Culture in Eighteenth-Century England." *Genre* 26 (1993): 219–52.

M'Crie, Thomas. *A Vindication of the Scottish Covenanters: Consisting of a Review of the First Series of the "Tales of My Landlord."* Philadelphia: James M. Campbell, 1843.

Mears, Abraham [Gamaliel ben Pedahzur]. *The Book of Religion, Ceremonies, and Prayers of the Jews, as Practiced in their Synagogues and Families*. London, 1738.

Mee, Jon. "Apocalypse and Ambivalence: The Politics of Millenarianism in the 1790s." *South Atlantic Quarterly* 95 (1996): 671–97.

———. *Dangerous Enthusiasm: William Blake and the Culture of Radicalism in the 1790s*. Oxford: Clarendon Press, 1992.

Mendelssohn, Moses. *Jerusalem, or On Religious Power and Judaism*. In *"Jerusalem" and Other Jewish Writings*. Translated and edited by Alfred Jospe, 9–110. New York: Schocken, 1969.

———. *Jerusalem, Or On Religious Power and Judaism*. Translated by Allan Arkush. Hanover and London: University of New England Press, 1983.

———. *Phaedon, oder über die Unsterblichkeit der Seele*. Berlin: Stettin, F. Bey, 1767.

Mendoza, Daniel. *Memoirs of the Life of Daniel Mendoza*. London, 1816. Reprint, edited with an introduction by Paul Magriel. London and New York: Batsford, 1951.

Meyer, Michael A. "Judaism as a Vehicle of the Enlightenment: The Contribution of Moses Mendelssohn." *Studies on Voltaire and the Eighteenth Century* 263 (1989): 571–4.

———. *The Origins of the Modern Jew: Jewish Identity and European Culture in Germany, 1749–1828*. Detroit: Wayne State University Press, 1967.

———. *Response to Modernity: A History of the Reform Movement in Judaism*. New York and Oxford: Oxford University Press, 1988.

Modder, Montagu Frank. *The Jew in the Literature of England to the End of the Nineteenth Century*. Philadelphia: Jewish Publication Society of America, 1939. Reprint, Cleveland: Meridian Books, 1960.

Montaigne, Michel de. *The Complete Essays*. Translated by Donald Frame. Stanford: Stanford University Press, 1957.

Monypenny, William Flavelle and George Earle Buckle. *The Life of Benjamin Disraeli Earl of Beaconsfield*. 6 vols. London: Murray, 1910–20.

Moore, George Foote. *Judaism in the First Centuries of the Christian Era, the Age of the Tannaim*. 3 vols. Cambridge: Harvard University Press, 1927–30. Reprint, 1966.
Morgentaler, Goldie. *Dickens and Heredity: When Like Begets Like*. London: Macmillan, and New York: St. Martin's Press, 2000.
Mosse, George L. "Jewish Emancipation: Between *Bildung* and Respectability." In *The Jewish Response to German Culture*, ed. Jehuda Reinharz and Walter Schatzberg, 1–16. Hanover, NH: University Press of New England, 1985.
Moylan, Christopher. *T. L. Beddoes and the Hermetic Tradition*. Belper, Eng: Thomas Lovell Beddoes Society, 1999.
Mullett, Michael. "Radical Sects and Dissenting Churches, 1600–1750." In *A History of Religion in Britain: Practice and Belief from Pre-Roman Times to the Present*, ed. Sheridan Gilley and W. J. Sheils, 189–210. Oxford: Blackwell, 1994.
Myers, Eric. *Jewish Ossuaries: Rebirth and Reburial*. Rome: Biblical Institute Press, 1971.
Nadler, Allan. *Rationalism, Romanticism, Rabbis and Rebbes*. New York: YIVO Institute for Jewish Research, 1992.
———. "Soloveitchik's Halakhic Man: Not a *Mithnagged*." *Modern Judaism* 13 (1993): 119–47.
Naman, Anne. *The Jew in the Victorian Novel*. New York: AMS Press, 1980.
Neil, W. "The Criticism and Theological Use of the Bible, 1700–1950." In *The Cambridge History of the Bible*. Volume 3: *The West from the Reformation to the Present Day*, ed. S. L. Greenslade, 238–93. Cambridge: Cambridge University Press, 1963.
Neusner, Jacob. *The Presence of the Past, the Pastness of the Present: History, Time, and Paradigm in Rabbinic Judaism*. Bethesda, MD: CDL Press, 1996.
———. *Talmudic Thinking: Language, Logic, Law*. Columbia: University of South Carolina Press, 1992.
Newman, Gerald. *The Rise of English Nationalism, A Cultural History: 1740–1830*. New York: St. Martin's Press, 1987.
Niebuhr, Carsten. *A Collection of Late Voyages and Travels ... Concerning the Present State of Society and Manners, of Arts and Literature, of Religion and Government, the Appearances of Nature, and the Works of Human Industry in Persia, Arabia, Turkey, &c*. London: J. Hamilton, 1797.
Ogden, James. *Isaac D'Israeli*. Oxford: Clarendon, 1969.
Ouseley, William. *Persian Miscellanies: An Essay to Facilitate the Reading of Persian Manuscripts with Engraved Specimens, Philosophical Observations, and Notes Critical and Historical*. London: Richard White, 1795.
Page, Judith. "Style and Rhetorical Intention in Wordsworth's *Lyrical Ballads*." *Philological Quarterly* (Summer 1983): 293–313.
Paine, Thomas. *The Age of Reason*. London: H. D. Symonds, 1795.
Paulding, James Kirk. *Chronicles of the City of Gotham*. New York: Carvill Press, 1830.
Perry, Thomas W. *Public Opinion, Propaganda, and Politics in Eighteenth Century England: A Study of the Jew Bill of 1753*. Cambridge: Harvard University Press, 1962.

WORKS CITED / 281

Philipson, David. *The Jew in English Fiction.* 5th ed. New York: Bloch, 1927.
Phillips, Watts. *The Wild Tribes of London.* London: Ward and Lock,1855.
Philo-Judaeis. *A Letter to Abraham Goldsmid, Esq. Containing Strictures on Mr. Joshua Van Oven's Letters on the Present State of the Jewish Poor. Pointing out the Impracticability of ameliorating their condition through the medium of Taxation and Coercion, with a Plan for Erecting a Jewish College, or Seminary, &c.* London: Blacks and Parry, 1802.
Pirke Aboth: The Ethics of the Talmud, Sayings of the Fathers. Translated and edited by R. Travers Herford. New York: Schocken, 1962.
Polanyi, Karl. *The Great Transformation.* Forward by Robert M. MacIver. New York: Rinehart, 1944. Reprint, Boston: Beacon Press, 1985.
Poliak, Abraham N. "Alroy, David." *Encyclopædia Judaica,* 2:750–1. Jerusalem: Keter, 1972.
Pollins, Harold. *Economic History of the Jews in England.* Rutherford: Fairleigh Dickinson University Press, 1982.
Popkin, Richard H. "David Levi, Anglo-Jewish Theologian." *Jewish Quarterly Review* 87 (1996): 79–101.
———. "Jewish Messianism and Christian Millenarianism." In *Culture and Politics from Puritanism to the Enlightenment,* ed. Perez Zagorin, 67–90. Berkeley: University of California Press, 1980.
Pratt, [Samuel?]. "Lines, Occasioned by the Death of Benjamin Goldsmid, Esq." *The European Magazine and London Review* 58 (October 1810): 244.
Prell, Riv-Ellen. *Fighting to Become Americans.* Boston: Beacon Press, 1999.
Preuss, Julius. *Biblical and Talmudic Medicine.* Translated and edited by Fred Rosner. New York: Sanhedrin Press, 1978. Reprint, Northvale, NJ: J. Aronson, 1993.
Prideaux, Humphrey. *The Old and New Testaments Connected in the History of the Jews and Neighbouring Nations.* 1st American, from the 16th London ed. to which is now added, The life of the author. 4 vols. Charlestown, MA, 1815.
Priestley, Joseph. *Inquiry into the Knowledge of the Antient Hebrews Concerning a Future State.* London, 1801.
———. *The Theological and Miscellaneous Works of Joseph Priestley.* Edited by J. T. Rutt, 25 vols. 1817–32. Reprint, New York: Kraus Reprint, 1972.
Prooftexts. Special Issue: The Anthological Imagination in Jewish Literature, Part 2, 17 (May 1997): 153–75.
Ragussis, Michael. *Figures of Conversion: "The Jewish Question" and English National Identity.* Durham, NC: Duke University Press, 1995.
———. "Representation, Conversion, and Literary Form: *Harrington* and the Novel of Jewish Identity." *Critical Inquiry* 16 (Autumn 1989): 112–43.
Rancière, Jacques. "The Myth of the Artisan: Critical Reflections on a Category of Social History." *International Labour and Working Class History* 24 (1983): 1–12.
Review of *Hebrew Tales,* by Hyman Hurwitz. *The Quarterly Review* 35 (January and March, 1827): 86–114.
Ricardo, David. "Notes on the Bullion Report." In his *Pamphlets and Papers, 1809–10.* Volume III of *The Works and Correspondence.* Edited by Piero

Sraffa and M. H. Dobb. Cambridge: At the University Press for the Royal Economic Society, 1951.

Richardson, John. *A Dictionary. Persian, Arabic and English, by John Richardson, to Which There Is Prefixed a Dissertation on the Languages, Literatures, and Manners of Eastern Nations.* 2 vols. Oxford: Clarendon, 1777–80.

———. *A Grammar of the Arabic Language, in Which the Rules Are Illustrated by Authorities from the Best Writers, Principally Adapted for the Use of the Honourable East India Company.* London: J. Murray, 1776.

Richmond, Charles and Paul Smith, eds. *The Self-Fashioning of Disraeli, 1818–1851.* Cambridge: Cambridge University Press, 1998.

Romaine, William. *An Answer to a Pamphlet, entitled, Considerations on the Bill to permit Persons professing the Jewish Religion to be naturalized; Wherein, the False reasoning, Gross Misrepresentation of Facts, and Perversion of Scripture, Are fully laid open and detected.* London, 1753.

Rosen, Jonathan. *The Talmud and the Internet: A Journey Between Two Worlds.* New York: Farrar, Straus and Giroux, 2000.

Rosenberg, Edgar. *From Shylock to Svengali: Jewish Stereotypes in English Fiction.* Stanford: Stanford University Press, 1960.

Ross, Marlon B. "Romancing the Nation-State: The Poetics of Romantic Nationalism." In *Macropolitics of Nineteenth-Century Literature: Nationalism, Exoticism, Imperialism,* ed. Jonathan Arac and Harriet Ritvo, 56–85. Philadelphia: Pennsylvania University Press, 1991.

Roth, Cecil. *Anglo-Jewish Letters (1158–1917).* London: Soncino Press, 1938.

———. *Benjamin Disraeli.* New York: Philosophical Library, 1952.

———. "The Haskalah in England." In *Essays Presented to the Chief Rabbi Israel Brodie on the Occasion of his Seventieth Birthday,* ed. H. J. Zimmels, J. Rabinowitz, and I. Finestein, 1:365–76. London: Soncino Press, 1967.

———. *A History of the Jews in England.* 3rd ed. Oxford: Clarendon Press, 1964.

———. *Magna Bibliotheca Anglo-Judaica: A Bibliographical Guide to Anglo-Jewish History,* new ed. London: Jewish Historical Society of England, 1937.

———. "Nelson and Some Jews." In his *Essays and Portraits in Anglo-Jewish History.* Philadelphia: The Jewish Publication Society of America, 1962.

Roth, Philip. *My Life As a Man.* New York: Holt, Rinehart and Winston, 1974.

———. *Portnoy's Complaint.* New York: Random House, 1969.

Rubens, Alfred. *Anglo-Jewish Portraits: A Biographical Catalogue of Engraved Anglo-Jewish and Colonial Portraits from the Earliest Times to the Accession of Queen Victoria.* London: The Jewish Museum, 1935.

——— "Portrait of Anglo-Jewry, 1656–1836." *Transactions of the Jewish Historical Society of England* 19 (1960): 13–52.

Ruderman, David B. *Jewish Enlightenment in an English Key: Anglo-Jewry's Construction of Modern Jewish Thought.* Princeton: Princeton University Press, 2000.

Ryan, Robert M. *The Romantic Reformation: Religious Politics in English Literature 1789–1824.* Cambridge Studies in Romanticism 24, gen. ed. Marilyn Butler and James Chandler. Cambridge: Cambridge University Press, 1997.

Samuels, M. *Memoirs of Moses Mendelssohn, the Jewish Philosopher.* 2nd ed. London: Longman, 1827.

Saperstein, Marc, ed. *Essential Papers on Messianic Movements and Personalities in Jewish History*. Essential Papers on Jewish Studies, gen. ed. Robert M. Seltzer. New York: New York University Press, 1992.

Schechter, Solomon. "Rabbi Elijah Wilna, Gaon." In his *Studies in Judaism*, first series. Philadelphia: Jewish Publication Society, 1896.

Scholem, Gershom G. "Toward an Understanding of the Messianic Idea in Judaism." In *The Messianic Idea in Judaism and Other Essays on Jewish Spirituality*. New York: Schocken, 1971.

Schor, Esther. *Bearing the Dead: The British Culture of Mourning from the Enlightenment to Victoria*. Princeton: Princeton University Press, 1994.

Schwarz, Daniel R. *Disraeli's Fiction*. New York: Macmillan, 1979.

Schweid, Eliezer. "Jewish Messianism: Metamorphoses of an Idea." In *Essential Papers on Messianic Movements and Personalities in Jewish History*, ed. Mark Saperstein, 53–70. Essential Papers on Jewish Studies, gen. ed. Robert M. Seltzer. New York: New York University Press, 1992.

Scott, Walter. *Ivanhoe*. Edited by Ian Duncan. Oxford: Oxford University Press, 1996.

———. *Miscellaneous Prose Works*. 3 vols. Edinburgh: Robert Cadell, 1841.

———. *Old Mortality*. Edited by Angus Calder. London: Penguin, 1975.

Scrivener, Michael. "Shelley and Radical Artisan Poetry." *Keats-Shelley Journal* 42 (1993): 22–36.

Segev, Tom. *One Palestine, Complete: Jews and Arabs under the British Mandate*. Translated by Haim Watzman. New York: Henry Holt, 2000.

Shannon, Richard. *The Age of Disraeli, 1868–1881: The Rise of Tory Democracy*. London: Longman, 1992.

Shapiro, James. *Shakespeare and the Jews*. New York: Columbia University Press, 1996.

Singer, Alan. "Aliens and Citizens: Jewish and Protestant Naturalization in the Making of the Modern British Nation, 1689–1753." Ph.D. diss., University of Missouri-Columbia, 1999.

Singer, S. "Early Translations and Translators of the Jewish Liturgy in England." *Transactions of the Jewish Historical Society of England* 3 (1896–98): 59.

Solomon ibn Verga. *Shevet Yehudah*. Adrianople, 1553.

Soloveitchik, Joseph B. *Halakhic Man*. Translated by Lawrence Kaplan. Philadelphia: Jewish Publication Society, 1983.

The Soncino Chumash: The Five Book of Moses with Haphtaroth. Edited by A. Cohen. New York: Soncino, 1983.

Sorkin, David. *Moses Mendelssohn and the Religious Enlightenment*. Berkeley and Los Angeles: University of California Press, 1996.

———. *The Transformation of German Jewry, 1780–1840*. New York: Oxford University Press, 1987.

Spector, Sheila A. "Blake as an Eighteenth-Century Hebraist." In *Blake and His Bibles*, ed. David V. Erdman, 179–229. Locust Hill Literary Studies No. 1. West Cornwall, CT: Locust Hill Press, 1990.

———. *"Glorious incomprehensible": The Development of Blake's Kabbalistic Language*. Lewisburg, PA: Bucknell University Press, 2001.

———. *"Wonders Divine": The Development of Blake's Kabbalistic Myth*. Lewisburg, PA: Bucknell University Press, 2001.

[Stephens, Alexander et al.]. *Public Character.* 10 vols. London: R. Phillips, 1798–1810.
Stern, David. "Introduction: The Anthological Imagination in Jewish Literature." *Prooftexts,* Special Issue: The Anthological Imagination in Jewish Literature, Part 1, 17 (January 1997): 1–7.
Stewart, R. W., ed. *Disraeli's Novels Reviewed, 1826–1968.* Metuchen, NJ: Scarecrow Press, 1975.
Stone, Harry. "Dickens and the Jews." *Victorian Studies* 2 (1959): 223–53.
Susser, Bernard. *The Jews of South-West England: The Rise and Decline of their Medieval and Modern Communities.* Exeter: Exeter Press, 1993.
Tannenbaum, Leslie. *Biblical Tradition in Blake's Early Prophecies: The Great Code of Art.* Princeton: Princeton University Press, 1982.
Taylor, James Stephen. *Jonas Hanway, Founder of the Marine Society: Charity and Policy in Eighteenth Century Britain.* London: Scolar, 1985.
Thompson, E. P. *Customs in Common: Studies in Traditional Popular Culture.* New York: The New Press, 1993.
Tovey, D'Blossiers. *Anglia Judaica, or A History of the Jews in England.* Oxford, 1738.
Trawick, Leonard M. "William Blake's German Connection." *Colby Library Quarterly* 13, 4 (1977): 229–45.
Trilling, Lionel. "Wordsworth and the Rabbis." In *The Opposing Self: Nine Essays in Criticism.* New York: Viking, 1955.
Tyson, Gerald P. *Joseph Johnson, A Liberal Publisher.* Iowa City: University of Iowa Press, 1979.
Valletine, N. I. *The Discourse of the Three Sisters: A Lamentation for Lord Nelson.* London: 1805.
Vincent, John. *Disraeli.* Oxford and New York: Oxford University Press, 1990.
Viscomi, Joseph. *Blake and the Idea of the Book.* Princeton: Princeton University Press, 1993.
Vital, David. *A People Apart: The Jews in Europe 1789–1939.* Oxford History of Modern Europe, gen. ed. Lord Bullock and Sir William Deakin. Oxford: Oxford University Press, 1999.
Vreté, Mayir. "The Restoration of the Jews in English Protestant Thought 1790–1840." *Middle Eastern Studies* 8 (1972): 3–50.
Wang, Orrin N. C. *Fantastic Modernity: Dialectical Readings in Romanticism and Theory.* Baltimore: The Johns Hopkins University Press, 1996.
Webb, R. K. "Religion." In *An Oxford Companion to The Romantic Age: British Culture 1776–1832,* gen. ed. Iain McCalman, 93–101. Oxford: Oxford University Press, 1999.
Weintraub, Stanley. *Disraeli: A Biography.* New York: Truman Talley Books/Dutton, 1993.
Welsh, Alexander. *The Hero of the Waverley Novels.* Princeton: Princeton University Press, 1963. Reprint, with new essays, 1992.
Werblowsky, R. J. Zwi. "Messianism in Jewish History." In *Essential Papers on Messianic Movements and Personalities in Jewish History,* ed. Mark Saperstein, 35–52. Essential Papers on Jewish Studies, gen. ed. Robert M. Seltzer. New York: New York University Press, 1992.

Whitmore, Daniel. "Bibliolatry and the Rule of the Word: A Study of Scott's *Old Mortality*." *Philological Quarterly* 65 (Spring 1986): 243–62.

Wilson, Douglas B. "Psychological Approaches." In *A Companion to Romanticism*, ed. Duncan Wu, 420–30. Oxford: Blackwell, 1998.

Wilson, Mona. *The Life of William Blake*. London: Nonesuch, 1927.

Wimsatt, W. K., Jr. "The Concrete Universal." In *The Verbal Icon: Studies in the Meaning of Poetry*. Lexington: University of Kentucky Press, 1954.

Wittaker, Jason. *William Blake and the Myths of Britain*. London: Macmillan, 1999.

Wolf, Lucian. "Lady Montefiore's Honeymoon." In *Essays in Jewish History*, ed. Cecil Roth, 233–58. London: The Jewish Historical Society of England, 1934.

Wolfenstein, Martha. "Two Types of Jewish Mothers." In *The Jews: Social Patterns of an American Group*, ed. Marshall Sklare, 520–34. New York: Free Press, 1958.

Wolfson, Susan J. "50–50? Phone a Friend? Ask the Audience?: Speculating on a Romantic Century, 1750–1850." *European Romantic Review* 11, 1 (Winter 2000): 1–11.

Wood, Jeanne. "'Alphabetically Arranged': Mary Hays's *Female Biography* and the Biographical Dictionary." *Genre* 31 (1998): 117–42.

Wordsworth, Dorothy. *Journals of Dorothy Wordsworth*. Edited by Ernest de Selincourt. Vol. 1. London: Macmillan, 1952.

Wordsworth, William. *Home at Grasmere*. Edited by Beth Darlington. The Cornell Wordsworth. Ithaca, NY: Cornell University Press, 1977.

———. "Home at Grasmere." In *Major British Poets of the Romantic Period*. Edited by William W. Heath, 239–47. New York: Macmillan, 1973.

———. *Poetical Works of William Wordsworth*. Edited by Ernest de Selincourt and Helen Darbishire. 5 vols. Oxford: Clarendon, 1940–49.

———. *The Prelude, or, Growth of a Poet's Mind*. Edited by Ernest de Selincourt and Helen Darbishire. 2nd ed. Oxford: Clarendon, 1959.

———. *The Prose Works*. Ed. W. J. B. Owen and Jane Worthington Smyser. 3 vols. Oxford: Clarendon Press, 1974.

Wu, Duncan, ed. *A Companion to Romanticism*. Oxford: Blackwell, 1998.

Yerushalmi, Yosef Hayim. *Zakhor: Jewish History and Jewish Memory*. Seattle: University of Washington Press, 1982.

Young, Robert. *Colonial Desire: Hybridity in Theory, Culture and Race*. London: Routledge, 1995.

Zatlin, Linda Gertner. *The Nineteenth-Century Anglo-Jewish Novel*. Boston: G. K. Hall, 1981.

Zizek, Slavoj. *The Plague of Fantasies*. London: Verso, 1997.

Index

Abrahams, Israel, 246 n.1
Abrams, M. H., 76 n.6, 255
Abravanel, Isaac, 162, 248 n.11
Ackroyd, P. R., 14 n.9
Adorno, Theodor W., 250
aggadah, 198, 199, 201
Aguilar, Grace, 12, 215–34
  as bridge writer, 215–16
  Works: *The Days of Bruce,* 216, 224–6; *Home Scenes and Heart Studies,* 218; *The Magic Wreath,* 216; *The Spirit of Judaism,* 219, 223, 232 n.8; *The Vale of Cedars,* 215, 217, 225, 226–30, 233 n.16; *The Women of Israel,* 219–23
Aguilar, Sarah, 219
Aikin, Lucy, 220
alchemy, 42, 43, 96–7
Alexander, Levy, 42, 49, 164, 171–2, 175 n.22
Alroy, David, 235, 246 n.2
Altmann, Alexander, 174 n.14
Anderson, Benedict, 31
Andreades, Andreas Michael, 56 n.11
Anglicanism, 3–5, 15 n.12
Anglo-Israelites, 4, 15 n.13, 85
Anglo-Judaica: history, 16 n.20; literature, 159–77
anti-Semitism, 7, 10, 11, 39, 43, 48, 51, 99, 114–17, 121, 123, 164, 168, 206, 226, 229, 236, 255, 257, 261 n.2
apologetic, Christian, 235–6
Arkin, Marcus, 57 n.16

Arnold, Matthew, 64
artisan writers, 175 n.19
Ascheim, Steven E., 262 n.3

Ba'al Shem Tov, *see* Israel ben Eliezer
Ballard, George, 219–20
Barnett, Arthur, 161
Baron, Salo, 246 n.2
Baumgarten, A. I., 14 n.7
Baumgarten, Murray, 140, 153 n.5, 154 n.21
Beddoes, Thomas Lovell, 10–11, 93–103
Bell, John, 188, 190
Benjamin of Tudela, 246 n.2
Berkeley, George, 182, 183
Bermant, Chaim, 49
Betham, Matilda, 220
Bible, 2–5, 15 n.12, 210, 220–3, 232 n.10
  exegetical tradition, 2–3
  high criticism, 3, 14 n.10
  translation, 2, 184
Blake, Robert, 247 n.5
Blake, William, 10, 140, 192; Works: *All Religions are One,* 87; *The Book of Thel,* 192; *The Book of Urizen,* 90 n.41, 192; *Europe, a Prophecy,* 192; *The Four Zoas,* 118; *Jerusalem,* 10, 79–90; *The Marriage of Heaven and Hell,* 84, 192, 193; *Milton,* 4, 79; *Songs of Innocence and of Experience,* 192; *Visions of the Daughters of Albion,* 192

Bloom, Harold, 12, 249–63; Works: "Agon: Revisionism and Critical Personality," 262 n.6; *The Anxiety of Influence,* 249–63
Blumenbach, Johann Friedrich, 183
Boerhaave, Hermann, 183
Bonnet, Charles, 89 n.8
Bosanquet, Charles, 142
Bradshaw, Michael, 98
Braham, John, 57 n.21
Brewer, John, 36 n.29
Britain, Ian, 13 n.1
"Britannia," 25–6, 30
Buckle, George Earle, 246 n.1, 247 n.5
Buffon, Georges, 183
Burke, Edmund, 39–40, 43, 56 n.10
Butler, Marilyn, 13 n.1

Calder, Angus, 119 n.3, 119 n.4
Cambridge History of the Bible, 14 n.9
Centilivre, Susanna, 39
Chaucer, Geoffrey, 139
Chavel, Charles, 66, 75 n.1
Cheyette, Brian, 13 n.3, 153–4 n.10, 233 n.18
Christensen, Jerome, 55
Christian Hebraism, *see* Hebraism, Christian
Cobbett, William, 38, 46–53, 171
Cole, G. D. H., 59 n.37
Coleridge, Samuel Taylor, 61, 142, 197, 198, 199, 203, 208, 211 n.2
Colley, Linda, 13 n.4, 21, 31, 34 n.5, 35 n.21
The Commercial Habits of the Jews, 49
conversionism, 116–17, 165, 195 n.21, 218, 225, 229–30, 231 n.4, 235–7, 248 n.11
Cope, S. R., 43
covenant, 70–1
Cranz, August, 89 n.3
The Crisis, or an Alarm to Britannia's True Protestant Sons, 32–3, 36 n.42

crypto-Jew, *see* maranno
Cumberland, Richard, 140, 160, 171

Dallaway, James, 188
Damon, S. Foster, 192
Davies, Lloyd, 10, 61–77, 77 n.37
Davis, Eliza, 144–6
Descartes, René, 14 n.10, 252
Dibdin, Thomas, 140
Dickens, Charles, 11, 139–55
  and anti-Semitism, 139–55
  Works: *Little Dorrit,* 147; *Oliver Twist,* 11, 140, 141, 142–3, 145; *Our Mutual Friend,* 140, 141, 142, 143, 146, 147–52
Dickson, P. G. M., 36 n.29
Dighton, Robert, 43
Disraeli, Benjamin, 8, 12, 16 n.26, 160, 179, 224, 225, 229, 233 n.15
  conversion, 195 n.21, 235–7
  Works: *Alroy,* 12, 235–48); *Coningsby,* 225, 233 n.15; *Lothair,* 233 n.15; *Sybil,* 225; *Tancred, or The New Crusade,* 8, 225, 233 n.15; *Vivian Grey,* 246 n.1
D'Israeli, Isaac, 8, 11–12, 13 n.1, 160, 236–7, 238, 247 n.7
  and Blake, 192–3
  and history, 179–81
  and philosophy, 181–4
  and the Talmud, 184–8
  Talmudical style, 188–92
  Works: *Amenities of Literature,* 179, 181, 186, 190, 191; "Aristotle and Plato," 181; *Calamities of Authors,* 194 n.11; *Commentaries on the Life and Reign of Charles the First,* 180, 195 n.19; *Curiosities of Literature,* 179–80, 195 n.21; *Flim-Flams,* 180, 182, 183, 184, 192, 194 n.5; *Genius of Judaism,* 180–1, 186, 187,

D'Israeli, Isaac – *continued*
Works – *continued*
190, 195 n.21, 237; *The Literary Character,* 179, 186, 187, 190; *Literary Miscellanies,* 191; *Mejnoun and Leila,* 188–9; "Modern Platonism," 182; "Orthography and Orthoepy," 186; "Rabbinical Stories," 195 n.21; *Romances,* 188–9; "Self-Characters," 191; "Shakespeare," 190; "The Talmud," 195 n.21; *Vaurien,* 180, 182, 192
Dryden, John, 109
Duncombe, John, 220

economy, British, 40
during French Revolution, 40
paper money, 40–41
Edgeworth, Maria, 11
and anti-Semitism, 121–37
Works: *Harrington,* 11, 121–37; *Moral Tales for the Young,* 134
Eliakim ben Abraham, *see* Hart, Jacob
Elijah ben Solomon Zalman, Gaon of Vilna, 10, 61, 62, 63, 75 n.1, 76 n.20
Eliot, George, 116, 118
Eliot, Thomas Stearns, 261 n.2
Emancipation (1858), 2, 16 n.21, 141, 143, 236
Emden, Paul, 42, 56 n.14
The Encyclopaedia Britannica, 64
Endelman, Todd, 13 n.4, 16 n.19, 16 n.20, 34 n.4, 49, 58 n.33, 119 n.1, 159, 163, 167, 168, 171, 174 n.18, 195 n.26, 247 n.7
Enlightenment, 2, 9, 81
"Erinaceus," 52–3
eschatology, 2–3, 14 n.8, 141
Jewish, 93–103
Evans, C. F., 14 n.9
exilarch, *see Resh Galuta*

Fay, Elizabeth, 12, 215–34
Felsenstein, Frank, 13 n.3, 34 n.4, 233 n.18
Ferris, Ina, 119 n.5
Fichte, Johann Gottlieb, 183
Fiedler, Leslie, 152 n.1
Fisch, Harold, 155 n.23, 248 n.12
Fraistat, Neil, 212 n.4
Francis, John, 42, 53–4
Freedman, Jonathan, 255, 260, 261 n.2
Fretwell, Katie, 57 n.24, 58 n.27
Freud, Sigmund, 13 n.2, 249–53, 255, 257, 259–60
Frye, Northrop, 192–3, 255
Fuseli, Henry, 80

Galchinsky, Michael, 219, 223, 231 n.4, 232 n.8
Gans, David ben Solomon, 246 n.2
Gaon of Vilna, *see* Elijah ben Solomon Zalman, Gaon of Vilna
Gelber, Mark H., 153 n.1
George III, 40
Gilman, Sander, 153 n.5, 175 n.24
Gnosticism, 249, 253, 255
Godwin, William, 182, 183–4, 194 n.9, 215
Goldschmid, Aaron, 42
Goldschmid, Aaron Asher, 47–8
Goldschmid, Abraham, 9, 37–60, 164, 175 n.22
public self, 39–46
suicide, 37–8
Goldschmid, Benjamin, 37, 46, 175 n.22
Goldschmid firm, 41–3
Goldschmid, Lionel, 46
Goodman, Judith, 57 n.24, 58 n.27
Gordon Riots, 122, 124, 131
Green, Ian, 15 n.12
Greenslade, S. L., 14 n.9
Grossman, Jonathan H., 153 n.2
Grotius, Hugo, 14 n.10
Groves, J. T., 44

halakhah, 10, 62, 64, 65, 66, 67, 68, 74, 75, 199, 202
Halakhic Man, 68–9, 71
Halevi, Uri, 42
Hamann, J. G., 61
Hanway, Jonas, 22–3, 24, 29–30, 34–5 n.8, 35 n.13
Hart, Jacob, 161–2
Hartman, David, 64, 67–8
Hartman, Geoffrey, 232 n.5, 250, 261 n.3
Ḥasidism, 61, 65–6, 67, 68, 74, 75 n.1
Haskalah, 2, 5, 8, 9, 62, 64, 65, 66, 67, 161, 170, 173
  English, 6–8, 11, 15 n.11, 16 n.19, 159, 197
  German, 5–6
Hayden, John O., 119 n.5
Hays, Mary, 218, 220
Hayyim of Volozhin, 75 n.1, 76 n.20
Hebraism, Christian, 15 n.11
Hegel, Georg Wilhelm Friedrich, 252
Heidegger, Martin, 76 n.20, 249
Heller, Deborah, 153 n.1
Hemans, Felicia, 218, 220, 222, 225
Henriques, H. S. Q., 137 n.5
ḥerem, 61, 172
high criticism, *see* Bible, high criticism
Hill, Christopher, 15 n.12
Hillel, R., 205, 207–8, 212 n.15
Hoad, Neville, 11, 121–37
Horner, Francis, 56 n.12
Horodetsky, Shmuel Abba, 66–7
Hughson, David, 45, 58 n.32
Hume, David, 183, 194 n.11, 195 n.19
Hurwitz, Hyman, 7, 12, 159–60, 197–213
  audience, 208–11
  literary theory, 198–204
  storytelling, 204–8
Husserl, Edmund, 76 n.20
Hutchinsonianism, 119 n.2
Hyman, Leonard, 211 n.2

Ibn Ezra, Abraham ben Meir, 3, 14 n.10, 170
Inquisition, Spanish, 233 n.17
Irving, Washington, 188
Israel ben Eliezer, 65–6, 75 n.1

Jamilly, Edward, 58 n.26
'the jew,' 11, 21–2, 139–40, 142, 233 n.18
Jewish and Christian Self-Definition, 14 n.7
Jewish crime, 142
Jewish Naturalization Bill (1753), 2, 7, 9, 10, 11, 14 n.6, 19–36, 122, 124–8, 141, 167, 236
  opposition, 20: Jewish threat to British finances, 28–9; Jews as anti-nation, 22–7; Jews as Christ killers, 25; Jews as king killers, 25–6; Jews as landowners, 30; Jews as perceived threat, 21–2, 31; Jews as persecutors of Christians, 27; Jews as treasonous, 25
  proponents, 32–3, 127–8
  provisions and passage, 19–20
Jews as race, 141, 144, 154 n.15
"J. M.," 37–8
Johnson, Edgar, 152 n.1
Johnson, Samuel, 250
Johnston, Kenneth R., 63, 73–4
Jones, D. W., 36 n.29
Jones, G. Lloyd, 15 n.11
Jones, William, 13 n.1, 188

Kabbalism, 42, 81, 82, 85, 94, 235, 253
Kant, Immanuel, 14 n.10, 61, 67, 183, 194 n.10
Karaites, 173, 187
Katz, David S., 13–14 n.4, 15 n.11, 16 n.20, 34 n.4, 119 n.1, 159, 167, 176 n.36, 177 n.60, 247 n.10
Kaufmann, David, 12, 249–63
Kaufmann, Peter, 262 n.13

Keats, John, 118, 203
Kerker, Milton, 153 n.1
Kermode, Frank, 218
Keynes, Geoffrey, 192
King, John, 168
King, Jonathan, 13 n.1
Klingenstein, Suzanne, 262 n.11

Lacan, Jacques, 94, 101, 249
Lackington, George, 164
Lamm, Norman, 75 n.1
Lampe, G. W. H., 14 n.9
Landon, Letitia Elizabeth, 216
Lane, Lauriat, 152 n.1
Laplanche, J., 262 n.7
Lavater, Johann Kaspar, 80, 83, 86, 89 n.8, 162–3
Leask, Nigel, 13 n.1
Lefevere, André, 210
Leibnitz, Gottfried Wilhelm von, 81, 183
Lemoine, Henry, 164
Lessing, Gotthold Ephraim, 14 n.10, 160, 170–1
A Letter from a Gentleman to his Friend Concerning the Naturalization of the Jews, 30
Levi, David, 7, 11, 15 n.11, 159–77
  as Anglo-Jewish example, 161–4
  as controversialist, 167–70
  Works: *Dissertations on the Prophecies of the Old Testament*, 168, 169–70; *Lingua Sacra*, 7, 161–7, 170, 172, 173; *A Succinct Account, of the Rites, and Ceremonies of the Jews*, 7, 164–5; translations of Bible and liturgy, 165–66, 171–2
  as writer, 164–7
Levinas, Emmanuel, 65, 68, 76–7 n.20, 184–5, 188
Levinson, Marjorie, 260
Levita, Elias, 3, 14 n.10
Lipowitz, Ina, 211 n.2
Locke, John, 127, 130, 188
Luppa, Joseph, 46

luz of the spine, 10–11, 94–6, 101, 102 n.4
Lyotard, Jean François, 153 n.10

Maidment, Brian, 175 n.19
Maimonides, 246 n.2, 248 n.11
Malthus, Thomas Robert, 184
mandrake, 97–9
maranno, 216–17, 218, 243–4
Marcus, Steven, 141
Martin, Bernard, 75 n.1
Maxwell House Haggadah, 176 n.33
Mayhew, Henry, 142
McCalman, Iain, 1
M'Crie, Thomas, 105–6, 107–8, 116–17, 120 n.15
medievalism, 224–5
Meldola, Raphael, 248 n.11
Mendelson, Alan, 14 n.7
Mendelssohn, Moses, 5–6, 10, 61, 63, 64, 162–3, 168–9, 170–1, 186, 187–8, 195 n.21, 236
  Jerusalem, 10, 79–90, 174 n.14
Mendoza, Daniel, 160, 162, 167
Meyer, Ben F., 14 n.7
Meyer, Michael A., 15–16 n.18, 163, 247 n.8
Michaelis, Johann David, 171
midrash, 197, 205–6, 218, 219, 222, 223, 225, 230, 232 n.5, 261 n.3
Mitford, Mary Russell, 220
Mitnaggedism, 61, 62, 65, 67, 68, 74, 75 n.1
Modder, Montagu Frank, 152 n.1
A Modest Apology for the Citizens and Merchants of London, 25–6
Montaigne, Michel de, 37
Montefiore, Judith, 208
Monypenny, William Flavelle, 246 n.1, 247 n.5
Mordechai, Rachel, 121, 130, 137 n.9
Morden, 44–5
More, Henry, 182
Mörschel, David Ernst, 89 n.3
Mortgen, Levi, 46

292 / INDEX

Mosse, George L., 262 n.3
Moylan, Christopher, 10–11, 93–103
Mullett, Michael, 15 n.15
Murray, John Fisher, 141–2

Nadler, Allan, 66, 68
Naman, Anne, 153 n.1
nationalism, 21–36, 153 n.6
Neil, W., 14 n.10
Nelson, Horatio. 46, 59 n.36
Neusner, Jacob, 185, 188, 191–2
New Criticism, 249, 253–5, 261 n.2
Newland, Abraham, 41–2, 43
Newman, Gerald, 21, 34 n.5
Newton, Isaac, 81
Niebuhr, Carsten, 188
Nietzsche, Friedrich, 249, 253
Nugent, Robert, 33–4 n.3

Ogden, James, 179, 188, 191, 192, 193, 194 n.8, 195 n.19, 195 n.21, 247 n.7
other, see "the jew"
Ouseley, William, 188, 189
Oxford Movement, 224, 230

Page, Judith W., 12, 197–213
Paine, Thomas, 88
Paulding, James Kirke, 54–5
Pelham, Henry, 33–4 n.3
Perry, Thomas W., 33 n.2, 33- 4 n.3, 34 n.4
Peterfreund, Stuart, 11–12, 179–96
Philo-Judaeis (pseud.), 45–6
Philo Judaeus (ca. 20 BCE–ca. 50 CE), 184–5
philo-Semitism, 10, 116, 118, 127, 141, 160, 171
Pirke Aboth, 65, 76 n.20
Pitt, William, 40
Plato, 188, 202–3
Polanyi, Karl, 42
Poliak, Abraham N., 246 n.2
Pollins, Harold, 56 n.8
Pontalis, J.-B., 262 n.7
Popkin, Richard H., 14 n.8, 174 n.13

Pratt, [Samuel?], 37–8
Prell, Riv-Ellen, 263 n.16
Priestley, Joseph, 88, 162–3, 168, 171, 176 n.36

Ragussis, Michael, 13 n.3, 116, 137 n.10, 137 n.12, 232 n.4
Rancière, Jacques, 175 n.19
Rashi, 232 n.10
Reformation, 3–4
Reform Judaism, 6, 8, 15–16 n.18, 159, 187, 195 n.21, 237, 245, 247 n.10
Reich, Benjamin Bernhard, 93–5, 99, 101, 102
Reid, Thomas, 183
Resh Galuta, 247 n.11
Ricardo, David, 13 n.1, 48
Richardson, John, 188–9
Richmond, Charles, 16 n.26
Romaine, William, 23–4, 29
"Romantic reformation," 5, 8, 15 n.15
Rosen, Jonathan, 204, 205
Rosenberg, Edgar, 233 n.18
Ross, Marlon B., 153 n.6
Roth, Cecil, 15 n.14, 16 n.20, 58–9 n.36, 161, 235, 247 n.5, 247 n.7
Roth, Philip, 250–1, 260; *Portnoy's Complaint,* 255–60
Rothschild, Nathan, 45
Rubens, Alfred, 57 n.22, 57 n.25, 58 n.31
Ruderman, David B., 13 n.3, 15 n.11, 16 n.19, 16 n.22, 105, 119 n.2, 159, 160, 168, 197, 211 n.2, 213 n.24
Ryan, Robert N., 15 n.15

Salvador, Joseph, 33 n.3
Sanders, E. P., 14 n.7
Saperstein, Marc, 14 n.8, 246 n.2, 246 n.3
Schechter, Solomon, 75 n.1
Schoenfield, Mark L., 9, 37–60
Scholem, Gershom G., 14 n.8

INDEX / 293

Schor, Esther, 11, 105–20, 120 n.22
Schwarz, Daniel R., 247 n.5
Schweid, Eliezer, 14 n.8, 246 n.3
Scott, Mary, 220
Scott, Walter, 11, 12, 60 n.51, 216, 225, 231 n.4; Works: *Ivanhoe*, 116, 118, 140, 215, 217, 219, 226–30, 231 n.3, 234 n.19, 234 n.20; *Old Mortality*, 105–20; *The Surgeon's Daughter*, 116; *Waverley*, 118
Scrivener, Michael, 11, 159–77, 175 n.19
Segev, Tom, 105
Shakespeare, William, 28, 217
Shammai, 205, 212 n.15
Shapiro, James, 34 n.4
Shelley, Mary, 216, 218
Shelley, Percy Bysshe, 118
Shneyur Zalman of Liady, 10, 61, 62, 75 n.1
Shylock, 29, 140–1, 148–50, 225
Sicher, Efraim, 11, 139–155
Singer, Alan H., 9, 19–36, 36 n.42
Singer, S., 176 n.33
Smith, Paul, 16 n.26
Solomons, Ikey, 154 n.18
Soloveitchik, Joseph, 65, 68, 74, 77 n.20
Sonnenfels, Joseph von, 89 n.3
Sorkin, David, 86, 88, 262 n.3
Spallanzani, Lazzaro, 183
Spector, Sheila A., 1–16, 12, 15 n.11, 15 n.13, 82, 90 n.29, 235–48, 177 n.60
Spiller, James, 44
Spinoza, Benedict, 14 n.10, 64, 67
Stephens, Alexander, 57 n.21
Stern, David, 212 n.6
Stone, Harry, 152 n.1
Susser, Bernard, 58 n.35

Talmud, 10–11, 94, 95, 184, 186, 187, 188, 197, 199, 201–2, 203–4, 205, 209–11, 212 n.6, 219, 220, 239–41
Tang, Abraham, 159–60

Tannenbaum, Leslie, 10, 79–90, 90 n.27, 90 n.41
Tatham, Frederick, 87
Taylor, James Stephen, 35 n.13
Thompson, E. P., 21–2
Tovey, B'Blossiers, 16 n.20
Trilling, Lionel, 63–4, 65, 71, 75, 207, 255
Tucker, Josiah, 36 n.42

Vallentine, N. I., 46
Van Oven, Joshua, 58 n.33, 159–60
Verga, Solomon ibn, 246 n.2
Vincent, John, 246 n.1
Vital, David, 15 n.17, 16 n.21, 247 n.9

Wandering Jew, 139, 140, 141, 149, 151
Wang, Orrin N. C., 249, 261 n.1
Watson, Richard, 88
Webb, R. K., 13 n.1
Weintraub, Stanley, 233 n.15, 247 n.5
Werblowsky, R. J. Zwi, 14 n.8, 246 n.3
Whitfield, George, 23
Wilson, Douglas B., 13 n.2
Wilson, Mona, 192
Wimsatt, William, 253–5, 259–60
Wolfenstein, Martha, 263 n.16
Wolff, Christian, 81
Wolfson, Susan K., 14 n.5
Wollstonecraft, Mary, 218, 222
Wordsworth, Dorothy, 62, 72, 76 n.4
Wordsworth, William, 10, 140, 198, 199, 202, 204, 207, 211, 261 n.3
and *Halakhah*, 61–77
and *Hasidism*, 65–7
Works: "Expostulation and Reply," 66; "Home at Grasmere," 62, 72–4; *Lyrical Ballads*, 12, 62, 198, 199, 202, 204–5, 206, 207; "Nuns fret not at their convent's narrow room," 62,

Wordsworth, William – *continued*
Works – *continued*
70; "Ode: Intimations of Immortality," 66; "Ode to Duty," 62, 71–2; Preface to *Lyrical Ballads,* 200, 202; *The Prelude,* 69–70; "A slumber did my spirit seal," 72; "Song for the Wandering Jew," 63; "Tintern Abbey," 62, 68, 69, 199

Wu, Duncan, 1

Yassif, Eli, 213 n.23
Yerushalmi, Yosef Hayim, 119 n.8
Yiddish, 187, 211, 258
Yorke, Philip, 33–4 n.3
Young England, 224–6, 229, 233 n.15

Zatlin, Linda Gertner, 232–3 n.13
Zionism, 6, 8, 11, 105, 118, 162
Zizek, Slavoj, 94, 99, 101